Houses
of the National Trust

LYDIA GREEVES

 National Trust

First published in Great Britain in 2008

This revised edition first published in 2013 by

National Trust Books
10 Southcombe Street
London W14 0RA

An imprint of Anova Books Ltd

ISBN 978 19078 9248 6

A CIP catalogue record for this book is available from the British Library.

21 20 19 18 17 16 15 14 13
10 9 8 7 6 5 4 3 2 1

Book Design by Lee-May Lim

Reproduction by Mission Productions Ltd, Hong Kong
Printed and bound by 1010 Printing International Ltd, China

This book can be ordered direct from the publisher at the website www.anovabooks.com, or try your local bookshop. Also available from National Trust shops and shop.nationaltrust.org.uk

Lydia Greeves is very grateful to all those in the National Trust who helped her with this new edition; to Pauline Buckle for her research on Duffield Castle; to John Barkham, Brian and Dill Hughes and Ellen Kenny for their hospitality on the road; and to Nicola Newman of Anova, who was a pleasure to work with.

Page 2: The haunting shell of the house at Lyveden New Bield in Northamptonshire is mirrored in the waters of the garden moat.

Contents

Foreword

by Simon Jenkins

The National Trust owns the most remarkable collection of houses of any country in the world. It opens to the public over three hundred properties in England, Wales and Northern Ireland, most of them with extensive gardens and parks. Formed over the course of the 20th century, mostly when such houses seemed unsustainable in private hands, it has not just sustained them but proved them popular. Some four million Trust members support them. Some 18 million visits are paid to them each year. This book is their tribute and their catalogue.

While some houses in this book are grand, many are modest and even quirky. For every Knole, Lyme, Petworth or Kedleston there is a Hardy's cottage, a Beatles house or a Birmingham back-to-back. Indeed in recent years the flow of larger properties to the Trust has almost ceased, as 'new rich' owners have come into play and as private trusts become more sophisticated. That said, each year brings another Tyntesfield, Seaton Delaval or Tredegar. Smaller properties, as well as gardens and landscapes, continue to arrive. Most recently we have acquired the extraordinary 575 Wandsworth Road in London, and Lord Nuffield's former house in Oxfordshire.

What is changing more radically is the style in which these houses are presented. There has been a loosening up, an end to the so-called dead hand of Trust identity. Houses are to allowed to speak for themselves. This programme of 'bringing houses to life' has been challenging for staff, who must decide what aspect or storyline to promote at any one time.

The result has been immensely popular with visitors. They can see houses in a changing light and, by acting as guests rather than passers-by, they can enter into their spirit. Fires are being lit at Petworth, pianos played at Stourhead, kitchens brought into use at Buckland Abbey. At Wray Castle in the Lakes, visitors are invited to fill what are currently empty places with their imagination, camping in rooms and even making their own tea.

We have also been able to bring to life the characters who created or infused these places. We can see William Armstrong, the armaments tycoon, at Cragside, or the eccentric collector Charles Paget Wade at Snowshill. We can compose poetry alongside Coleridge at Nether Stowey, or play croquet with the Jones's at Chastleton. We can watch a country house weekend at Upton or a tennis tournament at Hidcote.

A National Trust property is never wholly still, though there should always be stillness somewhere about it. I shall never forget my first visit to Fenton House in Hampstead. I looked out over the metropolis from an upstairs window in utter peace, broken only by the sound of a piano drifting up from the drawing room below. A Trust house should be what its founder Octavia Hill demanded, a place that takes people from the humdrum of life and refreshes and enriches them with the experience of beauty. I hope this book begins that enrichment.

Houses

of the National Trust

Introduction

The National Trust cares for a large and wonderfully diverse collection of buildings. Of those covered in this book, most are houses, but there is also a good representation of other types of building, from ruined castles and former monasteries, inns, chapels and follies, to the watermills, windmills, tithe barns and market halls which once played such an important part in the rural economy. Between them, they span almost a thousand years of history, from the time of William the Conqueror to the present day. Among the earliest is the remarkable one-storey Norman hall at Horton Court, deep in the Cotswolds, which was built for the prebendaries who were responsible for the church across the road. Dating from the same period is Corfe Castle, now a dramatic ruin standing high on the Purbeck Hills, but once an impregnable stronghold, one of the many built by William the Conqueror in the years after his victory at Hastings to consolidate his hold on his new kingdom. The most recent buildings include the terraced house on a post-war Liverpool estate where Paul McCartney and John Lennon, then in their teens, worked out their first songs and developed the individual sound that would come to define the Beatles, and three examples of modernist domestic architecture: 2 Willow Road, looking over London's Hampstead Heath; The Homewood, in leafy Surrey; and High Cross House, built for the headmaster of a progressive co-educational school in deepest rural Devon.

Although the preservation of buildings and their contents is now seen as a core aspect of the Trust's work, this has not always been so. For the first forty or so years of its existence, from its establishment in 1895 until the 1930s, the Trust was primarily concerned with the acquisition and protection of the countryside, a focus which partly reflects the principal aims of its founders, Octavia Hill, Robert Hunter and Canon Hardwicke Rawnsley. This indomitable trio had backgrounds in the Commons Society and the Lake District Defence Society and were only too aware that the beauty of England was being eroded by uncontrolled development. For them, the National

LEFT The Homewood, completed in 1938, is a study in concrete and glass, with a capacious balcony leading off the principal rooms.

Trust was primarily a vehicle for educating public opinion and for acquiring and safeguarding threatened landscapes that were worthy of protection. Among the first properties to come to the Trust were a stretch of coastline in Wales, part of Wicken Fen in Cambridgeshire, Brandelhow on the west side of Derwentwater in the Lake District, and the shingle spit of Blakeney Point in Norfolk.

The Trust's remit to preserve places of historic interest as well as natural beauty was at first interpreted as applying to small, ancient buildings, as typified by the two properties the Trust acquired in its initial ten years of existence. The first, bought in 1896 for £10, was Alfriston Clergy House, an exquisite fourteenth-century, half-timbered building that was in an advanced state of dilapidation. A few years later, in 1903, the Trust bought the tiny medieval manor known as the Old Post Office in the centre of Tintagel, which was threatened by redevelopment for the tourist trade. To be strictly accurate, the Old Post Office was the third building to be acquired by the Trust as, in 1900, Robert Hunter had negotiated the gift of the semi-ruinous Kanturk Castle, a fortified Jacobean manor in Co. Cork. When Ireland was divided in 1921, Kanturk lay in what is now known as the Irish Republic and in 1951 the Trust gave it to An Taisce, the National Trust for Ireland, on a thousand-year lease.

Significantly, these buildings came to the Trust without any contents and this was also true of Barrington Court, the Trust's first substantial property, which was bought in 1907. The purchase price and bill for initial repairs together came to the then massive sum of £11,500. Built of golden Ham Hill stone and with a roofline display of twisted finials, Barrington is a great Elizabethan mansion with an exterior that is as dramatic as that of Montacute, which lies only a few miles away. When bought, though, the house was a shell in an advanced state of dilapidation and without many of its fittings, which had been taken out and sold. Maintaining this property, which was a constant drain on the Trust's slender resources, proved to be a salutary lesson in the pressures and difficulties involved in caring for houses of this size and the need for endowments to cover ongoing expenditure. But anyone who has wandered through Barrington's atmospheric rooms or sat in the beautiful compartmental gardens with their Jekyll-inspired planting will know the Trust's decision was the right one.

Fortunately, in the years before the Second World War, just at the time when owners of great country houses were being faced with ruinous increases in taxation, death duties and running costs, a change in the Trust's status in 1937, which enabled the Trust to hold land and investments to provide for property upkeep, and the introduction of the Country Houses scheme in 1940, by which owners could transfer their houses to the Trust, together with a suitable tax-free endowment, while continuing to live there, paved the way for a number of the finest properties, together with their contents, to be gifted. Blickling was given to the Trust in 1940, Wallington was acquired in 1941, Cliveden in 1942, West Wycombe in 1943, Polesden Lacey and Lacock Abbey in 1944. Many more followed after 1946, when the government decided to accept houses and land in lieu of death duties and to hand suitable properties over to the Trust.

These great houses, and many more modest acquisitions, offer a unique record of changing tastes and fashions in architecture and decoration and house an unrivalled collection of precious and beautiful things. Moreover, unlike most museums and galleries, where what is on show has no connection with the building in question, the paintings, furniture, books and other contents in Trust properties are often intimately connected with the history of the house and of the family, or families, who have lived there and, in many cases, continue to live there. Bess of Hardwick herself probably worked on some of the Elizabethan embroideries and other hangings which are a unique feature of

Hardwick Hall; luminous landscapes by Turner at Petworth reflect the artist's friendship with the 3rd Earl of Egremont, who arranged for Turner to have a studio in the house; and a shoal of tiny glittering fish displayed at Ickworth, each a beautifully crafted silver scent bottle or vinaigrette, was acquired by the 3rd Marchioness of Bristol, whose husband was the great-grandson of the eccentric Frederick Hervey, the Earl-Bishop, who was responsible for building this most extraordinary of houses. Gifts and loans of furniture and paintings and the donation of particular collections, such as the display of delicate English drinking glasses at Mompesson House, have further enriched what is on offer and have enabled the Trust to refurnish those properties where, for whatever reason, the contents have been lost or diminished. At Clandon Park, for example, the enchanting porcelain birds which perch on gilded brackets and other surfaces in many of the rooms are from the bequest of Mrs Gubbay, whose fine eighteenth-century furniture and carpets are also on show in the house. In recent times, too, the Trust has benefited enormously from the loan of portraits from the National Portrait Gallery, whose paintings now account for the show of sixteenth- and seventeenth-century figures in the Long Gallery at Montacute in Somerset and for similarly appropriate displays at two properties in the north of England, Beningbrough and Gawthorpe.

But grandeur is only one side of the story. At many houses, as well as being conducted through the finely decorated show rooms, visitors are also able to see the extensive quarters, often grouped round a courtyard of their own, where an army of servants kept the establishment going, cooking meals of many courses for the dining room, cleaning clothes and linen, brewing beer and making butter, cream and cheese from milk brought in from the home farm. Some 40 servants were employed at Penrhyn Castle in the late nineteenth century, among them the men who tended to the 36 horses in the stables and the French chef who presided over the gastronomic dinners served to the Prince of Wales and his entourage during their visit to the house in 1894. A property may have a prettily tiled dairy, and at Ham House, the great brick palace set beside the Thames just upstream of Richmond, there is even a late seventeenth-century still house, where soaps, sweet-scented waters and ointments were prepared. At Llanerchaeron, in the depths of rural Wales, there are original cheese presses and cream pans made of slate in the buildings grouped round the late eighteenth-century service courtyard. These rare survivals are typical examples of the Trust's extensive collection of the kind of everyday objects that were once seen everywhere but are now uncommon, among them such things as leather fire buckets, double-handled creamware pottery jugs used for carrying milk from the dairy to the house, spits and other equipment for roasting meat over an open fire, and a range of carts, carriages and other conveyances. Particularly memorable is the large collection of early bicycles, one of them with a wooden frame as well as wooden wheels, that now hangs in one of the attics at Snowshill, the modest Cotswold manor which Charles Wade, that most individual of collectors, stuffed with a mix of household objects and more precious things.

As Snowshill shows, smaller properties can be just as fascinating as the grander and more imposing places. In many cases, too, more modest buildings enjoy magnificent settings, or take the intrepid visitor on excursions to remote corners of the countryside that would otherwise remain unseen. Anyone who has visited the gentrified farmhouse known as Plas-yn-Rhiw, set in a far corner of the long Llŷn peninsula, will remember the views over the sea towards the mountains of Wales, the tang of salt in the air, and the sense of being somewhere very remote, as much as the little granite-walled house itself, filled with the possessions of the indomitable Keating sisters. Similarly, visiting

Lindisfarne Castle, built on a dolerite crag at the southern end of Holy Island off the Northumberland coast, has all the ingredients of an adventure, not least because this intriguing place, created out of what was once a small Tudor fort, can only be approached over a causeway that is under several feet of water at high tide. And across country to the south, the Tudor hunting lodge of Newark Park, perched high on a spur of the Cotswolds, enjoys panoramic views over wooded slopes plunging to the Severn valley from the windows of the former banqueting room on the top floor.

Many smaller places have distinguished connections. A little stone cottage set high above the Tyne, and originally thatched with heather from the hills, was the birthplace of the engraver and naturalist Thomas Bewick; Compton Castle, a walled and towered medieval manor hidden in a fold of the soft south Devon countryside just inland from the sea, is the seat of the Gilbert family, whose Elizabethan forebears include the adventurer Sir Humphrey Gilbert, who claimed Newfoundland for Elizabeth I in 1583; and the half-timbered farmhouse at one end of the little Kentish village of Smallhythe was lived in by the actress Ellen Terry from 1899 until her death in 1928 and is full of mementoes of her life and work. Recently acquired is the comfortable and unassuming house, in a leafy village on the edge of the Chilterns, where the multi-millionaire and philanthropist William Morris, 1st Lord Nuffield, lived for 30 years.

Most numerous are the properties connected with writers, among them the little cob and thatch cottage where the poet and novelist Thomas Hardy was born in 1840, and which he immortalised in *Under the Greenwood Tree*; the elegant Georgian house on the banks of the Derwent in the little Cumbrian town of Cockermouth where William Wordsworth was born; weather-boarded Monk's House in the village of Rodmell, which Leonard Woolf and his wife Virginia bought as a country retreat in 1919 and where she wrote in a shed at the far end of the garden; and Bateman's, buried in a deep Wealden valley, where Rudyard Kipling produced some of his greatest work. In 2000, the Trust was gifted the Greenway estate on the banks of the Dart, where an atmospheric woodland garden plunging steeply to the river surrounds the plain Georgian house which Agatha Christie, most prolific of authors, and her husband bought in 1938 as a holiday home.

This book covers both the Trust's grandest places, such as Knole and Petworth, and the many lesser houses and other buildings that are open to visitors. All are worth seeing, but those described in the separate section at the back of the book are, on the whole, the kind of properties that would not detain you long, are not regularly open, or only to be seen by appointment, and do not justify a lengthy detour or a day out. This end section is rich in windmills and watermills, barns and dovecotes, monuments and follies and other small and mostly vernacular buildings, many of them, such as the Welsh farmhouse of Aberdeunant, or Sticklebarn Tavern in the Lake District, in beautiful surroundings.

Today the Trust is huge, but the philosophy and principles on which it rests remain unchanged. Most importantly, as its founders recognised, it is completely independent of government subsidy, relying for its income on the generosity of the public together with support from bodies such as the Heritage Lottery Fund, Historic Buildings Council and the National Heritage Memorial Fund, which may recommend a grant to make up an endowment or help meet the cost of a major acquisition. Increasingly, too, local authorities have provided financial assistance. Nevertheless, although rich in terms of what it holds, the Trust is always short of money. When Tyntesfield, a major example of Victorian Gothic architecture, was due to be sold by public auction in 2001, the necessary funds were only secured by a whirlwind appeal. The sum of over £20 million that was raised included a vital contribution from the National Heritage Memorial Fund. In 2009 the Trust had to dig deep into its own resources to come up with an adequate endowment for Seaton Delaval, John Vanbrugh's theatrical baroque house on the coast of Northumberland.

Secondly, as a result of an Act of 1907, which also gave the infant charity statutory authority, the Trust has the unique power to declare its properties and land inalienable, which means they cannot be sold or mortgaged. This is a priceless asset, which effectively means that anything gifted will be safeguarded for ever. Thirdly, and again this has been a principle since its early days, the Trust exists to conserve buildings and countryside for the nation, for all of us to enjoy. With the massive growth in membership and visitor numbers in recent years, this has inevitably led to a conflict between the demands of access and conservation. This raises dilemmas of which the Trust is acutely aware and accounts for, for example, very low light levels in some rooms and restrictions on visitor numbers.

Today, tourism, and the visiting of historic properties, is a major activity. But there is nothing new about it. As Jane Austen shows so clearly in *Pride and Prejudice*, when Elizabeth Bennet and her uncle and aunt go to visit Pemberley, Mr Darcy's grand country house, it was understood that people would turn up at these places and ask to be shown round. Elizabeth and the Gardiners are attended to by the housekeeper, 'a respectable-looking elderly woman', and it was part of a housekeeper's duties to act in this way when the owners were absent, a task that usually brought them a generous tip. Jane Austen was describing the world she knew, of the late eighteenth and early nineteenth century, but interest in country seats goes back at least another hundred years. When the indomitable Celia Fiennes travelled round England in the late seventeenth century, visiting the houses of the great was part of her itinerary. By the later eighteenth century, among the educated and leisured, it was commonplace. As Boswell recorded in his journal, he and Dr Johnson were taken round Kedleston in 1777 by the elderly Mrs Garnett, who was housekeeper there for over 30 years and whose portrait by Thomas Barber hangs in the house. When talking to visitors, she presumably referred to the printed catalogue of pictures and statues which she is shown holding in her hands. Some 240 years later, the Trust's guidebooks are the descendants of such catalogues.

A La Ronde

Devon
2 miles (3.2 kilometres) north of
Exmouth on the A376

On the northern fringes of Exmouth, with views across the Exe estuary, is a delightfully uninhibited late eighteenth-century *cottage ornée*. Looking rather like a dovecote for humans, A La Ronde is a small, sixteen-sided, three-storey house, with rough limestone walls and a steeply pitched conical roof – now tiled but originally thatched – topped off with tall brick chimneys. Dating from a time when Exmouth was a fashionable resort, it was built, almost certainly to designs by the Bath architect John Lowder, for two resourceful spinsters: Jane Parminter, daughter of a Barnstaple wine merchant, and her younger cousin Mary, who had both just returned from a nine-year Grand Tour. The design of the house, with wedge-shaped main rooms divided by triangular lobbies, and curious diamond-shaped windows on the exterior angles, is unusual enough; even more so are the decorative schemes of the Parminters.

These are rare survivals of the kind of time-consuming, intricate techniques involving paint and paper, shell and feathers, sand and seaweed, which were much indulged in by Regency ladies but which, due to their fragility, have mostly been lost. The interior of the property stands out, too, for the skilful use of awkward angles and corners, and for the survival of its original contents.

The main rooms are arranged around a central octagon. The eight doors off have marbled yellow and green architraves, ingenious seats fold down over the openings and there are unique painted chairs with octagonal seats. The west-facing drawing room has its eighteenth-century tub chairs and sofa, the original marbled skirting and painted pelmet and the Parminters' feather frieze, with a delicate pattern of downy concentric circles.

Pictures here include a large silhouette group of the Parminter family in 1783 and landscapes of paper, sand and seaweed, with feathery trees stretching out their microscopic branches. A chimney board with shellwork surrounding a watercolour of St Michael's Mount (*see* p.276) is a prelude to the gallery at the top of the house. Alas, so fragile that it can only be viewed on video, this is the Parminters' *tour de force*, with shell-encrusted recesses and a zigzag frieze setting off feathery bird portraits resting on moss and twigs.

Jane died in 1811, Mary in 1849. Partly due to Mary's will, which aimed to keep the house as it was and to allow only unmarried kinswomen to inherit, A La Ronde survived remarkably unaltered, despite the attentions of its only male owner, the Rev. Oswald Reichel, who added the third-storey dormer windows and roofline catwalk and introduced a dark Victorian note to some of the rooms. The family struggled to keep the property intact until increasing difficulties brought it to the National Trust in 1991.

OPPOSITE A La Ronde: this whimsical sixteen-sided house on the outskirts of Exmouth was built in the 1790s for Jane and Mary Parminter, who were cousins, and originally had dovecotes hanging from the eaves.
ABOVE LEFT The intricate decoration of the Shell Gallery took years of work to complete.

Alfriston Clergy House

East Sussex
4 miles (6.4 kilometres)
north-east of Seaford,
between the A27 and the A259,
in Alfriston village

Despite its name, this small, timber-framed thatched building looking over the green of a leafy South Downs village was probably built for a well-to-do farmer. It became known as the Clergy House because it was subsequently owned by the Church and it may have been the vicarage at some time in its history. Constructed in about 1350, it is typical of its date, with a central hall rising to the rafters flanked by two-storey blocks on either side, one containing the family's private apartments, the other service quarters. The hall has a rammed chalk floor of a kind local to Sussex, the lumps of chalk being laid and sealed with sour milk.

Bought in 1896 for only £10, Alfriston Clergy House was the first building to come to the National Trust, and is one of only a very few fourteenth-century houses surviving in such a little-altered state. It is surrounded by a small cottage garden.

BELOW Alfriston Clergy House, the first building to be acquired by the Trust, was bought in 1896 for £10. It was in a ruinous state and essential repairs were made only just in time to save it.

Anglesey Abbey and Lode Mill

Cambridgeshire
In the village of Lode, 6 miles (9.6 kilometres) north-east of Cambridge on the B1102

An interest in horse racing led Huttleston Broughton, later 1st Lord Fairhaven, and his brother Henry to purchase Anglesey Abbey in 1926. A typical stone Jacobean manor house with mullioned windows and tall chimneys, it was conveniently placed for Newmarket and the family stud near Bury St Edmunds and set in good partridge-shooting country. Apart from the vaulted monks' parlour, now the dining room, few traces remained of the Augustinian priory established here in the early thirteenth century from which the house takes its name.

Although his sporting interests were never neglected, over the next 40 years Lord Fairhaven transformed and extended the house, of which he was sole owner from 1932, and filled it with an exceptional and wide-ranging collection of works of art. His taste had been formed as a child in New York where his American mother, the oil heiress Carla Leyland Rogers, had furnished the family house with exquisite things, and where his parents moved in the same circles as the Fricks, Rockefellers and Vanderbilts. And there was no shortage of money. Lord Fairhaven's great wealth came not only from his mother but also from his English father, who made a fortune in American railroads.

Comfortable intimate interiors, where log fires were kept burning all day, were created with the help of the architect Sidney Parvin, who introduced panelling, antique stone fireplaces, a vaulted corridor, a stone spiral staircase and other 'period' touches. These rooms are the setting for carefully arranged groupings of fine furniture, clocks (of which 37 are on display), silver, tapestries, small bronzes and other statuary, and paintings. In the dining room, the medieval vaulting is complemented by a massive refectory table, at which the family still eat, and by a sixteenth-century carved oak cabinet, but elsewhere objects of very different date and character, some of which Lord Fairhaven inherited from his mother, are set harmoniously together. In the living room a goat modelled by the great eighteenth-century sculptor Michael Rysbrack sits on a late seventeenth-century inlaid Italian cabinet, a Regency clock devised as a pagoda stands against a French tapestry, and

ABOVE The Jacobean south front of Anglesey Abbey, with square-headed mullioned and transomed windows, dates from c. 1600, although the period porch was added in the twentieth century.

there are eighteenth-century English landscapes on the walls, one of them a Suffolk coastal scene by Gainsborough. Also here is a medieval wooden carving of St Jerome and the lion, with the beast depicted looking up at the saint affectionately.

Lord Fairhaven's exceptional collection of books, some with very fine bindings, are housed in the spacious and airy library, doubled in size by mirrors on the end walls, that was built on by Sidney Parvin in 1937–8. The 9,000 or so volumes now here, overlooked by John Constable's panoramic riverscape showing the opening of Waterloo Bridge in 1817, include rarities such as Saxton's atlas of the English counties of 1574–9 and many spectacular illustrated books from the period 1770–1820. Intriguingly, the shelves are made of elmwood taken from Waterloo Bridge when it was demolished in 1934. Two exquisite eighteenth-century silver chandeliers in this room, each carrying a royal crown, were designed by William Kent for George II.

Lord Fairhaven had a particular liking for nudes by the fashionable Victorian painter William Etty, about 20 of which now hang in the house. He also acquired a unique collection of views of Windsor, where he lived for a time in the Great Park. Displayed in the two-storey gallery designed by Sir Albert Richardson that was built onto the house in 1955, these paintings faithfully record changes in landscape and architecture over 350 years and range in style from the toy castle depicted in an early seventeenth-century canvas to William Daniell's mistily romantic view down the Long Walk, executed in the early nineteenth century. On the lower floor hang the three paintings for which this space was primarily created, a biblical scene by Aelbert Cuyp, and two of the sublime landscapes by Claude Lorraine that inspired the naturalistic gardens of the eighteenth century. In *The Landing of Aeneas*, each slave rowing the boat carrying the Trojan leader is an individual, two looking over their shoulders to see how far they are from the shore. Displays of fine silver in the gallery include the sculptor John Flaxman's *Shield of Achilles*, which was inspired by a description in Homer's *Iliad*.

To set off his house, Lord Fairhaven transformed 40 acres of unpromising fen into a garden on the scale of an eighteenth-century landscape. A composition in trees and grass against the backdrop of towering East Anglian skies, this is a place of long vistas punctuated by an urn, a statue or some

other eye-catcher. Broad avenues and walks, such as the wide grassy ride lined by double rows of horse chestnuts which runs for half a mile (0.8 kilometre) to the west of the house, provide a bold geometric framework, within which are some areas of very different character. Some are grand set pieces, like the curved border in the herbaceous garden, with its spectacular summer displays; others are more intimate and enclosed, such as the small sheltered lawn where William

ABOVE Lord Fairhaven's winter drawing room, where the paintings hung against Jacobean oak panelling include a serene landscape by Claude.

Theed's *Narcissus* contemplates his image in the still waters of a pond. Several vistas focus on the water-mill on the River Lode at the northernmost tip of the garden. A white weather-boarded building with a projecting lucarne (dormer window) on the fourth floor, the present structure dates from the eighteenth century, but there has probably been a mill here since the time of Domesday Book. The mill is once again a working water-mill, used for grinding flour.

Antony

Cornwall

5 miles (8 kilometres) west of
Plymouth via the Torpoint car ferry,
2 miles (3.2 kilometres) north-west
of Torpoint, north of the A374,
16 miles (25.7 kilometres)
south-east of Liskeard, 15 miles
(24 kilometres) east of Looe

Antony stands at the end of the long neck of land forming the far south-eastern corner of Cornwall, an isolated peninsula bounded by the estuaries of the rivers Tamar and Lynher to the east and north, and by the sea to the south. The best way of approaching Antony is by boat, as it has been for centuries, crossing to Cornwall by the car ferry from Plymouth to Torpoint rather than taking the much longer route by road over the Tamar Bridge. The house is beautifully set. The entrance front faces up a slight rise crowned by a wrought-iron screen, but at the back the ground falls away across terraces to a sweep of grass and woodland beyond. Attractively grouped clumps of trees frame glimpses of the Lynher and of the arches of Brunel's Saltash railway bridge crossing the Tamar estuary.

The Antony estate has been the property of the Carews, and their descendants the Pole-Carews and Carew Poles, since the early fifteenth century. The main block of the present house, an elegant two-storey rectangle faced with beautiful silvery-grey stone and ornamented only with the plainest of pediments marking the central bay and with pilasters framing the front door, was built by Sir William Carew between 1718 and 1724. The architect is as yet unknown. Red-brick colonnaded wings enclosing a courtyard on the south front, thought to have been designed by James Gibbs, were added a little later. It is a charming and entirely satisfying house, one of the best of its date in the West Country, and was built to be lived in, not as a show place: modest, oak-panelled rooms lead off the hall and upstairs there are only five principal bedrooms, the space for a sixth being taken up by the huge and elegant staircase.

Antony is exceptional for the quality of its furnishings and for the collection of family and other portraits. Queen Anne pier glasses in the saloon, where three long windows look out towards the Lynher, and a Soho tapestry hanging in the room next door, were made for the house, and other pieces that have always been here include a set of early eighteenth-century walnut-framed settees and chairs. At the same time, each

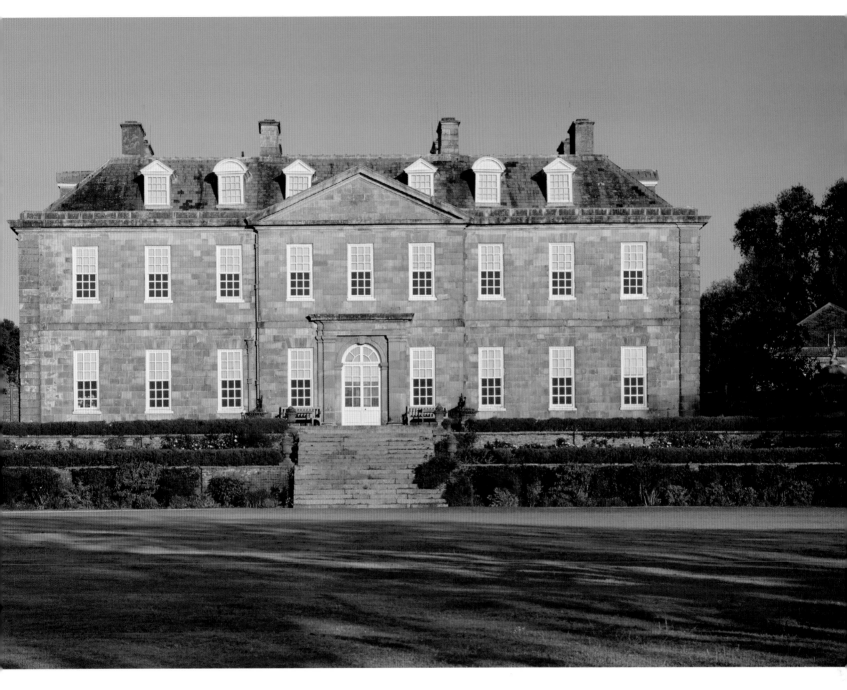

ABOVE LEFT This ship's figurehead greets visitors from one of the brick colonnades enclosing the forecourt.
LEFT: A detail of the rich carving on the mid nineteenth-century Italian alabaster urn standing in the porch.

ABOVE Antony's elegant north front looks across a sweep of grass to tree-framed vistas of the Lynher estuary.

generation of the family has continued to enrich the house, a recent acquisition being the endearing Chinese ceramic army from the Ming period (1368–1644) displayed over the fireplace in the tapestry room.

The portraits, including several works by Reynolds, enhance every room. Most memorable is the likeness of Charles I painted at his trial that hangs in the hall. The king is shown dressed in black wearing a large beaver hat, his sad eyes pouched with weariness. This is the last of a number of portraits that record Charles's final days and only here has the famous pointed beard turned grey. John Carew, who had sat in judgement on Charles, was himself executed at the Restoration. His tragic elder brother Alexander, whose portrait hangs in the library, suffered the same fate at the hands of the Parliamentarians, dying with a troubled and divided mind, uncertain which cause was right.

No such doubts assailed the historian Richard Carew, author of the great *Survey of Cornwall*, who inherited the estate in 1564. His striking portrait, painted in 1586 when he was 32, faces Charles across the hall. Two years later he must have seen the Armada sail up the Channel along the coast for which, as deputy lieutenant of the county, he was responsible.

Antony's landscaped setting, with tree-framed lawns sweeping down to the Lynher and views across to the opposite bank, is partly due to Humphry Repton, who was consulted in 1792 and produced one of his earliest Red Books at the house. The terraces above the lawns were once planted with parterres and there is a more formal garden to the west with clipped yew hedges, espaliered fruit trees, a sheltered flower garden and a knot garden. An eighteenth-century dovecote squats by the house; some striking modern sculptures, by William Pye and others, were commissioned by Sir Richard Carew Pole, who lives at Antony; and hidden in a tangle of woodland beside the Lynher (not owned by the National Trust) is a bath house of 1784, with a plunge bath.

Ardress House

Co. Armagh
7 miles (11.2 kilometres) from Portadown on the B28 Moy road, 5 miles (8 kilometres) from Moy, 3 miles (4.8 kilometres) from Loughgall, intersection 13 on the M1

Ardress House is not quite what it seems: the apparently Georgian entrance front disguises what was originally a seventeenth-century farmhouse, one room deep, the roof of which still rises above the urn-studded parapet. Moreover, the long two-storey facade with an impressive array of sash windows is partly a sham, one end of it being nothing more than a screen wall with false openings added in the interests of symmetry. There is a pedimented portico giving dignity and importance to the front door but it is not placed centrally between the windows on either side. The interiors of Ardress similarly reflect the gradual evolution of the house: intimate and homely rooms, and a worn flagged floor in the hall, contrast with grander later additions.

This piecemeal gentrification was partly the work of the architect George Ensor, who married the heiress of Ardress in 1760 and moved here from Dublin some 20 years later. Although he doubled the size of the house, a full remodelling was beyond his means and, apart from adding the classical portico on the entrance front, he concentrated his resources on an elegant new drawing room. Ardress's finest feature, the room is dominated by exceptional Adam-style plasterwork. An intricate pattern of intersecting circles and arcs round the central medallion on the ceiling, one of several showing figures and scenes from classical mythology, is picked out in muted tones of yellow, mauve and grey, with a rich blue as contrast. Whirls of foliage here are echoed in more extravagant loops and chains framing more medallions on the walls. Playful plaster cherubs along the frieze stand with the right leg crossed behind the left, except in one corner of the room, where the stance is reversed. This exceptional plaster decoration, among the finest in Ireland, was the work of the outstanding stuccadore Michael Stapleton, who is known for the magnificent interiors he created in eighteenth-century Dublin, where Ensor's brother John was a leading architect.

LEFT Gentrification of Ardress House in the mid eighteenth century accounts for the Georgian entrance front, which conceals an older building behind.
OPPOSITE One of the plaster medallions decorating the walls of the drawing room at Ardress House.

Stapleton and Ensor would have known each other, and may even have worked together.

The lawyer and author George Ensor II's additions to the house in the early nineteenth century, including the extended entrance facade and curving screen walls framing the garden front, are a more mixed bag. His new wing at the back of the house contains a cavernous dining room which can only be reached from outside, because an internal door would have upset the Stapleton plasterwork in the drawing room next door. The dining room is now hung with seventeenth-century Dutch and Flemish paintings on loan from the collection of the Earl of Castle Stewart, among them a rare signed picture by the Flemish artist J. Myts. The diminutive haloed figure of Our Lord on the road to Emmaus is portrayed in a Northern European setting, with gentlemen in frock coats and a cluster of steep-roofed half-timbered houses marking a little town in the distance.

Fine period furniture includes a locally made oak and applewood bureau-bookcase of 1725 in the little parlour, an oak Irish Chippendale sideboard with characteristic five-clawed feet and lion's mask decoration in the dining room and a pair of Neo-classical settees in the drawing room. A late eighteenth-century table made for the Speaker of the Irish Parliament is the one on which George V signed the Constitution of Northern Ireland when Ulster was formally separated from the rest of the country in 1921.

A cobbled yard behind the house is a reminder of the working farm Ardress once was, the outbuildings here including a dairy, a smithy, a cow byre, a threshing barn complete with horse-powered thresher, and a boiler house where large quantities of potatoes were cooked for the pigs. There is a formal garden and landscaped woodland near the house; beyond, the farmland, orchards and woods of the estate slope down to the Tall River.

The Argory

Co. Armagh
4 miles (6.4 kilometres) from Moy,
3 miles (4.8 kilometres) from the
M1, exit 14

The barrister Walter McGeough Bond's decision in the 1820s to build on his newly inherited land at Derrycaw was influenced by the terms of a very curious will. He and his three sisters had been left the bulk of their father's fortune, their unfortunate elder brother inheriting only £400, but Walter was not allowed to live at Drumsill, the family house, while two of his sisters remained unmarried. He was wise to provide himself with an alternative establishment as two of his sisters remained at Drumsill until they died, rich and eccentric old spinsters.

Walter McGeough Bond's house was completed in 1824, but in the early 1830s he employed the brothers Arthur and John Williamson, associates of the much more famous Dublin architect Francis Johnson, to remodel and extend it. Echoes of Johnson's austere style appear in the modest two-storey stone building set on a rise overlooking the Blackwater River, its plain Neo-classical facades given added interest by the lengthened centre windows that were introduced on the west and south in the late nineteenth century.

The drawing room, fitted out with mahogany furniture, sumptuous curtains and upholstery, potted plants, an abundance of cushions and *objets* and fur-draped chairs, is typical of The Argory's largely original interiors, which powerfully evoke the lifestyle of the Irish gentry during the early nineteenth century. The family traditionally entertained at tea-time and the white cloth on the dining-room table is set with china and silver as if awaiting guests. Tea was also occasionally taken at the round walnut table in the organ lobby on the first floor, where a magnificent instrument made by James Bishop of London was commissioned by Walter in 1822. Three surviving 1.8-metre (6-foot) barrels hold a selection of music chosen on the advice of Samuel Sebastian Wesley, nephew of the founder of Methodism, whose recommendations seem to have resulted in a mixture of suitably uplifting hymn tunes such as 'See, the conquering hero comes' and excerpts from *The Magic Flute*. The instrument can also be played manually.

Personal possessions in the bedrooms have a strong period feel. A wardrobe is filled with Lady Bond's early twentieth-

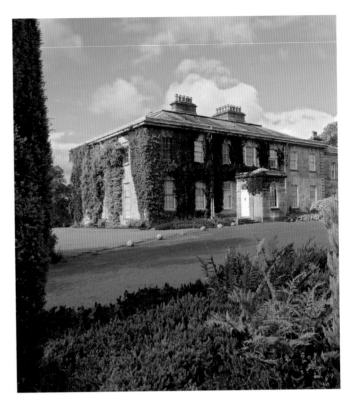

ABOVE The Argory's atmospheric interiors evoke country-house living in nineteenth-century Ireland.

century outfits, including fashionable narrow-waisted jackets and tiny Italian shoes. Another holds her hats. Ugly gas lamps disguised as candles on the dressing-tables are examples of The Argory's early nineteenth-century lighting arrangements, the most impressive being the six fittings with pale green conical shades that hang low over the billiard table. Originally oil, the fittings were subsequently converted to gas and run from the plant still to be seen in the stable yard, which was installed by the Sunbeam Acetylene Gas Company of Belfast in 1906 at a cost of £250.

A little Victorian rose garden leads into the pleasure ground sloping down to meadows fringing the Blackwater River. There is a pair of garden pavilions, of the same date as the house, linked by a long curving walk, and a wide lawn is studded with two yew arbours and a handkerchief tree and framed by shrub borders.

Arlington Court

Devon
7 miles (11.2 kilometres)
north-east of Barnstaple on
the A39

The plain, grey stone facades of this Neo-classical house are no preparation for the cluttered Victorian interior, where boldly patterned and coloured wallpaper sets off mahogany furniture and display cabinets overflowing with shells, snuffboxes, model ships, pewter and precious objects. The house was built in 1820 for Colonel John Chichester by the Barnstaple architect Thomas Lee and still has some decorative schemes of 1839, by the London firm of John Crace and George Trollop. But the collections are all the work of Rosalie Chichester, the last of the Chichesters of Arlington, who lived here for 84 years until her death in 1949.

Only child of the flamboyant and extravagant Bruce Chichester, who created the opulent staircase hall hung with yachting pictures more suited to a gentleman's club than a private house, Rosalie had been taken on two world cruises in her father's schooner *Erminia* before she reached her teens.

Perhaps fired by these early experiences, she was always an enthusiastic traveller, one of the many delightful photographs on display showing her with Chrissie Peters, her diminutive companion, in New Zealand, both of them in sensible shoes and heavy suits with skirts down to their ankles. The Pacific shells and other mementoes she brought back from her travels were added to her growing collections, among them such things as model ships, tea caddies, candle snuffers and paperweights as well as more exotic items. Although her stuffed birds, Maori skirts and African clubs are no longer in the house, and the National Trust had to make the rooms less crowded before they could be opened to visitors, Arlington is still full of Rosalie's treasures, including the largest collection of pewter held by the Trust. Her favourite piece, a slightly malevolent red amber elephant from China, is prominently

BELOW The main block of Arlington Court, marked by the single-storey porch, was built in a plain Greek Revival style in 1820; the service wing to the right was added in 1865.

displayed in the White Drawing Room, one of three sunny rooms that interconnect along the south front. Also in the drawing room is a thirteenth-century Flemish psalter and in the ante-room next door hangs a mystical watercolour by William Blake, which was found on top of a pantry cupboard in 1949.

On the first-floor landing another watercolour, of Miss Chichester's parrot Polly, reflects her passionate love of all living plants and creatures. This undoubtedly eccentric lady kept budgerigars and canaries in brass cages in the house and allowed her parrot to fly free and peacocks to wander in to the house from outside.

Shady lawns surrounding the house are planted with specimen trees, including an ash collection. Some distance away is a small formal garden laid out in 1865, where a conservatory against a high brick wall looks down over three grass terraces and a fountain pool guarded by metal herons, the birds of the Chichester crest. To the west of the house, beyond the little parish church filled with Chichester memorials, is the colonnaded stable block constructed by Rosalie's father. A modern extension here now displays one of the finest carriage collections in Britain. Largely dating from the nineteenth century, and brought together after the Trust took over the house, the exhibits range from carriages made for children and a pony carriage made for Queen Victoria to a travelling chariot that is known to have been driven to Vienna.

Arlington is the centre of a thriving agricultural estate, as it has been ever since the Chichester family came here in the sixteenth century. A walk leads down to the thickly wooded valley of the River Yeo, where two great piers on the lake half a mile (0.8 kilometre) below the house are all that was built of the suspension bridge Rosalie's father had planned to carry a grand new drive. The lake and woods, which have been rejuvenated by the Trust, are a haven for wildlife, as Miss Rosalie intended, and the Jacob sheep and Shetland ponies in the park are descendants of those she established here as part of her wildlife sanctuary.

RIGHT The Morning Room at Arlington Court, decorated with boldly patterned wallpaper by John Crace that was put up in 1839, forms one end of a long sunny gallery running down the south front.

Ascott

Bedfordshire
½ mile (0.8 kilometre) east of
Wing, 2 miles (3.2 kilometres)
south-west of Leighton Buzzard,
on the south side of the A418

Entrepreneurial talent rarely passes from generation to generation, but Mayer Amschel Rothschild (1744–1812), who founded the family banking business in Frankfurt during the Napoleonic Wars, was blessed with five sons whose drive and ambition matched his own. While one inherited his father's mantle, the others dispersed to Paris, Naples, Vienna and London to set up branches of the firm. The wealth generated by the activities of this extraordinary clan financed the collection in this rambling neo-Jacobean house overlooking the Vale of Aylesbury as well as the more flamboyant magnificence of Waddesdon Manor a few miles away (*see* p.336).

Ascott is the creation of Leopold de Rothschild, great-grandson of the founder of the family fortunes and son of Baron Lionel, the first Jewish British MP. The little Jacobean farmhouse he took over in 1876 is now buried in the gabled ranges, all black-and-white half-timbering and diamond-paned windows, added by the architect George Devey, and his assistant James Williams, in the years that followed, transforming the house into a massively overgrown cottage. But, despite Ascott's size, the rooms are pleasingly domestic in scale. Rothschilds live here still and the atmosphere is that of a beautifully furnished private house. Leopold's son Anthony removed most of the original Victorian décor in the 1930s and recently Sir Evelyn de Rothschild, Anthony's son, has again redecorated the rooms on show.

Predominantly Dutch and English paintings include Aelbert Cuyp's panoramic *View of Dordrecht*, its wide shallow canvas filling one wall of the low-ceilinged dining room. The town lies on the left, a low sun lighting up a row of gabled houses on the glassy river and giving a warm glow to the clouds heaped overhead. A faint mark in the centre of the painting shows where the canvas was once divided to be sold in two halves. A striking woman by Gainsborough, thought to be a likeness of the Duchess of Richmond, her flaming red curls set off by the silky sheen of her blue satin dress, is one of a number of fine English portraits at Ascott. There are three of Stubbs's distinctive horse studies, including the only known

canvas in which he shows mares without any foals (shown above), and a major work from the Italian Renaissance, Andrea del Sarto's arresting *Madonna and Child with St John*. Elegant eighteenth-century English furniture, such as the two oval pie-crust tables and the walnut and mahogany chairs covered with tapestry and needlework in the oak-panelled library, contrast with the contemporary French pieces elsewhere.

Anthony de Rothschild added paintings and English furniture to his father's collection and also introduced the oriental ceramics that are now such a prominent feature of the house. The earliest pieces are ceramics from the Han (206BC–AD220), Tang (618–906) and Sung (906–1280) dynasties, with the cream of the collection, in deep rich colours, from the Ming (1368–1644) and Kangxi (1662–1722) periods. These were the centuries that produced sophisticated, three-colour ware in vibrant shades of blue, purple and burnt yellow, such as the elegant vases decorated with flowing chrysanthemums.

But it is the paintings, one of the best small collections in Britain, that make a visit to Ascott so rewarding. And afterwards visitors can enjoy panoramic views to the Chilterns from the terraced lawns that fall away from the house.

ABOVE This serene picture by George Stubbs, the only known canvas in which this renowned horse-painter showed mares without their foals, is part of the exceptional Rothschild art collection at Ascott.

Ashdown House

Oxfordshire
2½ miles (4 kilometres) south of Ashbury, 3½ miles (5.6 kilometres) north of Lambourn, on the west side of the B4000

Set high up on the rolling, windswept Berkshire Downs, some 2 miles (3 kilometres) from the nearest village, is this unusual and appealing seventeenth-century house. Built of a pleasing combination of creamy chalk, quarried from the downs nearby, and honey-coloured Bath stone, Ashdown is square in plan and exceptionally tall and narrow, with three main storeys rising to a hipped roof and a crowning cupola. There is something Dutch about it, as if one of the contemporary town houses that are packed tightly along the canals of Amsterdam had been suddenly uprooted and put down in this isolated spot. The architect may have been William Winde (see, for example, p.49), who spent his early years with exiled Royalists in Holland and would have seen similar buildings in Leiden, Amsterdam and The Hague. Ashdown would look even more out of place in its downland setting were it not for the fact that its outline is broadened and softened by detached pavilions on either side, possibly added some 20 years after the main block was built in the early 1660s.

Appropriately enough, this singular place was constructed for the eccentric and endearing William, 1st Lord Craven. Also one of the richest men of his day, the 1st Lord was devoted to Charles I's sister, Elizabeth of Bohemia, who had reigned for only one winter with her husband Frederick when the forces of the Hapsburg emperor forced them into exile in 1620. Craven met Elizabeth in The Hague, where she and Frederick had taken refuge. He gave her unstinting support, particularly during the English Civil War, and offered her his London house when she returned to England after the Restoration.

Craven may have intended that Ashdown would be a refuge for the queen from plague-ridden London, or it may have been designed as a hunting lodge from which to watch the chase, which is why it is so tall. Whatever the truth, Elizabeth never came here, dying in 1662 before the house was completed. But she left the 1st Lord all her papers and pictures, and this legacy accounts for the portraits of the Winter Queen and her family that now enrich the interior. Presented to the National Trust by the Treasury from the Craven Collection in 1968, these portraits hang in the hall and on the staircase that rises

the height of the building. Echoing the strong associations of the exterior, all except three are works by or after two Dutch artists, Michel Miereveldt and Gerard van Honthorst.

The west front of the house is now set off by a formal parterre based on a seventeenth-century engraving, such as Winde might have designed. The twists and curves of box and gravel are best seen from the roof, and from here there are also spectacular views over the woodland round the house and to the Berkshire Downs beyond. Long breaks cutting through the trees mark the north–south ride that shows clearly on Kip's engraving of 1724.

OPPOSITE Delightful Ashdown House, perched high on the Berkshire Downs, may have been intended to serve as a grandstand for watching hunting and coursing on the open country around.
BELOW Among the portraits on show is Gerard van Honthorst's painting of Charles I's sister Elizabeth, who was queen of Bohemia for only one winter before being forced into exile. Like the other pictures from the Craven Collection, it was presented to the National Trust by the Treasury in 1968.

Attingham Estate

Shropshire
4 miles (6.4 kilometres)
south-east of Shrewsbury,
on the Telford road

Few family mottoes can be more apposite than that of Noel Hill, 1st Lord Berwick: 'Let wealth be his who knows its use.' This wily politician, who obtained his peerage through expedient loyalty to William Pitt the Younger, poured the fortune he inherited into this grandiose classical house, set, like Wallington (see p.338), in full view of a public road, from which it was devised to look as magnificent as possible.

Designed in 1782 by the individual Scottish architect George Steuart, and a rare survival of his work, Attingham consists of a main three-storey block linked by colonnaded corridors to pavilions on either side, with a classical portico rising the full height of the house on the entrance front. Seen from the bridge taking the road over the River Tern, the facade stretches 122 metres (400 feet) from pavilion to pavilion, while inside there are 80 rooms, an unusually large number for a house of this period. The layout of the interior is equally singular, with the rooms on the west side, including the library and dining room, making up a set of masculine apartments, and those on the east, including the drawing room, a set of feminine rooms.

On the 1st Lord's untimely death at the early age of 44, with Attingham not yet completed and furnished, the house passed successively to his two elder sons, who were responsible for the splendid Regency interiors. Acquisitions during a lengthy Grand Tour in Italy formed the basis of an extensive art collection built up by the 2nd Lord, who commissioned John Nash to add the grand picture gallery in 1805–7. One of the first to be built in a country house, this room is notable for the revolutionary use of curved cast-iron ribs to support the windows in the roof, an innovation that was to be used in the design of the Crystal Palace. Although the 2nd Lord's paintings were largely dispersed in the sale that followed his bankruptcy in 1827, a financial disaster that was precipitated by his marriage, at the age of 43, to a 17-year-old courtesan who helped him spend his fortune, the mixture of Italianate landscapes and copies of Old Masters now hanging two and three deep in the gallery conjures up the splendour of the original collection. A pair of Neapolitan landscapes by Philipp Hackert (1737–1807) includes a view of Pompeii showing the

small extent of the excavated area at the end of the eighteenth century and the garlanded vines that can still be seen in this part of Italy.

Nash was also responsible for the theatrical staircase, with a mahogany handrail inlaid with satinwood and ebony, which rises confidently to a half landing. In the drum-like space available, however, there was not room for the two flights into which the stairs divide to continue elegantly to the first floor, and Nash hid his unsatisfactory solution behind jib doors.

The Regency flavour continues in the dining room. Boldly decorated in deep red and gold, with gilded mouldings framing a show of portraits, the room is dominated by George Steuart's plasterwork design on the ceiling, with its gilded wreath of lacy vine leaves, and there are more vines decorating an original set of mahogany dining chairs. The tiny feminine boudoir on the other side of the house, with a domed ceiling painted with frail tendrils of foliage and medallions depicting cherubs set against rose-tinted clouds, has one of the most delicate late eighteenth-century schemes to survive in England and may be one of the few rooms to have been completed before the 1st Lord's death.

The paintings and furniture now seen in the house were largely collected by the diplomatist 3rd Lord – described by Byron as the only Excellence who was really excellent – during his 25 years in Italy. He was responsible for the elegant pale-blue drawing room filled with white and gold Italian furniture, some of which may have come from Napoleon's sister's Neapolitan palace, and for the glittering silver displayed in the old wine cellars, once stocked with some 900 bottles of sherry, port and Madeira.

Parkland dotted with mature oaks, elms, beeches and pines slopes gently down to the Tern. The initial layout, of 1769–72, was by Thomas Leggett, but the planting schemes reflect the hand of Humphry Repton, who produced a Red Book for Attingham in 1797. A grove of Lebanon cedars marks the start

BELOW The Scottish architect George Steuart designed Attingham's grandiose entrance front, dominated by a three-storey portico.

of Leggett's Mile Walk, which loops down to the river and returns past the walled garden.

The estate, some 1,500 hectares (3,707 acres) of farmland and woodland, stretches across the winding course of the River Severn. On the south side of the river, about 1½ miles (2.4 kilometres) south-west of the house, is Cronkhill, the individual Italianate villa that Nash built for the 2nd Lord in 1802 as an eye-catcher on a low ridge above the river. Built of brick faced in stucco, with round-headed windows and wide-eaved, low-pitched roofs, Cronkhill is delightfully asymmetrical, with a round tower at one end, an arcade enfolding two sides of the main block and a second tower, lower and square in plan, behind. A timber-framed seventeenth-century farmhouse that Nash refaced in brick forms a long south wing, balancing the composition. A pioneering example of the Picturesque style, Cronkhill's design may well have been inspired by the towered and stuccoed rural buildings, of a type seen in many parts of Italy, that often feature in Claude's idyllic landscape paintings, a couple of which were owned by Lord Berwick.

Essentially a residence for a gentleman farmer rather than anything grander, the house was built for Francis Walford, Lord Berwick's agent, who took over the running of the estate in 1804 and it is set close to a group of brick farm buildings. The main reception rooms, ornamented with simple Neo-classical mouldings and fireplaces, reflect the shape of the building: the drawing room, in the round tower, being octagonal; the library, in the other tower, being square; and the dining room, in the main block, rectangular. There is an elegantly curved cantilevered staircase and there are French windows giving access from the main rooms to the arcade, from where there are glorious vistas south over the River Severn and east to the Wrekin. One of Nash's most original buildings, both eye-catcher and viewpoint, Cronkhill marks a watershed in the design of the smaller country house and was to inspire many imitations, even if not as boldly conceived, some of them, such as the villas on the north-western edge of Regent's Park in London, in urban rather than rural settings.

LEFT The intimate boudoir designed for the 1st Lady Berwick at Attingham. In the interests of symmetry, it was given five doors, but only two of them give access into the room.

Avebury

Wiltshire
6 miles (9.6 kilometres)
west of Marlborough, 1 mile
(1.6 kilometres) north of the A4
Bath road, at the junction of the
A4361 and the B4003

The leafy village of Avebury is set in a shallow valley below the ridge of the Marlborough Downs. Immense stones incorporated in several buildings were taken from the prehistoric stone circle that is enmeshed with the village, like some surreal sculpture park, with grassy hollows showing where boulders were removed. In early Saxon and medieval times, when this pagan monument was feared, the village stood further west, outside the circle and its massive bank and ditch and close to the River Kennet, with the church set as a shield between the villagers and the prehistoric remains. Over time, as the stones lost their power, the village crept eastwards across the bank and into the circle, where the narrow main street is now lined with some fine eighteenth-century houses as well as earlier buildings, some of brick, some of flint or cob.

The National Trust owns most of the village and also the old manor on an originally monastic site outside the circle bank, beside the ancient St James's church. The manor's charming classical gateway is approached through what was the estate farmyard, past a thatched and weather-boarded great barn and a moss-encrusted sixteenth-century dovecote. Set back across a stretch of grass is a long, asymmetrical, many-gabled range, with tall chimneys and some stone-mullioned windows. This

BELOW Avebury Manor's rambling east range incorporates the oldest part of the building, dating from the mid-sixteenth century.

is the eastern and oldest wing of a rambling building set round three sides of a small courtyard. Incorporated within it is the modest house, one room deep, built by the upwardly mobile William Dunch in c.1557 and still in evidence in the massive roof beams and low, wide Tudor doorways of the kitchen. A more regular mid-eighteenth-century frontage on the south wing, with a roofline parapet, conceals the range added by James Mervyn in c.1600, although the playful classical porch, ornamented with fluted pilasters, was part of the Elizabethan facade. The spacious parlour with an elegant ribbed plasterwork ceiling extending into the garden from the south end of the Tudor range may also be an Elizabethan improvement, while on the western side of the house is a 1920s library in the same spirit as the old building, with a pretty flight of stone steps leading down into the garden. Interior remodelling of the south wing in the mid-eighteenth century accounts for the carved and pedimented doorways in the dining room and the deep coved ceiling in the room above, while some seventeenth-century oak panelling and other period features, such as the stone fireplace in the parlour, were introduced by Colonel and Mrs Jenner, who lived at Avebury from 1902 to 1929 and restored the house.

Acquired by the Trust in 1991 without any contents, and for many years let to a tenant, in 2011, as a result of an innovative collaboration with the BBC, the manor was refurnished to show how it might have looked at different times in its history. Nine modest rooms, two of them no more than intimate closets, were refitted in period styles taken from the sixteenth to the twentieth century in an approach that linked the house to people associated with it. Traditional skills and materials were used to make appropriate furnishings, although these are in many cases modern interpretations of period designs rather than direct reproductions.

In the parlour, the original plasterwork is now accompanied by an heraldic panel over the fireplace painted with William Dunch's new coat of arms, and by specially-made Tudor-style oak furniture and rush matting. In the Georgian dining room, some pieces of armorial porcelain and hand-painted Chinese wallpaper allude to the tenure of Sir Adam Williamson, who became governor of Jamaica; motifs on the wallpaper include illustrations of the kind of English trading ships that would have called at Jamaica, and of the

manor and stone circle. The bedroom above, with its eighteenth-century coved ceiling, is fitted out with a state bed and high-back chairs as part of a suite of rooms that could well have been prepared for Queen Anne when she came to dine at the manor; while an Art Deco parlour in the Tudor part of the house reflects the interests of the archaeologist Alexander Keiller, who lived here while excavating the stone circle in the late 1930s.

Some furnishings have been bought or salvaged rather than specially made and just a few, such as the semi-circular tables which stand either side of the fireplace in the dining room, are genuine antiques. All the rooms are based on historical parallels and evidence, such as the inventory made on Sir Adam's death in 1798, and a sale catalogue of 1902, but a sense that this is theatre rather than historic experience is heightened by some defiantly modern interpretations of the

BELOW In the Tudor bedroom, decorative oak panelling introduced by the Jenners complements the original plasterwork frieze, shown here before it was brightly painted as part of the recent transformation of the manor.

real thing. Dunch's parlour is lined by printed hangings imitating tapestry and some specially-commissioned paintings include three acrylics by Corin Sands, one of which is a take on the exotic bird paintings that were much admired in the early eighteenth century.

The manor is surrounded by a beautiful compartmental garden developed by Colonel and Mrs Jenner and laid out within an existing framework of Tudor and eighteenth-century

ABOVE Avebury's Georgian dining room, where the hand-painted Chinese wallpaper includes depictions of the manor and of the great stone circle which enfolds the village.

walls in brick and stone. There is much clipped yew and box and gateways give views out into the countryside and of the pinnacled tower of the church.

Baddesley Clinton

Warwickshire
¾ mile (1.2 kilometres) west of the
A4141 Warwick–Birmingham road,
at Chadwick End, 7½ (12
kilometres) miles north-west of
Warwick, 15 miles (24 kilometres)
south-east of central Birmingham

This exceptional medieval manor house set in an ancient park lies in a remnant of the Forest of Arden. Although only 15 miles (24 kilometres) south of Birmingham, the surrounding countryside, criss-crossed by a network of sunken lanes, still has an essentially medieval character, with the waves of former ridge and furrow showing in fields that are now under grass.

The present house, built round three sides of a courtyard, dates from the fifteenth century, but it is encircled by a moat that is probably much older and was dug to surround an earlier building. The only way into the manor is over the two-arched, eighteenth-century bridge that leads to the crenellated gatehouse. Grey walls punctuated with mullioned windows fall sheer to the water on either side and there are tall red-brick Elizabethan chimneys that form splashes of colour against the roof. Despite its guarded appearance, this is not a forbidding place. Its small panelled rooms, filled with mostly seventeenth- and eighteenth-century oak furniture, are intimate and homely.

Baddesley Clinton is a remarkable survival. From the early sixteenth century until 1980, when it came to the National Trust, this romantic moated house was lived in by generation after generation of the Ferrers family who, despite financial pressures, managed to preserve the manor and the estate. In 1940, when the house was first offered for sale, the estate lands were the same as those shown on a map of 1699. Succeeding generations have left their mark on the manor. Henry Ferrers, the Elizabethan antiquary who owned the house from 1564 to 1633, did much to embellish it, rebuilding the south range and introducing oak panelling, carved heraldic overmantels and richly coloured armorial stained glass. Much of this decoration survives, although some, such as the great stone chimneypiece now in the great hall, was once elsewhere. Although a Catholic, Henry seems to have avoided penalties for recusancy, despite the fact that the widow to whom he let the house in the late sixteenth century, when persecution was at its height, sheltered Jesuit priests here and created hiding places for them. One of these, formed

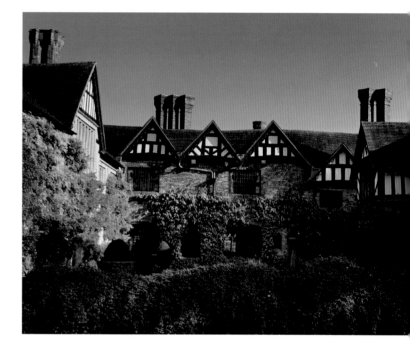

ABOVE The former courtyard at the heart of the house was transformed into a garden in 1889.

out of an old sewer and viewable through a glass panel in the kitchen floor, is where eight men evaded capture in October 1591, standing motionless with their feet in water for four hours. Then, in 1604, Henry was unwittingly involved in the Gunpowder Plot when his Westminster house, which he had let to one of the plotters, was used to store the gunpowder for blowing up Parliament. Although he was never penalised for his religion, Henry died heavily in debt and the family was further impoverished by taxation and appropriations during the Civil War. But this shortage of funds is probably the reason why Baddesley survived unchanged.

At the end of the nineteenth century, the manor's medieval character was further enhanced by an artistic quartet. In 1867 Marmion Edward Ferrers had married Rebecca Dulcibella Orpen, whose romanticised portraits of her friends and life at Baddesley are now a feature of the house. Two years later the couple were joined by Rebecca's aunt, Lady Chatterton, a romantic novelist, and her husband Edward Dering, who devoted his fortune to the house and estate. All four revelled in the antiquity of the place, added further stained glass and other embellishments and created the Catholic chapel, sumptuously fitted out with leather hangings decorated with flowers and birds in gold, pink and blue. Both Lady Chatterton and Rebecca liked to paint in the great parlour on the first floor of the gatehouse, lit by a great mullioned and transomed window inserted in the 1630s. Today, the high barrel ceiling, sparse furnishings and rippling reflections from the moat create a sense of airy spaciousness that contrasts with the dark intimacy of the rest of the house.

ABOVE An early eighteenth-century brick bridge is the only way across the moat which surrounds Baddesley Clinton, one of the most romantic of medieval manor houses.

Barrington Court

Somerset
2 miles (3.2 kilometres) north of the A303 between Ilchester and Ilminster, at the east end of Barrington village, ½ mile (0.8 kilometre) east of the B3168

Twisted finials and chimneys reaching skywards from every gable and angle transform Barrington's roofline into a forest of stone fingers. Although not as grand as Montacute only 10 miles (16 kilometres) or so to the east (see p.214), which it pre-dates by about 40 years, this fine mid-sixteenth-century house has the same indefinable charm, a blend of romance, fantasy and age. It is built to a characteristic Elizabethan E-plan, with long wings projecting either side of the original entrance court on the south front, and the honey-coloured facades with their generous mullioned windows and buttressed gables are typical of the best architecture of the day.

But, unlike its grander neighbour, Barrington was not designed for a high-flying politician. Although Henry Daubeney, the ambitious Tudor courtier who owned the estate in the early sixteenth century, may have begun a grand country seat here after he was created Earl of Bridgwater in 1538, he died bankrupt ten years later and Barrington was completed by William Clifton, a prosperous London merchant to whom the property was sold in 1552. William Strode, whose father had acquired Barrington in 1625, was responsible for the fine late seventeenth-century stable block in the style of Wren which sits beside the house.

Barrington still has an essentially sixteenth-century plan, but many of the original decorative features were torn out and sold during a long period of decline in the nineteenth century when the court became a farmhouse and, ultimately, was used to store cider and keep chickens. The first country house to be acquired by the National Trust, it was bought, in 1907, as an empty, derelict shell, with 'attics full of owls'. Deceptively authentic oak panelling, such as that lining the magnificent gallery that runs the length of the house on the top floor, and other decoration, including a remarkable honeycomb of wooden ribs covering the ceiling of the small dining room, was brought here by Colonel A. Lyle, who took a long lease on the house in 1920. With the help of his architect friend J. Edwin Forbes, Lyle restored Barrington and filled it with his collection of period woodwork taken from other derelict buildings.

The house is shown as it would have been just before the Lyles moved in, as a sequence of atmospheric, unfurnished rooms. The library in the east wing, lit by windows on three sides, is painted a soft sea-green as the Lyles had it and the great hall, with its Tudor gallery at one end and a sprung floor for dancing, is where the Lyles held a ball in 1925 to celebrate the restoration. Upstairs rooms interconnect as they would have done in Tudor times, there are plentiful period bathrooms, and some original features include a painted overmantel bearing the Strode arms in the former Great Chamber.

Barrington is approached from the west through an enchanting formal garden laid out in the brick-walled compartments of former cattle yards. Originally planted with advice from Gertrude Jekyll, the garden is enclosed on two sides by the moat Forbes created to evoke Barrington's Tudor origins.

RIGHT In the 1920s, Colonel Lyle enriched the house with period woodwork salvaged from elsewhere, such as these seventeenth-century oak doors.

ABOVE A great display of twisted finials and chimneys marks the roofline of the early Elizabethan Barrington Court, which was the first country house to be acquired by the Trust.

Basildon Park

Berkshire
Between Pangbourne and Streatley, 7 miles (11.2 kilometres) north-west of Reading, on the west side of the A329

This Neo-classical mansion standing high above the River Thames a little way upstream from Reading was built between 1776 and 1783 by the Yorkshire architect John Carr. One of Carr's best works and his only house in the south of England, it was commissioned by another Yorkshireman, Francis Sykes, who had bought the Basildon property in 1771. Sykes, later 1st Baronet, was one of those ambitious self-made men who returned from India with vast fortunes accumulated in the service of the East India Company. Although less corrupt than many, he appears to have been particularly wealthy and was able to spend lavishly on his new house. Several other men who had made themselves rich in India lived in the tranquil countryside round about, among them his friend Warren Hastings.

John Carr's Palladian villa, built of beautiful honey-coloured Bath stone, is both restrained and suitably grand. A pedimented portico, its massive columns standing out against a deep shadowy recess behind, dominates the three-storey entrance front. To either side, linked to the main house by screen walls that hide service courtyards, are two-storey pavilions, their pedimented facades echoing the design of the central block. Originally, all three parts of the house were linked internally but this is no longer so, the windows and doors on the screen walls being only dummies.

Carr's Neo-classical decoration in the hall, with its delicate plasterwork ceiling subtly coloured like expensive wrapping paper in pink, lilac, green and stone, survives unaltered. His magnificent staircase, lit from above by graceful lunettes and with an elegant wrought-iron balustrade that curves gently upwards, is little changed. But Francis Sykes did not finish his new house, perhaps because he never recovered from the investigation into his dealings in India which lost him his parliamentary seat and left him £11,000 poorer, or because of his disappointment in his sons, one dying young, the other a spendthrift. In 1838 the decline in the family fortunes forced his grandson to sell to the Liberal MP James Morrison, a similarly self-made man whose upward path in life had been eased by marriage to his employer's daughter. Now a merchant prince, he needed a suitably grand setting to display his considerable collection of pictures. Morrison employed his architect-friend J.B. Papworth to complete the house and he and his ten children lived here in style. This was Basildon's golden age. A fast train link with London brought many distinguished visitors, J.M.W. Turner and Bishop Samuel Wilberforce among them.

Sadly, with the death of Morrison's daughter Ellen in 1910, the contents were dispersed and the house remained empty for over 40 years. During this period Basildon survived a scheme to re-erect it in America (no purchaser could be found) and lost some sections of plasterwork which were sold to the Waldorf Astoria Hotel in New York. It was saved by the 2nd Lord and Lady Iliffe, who bought it in 1952, restored it with great skill and filled it with period furnishings and paintings, including portraits by Lely, Hoppner and Mytens as well as one or two twentieth-century works, such as Frank Salisbury's lovely painting of Lady Iliffe in a simple white dress, or Graham Sutherland's portrait of Lord Iliffe and watercolour studies for 'Christ in Glory', the tapestry that

BELOW A fortune made in Bengal in the service of the East India Company enabled Sir Francis Sykes to build Basildon Park, an outstanding Georgian mansion set high above the Thames.

hangs behind the altar in Coventry Cathedral. The grandest interior, at the centre of the garden front, is the Octagon Drawing Room, its three great windows looking out over the Thames and the beech woods beyond. Pompeo Batoni's vivid portrayals of seven of the apostles and God the Father clustered round the doors on either side of the room are typical of the fine seventeenth- and eighteenth-century Italian paintings that Sir Francis Sykes might have acquired on a Grand Tour, and the deep red of the walls on which they are displayed is in accord with eighteenth-century taste.

Parkland studded with carefully placed chestnuts, beeches and limes still comes right up to the entrance front, as it did in

ABOVE The richly decorated hall at Basildon Park would have been used for the kind of grand entertaining that was a feature of country-house life in the eighteenth century.

Sir Francis Sykes's day. James Morrison added the balustraded terrace walk that now frames a lawn at the back of the house, and he also introduced the pair of carved stone dogs on the north side of the grass, which he bought on a trip to Italy in 1845–6. Lord and Lady Iliffe were responsible for most of the other garden ornaments and the present sympathetic planting, such as the white rambling rose on the terrace balustrade and the magnolia on the house.

Bateman's

East Sussex
½ mile (0.8 kilometre) south of Burwash on the A265; approached by road leading south from the west end of the village.

This modest Jacobean house lies deep in the Sussex Weald, in the richly wooded Dudwell valley. Built in about 1634, as the date over the porch records, and constructed of sandstone from a quarry just across the lane, it has traditional gabled facades, stone-mullioned windows and a massive central chimney-stack formed of six brick columns.

A tradition that the house was built by a local ironmaster may reflect the fact that the Wealden iron industry was at its height in the early seventeenth century, when there were several forges on the River Dudwell.

The particular interest of this modest building lies in its association with Rudyard Kipling, who bought the property in 1902 and lived here until his death in 1936. The great man broods over the stairs in a painting by John Collier, his dark three-piece suit slightly too big for him, the eyes behind the glasses tinged green and blue. In tune with Edwardian appreciation of seventeenth-century furniture and design, he and his wife created interiors that perfectly complement the building and which are still as the Kiplings left them. At the top of the stairs is the book-lined study where Kipling wrote, flinging himself down on the day-bed to smoke and review what he had done, or when inspiration deserted him. The room is still much as he had it, although much tidier. The long early seventeenth-century walnut refectory table under the window where he worked still has his array of 'writing tools' and 'essentials', among them a canoe-shaped pen tray, boxes of clips and pins flanking the blotter and a fur seal he used as a paperweight. The large Algerian wastepaper basket beside the desk was where he threw discarded drafts of the stories and poems that he wrote and rewrote, honing what are now classics of the English language.

Kipling produced some of his greatest works here, including *Puck of Pook's Hill*, called after the hill visible from the house, *If* and *The Glory of the Garden*. For these he drew his material from the Kent and Sussex countryside, no longer looking east to the India of his childhood for inspiration. But the house also reflects his strong links with the sub-continent, with oriental rugs in many of the rooms and Kipling's large collection of Indian artefacts and works of art on display in the parlour and study. His delightful bookplate shows a diminutive figure reading on top of an elephant.

The peaceful garden running down to the River Dudwell owes much to the Kiplings, who laid out paths and hedges, planted the rose garden and created the pond, paying for the work out of the £7,700 he received for the Nobel Prize in 1907. Kipling's sundial is engraved with the words 'It is later than you think'. As might be expected from the author of *Kim*, the pond was designed with young people in mind, shallow enough for his children and their friends to use for boating and bathing. It is immortalised in the visitors' book, where the initials FIP stand for 'fell in pond'. There are two eighteenth-century oasthouses near the house and beyond, in a garage beside the potting sheds, is the Rolls-Royce Kipling bought in 1928. On the river, where the garden becomes half-wild, with trees and bulbs in long grass, is an eighteenth-century water-mill. Kipling converted it to produce electricity when he first came to Bateman's, but it has now been restored for grinding flour.

ABOVE The study at Bateman's is where Kipling worked, sitting at the table by the window and writing on pads of blue paper that were specially made for him.

ABOVE Bateman's, a serene early seventeenth-century house built of local sandstone and oak, is where Rudyard Kipling wrote some of his best-known books.

Bath Assembly Rooms

Bath & NE Somerset
In Alfred Street, north of Milsom Street, east of the Circus

Although Bath had been known as a spa since Roman times, it was only under the influence of Beau Nash's forceful personality in the eighteenth century that what had been a provincial watering place was turned into an international resort. Visionary town planning and elegant architecture by John Wood and his son transformed the city and created a suitable setting for fashionable society. By 1769, when work started on the Assembly Rooms – the third set to appear in the town – John Wood the Elder had died, leaving Queen Square and the Circus as his showpieces. John Wood the Younger was carrying on his father's work, designing beautifully proportioned streets, terraces and public buildings to fill his father's layout, a scheme that would be crowned by Wood the Younger's Royal Crescent, completed in 1775.

His elegant Assembly Rooms, just east of his father's Circus, are straight from the world of Jane Austen, a place where the company could amuse themselves with dancing or playing cards, strolling from one pursuit to another as the fancy took them and refreshing themselves with ices and claret cup or by drinking tea. The Rooms are impressively set across a wide pavement, with two rather austere classical facades to either side of the central pedimented entrance. This plain exterior gives no hint of the splendours within. The magnificent 30-metre (100-foot) ballroom rises through two floors to a high coved ceiling, with Corinthian columns picked out in white against blue flanking windows at the level of the second floor and lining the interior wall. The largest eighteenth-century room in Bath, it would have been filled with 800 to 1,200 people on ball nights. The five great candlelit chandeliers illuminated the glittering company and an orchestra set on a stage at one end provided music for the dancing. Those who came here were expected to conform to certain standards of dress and behaviour, as laid down by the Master of Ceremonies. Captain William Wade, the Rooms' convivial and decorative host from their opening in 1771 until 1777, still scrutinises visitors from Gainsborough's full-length portrait. His published rules included instructions on where to sit, as well as exhortations such as 'no Lady dance country-dances in a hoop of any kind'.

The lofty tea-room, with a double screen of columns at one end, is similarly splendid. Completing the original suite was the Octagon, or card-room, where an organ was provided to entertain the company when card-playing was banned on Sundays, but in 1777 another card-room was added to cope with the numbers who flocked here. Concerts graced by such celebrities as Johann Strauss and Liszt continued to be popular, but the Assembly Rooms lost their appeal in the nineteenth century, closing at the start of the First World War. They were restored by the City of Bath after they had been presented to the National Trust in 1931, only to be severely damaged by bombs in 1942. Reconstruction began in 1946, initially under the close supervision of Sir Albert Richardson, whose determination ensured the accurate reproduction of original features. Subsequent redecoration, and major restoration in the late 1980s, has been based on original colour samples found in the City Archives, thus re-creating the complete eighteenth-century scheme. A Museum of Costume (not owned by the Trust) is housed in the basement.

ABOVE LEFT After incendiary bombs gutted the Bath Assembly Rooms in 1942, every detail of the plasterwork and other decoration was re-created.
RIGHT The magnificent ballroom was filled with dancers on ball nights. Spectators looked on from settees arranged in tiers along the walls and an orchestra set on a stage at one end provided music for the dancing.

The Beatles' Childhood Homes

Woolton and Allerton
Liverpool

The distinctive musical voice of the Beatles, the sound of the '60s, was born in two unremarkable houses in the suburbs of Liverpool. Set less than a mile (1.6 kilometres) apart on either side of Allerton Park, but in different leagues socially, are the childhood homes of John Lennon and Paul McCartney, whose song-writing partnership was the engine behind the Beatles' success. No. 20 Forthlin Road, where the McCartney family moved in 1955, when Paul was 13 and his brother Michael 12, is part of the Mather Avenue estate, built between 1949 and 1952 by Liverpool Council.

A two-storey, brick-built house with three rooms on each floor, there is nothing special about No. 20, although the city architect, Sir Lancelot Keay, planned the estate well, specifying good materials and such modern conveniences as an inside toilet, which the McCartneys' previous house had not had.

Where Forthlin Road is part of a terrace, Mendips in Menlove Avenue, where John came to live in 1945 at the age of 5, is a 1930s pebble-dashed semi designed to appeal to the aspiring middle-classes who would value its bay windows, leaded panes, Art Nouveau-style stained glass and other tasteful features, such as Art Deco fireplaces. At Mendips, John was brought up by his mother's sister, Aunt Mimi, and her husband George, who, childless themselves, gave John the

ABOVE LEFT The houses are full of period details.
BELOW The living room at Forthlin Road has been re-created as the McCartneys had it, with protective coverings on the arms of the suite and runners sewn together covering the floor.

stable and loving home he needed after his parents' marriage had fallen apart. After George's sudden death in 1955, it was the rock-like Mimi who kept John's teenage rebelliousness within bounds. Early experiences and interests fed through into John's later writing, among them his love of nonsense verse, which was a continuation of his childhood enthusiasm for the fantasy world of Lewis Carroll, and his use of lyrics inspired by newspaper headlines, which was rooted in the fact that Uncle George used the *Liverpool Echo* to teach John to read. The teenage Lennon would sit writing poetry and songs in the front room, encouraging Mimi to keep what he threw aside because he 'would be famous one day'. And he practised the guitar which he had badgered his mother into getting him until his fingers were raw.

Paul had the advantage of being part of a musical household. His father Jim, who brought up the boys after their mother died not long after the move to Forthlin Road, played show tunes on the upright piano which dominated the living room; he rigged up extensions from the radio so the boys could listen to Elvis, Fats Domino and other idols while they were in bed; and, inspired by seeing Lonnie Donegan at the Liverpool Empire in 1956, Paul bought an acoustic guitar on which, like John, he practised for hours.

When Paul was 15 and John 17, the boys met at a church fête in Woolton where John was performing with his skiffle group. Paul joined the band and he and John started to compose songs at Mendips, among them 'Please Please Me'. But, although Mimi warmed to John's new friend, the noise they made did not go down well. They tried taking refuge in the glazed porch, which has an ideal bathroom acoustic, but then retreated to Forthlin Road. Paul was still at school, John at art college, but they would both play truant in the afternoons and practise undisturbed while Jim was out at work. 'Love Me Do' and 'I Saw Her Standing There' both came out of these afternoon sessions, and the lyrics they scribbled down in a school exercise book immortalised places in the neighbourhood, such as Penny Lane and Strawberry Field.

Paul's friend George Harrison, whom he had got to know on the bus to school, joined them in 1958 and in 1960, with Pete Best playing the drums, they began to call themselves the Beatles and got their first big break, in Hamburg. A year later they had their debut at Liverpool's Cavern Club and their new

ABOVE The kitchen at Mendips, where John's Aunt Mimi would cook his favourite meal of egg and chips.

manager, Brian Epstein, whose father had sold Jim his upright, had got them an EMI recording contract; in 1962 Ringo Starr replaced Pete, and in 1963 the boys took off, with concerts all over the country, recording sessions and television and radio appearances.

At Forthlin Road, Jim and Michael were increasingly besieged by fans, and in 1964 Paul bought his father a new house five miles from Liverpool. No. 20 was sold to the Jones family, who lived here for 30 years and made a number of changes, such as replacing the sash windows. The National Trust acquired the property in 1995, and has returned it to what it would have looked like when the McCartneys were living in the house. The back garden still has its original coal shed and outside WC, and there are displays of Beatles memorabilia loaned by Hunter Davies and evocative photographs by Michael McCartney.

Mimi stayed on at Mendips after the Beatles became famous, but in 1965, when she retired to a bungalow that John had bought her in Dorset, the house was sold. John's second wife, Yoko Ono, generously bought the house when it came up for sale and gave it to the Trust in 2002. Now presented with a 1950s interior, it conjures up the world of Lennon's formative years with authentic touches such as the posters in his former bedroom.

Beatrix Potter Gallery

Cumbria
In Hawkshead, next to the
Red Lion Inn

Like Hill Top, the little farm she purchased in 1905 (*see* p.168), and the village of Sawrey, the nearby market town of Hawkshead was captured in several of Beatrix Potter's delicate illustrations for her children's books. A cluster of small limewashed houses ranged round three squares and along two main streets, the town still looks very much as she knew it in the late nineteenth and early twentieth centuries. Next to the Red Lion Inn, overlooking one of the squares in the centre of town, is the low, cream-coloured building where Beatrix Potter went to consult the local solicitor W.H. Heelis & Son on her property purchases in the district, all of which were to come to the National Trust. William Heelis, the junior partner she saw regularly over the years, not only gave advice on her acquisitions, but also kept an eye on her property when she was away and attended sales on her behalf. In 1912 he asked her to be his wife.

Four small rooms, two of which were created out of the large upstairs office that William shared with his uncle and cousin, are now the setting for a changing exhibition of Beatrix Potter's sketches and watercolours. There are also photographs of the Heelis and Potter families and of some of Beatrix's farms. Downstairs, what was the clerks' room has been refurnished as a nineteenth-century solicitor's office, using some of the original desks and furnishings.

ABOVE Part of the Beatrix Potter Gallery has been fitted out as a nineteenth-century solicitor's office, using some of the original furnishings of W. H. Heelis & Son.

Belton House

Lincolnshire
3 miles (4.8 kilometres)
north-east of Grantham on the
A607 Grantham–Lincoln road

Belton is at peace with the world. Built in the last years of Charles II's reign to an H-shaped design by the gentleman-architect William Winde, its simple Anglo-Dutch style seems to express the confidence and optimism of Restoration England. Symmetrical honey-coloured facades look out over the tranquil, wooded park, the grandeur of the broad flight of steps leading up to the pedimented entrance front offset by domestic dormers in the steeply pitched roof and a delightful crowning cupola.

The interiors reflect Belton's long association with the Brownlow and Cust families, descendants of the ambitious and wealthy Elizabethan lawyer who bought the estate in 1609. Family portraits hang in almost every room, from Reynolds's imposing study of Sir John Cust, Speaker of the House of Commons from 1761–70, which greets visitors in the marble hall, to Lord Leighton's magical portrait at the top of the stairs of the last Countess Brownlow as a young woman, the colour of the bouquet she holds against her long white dress echoed in the autumnal trees behind.

High-quality decorations and furnishings, including magnificent wall mirrors, a brilliant-blue Italian lapis lazuli cabinet and the remnants of an extensive collection of Old Masters, speak of wealth well spent. Glowing panelling lines the formal seventeenth-century saloon in the middle of the house, setting off delicate limewood carvings with minutely realised fruit and flowers that suggest the hand of Grinling Gibbons. Early eighteenth-century gilt wall mirrors between the three long windows looking onto the garden reflect two sets of Charles II walnut chairs arrayed on the pink and green Aubusson carpet, their seats and backs upholstered in faded crimson velvet and a host of cherubs adorning the frames. Two more cherubs, their grumpy expressions perhaps due to their rather precarious position, perch uncomfortably on the monumental reredos in the largely unaltered north-facing chapel, where an exuberant baroque plaster ceiling by Edward

Goudge contrasts with James Wyatt's Neo-classical compositions of the 1770s in other parts of the house.

Apart from the silver awarded to Speaker Cust for his service to the House of Commons, and the fine porcelain seen in almost every room, such as the massive blue and white Chinese Kangxi vases in the marble hall, some of the most prized pieces at Belton are the vast garden scenes by Melchior d'Hondecoeter acquired by the 3rd and last Earl. He and his wife presided over a golden age in the late nineteenth century, when Belton was sympathetically restored. The last Earl also made changes to the garden, adding a final layer to the harmonious blend of styles and periods that characterises the grounds. To the north of the house is his re-creation of a baroque Dutch layout, a formal composition of clipped yew and

RIGHT Grinling Gibbons may have carved the limewood garland framing this portrait of 'Old' Sir John Brownlow, the seventeenth-century sheep farmer who founded the family fortunes.

ABOVE A fortune made from sheep farming and the law financed the building of Belton House in 1685–88. The north front looks over nineteenth-century formal gardens.

gravel walks punctuated by urns and pieces of sculpture, among them an eighteenth-century sundial clasped by Father Time. Further from the house is the more extensive sunken Italian garden dating from 1810 that was designed by Jeffry Wyatville and is overlooked by Wyatville's elegant orangery of 1820.

The last Earl's Dutch garden was based on an engraving of the original elaborate baroque layout. A lime avenue sweeping east across the park to a tall prospect tower silhouetted against the sky is a remnant of this scheme, and a little Palladian temple facing across a short canal on the east side of the garden, and an unrestored Picturesque wilderness to the west, are also survivals of earlier layouts, as depicted in a number of eighteenth-century paintings of the house and grounds in the breakfast room. Twentieth-century portraits hanging here include a likeness of the 6th Lord Brownlow, Lord in Waiting to Edward VIII during his brief reign and a close friend of the king. Edward VIII stayed several times at Belton, perhaps deriving strength from the serenity of his surroundings.

Beningbrough Hall and Gardens

North Yorkshire
8 miles (12.8 kilometres)
north-west of York, 2 miles
(3.2 kilometres) west of Shipton,
2 miles (3.2 kilometres)
south-east of Linton-on-Ouse

This great baroque house is set on a slight rise above the water meadows of the Ouse. Built of red brick and stone, with long sash windows lighting the two principal floors and little pavilions crowned with cupolas either side of the main block, it is a product of the cultivated, secure decades of the early eighteenth century and was largely complete by 1716. Ornate stonework, including two lifelike horses struggling to escape sculptured drapery, marks the central bay, a splayed flight of steps rises to the entrance and tiny casements in the attic storey are squeezed in between the massive console brackets supporting the prominent cornice.

Beningbrough was built for John Bourchier, whose family had acquired the property by marriage in the previous century, but it is not known exactly who designed the house. The talented local carpenter-architect William Thornton, who oversaw construction, may have done more than just supervise the work; there may have been advice from the architect Thomas Archer, who had studied continental baroque at first hand; and Bourchier, who had seen contemporary buildings in Italy, may also have played a part. Certainly, much of the exterior detailing, such as the paired brackets supporting the cornice, is taken from Italian baroque buildings, and the treatment of the imposing stone-flagged entrance hall, rising through two storeys on the north side of the house, may well have been influenced by the grand baroque palaces Bourchier saw in Rome.

The interior plan, with its formal, strongly axial layout, is marked by the kind of spatial effects characteristic of baroque architecture. There are long vistas down the corridors running the length of the house on both floors, the lower closed by the greenery of the conservatory at one end, the upper with openings into the entrance hall. Another feature is the exceptional woodcarving that stands out in high relief on the friezes and overmantels of the pine-panelled rooms, decoration that was usually executed in plaster being here realised in wood. This was probably the work of French Huguenot craftsmen employed by Thornton, who was closely associated with a group that had established themselves in the north of England. Despite the sale of the contents in 1958, the interior is furnished in period style. Some exceptional pieces and pictures were bought back by the National Trust, while others are from a bequest by Lady Megaw, and the house has benefited from the loan of oriental porcelain by the Ashmolean Museum and from an imaginative partnership

BELOW Beningbrough Hall, built in the early eighteenth century, is notable for baroque spatial effects, such as the long vistas across the house, and for the quality of the panelling and other woodwork.

with the National Portrait Gallery, as a result of which Beningbrough's eighteenth-century interiors now display an outstanding collection of period portraits.

Running across five bays on the first floor of the garden front is the impressive saloon, with giant fluted pilasters framing the windows and punctuating interior walls. Decorated in grey and gold and hung with portraits, this grand architectural space would have been used for balls and large family gatherings. The formality of early eighteenth-century life comes through in the apartments on the ground floor, where suites of rooms were used for receiving visitors as well as sleeping. There is magnificent upholstery on a trio of state beds and stepped shelves over the fireplaces in the intimate closets at the corners of the house, where only the closest friends would have been admitted, are crowded with oriental porcelain in the fashion of the time. Contemporary taste for the eastern and exotic is also reflected in pieces of lacquer work, among them a Chinese cabinet in one of the dressing rooms with sections of Chinese screen set into the panelling above.

The paintings, illustrating many of the great figures of the day and work by most of the leading portraitists, are a feature of all the furnished rooms. Here are canvases by Ramsay, Angelica Kauffman, Highmore, Hudson, Reynolds, Gainsborough, Batoni and, above all, Kneller, whose studies of members of the politically influential Kit-Cat Club, all painted to the same format and in identical frames, hang two deep in the dining room. Like the show of eighteenth-century royalty in the entrance hall, these Kit-Cat portraits, nearly half of those Kneller produced, are among the paintings on loan from the National Portrait Gallery. So, too, is the poignant portrait of the bedridden actress Peg Woffington, who was stricken with palsy during her last performance. In addition, there are extensive interactive displays and a separate, changing exhibition of paintings from the gallery on the top floor.

A door in the wall of the cobbled yard opposite the nineteenth-century laundry leads into the garden spread along the south side of the house. Two formal layouts are enclosed by yew hedges and set round a fountain pool and the walled garden is planted with fruit trees and box-edged beds. The view south over the ha-ha to the water meadows has a feeling of the eighteenth-century landscaped park that once surrounded the house.

Benthall Hall

Shropshire
1 mile (1.6 kilometres) north-west of Broseley on the B4375, 4 miles (6.4 kilometres) north-east of Much Wenlock, 6 miles (9.6 kilometres) south of Wellington

Although the estate lies only a couple of miles from Coalbrookdale, the traumas of the Industrial Revolution passed Benthall by, isolated as it is on a plateau above the River Severn, with precipitous wooded slopes falling to the river. Seat of the ancient Benthall family, whose origins stretch back to Anglo-Saxon times, the estate was sold away from the family in 1843 but was bought back in 1934 and Benthalls live here still. With its tall moulded brick chimneystacks and mullioned and transomed windows, the house has changed little since it was built in the late sixteenth century. The south front that looks towards the Shropshire Hills is charmingly asymmetrical. The projecting porch is off-centre, two-storey bay windows are spaced unequally to either side, and there is a shallow wing at the west end. Nothing lines up with the gabled roofline. Five stone tablets set in a playing-card pattern above the door in the porch, perhaps alluding to the wounds of Christ, were probably advertising the family's Catholic sympathies, and these may also account for the hiding place under the floor in the little room above.

Early seventeenth-century interiors include a carved staircase of c.1618, with grotesque heads adorning the massive newel posts and the leopard of the Benthall crest proudly displayed on the panel at the turn of the stairs. In the sunny, welcoming drawing room, lit by windows facing south and west, an elaborate white plaster ceiling and frieze merge with off-white oak panelling. Lions, horses, stags, griffins and other mythical creatures look down on the room from their plaster roundels. Rococo chimneypieces of c.1760 here and in the dining room were added by T.F. Pritchard, whose Iron Bridge, spanning the River Severn just to the north, is perhaps the most evocative symbol of the Industrial Revolution.

The intimate tree-shaded garden owes much to tenants who lived in the house in the nineteenth century. The terraces, rockeries, rose garden and shrub banks were established by Robert Bateman, who came to Benthall in 1890 and whose father had created the individual layout at Biddulph Grange in Staffordshire (also owned by the National Trust). The distinguished botanist George Maw and his brother, who rented the house earlier in the century, were responsible for the display of autumn and spring crocuses and started a tradition of peopling the garden with unusual plants. An avenue of horse chestnuts to the south of the house follows the line of the original drive and earthworks in grassland to the north mark the site of the medieval village, which was destroyed by besieging Royalists in the Civil War.

BELOW Benthall Hall from the south-west, with a sixteenth-century chimneystack of moulded brick rising from the end wall.

Berrington Hall

Herefordshire
3 miles (4.8 kilometres) north
of Leominster on the west
side of the A49

Berrington is the creation of Thomas Harley, the 3rd Earl of Oxford's remarkable son, who made a fortune from banking and from supplying pay and clothing to the British army during the American War of Independence. He became Lord Mayor of London in 1767 at the age of 37. The architect of his austere three-storey house, with its domestic quarters clustered round a courtyard behind, was the young Henry Holland, who was to go on to build Carlton House for the Prince Regent.

The house is set above the wide valley of a tributary of the River Lugg, with views west and south to the Black Mountains and Brecon Beacons. This was the site advised by 'Capability' Brown, whom Harley took to see the estate in 1775, shortly after he had acquired it, and who was to landscape the park, creating the lake with its artificial island (Berrington is one of the best examples of his work). Holland, who was Brown's son-in-law, started on the house three years later.

Approached through an entrance lodge built in the form of a triumphal arch, the rather plain Neo-classical exterior with a wide flight of steps leading to the pedimented portico on the entrance front gives no clue to the lavishness of the interior. Feminine plaster ceilings now decorated in muted pastel colours adorn the principal rooms. Holland is at his most fanciful in the drawing room, where painted roundels on the ceiling, thought to be by Biagio Rebecca, are set off by white plaster cherubs leading seahorses by blue ribbons over a lavender background. Biagio Rebecca probably also executed the prominent grisaille panels in the library, deep shadows in those showing eminent Englishmen of letters on the ceiling giving them a three-dimensional quality, as if they were made of plaster. Bacon and Chaucer are easily recognisable; Alexander Pope is the only one of the eight to be shown in full profile.

Holland's most original interior at Berrington is the staircase hall. Rising to a delicately treated glass dome, it shows an extraordinary ability to use perspective and space to dramatic effect, as in an engraving by Piranesi. The rooms are set off with a collection of French furniture, including pieces that belonged to the Comte de Flahault, the natural son of Talleyrand, and Napoleon's stepdaughter Hortense.

In the dining room, four panoramic sea paintings, three of them by Thomas Luny, are a tribute to the distinguished Admiral Rodney. Father-in-law of Harley's daughter Anne and one of the most eminent admirals of the eighteenth century, he played a prominent role in the American War of Independence. The paintings show important incidents in the war at sea, in which Rodney was in action against the French and Spanish, who had allied themselves with the rebellious Americans. Two large pictures at either end of the room are of the Battle of the Saints on 12 April 1782, an engagement that Luny, who served as a purser, may have witnessed. One is a morning scene showing Rodney breaking the French line; the other depicts the surrender of the French flagship in the evening of the same day.

More poignant reminders of members of the Cawley family, to whom the estate was sold in 1901, hang in Lady Cawley's room. One of the photographs shows the 1st Lord Cawley and his four sons on horseback in front of the house, ready for a day's hunting. A few years later three of the young men had lost their lives in the First World War.

OPPOSITE The columns of the great portico at Berrington Hall were carefully spaced so as to allow uninterrupted views over the valley below from the windows of the hall.

ABOVE The finest of the interiors created by Henry Holland at Berrington is the staircase hall, with its screens of scagliola columns, delicate glass dome and bold spatial effects.

Birmingham Back to Backs

West Midlands
On the corner of Inge Street and Hurst Street, opposite the Hippodrome Theatre, Birmingham

When Birmingham was growing rapidly as an industrial centre in the late eighteenth and early nineteenth centuries, developers threw up street after street of brick-built, back-to-back houses, with one of each pair forming part of a terrace in front, the other looking over a courtyard behind. Three storeys high, but with just one room on each floor, and with windows only on one side, these houses were home to sizeable families, and often to their relatives and a lodger as well, all of whom had to use the communal privy and wash-house in the court. Cheap, high-density housing like this covered acres of Leeds, Liverpool and other industrial towns as well as Birmingham, but during the nineteenth century, as many became disease-ridden slums, increasing concern about public health led to controlling legislation. The 1858 Public Health Act, which allowed local councils to prohibit back-to-backs, was followed by the 1908 Housing Act, which made them illegal. Building back-to-backs was banned in Birmingham in 1876, but many existing courts survived until the slum-clearance programmes that followed the Second World War.

Court 15, Inge Street, which was lived in until 1966, is the only complete survival of a courtyard of early nineteenth-century back-to-backs. The housing forms an L-shape, with three pairs of back-to-backs on Inge Street adjoining a terrace of five blind-back houses on Hurst Street. These tenements make up the north and west sides of the inner court: on the east is a tall brick wall that was once the blind back of housing in an adjacent yard and the south side is closed by a modern brick wall. During most of the nineteenth century the court was occupied by artisans – button makers, leather workers, locksmiths and the like – some of whom worked from home, using one room in the house as a workshop. On Hurst Street, the lower floors were all converted into shops by 1900.

A tunnel entrance from Inge Street leads into the brick-paved yard, where two communal wash-houses survive, the water for them once heated in coppers over a brick hearth. Four back-to-backs have been fitted out to show what life in Inge Court and Hurst Street was like at different times in their

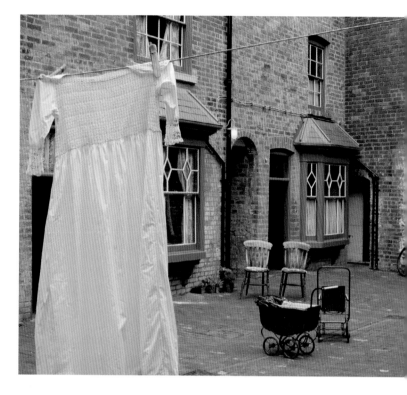

ABOVE These two houses only have a frontage onto the yard and have been given bay windows to let in more light. There were people living here until 1966.

history. Reconstructions have been based on what is known of the families and individuals who lived here, and provide authentic re-creations of period furnishings and lifestyles. One is based on the life of a Jewish watchmaker and his family, whose well-kept house includes artefacts such as a Seder plate for Passover and a nine-branched candlestick; another, with damp and peeling wallpaper, shabby clothes and little to be seen in the cupboards, reflects the day-to-day existence of the struggling Mitchell family, who were here during the recession and unemployment of the 1930s; while the most recent interior is based on the life of an immigrant from the West Indies, George Saunders, who opened a tailor's shop in the court, using the upper floors of the tenement as a workroom and for storage. A water pump has been reinstated in the courtyard and washing lines, a hoop and an old pram give the place a lived-in atmosphere.

Blickling Estate

Norfolk
On the north side of the B1154,
½ mile (0.8 kilometre) north-west
of Aylsham on the A140, 15 miles
(24 kilometres) north of Norwich,
10 miles (16 kilometres) south of
Cromer

A winding road from Aylsham leads to this serene Jacobean mansion set in almost 2,000 hectares (4,800 acres) of gently undulating park and estate in a loop of the River Bure. Built of warm red brick with stone dressings, Blickling has curving Dutch gables, generous leaded windows, massive chimneystacks and corner turrets carrying gilded weather vanes. On the southern entrance front, long, low service wings, their lines continued by yew hedges, frame the approach. The house was designed for Sir Henry Hobart, James I's distinguished Chief Justice of the Common Pleas, by Robert Lyminge, who transformed an existing medieval and Tudor manor. No trace of this manor can be seen, but its ghost lives on in the dry moat ringing the house, now planted with roses, hydrangeas and hostas, and in many features of the layout and dimensions of the new building, such as the double courtyard plan. Further remodelling in the eighteenth century by Thomas and William Ivory for John Hobart, the 2nd Earl of Buckinghamshire, resulted in a house that is a harmonious combination of Jacobean and Georgian, the later work, to the north and west ranges, blending beautifully with the earlier, more solid styling.

Rich and showy Jacobean decoration and fittings show Sir Henry spared no expense in creating interiors to match his status. The 1620s staircase, with carved figures on the newel posts, is a striking feature of the portrait-hung great hall, to which it was moved in 1767, while the south drawing room at the end of the east range, once the great chamber of the Jacobean house and the room where Charles II was entertained in 1671, still has its outstanding plasterwork ceiling by Edward Stanyon and the original ostentatious chimneypiece. An ante-room off the drawing room leads into Sir Henry's spectacular Long Gallery, running 37.5 metres (123 feet) down the east front and adorned with another intricate plaster ceiling by Stanyon. Here, his decoration intermingles heraldic motifs, including a generous display of the Hobart bull, with delightful depictions of the senses. In one panel a stag listens entranced to a man playing the mandolin, his lady following the music for him with her finger; in another, a

BELOW Blickling's Jacobean east front, with large windows lighting the Great Chamber and Long Gallery, looks over a formal parterre to a terrace walk giving views over the pastoral landscape towards Aylsham.

woman lifts a brimming glass to her lips, her lap full of luscious fruit. In about 1745 the gallery was converted into a library to accommodate the books inherited from Sir Richard Ellys, a distinguished theologian and antiquary who, with an eye for the rare, curious, old and beautiful, assembled an outstanding collection of works, recognised as such by his contemporaries in the early eighteenth century. The 12,000 volumes housed at Blickling, which form one of the most remarkable country-house libraries in England, include a very rare Eliot Indian bible printed in Massachusetts in 1663, a unique maritime atlas of the same period, spectacular books of engravings and books from the Aldine Press in Venice, several of which are in contemporary bindings. J.H. Pollen's delicately painted frieze above the bookcases, full of timid rabbits and other wildlife of the Norfolk countryside, is part of the Pre-Raphaelite mural decoration commissioned by the 8th Marquess of Lothian shortly after he inherited the house in 1850.

A door from the gallery leads into one of the rooms fitted out in 1778–82 to display the works of art acquired by the 2nd Earl during his congenial three-year posting as Ambassador to the court of Catherine the Great. There are only three paintings here now, but the room still displays the magnificent tapestry, given to the 2nd Earl by the empress as a parting present, which shows Peter the Great triumphing over the defeated Swedish army at Poltawa in 1709.

An RAF museum in the east wing, with displays of photographs and of equipment, clothing and other memorabilia, is a reminder of the role Blickling played in the Second World War, when aircrews from RAF Oulton, a satellite Bomber Command airfield just to the west of the estate, were billeted in the house and in Nissen huts in the grounds.

A formal garden remodelled by Norah Lindsay in the 1930s and flanked by formal wilderness areas with wooded walks borders the Jacobean east front, and a path leads on from here to a little early eighteenth-century temple set high on a massive terrace. Rolling wooded parkland landscaped in the eighteenth century stretches away to the north and west of the house, with beeches, sweet chestnuts and huge mature oaks framing a long, sinuous lake.

LEFT The atmospheric Jacobean Long Gallery was once used to display portraits, but now houses one of the most exceptional country-house libraries in England.

Bodiam Castle

East Sussex
3 miles (4.8 kilometres) south of Hawkhurst, 1 mile (1.6 kilometres) east of the B2244

By 1372, halfway through the Hundred Years War, England had lost control of the Channel and had begun to suffer devastating French raids. The Sussex ports of Winchelsea and Rye had both been destroyed a few years earlier; the manor of Bodiam, lying only some 10 miles (16 kilometres) from the coast and at the furthest navigable point of the River Rother, must have seemed similarly vulnerable. In 1385, Sir Edward Dalyngrigge, a veteran of the wars in France and an important figure in the defence of Sussex, asked Richard II for permission to fortify his house.

Rather than improving his manor, Dalyngrigge chose to build anew, on a site that gave a view of the river and a strategic bridge. Work started in 1385 and the fine, four-square castle which still stares south across the Sussex marshes was completed some three years later. Built just before siege artillery changed the approach to castle design, Bodiam's strength lay in the height and might of its tower-studded circuit walls, which rise sheer from a broad moat. The massive gateway, bristling with machicolations and gunports, is reached from the north bank across three bridges and two islands. Originally, to repel any attacker, this approach involved a dog-leg to the west bank, three drawbridges and an outlying barbican, the remains of which stand on one of the islands. A ground-hugging Second World War pillbox by the path up from the car park shows how much defensive thinking has changed.

Although now in ruins, enough of the interior survives to give a vivid picture of the realities of castle life. The deep well and the remains of a pigeon loft suggest the preoccupations of a garrison expecting to be besieged, but in fact the French threat soon receded and the remnants of traceried windows and a number of fireplaces tell a different story. Like many contemporary buildings in France and England, which Dalyngrigge must surely have seen, Bodiam combines domestic comfort with the trappings of defence and it is very likely the castle was built to be a status symbol as much as a fortress. The great courtyard beyond the gatehouse is surrounded by the outlines of domestic accommodation, including a traditional great hall with adjoining buttery, pantry and kitchen, such as would have been found in any mansion of the period, and personal chambers for Dalyngrigge and his wife. Separate quarters, each suite with its own fireplaces and garderobe, were provided for his household, with additional provision for a military garrison. A chapel catered for the spiritual needs of the retinue and their lord. The emphasis on the castle as a grand residence also comes through in the recently identified remains of landscape gardens beyond the moat. Dips and hollows in the grass mark what was a series of ponds and there was a terrace on the hill above from which to admire the castle and its setting.

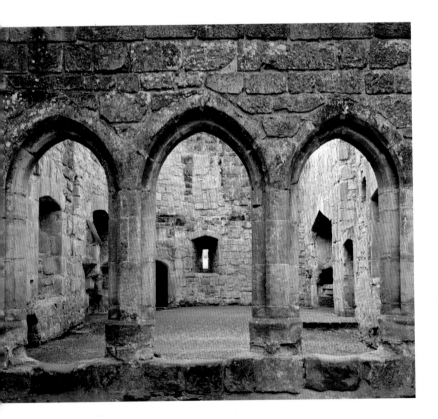

LEFT These three arches connected the great hall to the kitchen range. The two outer doorways gave access to the buttery and pantry, the taller central one to a passage leading to the kitchen.
OPPOSITE Bodiam looks everything a castle should be, with a massive gatehouse protecting the entrance on the north front and a wide moat, here frozen and snow-covered.

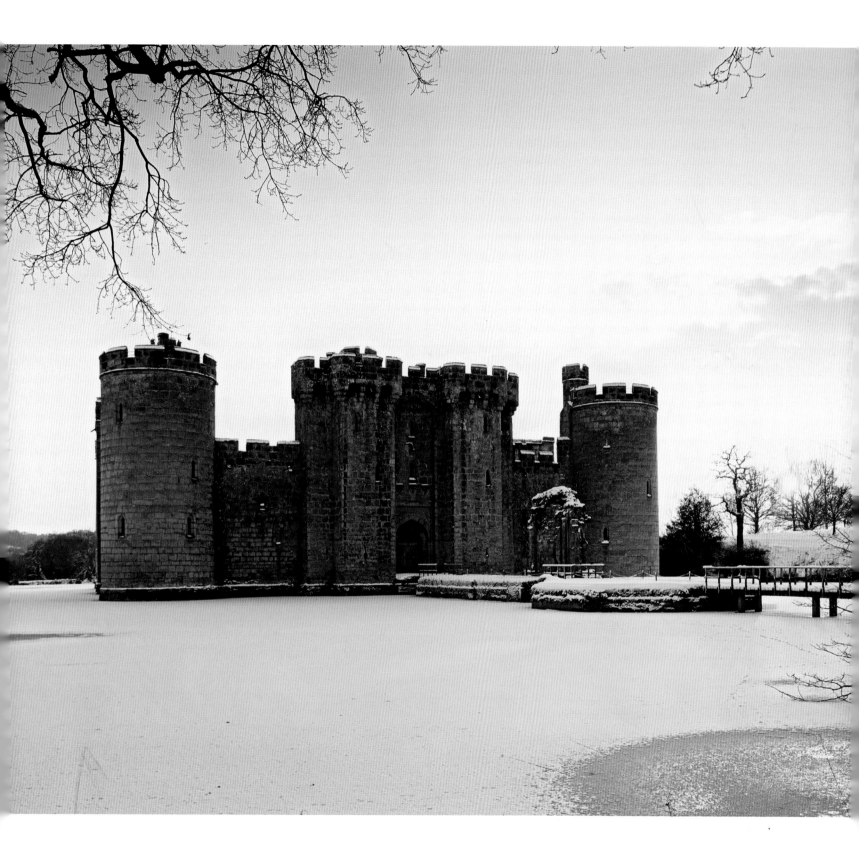

Brockhampton Estate

Worcestershire
1½ miles (2.4 kilometres) east of
Bromyard, on the north side of the
A44 Worcester road

The undulating oak-studded parkland of the Brockhampton estate falls away steeply into a deep, leafy valley. In the depths of the valley, reached by a private road that seems to descend for miles, is an enchanting timber-framed medieval manor house surrounded on three sides by a moat. A little gatehouse is set over the moat, its upper floor jettied out over the lower and the whole thing so warped and twisted that it lurches crazily. Set back 15 metres (50 feet) or so, and facing south across a grassy court, is the manor itself, an L-shaped building in which a great hall open to the rafters filling the stub of the L is attached to a two-storey wing. Red-brick chimneys rear up from the end walls.

When the manor was built, probably some time between 1380 and 1400, only a generation had passed since the devastations of the Black Death, which massively reduced the population of England. Crumbling walls on the fringes of the Malvern Hills to the east were typical of abandoned settlements on marginal land, and the economic depression of these years also saw the fragmentation of many great estates. But the middling landowners with modest holdings in well-endowed country were better placed to survive and prosper. John Domulton, a descendant of the Brockhampton family,

which was here from at least the twelfth century, may have been just such a man. His house is small and unpretentious, but it was comfortable for its day. A great chamber, for the family to distance themselves from their servants and retainers, once filled the upper floor of the wing. The moat which originally encircled the house may well have been necessary in the unsettled country of the Welsh Marches, but may also have been regarded as a status symbol. The gatehouse is a later addition, dating from the fifteenth century.

Massive timbers from the estate were used to build the house and there is woodwork of high quality here, particularly evident in the framework and roof of the hall. A ruined Norman chapel in the farmyard to the west of the house was probably built by the Brockhamptons in about 1180 and high in the parkland above, with panoramic views over a deeply rural landscape, is the mid-eighteenth-century red-brick Brockhampton Court (not open), built to replace the old manor far below. The Court was left to the National Trust, with the rest of the property, in 1946 by Colonel John Talbot Lutley, who wanted Brockhampton preserved as an example of a traditional agricultural estate.

BELOW Medieval Lower Brockhampton lies deep in a leafy valley, with an enchanting gatehouse, its timbers twisted out of shape, straddling the moat which still surrounds three sides of the manor.

Buckland Abbey

Devon
6 miles (9.6 kilometres) south of Tavistock, 11 miles (17.7 kilometres) north of Plymouth

Francis Drake's tiny *Golden Hind* left Plymouth on a cold winter's day in December 1577 and did not return until nearly three years later, on 26 September 1580. This historic voyage was the first circumnavigation of the globe by an Englishman, involving what must have been a terrifying passage across the unknown expanses of the Pacific Ocean. A national hero on his return, Drake needed a house that reflected his newly acquired status, ironically choosing to purchase the abbey that had been so recently converted by his rival, Sir Richard Grenville. It was from here that Drake planned his assault on the Spanish Armada a few years later.

Set among sloping green lawns and exotic trees and shrubs on the edge of the sleepy Tavy valley, Buckland Abbey is rich in associations with Drake. There are many echoes too of the great Cistercian monastery that was founded here in 1273 and which was dissolved in 1539, passing to Richard Grenville two years later. Like Lord Sandys at Mottisfont (see p.218), Grenville chose to convert the thirteenth-century abbey church rather than using the domestic buildings of the community. The abbey's great crossing tower, its south wall marked clearly with the roofline of a demolished transept, dominates the house, there are blocked arches and traces of monastic windows and, inside, the tracery of the chancel arch and ancient mouldings can be seen.

Presented in association with Plymouth City Museum and Art Gallery, the interior is a mix of museum-like exhibits and furnished rooms. Imaginative displays in the long gallery running the length of the top floor outline the history of the abbey from medieval times to the present day. Carved stones, pieces of tracery and floor tiles help recall the monastic community that lived here for some 300 years, growing gradually richer on an income derived from tin mines in the Tavy valley as well as from the tenants on their estates. Drake's coat of arms over the fireplace, on which a fragile ship is

RIGHT At Buckland Abbey, Sir Richard Grenville converted the monastery church into a country house, leaving the outline of a demolished transept on what had been the church tower.

guided by the divine hand of providence, heralds the displays on the floor below. Gorgeous flags, one showing the golden leopards of England on a red ground, may have flown on the *Golden Hind*. Other cases contain Elizabeth I's commission of 5 March 1587, giving Drake command of the fleet with which he 'singed the King of Spain's beard'; Armada medals, the first ever struck to commemorate a historical event; and finds from Spanish ships that foundered off Ireland. A fascinating document details the Armada accounts from December 1587, early entries covering payments – 'to drummers, carpenters, cooks, mariners, surgeons' – concerned with preparations to meet the Spanish, later months including terse references to engagements. Marginal notes in Treasurer Lord Burghley's thin, spidery hand record sums reimbursed, such as the payment in October 1588 to cover the loss of a fireship. Here, too, is Drake's drum, which was with him on his epic voyage and when he died of dysentery off Panama in 1596. It is said to beat if England is ever in danger.

The only complete interior surviving from these times is the sixteenth-century great hall. Dating from Sir Richard Grenville's conversion of the abbey, it is warmly panelled in oak and decorated with an elaborate ceiling and a holly and box frieze adorned with carved figures. Contemporary plasterwork on the end walls symbolising Grenville's retirement to Buckland shows his shield hanging on a tree and a large pile of discarded arms. A Georgian dining room hung with two characteristic seascapes by Van de Velde the Younger and other seventeenth-century Dutch works, and the elegant staircase curling up through four floors, were added as part of late eighteenth-century improvements.

A picturesque group of granite outbuildings with lichen-stained roofs includes an ox-shed introduced by the agricultural improver William Marshall, who spent four years at Buckland in 1791–4. Close by the abbey is the huge, heavily buttressed monastic barn, built in about 1300. Almost 49 metres (160 feet) long, it is one of the largest in Britain, eloquently suggesting the wealth of the community. Sinuous box hedges like window tracery enclose a little herb garden planted beside the barn, where it is easy to imagine white-robed figures moving silently from bed to bed collecting lovage, balm or sweet cicely. There is a re-creation of an Elizabethan garden too.

LEFT Georgian alterations at Buckland Abbey included the insertion of this splendid staircase, which rises right through the house. A gate on one of the half-landings kept dogs from the upper floors.
RIGHT Buscot's south front, with a steep flight of steps, flanked by bronze centaurs, rising to the pedimented entrance bay.

Buscot Park

Oxfordshire
Between Lechlade and Faringdon,
astride the A417

This extensive estate straddling the River Thames in the fertile valley above Oxford was the scene of an agricultural experiment in the nineteenth century, when a rich Australian, Robert Tertius Campbell, turned Buscot into the most progressive farm of its time, largely given over to sugar beet. His grandiose schemes, which eventually overwhelmed his resources, included a distillery for converting the sugar into spirit and over 6 miles (9.6 kilometres) of railway for bringing in the crop.

In 1889, two years after Campbell died, Buscot was sold to Alexander Henderson, later 1st Lord Faringdon, politician, financier and connoisseur, who was responsible for some of the finest paintings in the important collection that is now such a feature of the house. The 1st Lord's son died before him and it was his grandson, the 2nd Lord, who inherited. A prominent socialist, he was as enthusiastic about art as his grandfather.

The house, built in 1780–3 for Edward Loveden Townsend on a rise above the flatlands of the Thames, is a plain Neo-classical composition, with a pediment marking the south-facing entrance facade and two generous bays rising the height of the building on the north front. The pavilions to either side, and the imposing flight of steps flanked by bronze centaurs leading up to the entrance, were added by Geddes Hyslop in the 1930s for the 2nd Lord, who also did much to reinstate the original character of the house, removing nineteenth-century alterations. The interiors, in particular the three interconnected rooms on the north front which look over a grassy fountain terrace to the Thames valley beyond, are both sensuous and cultivated, with extravagant chandeliers, inlaid and painted Regency and Empire furniture (including neo-Egyptian pieces by Thomas Hope), a fine collection of oriental porcelain, bronzes and other *objets*, richly coloured carpets and gleaming mahogany doors.

The hang of the Faringdons' catholic art collection gives character to each room. An original filigree ceiling looks down

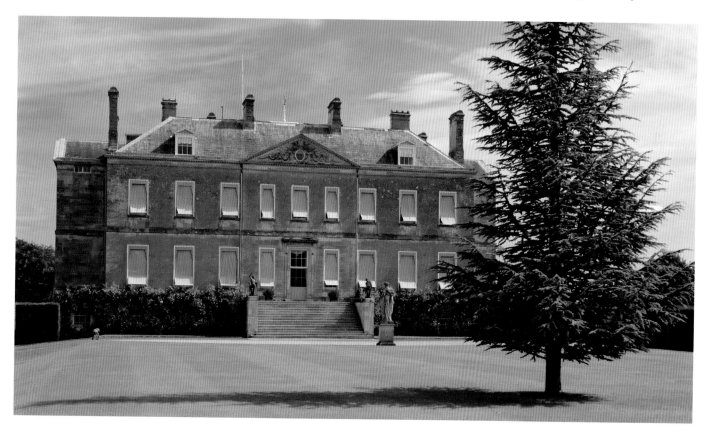

on the Italian paintings in the drawing room, among them Giovanni Pace's powerful *St Jerome*, Palma Vecchio's strangely asymmetrical *Marriage of St Catherine* and a tondo by Botticelli. Here, too, is the delightful *Rest on the Flight into Egypt* attributed to Andrea Previtali, in which the Holy Family are shown enjoying a substantial picnic of bread and cheese, the food carefully set out on a white cloth on the ground. There is a shadowy portrait by Rembrandt among a show of Dutch Old Masters, English eighteenth-century works include portraits by Reynolds and a sketchy Gainsborough landscape, and there is a display of Old Master drawings. A number of canvases reflect the 1st Lord's interest in the Pre-Raphaelites, perhaps inspired by his neighbour, William Morris, whose house at Kelmscott lies close by over the fields. Works by Rossetti and Millais are overshadowed by Burne-Jones's cycle based on the Sleeping Beauty story, the *Legend of the Briar Rose*, which runs round the walls of the saloon in richly coloured panels on a gilded ground. The knight who has come to wake the beautiful princess faces her across the room, as if he has to fight his way through the rose forest on the walls to reach her, past the sleeping knights entangled in thorny branches and the old king himself, slumbering on his throne, his grey beard reaching to his waist.

As the comfortable sofas, piles of books and family photographs suggest, Buscot is still lived in, by the 3rd Lord and his wife, and the collection is still being added to. A number of late twentieth-century paintings include an intriguing portrait of the poet and artist Ian Hamilton Finlay by Eileen Hogan and there are two arresting pieces, in glass on copper, like still Mediterranean rock pools, by Colin Reid. The extensive grounds, too, have continued to evolve. Innovations by the present Lord and Lady Faringdon, such as the inspired ornamental planting of the walled garden, have further enhanced the existing layout, with an Italianate water garden created by Harold Peto between 1904 and 1913 linking the house to the lake in the eighteenth-century parkland and radiating avenues through the flanking woodland, each focused on an urn, an Italian wellhead or some other feature.

Calke Abbey

Derbyshire
9 miles (14.4 kilometres) south of Derby, on the A514 at Ticknall between Swadlincote and Melbourne

Set some distance from any public road, Calke Abbey lies hidden in a fold of the landscape in a beautiful eighteenth-century park, insulated from the world by thousands of trees grouped in picturesque clumps and windbreaks and framing a chain of ornamental ponds. Built in 1701–4, it is an imposing three-storey baroque house set round a courtyard and with corner pavilions decorated with fluted pilasters. But behind the symmetrical grey sandstone facades are substantial remains of an Elizabethan building and the abbey's low-lying position, in a hollow of the park, reveals its earlier, monastic origins, some of the fabric having probably been recycled from the priory of Austin canons that was established here in the early twelfth century. Substantial remodelling by William Wilkins the Elder between 1789 and 1810 for Sir Henry Harpur, 7th Baronet, accounts for the pedimented entrance portico, the roofline balustrade and the suite of reception rooms on the first floor, of which only the dining room, with its Neo-classical decoration, and the library, where the rolled-up maps attached to the bookshelves are among the fittings supplied in 1806–7, are as he designed them.

Like Kedleston Hall only a few miles to the north (*see* p.180), Calke has been in the hands of the same family for hundreds of years, each generation of the Harpurs and Harpur Crewes contributing to the extraordinary individuality of the house. More remarkably, little has been changed since the mid-nineteenth century, providing a unique insight into mid-Victorian England.

William Wilkins's drawing room still has the striking gold and white wallpaper that was hung in 1841–2 and it is still as cluttered as it appears in a photograph of 1886, crowded with chairs and stools, numerous occasional tables and ornaments under glass domes. Display cases full of glistening polished stones are no preparation for the contents of the room next door, the saloon remodelled by Henry Isaac Stevens in 1841. Stevens's coffered ceiling decorated with the Harpur boar and his elegant panels hung with family portraits fade into insignificance beside the cases of stuffed birds and geological specimens and the stag trophies mounted on the walls. A noble head even looks down on Tilly Kettle's charming portrait of Lady Frances Harpur and her son, the future 7th Baronet, painted in *c.*1766.

These unusual exhibits reflect the interests of Sir Vauncey Harpur Crewe, the idiosyncratic recluse who inherited Calke in 1886 and filled the house with his collections. Increasingly unpredictable, Sir Vauncey took to communicating with his servants by letter, would make off into the woods when his wife entertained, and forbade his tenants to cut the hedges so as to provide maximum cover for the birds. Carriages now displayed in the stable yard reflect his insistence that motor vehicles should not be allowed on the estate.

Sir Vauncey seems to have had nothing in common with the three Georgian baronets, two Sir Henrys and Sir Harry, whose keen interest in the turf is commemorated by paintings of racehorses by Sartorius and Sawrey Gilpin in the library, by three florid eighteenth-century racing cups and, in the case of Sir Harry, by the riding school added to the impressive brick stable block in 1767–9. Lady Caroline, wife of the 5th Baronet, one of the Henrys, was given the sumptuous early eighteenth-century state bed, its beautiful Chinese silk hangings, embroidered with dragons, birds, deer and other traditional motifs in rich blues, reds, greens and oranges, still as fresh as when it arrived. This exceptional survival was found in a packing case in the former linen closet, and many more treasures lay forgotten behind closed doors or languishing in outhouses, among them Victorian dolls in mint condition, books full of dried flowers, a Georgian chamber organ and a harpsichord by Burkat Shudi. Household objects that would have been thrown away long ago in other establishments, such as an array of lamps that was in use until electricity was installed in 1962, have also survived here.

After Sir Vauncey died in 1924, apart from a brief period during the Second World War, when some evacuees and, later, soldiers were billeted here, the house slowly shut down.

Charles Harpur-Crewe, who inherited in 1949, was even more socially retiring than Sir Vauncey and, increasingly, only a core of habitable rooms was occupied. The extensive servants' quarters were shut up, and other rooms became

filled with the wreckage of unwanted things. These rooms, and the long bleak corridors connecting them, are shown as they were found and are deeply atmospheric. Wallpaper is stained and peeling, great cracks snake across ceilings, and paintwork is chipped and flaking. Seen with the shutters largely closed, the effect is of a place turned in on itself, of abandonment as much as decay. In the bowels of the building is the old kitchen and a series of cave-like wine and beer cellars and, from the north side of the courtyard, where grass grows between the paving stones, a long, dimly lit, brick-vaulted tunnel winds far underground to emerge in the brewhouse in the stable block.

Several members of the family lie buried in the graveyard and vaults of the little church, which crowns a rise to the south of the house. Although apparently of the nineteenth century, its appearance is due to a remodelling, in 1827–9, of a simple Elizabethan building, some parts of which, such as the roof trusses, were re-used. Nearby, hidden by a screen of trees, are the late eighteenth-century walled gardens, a combination of the ornamental and the practical. Mixed borders against the walls and geometrical beds in the lawn of the flower garden echo Victorian planting schemes, and neat rows of fruit and vegetables, many of them varieties that were known in the 1770s when the garden was created, have been planted in the original physic garden. A vast grassy arena at the top of the slope with an orangery on the north side and views over Staunton Harold reservoir was once the kitchen garden.

When Charles Harpur-Crewe died in 1981, while setting mole traps in the park, his brother Henry, who inherited the estate, faced death duties of £8 million. Despite the problems involved, including interest mounting up at the rate of £1,500 a day, Henry was determined to preserve Calke and, four years later, after special grants from the National Heritage Memorial fund and English Heritage, a successful public appeal and an anonymous donation, it was successfully transferred to the National Trust. Essential repairs meant that it was 1989 before the house could be opened to the public.

LEFT The plain baroque south front of Calke Abbey, completed in 1703, was embellished with a classical portico in 1806–8.

ABOVE This bleak scullery on the north side of the kitchen conveys the desolation of Calke's abandoned rooms.

Canons Ashby

Northamptonshire
On the B4525
Northampton–Banbury road

Set in the rolling, thinly populated country of south Northamptonshire, this ancient courtyard house reflects the bookish, conservative and never very wealthy family who lived here for 400 years, gradually altering and adding to the place but never rebuilding it. Little has changed since the early eighteenth century when the motto 'Antient as the Druids' was inserted over the drawing room fireplace. A lime avenue from the garden leads to an unexpectedly grand church, all that remains of the Augustinian priory that gave Canons Ashby its name and which once dominated a thriving medieval village, now only bumps and furrows in the grass. Although reduced to a quarter of its former length, the church is impressive; there is a striking red and white arcade on the west front and the massive pinnacled tower can be seen for miles.

John Dryden's modest H-shaped Tudor manor, built with material from the demolished east end of the church, now forms the great-hall range of the house, with its unusual squat tower like an echo of a Cumbrian pele rising over the south front. The wings to the east, enclosing the cobbled internal courtyard, were added by his son Sir Erasmus, the 1st Baronet, in the 1590s. Unlike the finished stone and brickwork of the exterior, the courtyard walls are rough and irregular, patterned with lichen and moss and set with leaded casement windows.

Painted decoration uncovered by the National Trust in the 1980s dates from Sir Erasmus's time. Some of it, such as the illustration of a story from the Old Testament with a great sailing ship at anchor in front of a walled city, is in grey-blue monochrome, but the array of crests and devices in the servants' hall is in full colour. Intriguingly, some of the symbols here, such as set squares and dividers, point to a connection with early freemasonry in Scotland, over a century before it was organised in England. Sir Erasmus was also responsible for the vast chimneypiece in the drawing room, but it was his son who added the striking domed ceiling, every inch of it crowded with elaborate plasterwork featuring thistles and pomegranates on stylised curving branches. Three long sash windows lighting this room, added when Edward Dryden remodelled the south front in 1710, look out over a rare survival of a formal garden of the same date, with a vista down a flight of terraces falling away from the house to a grand baroque gateway and across the park beyond. Enclosing walls are all of a piece.

Edward Dryden was also responsible for Canons Ashby's dignified west front. This now faces onto a grassy court but for centuries, from 1550 to c.1840, it was used as the main entrance to the house. An imposing baroque doorway dominates the facade, and Edward probably commissioned the sculptor Jan Van Nost to supply the leadwork coat of arms above the entrance and figures for the garden, of which only a statue of a shepherd boy survives. He also purchased the exquisite needlework-covered furniture in the Tapestry Room, with flowers and pastoral scenes embroidered on the seats and backs.

The present approach to the house, across the cobbled courtyard and up steps into the great hall, was arranged by Sir Henry Dryden, the much-loved Victorian squire of Canons Ashby who was known as the Antiquary. Fired by a lifelong interest in medieval architecture, Sir Henry measured and recorded all aspects of the house, down to the catches on the casement windows, and largely preserved it as it was, his only major addition being the oak bookcases in the little library where he wrote his learned articles. Leather-bound volumes now filling the shelves include the works of the three important literary figures associated with the house: the poet Edmund Spenser (1552–99), author of The Faerie Queene, who was a cousin of Sir Erasmus Dryden's wife; the poet laureate John Dryden, who visited the house as a very young man in the 1650s to pay court to his cousin, daughter of the 3rd Baronet; and the playwright and novelist Samuel Richardson (1689–1761), who is said to have written much of Sir Charles Grandison, his improbable moral tale about a virtuous paragon, at Canons Ashby.

The house is shown through Sir Henry's life and times and his meticulous records and period photographs have been used to re-create the Victorian planting of the terraces, with island beds and topiary yew on the grassy upper levels giving way to fruit and vegetable gardens framed by apples and pears on the lower terraces.

OPPOSITE A huge pendant hangs from the centre of the plasterwork ceiling that was added to the drawing room in the 1630s.

ABOVE Sixteenth-century ranges flanking John Dryden's Tudor staircase tower on Canon Ashby's south front are hidden behind early eighteenth-century embellishments.

Carlyle's House

London
24 Cheyne Row, London SW3 – off Cheyne Walk, between Battersea and Albert Bridges on Chelsea Embankment

When the historian and philosopher Thomas Carlyle and his wife Jane moved to London from Scotland in 1834, they decided to rent this unpretentious, red-brick Queen Anne house in the then unfashionable area of Chelsea. Tall and narrow, with two rooms and a closet on each floor and a strip of a garden behind, this is where they lived until their deaths, hers in 1866 and his 15 years later, furnishing the house with good but unremarkable Victorian pieces and a wealth of books and pictures. Still filled with the Carlyles' possessions, the walls crowded with photographs, watercolours and drawings of themselves, their families and places they loved, this otherwise unexceptional house conveys a remarkable impression of the great man and his lively and intelligent wife.

The basement kitchen with its cast-iron range and old stone sink, originally filled by pumping water from a well beneath the floor, is very little changed. Here Carlyle retreated to smoke so as not to offend his wife, and this is where their maid slept at night. Upstairs is the book-lined drawing room which the Carlyles enlarged in 1852, inserting the Victorian fireplace. Jane bought the green sofa second-hand in 1835 and decorated the screen covered with cut-outs that stands in a corner, while the reading chair was a present to Carlyle on his 80th birthday. It was in this room that Carlyle wrote *The French Revolution*, the work that was to establish his reputation, painstakingly rewriting the manuscript of the first volume after it had been accidentally burned while on loan to John Stuart Mill. In the attic room filling the top of the house, which the great man built on in 1853 in a vain attempt to provide himself with a soundproofed study, a fragment of manuscript is all that remains of the original draft. Among many other mementoes on display here now is the buff dressing gown Carlyle is wearing in a poignant watercolour by Helen Allingham, painted when the writer, beard and hair both snowy white, was 84.

While Carlyle wrote with vision about the condition of mankind, his wife is remembered for her witty and caustic correspondence with family and friends, and for the wide circle of eminent figures she received in Cheyne Row,

Dickens, Tennyson, Browning, Thackeray, Ruskin and Darwin among them. While Thomas Carlyle's reputation has dimmed over the years, Jane's stature has grown, and her observant letters are now regarded as among the best in the English language.

BELOW Carlyle's hat still hangs by the garden door in the hall of the red-brick terraced house in Chelsea where he and his wife Jane came to live in 1834 and which is filled with their belongings.

Castle Coole

Co. Fermanagh
1½ miles (2.4 kilometres) south-east of Enniskillen on the A32 Belfast–Enniskillen road

This austere white palace, James Wyatt's masterpiece, is one of the finest Neo-classical houses in the British Isles. Built between 1789 and 1795 for Armar Lowry Corry, Viscount and later 1st Earl of Belmore, it was designed to provide a suitably grand setting for a newly ennobled member of the peerage and also to surpass Florence Court across Lough Erne to the south, the house that had recently been embellished by Lowry Corry's brother-in-law, Lord Enniskillen (*see* p.140).

The shady path up from the car park by the stables suddenly emerges on the grass in front of the house to give an oblique view of the dazzling entrance facade faced in creamy Portland stone. A pedimented portico rising the height of the house is echoed in colonnaded wings linking the main block to pavilions on either side, a rather old-fashioned Palladian design, reminiscent of Robert Adam's Kedleston (*see* p.180), which may reflect the fact that Wyatt had to work with the foundations for a scheme of *c.*1785 by the Irish architect Richard Johnston. This constraint clearly did not dim his enthusiasm. The quality of the interior detailing is superb: fine plaster ceilings by Joseph Rose and carved chimneypieces

ABOVE Castle Coole, built in the 1790s, is a palace of a house, whose architect, James Wyatt, never actually visited the site, sending drawings from London to be implemented, and adjusted, by the local clerk of works.

by Richard Westmacott are matched by similarly superior craftsmanship in the joinery of doors and floors. Unusually, a complete set of building accounts and many drawings have survived and these show that Wyatt even designed furniture and curtains. But he never visited Castle Coole, leaving his plans to be realised, and often altered, by the clerk of the works, Alexander Stewart. Rose and Westmacott too worked from afar, providing decorative features in London that were then shipped to Ireland. The Portland stone cladding of the exterior was brought by boat from Dorset to a special quay built at Ballyshannon and then taken by cart and barge up Lough Erne.

Sadly, Lord Belmore's ambitions far outstripped his purse, exhausting his funds before his new mansion was fully fitted out. Wyatt's chastely elegant interiors were furnished in an opulent Regency style between 1802 and 1825 by Belmore's son, whose relish for the job matched that of his father. The 2nd Earl spent over £26,000, more than it cost to build the house, with the fashionable Dublin upholsterer John Preston, whose fine furnishings include one of the few state beds in Ireland. Extensively restored by the National Trust to reflect its early nineteenth-century appearance, Castle Coole is an intriguing blend of classical and Regency. The dignified entrance hall, with a screen of mock-marble columns and statues in niches, is painted a welcoming pink as it was by the 2nd Earl. In contrast, grey scagliola pilasters ringing the oval saloon beneath Joseph Rose's delicate ceiling echo the original colour scheme, while stoves set in niches and the curved doors following the line of the walls are again strongly reminiscent of designs for Kedleston.

The saloon is the centrepiece of the north front, dividing rooms of very different character. The dining room on one side, still lit only by candles, is pure Wyatt, with fan-like plaster tracery arching over the curtainless windows, slate-green walls hung with family portraits and a delicate classical frieze. There is gleaming gold plate on Wyatt's sideboard, which was produced in 11 weeks by two joiners in 1797. The drawing room at the other end of the house is furnished with gilt couches and chairs upholstered in salmon pink and with a richly patterned nineteenth-century Aubusson carpet. The library across the hall is more comfortable, with a plentiful supply of cushions and bolsters lying casually on the red velvet

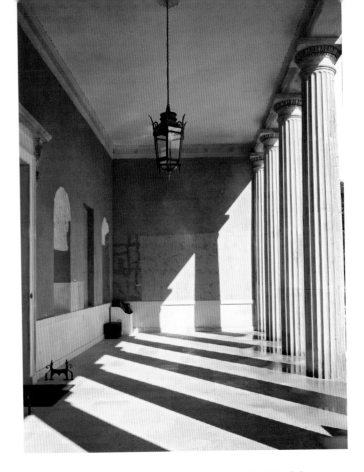

ABOVE As this view down one of the colonnades shows, Castle Coole has an austere and sculptural beauty.
OPPOSITE The oval saloon at Castle Coole, where even the mahogany doors are curved, is fitted out with opulent Regency furnishings which act as a foil for the cool Neo-classical decoration.

of the masculine Grecian sofas. The heavy folds of the crimson curtains with their plump tassels are immortalised in white marble on Westmacott's extraordinary chimneypiece, executed while Wyatt was employed on the house but not to the architect's surviving design. Substantial servants' quarters in the basement reflect the number of staff that would have been necessary for a house of this quality.

Castle Coole looks out over a wooded park that was landscaped in the late eighteenth century and slopes gently down to Lough Coole, the site of a previous house. The double oak avenue, along which Castle Coole has been approached since about 1730, has been replanted and will reach maturity some time in the middle of the century.

Castle Drogo

Devon
4 miles (6.4 kilometres) south of the A30 Exeter–Okehampton road via Crockernwell; or turn off the A382 Moretonhampstead–Whiddon Down road at Sandy Park

When Julius Drewe, the self-made millionaire, retired from his retailing business in 1889 aged only 33, he was determined to set himself up as a country gentleman. Fired with the belief that he was descended from a Norman baron and that the family name had been given to the Dartmoor village of Drewsteignton, he resolved to build a castle on the land that he thought had once belonged to his remote ancestors. Although the initial grandiose plans were massively scaled down, Castle Drogo, set on moorland to the west of the village and built of local granite, looks both suitably medieval and as if it is rooted in the landscape.

As the spectacular views from the roof confirm, the site, on a spur high above the gorge of the River Teign, was well chosen. A road runs along the top of the bluff, but the castle is far more impressive if approached by the steep path leading up from the river far below, when a jumble of granite walls and towers topped by battlements and pierced by mullioned windows suddenly rears up from the bracken-covered hillside ahead. A massive entrance tower with twin octagonal turrets on the west front has a genuine portcullis and the heraldic Drewe lion is proudly displayed over the entrance arch.

This ambitious building was commissioned in 1910 from Sir Edwin Lutyens, then at the height of his powers and with the transformation of Lindisfarne Castle already behind him (see p.200). The great architect's interiors, with much use of bare stone and unpainted woodwork, initially seem as unwelcoming as the outside. But the use of space is always interesting and carefully designed. The main corridor leading from the entrance hall, for example, is an architectural tour de force, with an intriguing interplay of domes and vaults. And, as the plentiful windows suggest, Lutyens in fact created a comfortable country house within the fortress-like exterior. A stately staircase lit by a huge east-facing window links the dining room to the airy, panelled drawing room, where soft green walls and chintz-covered sofas, and windows on three sides, create a restful, luxuriant atmosphere. Similarly, the agreeable bathrooms, one with an elaborate shower arrangement, were designed with pleasure in mind. Exotic Spanish furniture in several of the rooms was acquired as a result of the spectacular bankruptcy of the banker Adrian de Murrieta, friend of the Prince of Wales (the future Edward VII) and extravagant social butterfly, whose vast red-brick Sussex mansion Drewe purchased in 1899.

Lutyens took as much care with the extensive servants' quarters in the bowels of the castle as he did with the rest of the house. A round beechwood table and other fittings in the

LEFT Castle Drogo's entrance tower has a workable portcullis, operated by a winch in one or the turrets, arrow slits and the heraldic Drewe lion carved in relief above the archway.
OPPOSITE The long corridor linking the hall with the drawing room at Castle Drogo, with its walls of unplastered granite, shows how Lutyens ingeniously combined tunnel vaulting with shallow domes.

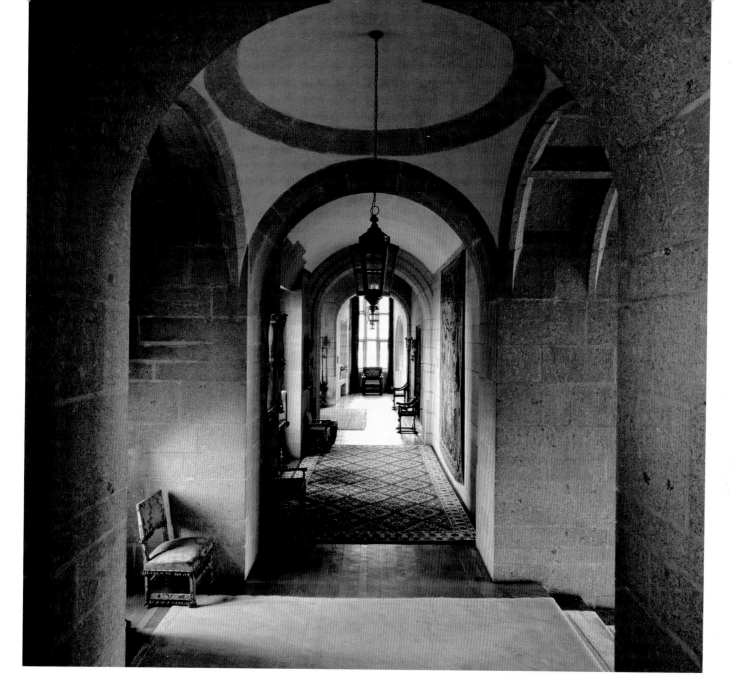

lofty kitchen, lit only through a lantern in the roof, were made to his design, as were the oak cupboards, table and teak sinks in the substantial pantry.

Lutyens was also involved in the formal garden to the north of the house, where yew hedges are clipped in geometric shapes and granite steps lead up a flight of terraces, although the layout and planting probably owe more to the garden designer George Dillistone, who had worked for Julius Drewe at Culverden in Kent and was employed at Castle Drogo from 1922.

Sadly, Julius Drewe died only a year after the castle was completed in 1930, but he must have been pleased with his progress in life. Whereas *Burke's Landed Gentry* ignored his similarly wealthy retailing rivals Lipton and Sainsbury, the land Drewe acquired with the fortune amassed from his Home and Colonial Stores gained his inclusion.

During a five-year programme of building works starting in 2013, visitors will be able to see rooms that have not been open before and work in progress.

Castle Ward

Co. Down
7 miles (11.2 kilometres) north-east of Downpatrick, 1½ miles (2.4 kilometres) west of Strangford village on the A25, on the south shore of Strangford Lough, entrance by Ballyculter Lodge

Castle Ward, crowning a gentle slope above Strangford Lough, is a very Irish house. Although built at one period, from 1762–70, it is classical on the west side, with a central pediment supported by four columns, and Gothick on the east, with battlements, pinnacles and ogival windows. This architectural curiosity is a result of the opposing tastes of Bernard Ward, later 1st Viscount Bangor, and his wife Lady Anne. Each favouring a particular style, they agreed to differ. The interior also reflects the Wards' eccentric approach, with the rooms on his side of the house, the hall, dining room and library, decorated in a Palladian idiom, while those on the east, the saloon, morning room and boudoir, are in an ornate and opulent Gothick, with pointed doors and plaster vaulting. The versatile architect is unknown, although tradition has it that, like the stone of which the house is built, he may have come from Bath (the stone was brought from England in Lord Bangor's own ship and unloaded in Castle Bay below the house).

The stylistic division of Castle Ward was followed by the separation of Bernard and Anne, and by her departure for Bath. By the time the 1st Viscount died, their eldest son,

BELOW Castle Ward's battlemented Gothick facade overlooking Strangford Lough is matched, on the other side of the house, by a coolly classical entrance front.
OPPOSITE The boudoir on the Gothick side of Castle Ward has a billowing, tent-like plaster ceiling which was based on drawings of the fan vaulting in Henry VII's chapel in Westminster Abbey.

ABOVE Castle Ward's classical west front, with a pediment carrying the Ward arms, reflects the conventional taste of the period.

Nicholas, was insane and the estate was divided between his two younger brothers, one of whom, after moving Nicholas to Downpatrick, removed most of the contents of the house. But the elaborate decorative schemes have survived almost unaltered. Three-dimensional plaster motifs stand out white against the green walls of the hall: here a festoon of musical instruments, including drums and tambourines, across the room a cluster of agricultural implements, a harrow, axe and billhook. A pedimented door leads into the Gothick saloon, where ogival mirrors between the ecclesiastical traceried windows reflect a cluttered Victorian interior, with photographs on many surfaces, stuffed birds under a glass case, a gossip seat and feathery dried flowers. Lady Bangor's sitting room next door, transformed by the voluptuous curves of the Gothick ceiling into a large pink tent, is even more exuberant. There could hardly be a greater contrast with the restrained treatment of the elegant cantilevered staircase, which has a Venetian window on the half-landing and a frieze of acanthus-leaf scrolls on the walls.

Steps lead down past an impressive array of bells to the kitchens, housekeeper's room and wine cellar in the basement, connected by a long whitewashed tunnel to the Victorian laundry, stables and servants' quarters set round a courtyard apart from the house, as was the fashion in eighteenth-century Ireland. A former billiard room in the basement is devoted to the exceptional Mary Ward (*d*.1869), scientist, painter and wife of the 5th Viscount Bangor. Her delicate watercolours of wildlife and atmospheric views of the house and estate are on show and cases are filled with her collections of butterflies and insects. Most remarkable are the fruits of her pioneering work with the microscope: magnified images of the eye of a dragonfly, like a blue honeycomb, and of the silvery scales of the jewel beetle.

Castle Ward has one of the most beautiful settings of any house in Ulster, with an eighteenth-century landscape park, in the English style, sloping down to the lough and views over the water framed by mature oaks and beeches. To the north of the house is the Temple Water, a serene artificial lake created in the early eighteenth century which is overlooked by a little classical temple. The formal Victorian garden near the house is different in character, with grassy terraces planted with palms and roses rising from a sunken, brightly flowering parterre to a line of Irish yews and a pinetum beyond.

Corn- and saw-mills, a drying kiln and slaughterhouse set round a yard near the Temple Water were once the centre of a thriving agricultural estate. Here, too, is the early seventeenth-century tower-house which the Wards built soon after they came to Ireland from England. Nearby is a row of slate-roofed late Victorian cottages that were provided for estate workers. Only a few decades before, in 1852, the village of Audleystown had been destroyed and its inhabitants transported to America to improve the view from the house. As the accounts in the estate office reveal, some left still owing rent.

Charlecote Park

Warwickshire
1 mile (1.6 kilometres) north-west
of Wellesbourne, 5 miles
(8 kilometres) east of Stratford-
upon-Avon, 6 miles (9.6
kilometres) south of Warwick on
the north side of the B4086

Charlecote has been the home of the Lucy family and their ancestors for some 800 years. The present house, begun by Sir Thomas Lucy in the mid-sixteenth century, stands on the banks of the River Avon at the centre of an extensive wooded deer-park grazed by fallow deer and a herd of rare Jacob sheep. The estate is within easy reach of Stratford and there is a story that Shakespeare was caught poaching here and brought before Sir Thomas Lucy, the resident magistrate, in Charlecote's great hall. Perhaps the young playwright vaulted over the rough oak paling that still surrounds most of the park and has been perpetuated since Elizabethan times. Shakespeare would have been fined, and possibly flogged, and the story goes that he took his revenge some years later by portraying Sir Thomas as the fussy Justice Shallow in *The Merry Wives of Windsor*. Alas, despite a reference to the Lucys' ancient coat of arms, of which Sir Thomas was known to have been very proud, the story is probably just that.

The house is built of red brick to a pleasingly irregular E-shape. With banks of decorative chimneys arrayed across the roofline and octagonal corner turrets crowned with gilded weathervanes, Charlecote seems to sum up the very essence .of Elizabethan England, especially when the brickwork is mellowed and burnished by the sun. Queen Elizabeth I spent two nights here in 1572, an occasion that is proudly celebrated in the display of her arms over the two-storeyed porch. With the exception of the porch, however, most of the present building is the result of 'Elizabethan' restoration in the mid-nineteenth century by George Hammond Lucy and his wife Mary Elizabeth, who not only refitted every room but also extended the house to south and west, obscuring much genuine Elizabethan brickwork in the process. The general effect is rich and lush, reflecting advice from the designer and antiquarian Thomas Willement, who, as well as advising on neo-Elizabethan plasterwork ceilings and other period features, even produced convincing Elizabethan versions of such things as fitted bookshelves and pile carpets, unknown in the sixteenth century. The Willement touch is particularly evident in the sunny and comfortable library, where he designed the Elizabethan-style bookcases to house the Lucys' fine collection of books, which includes a late fourteenth-century Book of Hours, and also the carpet, the wallpaper and matching chintz covers on the furniture, and the fire grate and door stops. Apart from the family paintings, which hang in every room, George Hammond Lucy was also responsible for most of the furnishings, many of which came from the 1823

BELOW The great hall at Charlecote Park is hung with portraits of the Lucy family who have been living on this site since at least the twelfth century and who still inhabit the house.

ABOVE Charlecote's entrance front dates largely from the nineteenth century, but the porch with its classical columns is an Elizabethan survival and carries the arms of Elizabeth I, who came here in 1572.

sale of the contents of William Beckford's Fonthill Abbey in Wiltshire. The most expensive purchase was the arresting sixteenth-century Italian marble table in the hall, which came from the Borghese Palace in Rome and is inlaid with brightly coloured birds and a slab of onyx like a section through a fossilised tree. Mary Elizabeth, who carried on altering and furnishing the house after George's death in 1845, created the drawing-room wing and purchased the gigantic, ornately carved neo-Elizabethan buffet that dominates the dining room.

Two generations earlier, in the mid-eighteenth century, George Lucy, a cultivated and much travelled bachelor, had employed 'Capability' Brown to redesign the park, sweeping away the seventeenth-century water gardens (shown in the painting above Shakespeare's bust in the great hall) and

altering the course of the River Hele (now the Dene) so that it cascaded into the Avon within sight of the house. George Lucy was also responsible for introducing the Jacob sheep, which he brought back from a trip to Portugal. The balustraded formal garden between house and river, with steps into the Avon, is a nineteenth-century addition.

Some of the earliest parts of the house are in the extensive outbuildings, where the stable block includes a brew-house that was in operation until the 1890s, a wash-house, and a coach-house displaying a collection of vehicles used at Charlecote in the nineteenth century. But only the rose-pink gatehouse with its fretwork stone balustrade survives unaltered from Sir Thomas Lucy's original Tudor mansion, a tantalising taste of what has been lost.

Chartwell

Kent
2 miles (3.2 kilometres)
south of Westerham

Winston Churchill, whose house this was, once declared that he bought Chartwell 'for that view'. Set on the side of a little Kentish valley, it looks over the garden that falls away steeply below to wooded slopes across the combe and the soft countryside leading onward to the Weald. There are vistas from almost every room and, as the many doors to the garden suggest, a sense of a house linked intimately with its surroundings. This serene setting, still breathtakingly beautiful, was to provide Winston Churchill with inspiration and strength for over 40 years, from 1922 until he left Chartwell for the last time in 1964.

The appeal of this unpretentious red-brick house, with its comfortable airy rooms created by Philip Tilden out of a gloomy Victorian mansion, lies in its powerful reflection of a great and complicated man, whose spirit still seems to linger on here. His bold and colourful paintings hang throughout the house, some, such as the simple study of a magnolia on an upper landing, tranquil still-lifes, others recording landscapes he loved, in France, Italy and Morocco as well as around Chartwell. A half-finished canvas stands on the easel in his garden studio, paints laid ready nearby. Finished pictures hang four and five deep on the walls round about. In the airy, flower-filled drawing room, a card table is set for the bezique he so much enjoyed, and a painting over the fireplace records one of the finest colts from his racing stable. A velvet siren suit, his characteristic wide-brimmed hats and cigar boxes also suggest a man who relished the pleasures of life.

But there are other mementoes too. In the lofty study, with its high roof open to the rafters, is the wide mahogany stand-up desk at which Churchill liked to work. His *A History of the English-Speaking Peoples* and *The Second World War* were mostly composed in this room. Here he reflected on the

BELOW Chartwell, the home of Winston Churchill from 1922 until 1964, looks out over terraced gardens laid out by the Churchills and the soft wooded countryside of Kent and Sussex beyond.

ABOVE Seven round-headed windows looking over the garden light the dining room, where dinner, served at eight, was usually accompanied by champagne.

growing power of Germany during the 1930s, a threat that he felt was perceived by him alone. The study is still essentially as he left it, crowded with family photographs, a dispatch box on the table. A portrait of his father hangs by the fire and a drawing of his mother confirms her exceptional beauty. Elsewhere, medals, uniforms and other reminders of a life devoted to his country include Churchill's terse directive to Field Marshal Alexander, instructing him to expel the enemy from North Africa, and the field marshal's equally short reply, informing the prime minister that he had done so. Chartwell is also very much a family house. The signatures of Lloyd George, Balfour and Field Marshal Montgomery in the visitors' book are interspersed with the more tentative efforts of the four young Churchills' friends and cousins. And it was the children who decided to mark their parents' 50th wedding anniversary by planting the borders filled with 32 varieties of golden roses that run in a long corridor down the old kitchen garden, close by the wall that Churchill built when he was in the political wilderness before the Second World War.

A loose framework of hedges and walls, with steps from one level to another, divides the spacious garden falling away to the lakes in the depths of the combe. Stretches of trees and grass are complemented by planting schemes reflecting Lady Clementine Churchill's love of cool colours and simple and direct effects. Her walled rose garden lies to the east of the house and there are many butterfly-attracting plants. Most evocative is the secluded pond, where an ample garden chair marks the spot where Churchill came daily to feed his golden orfe and ponder life.

Chastleton House

Oxfordshire
At Chastleton off the A44, 4 miles
(6.4 kilometres) south-east of
Moreton-in-Marsh

On the fringes of the Cotswolds, eastwards into Oxfordshire, is an unspoilt landscape of well-wooded farmland and limestone villages. Less than a mile (1.6 kilometres) off the main road from Oxford to Evesham, a leafy narrow lane runs steeply up through a straggle of cottages. At the top of the village, set back across a grassy court beside a stump-towered church, is a square, many-gabled Jacobean house. Of mellow local stone, with tall, three-storey ranges set round a tight internal court and mullioned windows, Chastleton is a charming and unaltered example of the kind of manor house which must have adorned a thousand English villages, lived in by families untouched by high office and national events. There are sophisticated touches, such as the arresting south front, with its show of glass and advancing bays, and some fine plaster ceilings, but much else, such as the rough and mossy dry-stone walls lining the entrance court, is rustic and ad hoc.

BELOW Jacobean Chastleton House, built of mellow local stone, lies on the fringes of the Cotswolds, with only an archway separating it from the straggle of cottages making up the village.

ABOVE Decorative panelling embellishes many of Chastleton's atmospheric interiors.

OPPOSITE One of the two battlemented staircase towers at Chastleton overlooks the topiary garden to the east of the house, where the 24 box figures are being allowed to become increasingly amorphous.

Until it came to the National Trust in 1991, Chastleton had been in the hands of the same family for almost 400 years. Built *c.*1610–12 for Walter Jones, a successful wool merchant, who bought the estate in 1602 from Robert Catesby, the future Gunpowder Plotter, it had been owned by Jones's descendants ever since, with tapestries and furniture identifiable on the inventory taken after his death in 1632. Early prosperity did not last. Although the family was staunchly royalist in the Civil War, when Arthur Jones is said to have evaded a Roundhead search party after the Battle of Worcester by hiding in a secret chamber, there were few rewards at the Restoration, and growing financial difficulties culminated in Henry Jones's imprisonment for bankruptcy in 1755. Chastleton's character comes from the slow accumulation of contents in a house that, like an old coat, was sometimes cut to fit but never drastically altered or updated.

Above a substantial basement, where the smoke-blackened kitchen ceiling, said to ensure the family's luck, remains unwhitewashed, is a sequence of parlours and chambers, some tapestry-hung and the grander with carved chimneypieces of stone or wood and decorative plasterwork. Panelling, now dark with age and dirt, is used like wallpaper, and there are pegged plank doors, undulating floors and deep windowsills. The plan is conservative, centred on a traditional great hall, with an oriel window lighting the high-table end and a carved strapwork screen, and with staircases in crenellated towers to either side of the house. The most ornate interior is the great chamber, where the overmantel, carved with the arms of Jones and his wife, still has much of its rich red, blue and gold colour scheme and the ceiling is an extravaganza of trailing vines and hanging pendants; the most glorious is the bare and airy long gallery on the third floor, with its silvery panelling and plasterwork barrel ceiling. The long refectory table in the hall, leather chests in the gallery, and the blue and red flamestitch hangings lining a little closet are among the furnishings given on the 1633 inventory; a brief burst of refurbishment after 1697, when Walter Jones married the forceful Anne Whitmore, accounts for the James II walnut chairs and exquisite Queen Anne crewel-work; and the family's poverty ensured the survival of some seventeenth-century woollen hangings that were once commonplace and are now very rare. There is also an unbroken run of family portraits, including works by Kneller and Hudson, and a leather-bound bible in the library is said to have been used by Charles I on the scaffold. All is seen in a shadowy half-light, brightened by shafts of sunlight through leaded casements.

It was Anne Whitmore who probably laid out the topiary garden to the east of the house, with a yew circle embracing 24 box figures. Once an impressive display of arboreal sculpture, these are now a collection of intriguingly individual amorphous shapes. To the north is a sequence of grassed terraces where a lawn laid out for croquet recalls the nineteenth-century Walter Jones Whitmore, who first codified the rules of the game. In a field beyond the garden, on a sightline from the house, there is a mature oak, said to have grown from an acorn off the Boscobel tree that sheltered the fugitive Charles II, and a delicious eighteenth-century dovecote stands in the parkland rising to the summit of Chastleton Hill.

Chedworth Roman Villa

Gloucestershire
3 miles (4.8 kilometres) north-west of Fossebridge, off A429 Cirencester–Northleach road

At the top of a peaceful wooded combe in the depths of the Cotswolds, low limestone walls, the stumps of former columns, terraces cut into the hillside and bumps and hollows in the grass mark the site of what was once one of the grandest villas of Roman Britain. These remains trace out three long wings, one storey high and one room deep, which were arranged round two courtyards running down the hill. Covered galleries fronted each wing and a cross gallery divided the more prestigious upper courtyard from what lay below. At the highest point of the site, an octagonal pool filled by a spring from the hillside marks the remains of a water shrine. The villa faces east, with glorious views down the combe to the pastoral Coln valley, from which it would have been approached.

Although parts of the villa date from the late second century, when three simple buildings and a bath house were constructed here, the remains are largely from the mid-fourth century. This period was a golden age, when the Romanised British aristocracy built villas to rival those of the Mediterranean world, many of them on the fertile estates of the Gloucestershire Cotswolds. Chedworth, only a few miles from the important Roman town of *Corinium Dobunnorum* (Cirencester) and from the great Roman highway of the Fosse Way, running from Exeter to the Humber, was particularly well placed. Who lived here is not known, but the owner must

have been a man of some consequence, one of the British elite who headed up a sizeable household of servants and slaves.

Although the walls are nowhere more than a foot or two above the ground, this remarkable place, which for centuries lay buried beneath soil and woodland, still has substantial remains of the lavish decoration and up-to-the-minute technology with which it was fitted out. Water from the spring at the top of the valley was fed by gravity to two sets of baths, one the equivalent of a modern sauna, where the stream filled a deep plunge pool, the other providing the steamy heat of a Turkish bath. Stone channels in the floor of the communal latrine were kept clean by running water, and the spring also fed taps in the kitchen. Pillars of brick and stone exposed in some rooms were part of the sophisticated heating system, which channelled hot air under the floors, and fragments of painted plaster suggest once-vivid colour schemes and paintwork that simulated marble. Most memorable are the villa's mosaic floors, their *tesserae*, in shades of white, olive, blue, grey, brown and red, mostly made of stones from local sources. The designs are predominantly geometric, using patterns seen across the Roman empire, but the impressive floor in the dining room in the west range includes Bacchic scenes, featuring drunken satyrs, and representations of the four seasons, Winter warmly clad, like an ancient Briton, in a hooded cloak, a hare dangling from one hand, wood clasped in the other.

The prosperity and political stability that underlay Chedworth did not last. The withdrawal of Roman power in AD410 was followed by the collapse of the Romanised way of life, and it seems the villa became part of a farm and was then abandoned, to be gradually absorbed by the surrounding woods. Over the years, stones were taken for use elsewhere and, in the seventeenth century, the ruins were used to feed a lime kiln, but generally the villa was forgotten. It was uncovered in 1864 by James Farrer, the uncle and guardian of the 3rd Lord Eldon, on whose land Chedworth lay. His interest sparked by a gamekeeper, who showed him fragments of mosaic picked up in the woods, Farrer dug out the remains, rebuilt parts of the walls and added protective coverings to the best rooms and mosaics. He also built the little museum displaying finds and carved stonework which stands in the middle of the site, at one end of the mock-Tudor hunting lodge added by Lord Eldon in 1866.

Cherryburn

Northumberland
Off the A695 at Mickley,
11 miles (17.7 kilometres)
west of Newcastle

A roughly built sandstone cottage set high above the deep green valley of the Tyne was the birthplace of the eminent engraver and naturalist Thomas Bewick (1753–1828), known for his closely observed engravings, carved in box, of the creatures that populated the Northumbrian countryside. At the age of 14, Bewick was apprenticed to a leading engraver in the nearby town of Newcastle, who, working with copper and silver, taught the boy how to produce the precise and delicate effects he was later to realise in wood. Once his apprenticeship was over, Bewick went into partnership with his old master and, in November 1785, on the day his father died, began working on the box engravings for the delightful company of animals which illustrate *A General History of Quadrupeds*, the book that would bring him to the attention of a wider world. Published in 1790, the *General History* was an instant success and was followed, a few years later, by two volumes on British birds, the illustrations for which Bewick drew from the life.

The cottage, originally heather-thatched but now tiled and somewhat smaller than it was in Bewick's childhood, looks over a sloping cobbled yard to the substantial farmhouse built in the late 1820s by Thomas's brother William, who took over the family smallholding and partly demolished his former home, using what remained for stabling. Although the bedroom under the roof from where Bewick watched the changing seasons did not survive William's attentions, what remains of the cottage has been reconstructed as it was in Bewick's day on the basis of detailed drawings made by his son Robert, and Bewick's desk and other mementoes and a splendid collection of his publications acquired with the help of the National Heritage Memorial fund are on display. Bewick himself lies in the graveyard of Ovingham church, less than a mile (1.6 kilometres) away across the valley.

OPPOSITE Like all Chedworth's mosaics, this geometric design, from the corridor of the west wing, dates from the fourth century.
LEFT The life and work of the engraver Thomas Bewick are captured at Cherryburn, where the National Trust owns both the sandstone cottage where he was born in 1753 and the family farmhouse built in the 1820s.

Chirk Castle

Wrexham
½ mile (0.8 kilometre)
west of Chirk village off
the A5

Chirk Castle is an elegantly appointed house within the carapace of a medieval fortress. The long drive from the baroque entrance gates – a filigree of white ironwork – leads up through the undulating oak-studded park. The castle, appearing suddenly on the brow of the hill, is unexpectedly menacing, with drum towers projecting from battlemented fourteenth-century walls.

A pointed archway marked with the grooves of a portcullis leads into the internal courtyard. Here the west range still has the character of the stronghold Roger Mortimer started in c.1295 as part of Edward I's campaign to subdue the Welsh. Deep underground, reached by a spiral staircase in the thickness of the walls, is a dungeon hollowed out of the rock, only two narrow beams of light reaching those who were incarcerated here. In the courtyard outside a great shaft falls 28.5 metres (93 feet) to the castle well.

These reminders of the turbulent Middle Ages contrast with the later interiors commissioned by the Myddelton family who came to Chirk in 1595, when the castle was sold to the merchant and financier Thomas Myddelton I. In the late eighteenth century, Joseph Turner of Chester created an elegant staircase and a suite of state apartments in the fashionable Neo-classical style within the massive walls of the north range. Gothic touches by A.W.N. Pugin, who was commissioned to redecorate the castle in the 1840s, have been mostly toned down or removed, but some of the strong colour schemes and other details introduced by this exceptional man remain. The sumptuous saloon, with gilded doors and dados and a red and white chimneypiece of Sicilian marble, is graced with an Adam-style coffered ceiling, coloured a brilliant blue by Pugin and his collaborator J.G. Crace and inset with Greek mythological scenes by the Irish painter George Mullins. Mortlake tapestries hang on the walls and the fine contemporary furniture includes pier tables and mirrors by Ince & Mayhew, a pair of stylish serpentine settees and the earliest signed harpsichord, of 1742, by Burkat Shudi, the intricate marquetry of the interior depicting eagles with outstretched wings. Among the seventeenth- and eighteenth-century family portraits hanging in these rooms are pictures of Richard Myddelton and his wife, who commissioned the state apartments, by Francis Cotes, and two rare portraits by the Flemish landscape painter Peter Tillemanns.

A door from the drawing room leads into the 30-metre (100-foot) long gallery that fills the first floor of the east range. Created in the 1670s, when Sir Thomas Myddelton IV, 2nd Baronet, repaired the extensive damage that Chirk had sustained in the Civil War, the gallery is more than twice the size of the saloon and is little changed, apart from the addition of a ribbed heraldic ceiling and fireplace tiles by Pugin. Dark oak panelling, perhaps by the gentleman-architect William Winde, is grandly conceived, with massive broken pediments crowning the doors and a bold cornice of carved acanthus leaves running above a show of early portraits. Among the few pieces of furniture, all of them probably part of the original contents, is a delicate seventeenth-century Dutch cabinet of ebony inlaid with tortoiseshell and ivory. The silver-encrusted interior is decorated with scenes from the life of Christ that were painted in the Antwerp studio of Frans Francken the Younger, one of which shows Our Lord blessing children against the backdrop of the gabled facades of a Flemish town. Declining a peerage from King Charles II, who had spent two nights at Chirk during the Civil War, Sir Thomas Myddelton II, grandfather of the 2nd Baronet, accepted this cabinet instead.

In 1820, an open colonnade beneath the gallery was transformed by the Chester architect Thomas Harrison into a suite of neo-Gothic family apartments. Subsequently redecorated by Pugin, these still contain Harrison's fan-vaulted ceilings and many features made for Chirk in the 1840s, such as the delightful metalwork door plates and knobs, firebacks and gasoliers supplied by John Hardman & Co. to Pugin's designs and Pugin's stone fireplace in the drawing room. Chirk's exceptional library is also in this range, the many rare sixteenth- and seventeenth-century books that it contains including a copy of the first popular edition of the Welsh bible, which was sponsored by Sir Thomas Myddelton, the purchaser of the estate, in 1630.

ABOVE Chirk Castle, built in the thirteenth century as part of Edward I's campaign to subdue the Welsh, was later converted into a country house, as its generous windows suggest.
OPPOSITE There are many rare sixteenth- and seventeenth-century books in Chirk's exceptional library.

These neo-Gothic rooms are fitted out in a 1930s idiom to reflect the life of Thomas, 8th Lord Howard de Walden, the shy and eccentric millionaire and patron of the arts who leased Chirk from the Myddeltons from 1911 to 1946. Specially commissioned furniture reproduces that shown in period photographs and in a portrait of the family by Lavery, a Gothic suit of armour commissioned from Felix Joubert, on loan from Dean Castle, reflects the 8th Lord's passion for medieval pursuits, and paintings and other works of art on loan from the family, the Tate and the National Gallery of Wales include a portrait of the 8th Lord by Augustus John, a bust by Rodin, and views of the castle and surrounding countryside by Wilson Steer.

Chirk lies in an oak-studded park, landscaped by William Emes in the late eighteenth century. The garden falls away on the east side of the castle, where the walls are softened by climbers. A show of topiary includes a massive hedge cut to resemble a battlemented wall; a sunken rose garden is centred on a sundial; and a mixed border flanking an expanse of grass was established by Colonel and Lady Margaret Myddelton, who restored the garden after the Second World War. A lime avenue hidden in woodland is the only survival of a seventeenth-century formal layout, and a little pavilion sits at one end of a long terrace, the views from here taking in a great sweep of the Welsh borders.

Clandon Park

Surrey
At West Clandon on the A247,
3 miles (4.8 kilometres) east of
Guildford on the A246

Clandon looks as if it would be more at home on the corner of a piazza in Venice or Florence than set down in the Surrey countryside. A massive four-square block of a house, three storeys high and 11 windows wide on the long garden facade, it is built in the reddest of brick with stone dressings and with a central pedimented section of stone on the entrance front. There is a roofline balustrade, but nothing rises above it to relieve the austere geometry of the building.

This individual Georgian country house, built in about 1731, owes its appearance to the Italian Giacomo Leoni and is one of only five surviving buildings by this Venetian architect in England (*see also* Lyme Park, p.204). The interior is as grand as the exterior, its most impressive feature being the richly decorated formal Marble Hall rising through two storeys. Here, the proportions are Palladian, with an impression of light and space, but some of the decoration is decidedly baroque. Classical statues are set in niches at the level of the first floor, but above them is a freely modelled theatrical plasterwork ceiling by Artari and Bagutti. Life-like slaves supporting the central relief are perched on the cornice with one leg over the edge, as if they could leap down at any moment. Decorated in shades of white, and with a marble floor and intricately carved marble chimeypieces over the two fireplaces, the hall appears cool and serene, refreshingly so on a hot August afternoon. Leoni even extended the marble floor into the grand saloon next door, as if Clandon were a Mediterranean villa.

Clandon was built for Thomas, 2nd Baron Onslow, to replace the Elizabethan house his great-grandfather had acquired in 1641, and it has remained in the family ever since. The Onslows have traditionally followed political careers; the three who served as Speakers of the House of Commons are commemorated in portraits in the Speaker's Parlour. Here too is the 'vinegar' bible that Arthur Onslow, Speaker from 1728–61 and the most famous of the three, presented to St Margaret's, Westminster, its name deriving from a misprint in the parable of the vineyard. The Maori meeting house in the grounds, its steeply pitched thatched roof reaching almost to the ground, is a memorial to another eminent Onslow, the 4th Earl, who was governor of New Zealand from 1888–92 and who also rescued Clandon from half a century of neglect by his great-uncle.

Most of the original contents have been sold or removed over the years, but Clandon is now filled with magnificent furniture, porcelain, textiles and carpets acquired by the connoisseur Mrs David Gubbay in the 1920s and 1930s. Apart from the English eighteenth-century furniture, which includes fine satinwood and marquetry pieces, the most striking feature of the collection is the array of seventeenth- and eighteenth-century porcelain Chinese birds. About 50 of these vividly plumaged creatures perch on baroque brackets or sit on tables and mantelpieces, the many species represented including a pair of elegant fragile cranes in the Green Drawing Room and brilliantly blue parrots, red and green pheasants and plump ducks in the Hunting Room. A spectacular phoenix presides over the state bedroom, where the four-poster and accompanying chairs were probably made for Sir Richard Onslow, father of the builder of the house. Clandon now also houses the Queen's Royal Surrey Regimental Museum in the basement.

ABOVE LEFT These enchanting ducks are from a large collection of porcelain Chinese birds which are on display throughout Clandon Park.
OPPOSITE Clandon's vast Marble Hall, and the adjoining saloon, were used for entertaining large gatherings; in good weather, the outside doors would be thrown open to give views of the garden and park.

Claydon

Buckinghamshire
In Middle Claydon, 13 miles
(20.9 kilometres) north-west
of Aylesbury, 3½ miles
(5.6 kilometres) south-west
of Winslow

A combination of ambition and gullibility led Ralph, 2nd Lord Verney, to create one of the most extraordinary houses in England. Inheriting the family estate in 1752, Verney initially contented himself with reconstructing and extending his father's old-fashioned Jacobean manor house, but some ten years later he embarked on a far more grandiose scheme for a great west front, partly, it seems, to produce a house to rival that of his much richer neighbour, Earl Temple of Stowe. The restrained classical exterior of the surviving west wing conceals extraordinary decoration by Luke Lightfoot, an eccentric and difficult genius variously described as cabinetmaker, master-builder and surveyor, but emerging at Claydon as a carver of unique talent.

Lightfoot's work in the North Hall and Chinese Room is in a class of its own. Ceilings, overmantels, doors and alcoves are encrusted with lacy white woodwork. Herons, swan-like birds and fantastic wyverns with barbed tails perch on the tracery. Necks are coiled and snaky, wings outstretched, claws extended. Tiny bells hang from the roof of the built-in pagoda-like feature in the Chinese Room, which was fitted out when the fashion for chinoiserie in eighteenth-century England was at its height. Carvings resembling oriental summerhouses, with trelliswork connecting the supporting columns, surmount the doors. Bamboo furniture made in Canton in about 1800 completes the effect.

Lightfoot's extravagance and the failure of a speculative housing project in which he had persuaded Lord Verney to invest led to his dismissal before the house was completed. Exquisite plasterwork adorning the saloon and staircase is by Joseph Rose, who was employed at Claydon after 1768. Working in plaster where Lightfoot worked in wood, Rose used conventional classical motifs but executed them with skill and ingenuity to create two of the finest Georgian interiors in England. The stairs are one of the marvels of Claydon, with delicate ears of corn quivering in the ironwork scrolls that make up the balustrade and a jigsaw of box, mahogany, ebony and ivory forming the parquetry treads.

Growing financial difficulties, unrelieved by lawyers employed to help manage mounting debts, led to the sale of the contents of the house in 1783, and Verney's grandiose ballroom and huge rotunda by the architect-squire Sir Thomas Robinson were demolished by his niece when she succeeded to the estate. The Javanese musical instruments filling the museum room, an assortment of gongs and wood and

LEFT This intricate doorcase in the Chinese room at Claydon House is typical of the outstanding decoration by the brilliant Luke Lightfoot, who created in wood what others would have realised in plaster.
RIGHT Claydon House as it is today, with a handsome front overlooking the park, was once a wing of a much grander mansion, with a vast ballroom, much of which was demolished in the 1790s.

bamboo xylophones collectively known as a gamelan, were a present to Sir Harry Verney, 2nd Baronet, who inherited the property in 1827. Florence Nightingale would have seen this exotic gift from Sir Stamford Raffles, lieutenant governor of Java, when she came to visit her elder sister Frances Parthenope, Sir Harry's wife. The room where she always slept is decorated as it was in her day, her sitting room has been re-created, and there are many mementoes of this

formidable woman, among them letters she wrote as a young girl, a watercolour of her pet owl, and reminders of the privations she endured in the Crimea, two photographs showing how thin and frail she looked on her return. Unfortunately there is no record of what this most Victorian of ladies thought of the extravagant rococo decoration of her sister's home.

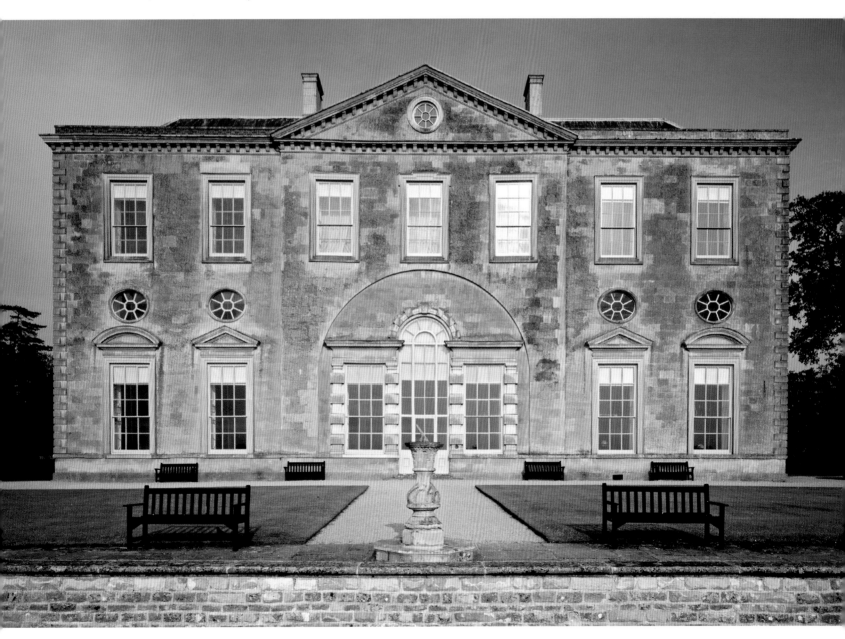

Clevedon Court

Somerset
1½ miles (2.4 kilometres) east of
Clevedon, on the B3130

During the nineteenth century, the seaside village of Clevedon was transformed into a fashionable resort with Italianate villas, a pier and a Royal Hotel. But the Eltons of Clevedon Court who had done so much to improve the town lived on in the remarkable medieval manor that Abraham Elton I, a Bristol merchant, had acquired in 1709.

Seen from the south, Clevedon is a picturesque assemblage of low, stone-built ranges, mullioned windows, steeply pitched roofs and tall chimneys, all set against the thick woods of Court Hill. Despite some later additions, Sir John de Clevedon's early fourteenth-century house has survived virtually unchanged, its buttressed walls and the portcullis groove on the projecting two-storey porch suggesting that he needed to build with defence in mind. At the north-east corner of the house is a massive four-storey tower, with arrow-slit windows, which may be earlier than the rest of the building but is probably part of Sir John's fourteenth-century work. Carved out of the hillside and rising sharply behind the house are terraced gardens, planted with tender shrubs and adorned with two summerhouses.

Finely crafted fourteenth-century arches on the right of the traditional screens passage bisecting the house were openings to the medieval buttery, kitchen and pantry. To the left is the great hall, now embellished with an eighteenth-century coved ceiling and thickly hung with a mixed bag of Elton family portraits. Sir Abraham, the 1st Baronet, dressed in his scarlet robes as Mayor of Bristol, proudly surveys the descendants who were to enrich Clevedon with literary and artistic associations. A cartoon of William Makepeace Thackeray at the top of the stairs, a shock of white hair standing out from his head and pince-nez on his nose, recalls the novelist's friendship with Sir Charles, the 6th Baronet, a gifted poet whose elegy for his two drowned sons moved his

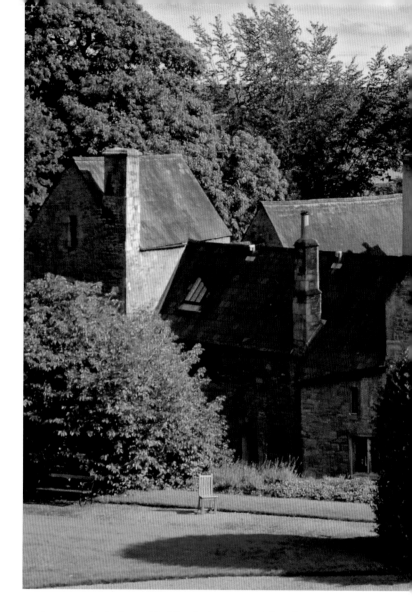

contemporaries to tears. Sir Charles's youngest daughter Jane, with whom Thackeray fell hopelessly in love, was immortalised as Lady Castlewood in *Henry Esmond*, much of which was written in the house. The poet-baronet's circle also included Lamb and Coleridge, and Tennyson composed his elegy 'In Memoriam' for Sir Charles's nephew Arthur Hallam, who was a close friend of Tennyson and died tragically young.

The family's artistic streak appeared again in Sir Edmund Elton, whose Eltonware pots and vases made of clay from the estate, most of them in rich, dark colours but some pieces of a striking sea-blue with metallic glazes, are displayed in the old kitchen and whose vivid portrait by Emmeline Deane hangs in the hall. This remarkable self-taught man began his career as a potter in about 1880, building up an international reputation for his work. Fragile glass walking sticks, some shot through with spirals and twists of colour, glass rolling pins and improbable pipes tinged rose-pink, crimson and blue are part of the collection of high-quality local Nailsea glass which is also shown in the house.

Another side of Victorian Britain emerges on the stairs, where boldly patterned wallpaper by G.F. Bodley shows off a number of prints and engravings illustrating triumphs of engineering in the late eighteenth and nineteenth centuries, from Abraham Darby's iron bridge at Coalbrookdale, constructed in the 1770s, to the Menai Strait, Severn and Clifton suspension bridges and a host of viaducts and aqueducts that were vital to the achievements of the age. A tall red and green Eltonware candlestick, designed with Sir

OPPOSITE The window of Clevedon Court's medieval chapel, filled with a net of stone tracery, stands out on the south front of this ancient house.
ABOVE Clevedon as seen from the garden terraces cut into the hill behind, with the four-storey medieval tower on the extreme left, and the great hall range dominating the main part of the house.

Edmund's characteristic flair, stands in the tiny first-floor chapel that was part of John de Clevedon's manor and originally consecrated in 1321. A net of stone tracery across the south wall, filled with brilliantly coloured Victorian stained glass by Clayton and Bell, not only recalls the patron saint of fishermen to whom the chapel was originally dedicated but also the Bristol Channel only a mile (1.6 kilometres) or so to the west, where the little islands of Flat Holm and Steep Holm stand out black against the sea in the light of a setting sun.

Cliveden

Buckinghamshire
3 miles (4.8 kilometres) upstream from Maidenhead, 2 miles (3.2 kilometres) north of Taplow and the A4

This three-storey Italianate palace floating on a chalk terrace high above the River Thames is a *tour de force* by Sir Charles Barry, who is best known for designing the Houses of Parliament. Built in 1850–1 for the Duke and Duchess of Sutherland, it replaced two earlier houses that had been destroyed by fire, the first a Restoration house by William Winde for the 2nd Duke of Buckingham, which burned down in 1795, the second a Georgian-style house designed in 1827–30 for Sir George Warrender by the Edinburgh architect William Burn, who made use of the foundations and surviving wings of the earlier building. Cliveden had just been sold to the Sutherlands when it was burned down again in 1849. The smoke from the fire alerted Queen Victoria as she came out of chapel at Windsor and she sent fire engines from the castle, which is only 5 miles (8 kilometres) away, but the house was largely gutted. An inscription running below the roofline records the seventeenth-century building, much of whose character and shape Barry preserved, as well as the construction of the present mansion. The two wings surviving from the original house, added on by Thomas Archer for the Earl of Orkney, Cliveden's new owner, in 1706 and linked to the main block by curved corridors, flank a great sweep of gravel on the entrance front, from where the drive, shaded by an avenue of limes, runs straight to an extravagant marble fountain by Thomas Waldo Story. Ornate stables on the west side of the forecourt, with a top-heavy clock-tower rising high above them, were added in the 1860s.

From the south, Cliveden is more of a piece and more imposing. Here, Barry's main block, with an urn-studded roofline parapet, rises grandly over a long arcaded terrace, 28 arches wide, which extends far beyond it on either side. A legacy of the Restoration house, this magnificent feature was embellished in the eighteenth century by a central double staircase that descends in elegant elbows of stone to a grassy platform. Immediately below the arcade, on a bank above the grass, is the weathered stonework and mellow brick of an early seventeenth-century balustrade, its central opening framed by elaborate pedestals, which was brought here from the Villa Borghese in Rome in 1896.

The Borghese balustrade was introduced by William Waldorf, later 1st Viscount Astor, who bought Cliveden in 1893. Lord Astor also commissioned J.L. Pearson, then in his mid-seventies, and his son Frank to remodel the interior of the house, but some of the painted decoration introduced by the Duchess of Sutherland still survives on the staircase ceiling, where figures by the French émigré artist Auguste Hervieu depict the Sutherland's four children in the guise of the seasons. Of the three rooms shown (Cliveden is now a hotel), the most seductive is the French dining room, lined with green and gold rococo panelling and with a marble chimneypiece and painted overdoors, all of which came from a mid-eighteenth-century hunting lodge near Paris. Pearson's capacious, low-ceilinged, oak-panelled hall, with a carved stone chimneypiece of *c.*1525 from a French chateau at one end and early eighteenth-century Brussels tapestries on the walls, is dominated by Sargent's vivacious portrait of Nancy Astor, wife of the 2nd Viscount. Given the house and its contents as a wedding present by William Waldorf in 1906, Nancy and her husband made Cliveden famous as a centre of literary and political society before the First World War, entertaining Henry James, Rudyard Kipling, Curzon and Churchill here. The house parties continued between the wars, when the so-called Cliveden Set, supporting Chamberlain and appeasement, were seen as politically significant, but the guest list, which included Charlie Chaplin, was as eclectic as ever. Only a few years later, during the Second World War, Lord Astor decided to give Cliveden to the National Trust, but the family continued to live here until 1966, and it was during these years that Cliveden was caught up in a sensational political scandal. It was here, in 1961, that John Profumo, Secretary of State for War, began his liaison with the

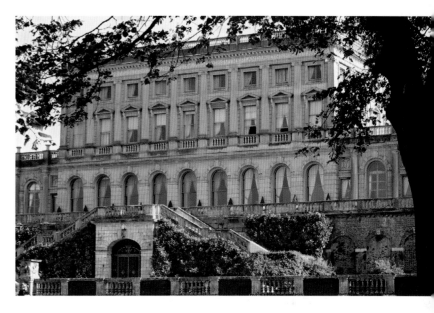

ABOVE Barry's south front is carried on Winde's arcaded terrace.
OPPOSITE The rococo panelling in Cliveden's seductive French dining room came from an eighteenth-century hunting lodge outside Paris.

call-girl Christine Keeler, a relationship that was to end his political career and seriously undermine the government of the day when it was revealed, two years later, that Keeler was also having an affair with the Soviet naval attaché Evegeny Ivanov.

The rustic cottage on the banks of the Thames where Christine Keeler stayed lies in the extensive wooded grounds, ornamented with garden buildings, Italian sculpture and other features, that surround the house and stretch down to the river. There are long walks and drives through the trees and magical views over the river and its still pastoral valley. Much of the landscaping dates from the early eighteenth century, when Charles Bridgeman laid out avenues and rides and created the grass amphitheatre carved into the hill for Lord Orkney. The box-hedged parterre on the great grass terrace to the south of the house was also first devised, by Orkney himself, at this time. The 1st Viscount Astor, as well as introducing the Borghese balustrade, was responsible for the informal water garden, with stepping stones leading to a pagoda on an island, and for converting the Octagon Temple, one of two ornamental buildings designed by Giacomo Leoni for Lord Orkney, into a family chapel and mausoleum. The magnificent yew maze which Astor sketched out the year he came to Cliveden has recently been replanted.

Clouds Hill

Dorset
9 miles (14.4 kilometres) east of Dorchester, ½ mile (0.8 kilometre) east of Waddock crossroads on the B3390, 1 mile (1.6 kilometres) north of Bovington Camp

This little brick and tile labourer's cottage on the slopes of Clouds Hill was a haven for T.E. Lawrence, better known as Lawrence of Arabia. After the First World War, in which he had played a major role in the campaign for Arab independence in the Middle East, Lawrence needed a retreat where he could recover from his experiences and pursue an undemanding occupation. An attempt to join the RAF under an assumed name ended in exposure and dismissal and in 1923 he tried again, enlisting as a private in the Tank Corps at Bovington Camp under the name T.E. Shaw. Clouds Hill, which he first rented and then bought, was just a mile (1.6 kilometres) from the camp. Its tiny rooms with their simple, even austere furnishings are as Lawrence left them, a direct reflection of his monastic way of life and complex personality. His books have gone from the shelves lining the downstairs room, but the wind-up gramophone with a huge horn on which he used to play Mozart and Beethoven still dominates the music room in the roof and his cell-like bedroom, lit by a porthole window which came from a 1914 battle cruiser, is as it was.

Here Lawrence would come to read or write by the fire whenever he could get away from the camp, finding the peace he needed to work on his revision of *Seven Pillars of Wisdom*. Friends were served picnic meals washed down with water or Lawrence's own blend of China tea, but never with alcohol.

For Lawrence the cottage was an earthly paradise. He rejoined the RAF in 1925 but came back to Clouds Hill to live out his days on his discharge in 1935 at the age of 46. Five days later he was dead, killed in a fatal crash when returning to the cottage from Bovington Camp on his motorcycle. The shed where he kept his machine is now used for an exhibition on Clouds Hill and Lawrence's life and times.

BELOW In the downstairs room at Clouds Hill, which was once lined with his books, T. E. Lawrence used to read by the fire in the evenings, sitting in the armchair that he had designed.

Clumber Park

Nottinghamshire
4½ miles (7.2 kilometres) south-east of Worksop, 6½ miles (10.4 kilometres) south-west of Retford, 1 mile (1.6 kilometres) from the A1 and the A57, 1 mile (1.6 kilometres) from the M1, junction 30

At the heart of the extensive former park of the Dukes of Newcastle, framed by specimen trees and rhododendrons, is the High Victorian Gothic chapel which G.F. Bodley built for the 7th Duke in 1886–9. Like the 1st Marquess of Ripon, who was responsible for an equally splendid chapel at Studley Royal to the north (*see* p.141), the duke was a passionate Anglo-Catholic. As well as building the chapel, he also provided a house and school for the boys of the choir.

Heavily buttressed walls, tall Gothic windows and a soaring 55-metre (180-foot) spire give the chapel the look of a parish church. Inside, it seems like a miniature cathedral, the vaulted roof in shadow high above the nave. Six brass candlesticks stand conspicuously along the elaborately carved rood screen, and ornate Flemish-style chandeliers light the Rev. Ernest Geldart's walnut and oak choir stalls, with musical angels carved out of limewood looking down from crocketed canopies. Stained glass by C.E. Kempe, rich tapestries and hangings and velvet and silk altar frontals, including an early work by J.N. Comper, add to the sumptuous effect of this masterpiece of Gothic Revival architecture.

The chapel is the main focus of the nineteenth-century pleasure grounds. The Italianate great house that was once here, designed by Sir Charles Barry to replace an earlier mansion that burned down in 1879, was largely demolished in 1938. Only the duke's study remains, but the outlines of the rest of the house are marked by paving stones in the grass.

The attractive stable block survives, its clock tower crowned by a whimsical cupola, and impressive late nineteenth-century glasshouses, with a central palm house projecting in a fan of glass, overlook the walled kitchen garden.

The nineteenth-century plantings and estate buildings were added to a landscape park that was created in the late eighteenth century out of heathland and focused on an L-shaped serpentine lake with wooded islands dotted down its length. Two classical temples and a balustraded bridge are the work of Stephen Wright, who designed the first house here, and the decorative lodges and gate piers at the park's many entrances are also his.

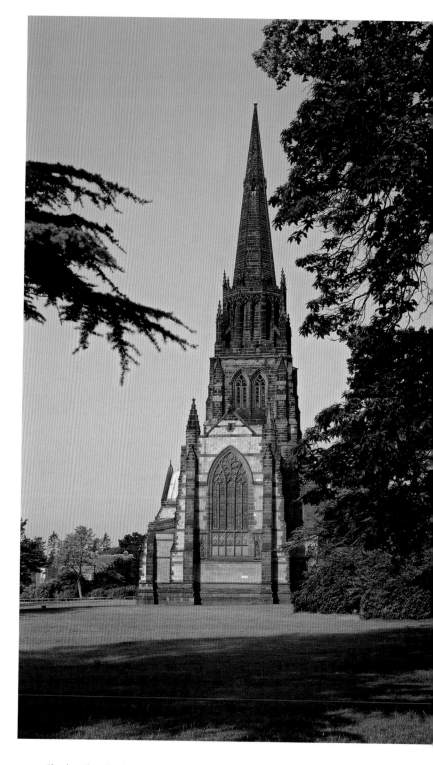

ABOVE Clumber Chapel, as large as a parish church, was built in 1886–9 by G. F. Bodley, who re-used stone from a chapel left unfinished twenty years before.

Coleton Fishacre

Devon
2 miles (3.2 kilometres) from
Kingswear; take Lower Ferry road,
turn off at the tollhouse

Near the mouth of the Dart estuary, on the headlands east of the river, a deep combe runs steeply down to the wooded cliffs above Pudcombe Cove. At the top of the valley, with its back against the slope, is a long, low house, with mullioned windows, tall chimneys and steep tiled roofs. Below, filling a natural amphitheatre, is a richly planted garden. Architectural near the house, with terraces, steps and walls continuing the lines of the building, the garden becomes wilder and more jungle-like as it nears the sea. Both house and garden were created in the 1920s for Rupert and Lady Dorothy D'Oyly Carte, who had spotted the valley while sailing along the coast and saw its potential for a place in the country. Son of the impresario who promoted Gilbert and Sullivan, Rupert was by then running the company that produced their operettas and also his father's other enterprise, the Savoy Hotel. While Lady Dorothy lived at Coleton Fishacre, Rupert came down from London for weekends, often bringing distinguished guests such as the conductor Sir Malcolm Sargent. After Rupert's death in 1948, the house was sold and the contents largely dispersed. The present furnishings have mostly been introduced by the National Trust, who have been able to draw on the 1949 inventory and photographic evidence.

The house, its walls now softened by climbers and shrubs, is built of Dartmouth shale quarried from the combe and roofed with Delabole slates. Begun in 1923, it was designed by Oswald Milne, a former protégé of Sir Edwin Lutyens, in an

ABOVE Art Deco alabaster light fittings, a cool green 1930s carpet by Marion Dorn, and the strong yellow cushions in the Saloon at Coleton Fishacre offset the spare modernism of walls and ceiling.
OPPOSITE Set at the head of a small Devon valley running down to the sea, Coleton Fishacre was built in the 1920s as a weekend retreat and includes accommodation for a chauffeur and the family Bentley.

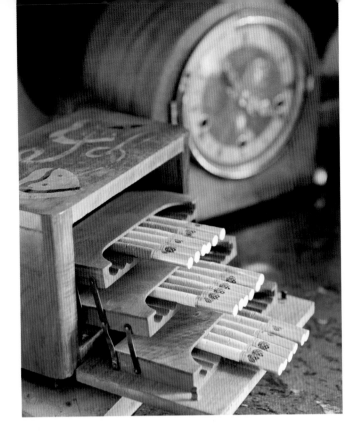

ABOVE These playful cigarettes evoke weekend parties, when a ship's bell was rung to summon guests back from the cove for pre-dinner drinks.

Arts and Crafts idiom, with much attention to craftsmanship and materials and with a flowing roofline that unites the rather rambling layout. While his treatment of the exterior looks back to the late nineteenth century, Milne's Art Deco interiors are very much of their time. The impression is of a comfortable, unpretentious family house but also of a kind of spare modernism, relieved by strong splashes of colour, original honeycomb ceiling lights and other details. Rooms are low ceilinged, walls are often roughly plastered, with smooth coves marking junction points, and there are deep windowsills lined with black Staffordshire tiles and much use of limed oak and pine. Long passages on both floors are bland and impersonal, but the main rooms have individuality and character.

At the west end of the house, angled out from the main building so as to give clear views over the garden, is the saloon. Entered down a theatrical flight of steps, and almost 12 metres (40 feet) long, the room is dramatically furnished in yellow and green, including original carpets made in the 1930s by the designer Marion Dorn. A little library filling the bay on the garden front is fitted out with pine shelves and is

dominated by George Spencer Hoffman's delightfully rose-tinted bird's-eye view of Coleton Fishacre, setting the house and combe in an enchanting blue-green patchwork of fields and lanes bounded by the sea. The original ultramarine scagliola table top and lapis lazuli bell-push in the dining room at the east end of the house bring the sea indoors and, whenever the weather was clement enough, meals were taken in the airy vine-hung loggia, with views deep into the valley, which lies beyond.

Upstairs, where almost none of the D'Oyly Cartes' furniture survives, the rooms have been fitted out with 1930s-style oak pieces from Heal's. Lady Dorothy's bedroom has been re-created from photographs and the black-and-white floral fabric designed by Raoul Dufy that was used for the curtains, cushions and seat-covers, and the near-black carpet, have been reproduced. Original features include splashes of colour from blue-green glass tiles round the basins in every room and period bathrooms with sunken baths and pictorial tiles by the young Edward Bawden. A glitter of gold on the stairs comes from the gleaming cupolas and crosses in a painting of St Mark's, Venice by W.R. Sickert, which had belonged to Bridget D'Oyly Carte and has been loaned back by the British Council. In the substantial servants' quarters at the east end of the house, a double sink in the kitchen is supported on sections of the railway track that was used to bring stone from the garden quarry.

Even before the house was completed, Rupert and Lady Dorothy were planting shelter belts to protect the valley from the prevailing wind and together they planned every detail of the garden, capitalising on the drama of the site, with its panoramic views, and on the presence of a little stream rushing headlong to the sea. Paths contour round the sides of the combe, follow the stream, or zigzag steeply up and down, with steps linking different levels. An upper path from the lawn by the loggia leads along the north side of the valley to the vine-hung gazebo, perched high above the quarry. The lower garden is spread out below, filled with colour in spring from a display of rhododendrons, azaleas, magnolias, dogwoods, camellias and Chilean fire trees. Mature specimen trees flourish throughout the garden and always there is the sea beyond, with a gate leading from the lower garden out onto the cliffs above Pudcombe Cove.

Compton Castle

Devon
At Compton, 4 miles (6.4 kilometres) west of Torquay, 1 mile (1.6 kilometres) north of Marldon

A delight of towers, battlements and buttresses, this fairytale place, more fortified manor than castle, is hidden in a deep and lush south Devon valley 2 miles (3.2 kilometres) from the sea. A heavy wooden door in the high defensive wall of the north front leads into the stone-flagged courtyard round which the house sprawls on three sides. Opposite the entrance is the reconstructed great hall, rebuilt in 1955 to its original medieval form and rising two storeys to an oak-timbered roof. A stone spiral stair leads to the solar on the first floor of the west wing and this side of the court is closed by a little chapel, its great traceried window on the north front still protected by the original defensive grille. Beyond the hall, in a corner of what was a second yard behind, is the splendid kitchen, with a hearth with bread ovens at each end filling the end wall. Five towers, all provided with garderobes, are incorporated in the house and a sixth, the watch-tower, is set into the south-east corner of the massive curtain wall that surrounds the castle.

This magical fortified house, one of very few to survive so unaltered, was built between the fourteenth and sixteenth centuries. The fortifications date from the reign of Henry VIII, when the Gilbert family, who had lived here from the mid-fourteenth century and had recently built a manor on the Dart (see Greenway, p.149), probably felt threatened by the French raids on Teignmouth a few miles north along the coast and on Plymouth to the west. Although the new defences did not make the manor impregnable, they would have deterred attack from a roving shore party.

Two Gilbert boys born in the mid-sixteenth century, half-brothers to Walter Raleigh, were among the small group of Westcountrymen who earned a place in the history of Elizabethan England. John, the eldest, who became Vice Admiral of Devon, played a major part in the defences against the Armada, providing for a possible landing in Torbay. And it was he who reported to Sir Francis Walsingham that Francis Drake had captured the Spanish galleon *Nuestra Señora del Rosario*, which was brought into the estuary of the River Dart nearby.

His younger brother Humphrey was one of the brave men who crossed the Atlantic in fragile ships in a wave of colonisation and expansion. Armed with the first Letters Patent granted by the Crown for the 'planting' of an English colony, he claimed Newfoundland for his queen on 5 August 1583, sadly drowning when his tiny ship *Squirrel* foundered on the return voyage. His torch was picked up by his half-brother, Sir Walter Raleigh, but the settlement Raleigh's expedition established on an island off what is now North Carolina was subsequently abandoned and it was Humphrey's youngest son, Raleigh Gilbert, who in 1607 founded the first permanent English colony in North America, calling it Jamestown after the new king.

The confidence of the age, which elsewhere led to the building of prodigy houses such as Hardwick (*see* p.161) or Wollaton Hall in Nottinghamshire, here led men to risk their lives in a quest for new lands, preserving Compton Castle as an unaltered medieval manor. Sold by the Gilbert family in 1785, and neglected for over a century, the house was bought back in 1931 in a ruinous state and restored by Commander and Mrs Walter Raleigh Gilbert, who refurnished it as a family home and whose portraits by Denis Fildes hang in the solar. Gilberts live here still.

BELOW A jumble of towers, gabled roofs and buttressed walls marks Compton Castle, a magical fortified house buried in a lush Devon valley only a few miles from the sea.

Corfe Castle

Dorset
On the A351 Wareham–Swanage road

The ruins of Corfe Castle rise like jagged teeth from the summit of a steep chalk hill that guards the only natural route through the Purbeck Hills. Although now reduced to broken walls and towers, this monument to the power of medieval kings is still architecturally striking and still dominates the little village huddled below. Strategically placed and the most defensible of all English castles, Corfe was eventually undone by treachery, not by the might of a besieging army.

Although there may have been a royal hunting lodge at Corfe in Saxon times and there is a tradition that the child-king Edward the Martyr was murdered here in 978, the castle was begun by William the Conqueror, whose fortifications formed part of the network of carefully placed strongholds with which he consolidated his hold on his new kingdom after 1066. These early Norman defences were gradually strengthened, with wooden features such as the original timber palisade being slowly replaced in stone. The massive keep crowning the hilltop, still rising some 22 metres (70 feet) in dramatic fingers of stone, was completed during the reign of Henry I, who imprisoned his elder brother Robert, Duke of Normandy here in 1106. The tower-studded curtain wall looping round the crest of the hill was a later addition, dating from the early years of the reign of King John (1199–1216), when Corfe's position so close to the south coast became of considerable importance in the renewed war with France. After the loss of Normandy in 1204, the castle was in the first line of the king's defences against a French invasion.

In a time when monarchs would travel round their kingdoms administering justice and enforcing loyalty by their presence, Corfe was a centre for government and administration as well as a stronghold. Part of the huge sum of £1,400 spent on building operations at Corfe during John's reign went to construct the king's 'Gloriette', a tower-house arranged round a courtyard in the topmost inner ward. The quality of the surviving masonry shows that this was a

LEFT The ruins of Corfe Castle, standing high on the chalk ridge crossing the Isle of Purbeck, are dominated by the remains of the great twelfth-century keep at its heart.

building of distinction, a compactly planned domestic residence fit for a monarch, with a great hall, chapel and parlour, and chambers for the queen overlooking a garden.

Apart from a brief period in the mid-sixteenth century, Corfe remained in royal hands until Elizabeth I sold it to Sir Christopher Hatton. About 50 years later the castle and estate were bought by Sir John Bankes, a staunch Royalist, who also purchased the neighbouring property of Kingston Lacy (see p.184). Of major strategic importance to both sides in the Civil War, Corfe was twice besieged. In 1643 Lady Bankes, who must have been a woman of strong character, held the castle against a force of local Parliamentarians in her husband's absence, but in the winter of 1645–6 Corfe was again attacked and fell through the treachery of one of the defenders, who arranged for enemy troops, disguised as reinforcements, to enter the castle. The victorious Roundhead colonel, impressed by Lady Bankes's courage, not only allowed the garrison to depart but also permitted his spirited opponent to take the keys of the castle with her; they now hang in the library at Kingston Lacy. Corfe was deliberately ruined, leaving only the romantic remains that inspired one of Turner's evocative watercolours.

BELOW A great ditch dug in 1207 and a formidable towered gatehouse guarded the approaches to Corfe's massive keep in the innermost part of the castle.

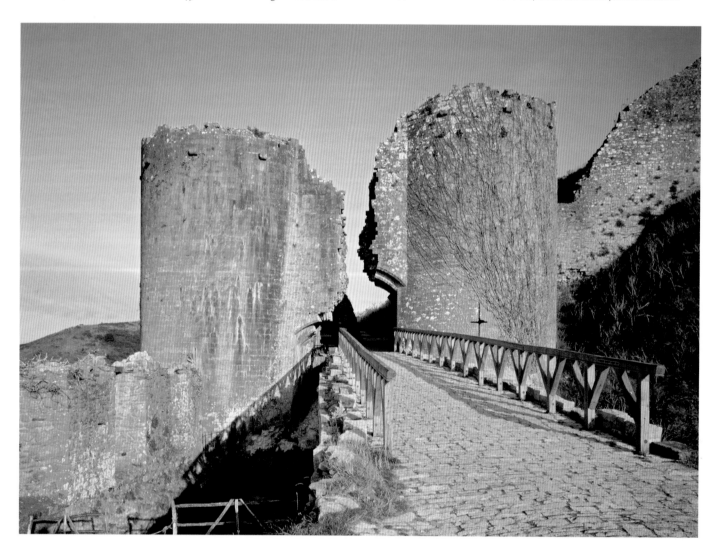

Cotehele

Cornwall
On the west bank of the Tamar, 1 mile (1.6 kilometres) west of Calstock by footpath (6 miles/ 9.6 kilometres by road), 8 miles (12.8 kilometres) south-west of Tavistock

The River Tamar, dividing Devon from Cornwall, has proved one of the most effective natural boundaries in England. Until 1962, when a suspension bridge was opened at the mouth of the river to link Plymouth and Saltash, the first road crossing was 15 miles (24 kilometres) upstream as the crow flies, but almost double that distance following the twists and turns of the river. For the villages and hamlets along its banks, the Tamar was for centuries the only effective route to the outside world. So it was for this Tudor courtyard house built by Sir Richard Edgcumbe and his son Sir Piers between 1485 and c.1540.

Low granite ranges set round three courtyards lie at the head of a steep valley running down to the river. The approach, past Sir Richard's massively buttressed barn and through a battlemented gateway tower, the arch of which is just wide enough to admit a loaded packhorse, signals the ancient character of the place. The rooms are small and mostly dark, reached by flights of worn stone steps and through massive wooden doors in granite archways. Three Tudor windows light the dais end of Sir Richard's medieval great hall, where an oak refectory table is set in the middle of the rough lime-ash floor and whitewashed walls rise the height of the house to a decorative timber roof. Adam and Eve are carved on one of the early seventeenth-century chairs at either end of the table, and the walls are hung with a collection of arms and armour that includes Elizabethan matchlocks, Civil War breastplates and lobster-tail helmets as well as some exotic pieces, such as long Indian swords.

The family chambers, with their large Tudor fireplaces and richly coloured hangings used like wallpaper, seem more inviting. On the late seventeenth-century bacchic tapestries adorning the little Punch Room, naked figures treading huge vats of grapes as if indulging in a communal bubble bath are clearly preparing a vintage to fill the arched niches in the cupboard-like wine cellar in one corner. In the Red Room upstairs, rich crimson drapery on the huge four-poster is set off by faded seventeenth-century arras on the walls, children at play with marbles and hoops on three of the panels contrasting with the scene of nightmarish violence by the bed illustrating the death of Remus. Across the landing, steps lead up to the rooms in the three-storey battlemented tower that was added on in 1627. At the top of the tower, reached by a steeply winding stair, are two bedrooms, one of them reputedly slept in by Charles I in 1644 on his march from Liskeard to Exeter, while some intriguing and exotic ebony furniture in the old drawing room that fills the floor below, once thought to be Tudor, is now regarded as having come from southern India, and to have been made, in some cases, as long ago as the early 1600s. Only a few decades after the addition of the tower, at the end of the seventeenth century, the family deserted Cotehele for Mount Edgcumbe, their much grander seat overlooking Plymouth Sound, and the old house was left largely undisturbed for 200 years, although the antiquarian interest of the place was already being recognised in the eighteenth century, when various royal parties were taken up the Tamar to visit the house. Even when the widow of the 3rd Earl of Mount Edgcumbe returned here in 1862, thus initiating another period of family occupation, much of the house remained unchanged. The east wing was improved and updated to provide modern comforts, such as central heating, but the new work was carefully designed to blend with the old.

This nineteenth-century wing looks over a luxuriant garden, sheltered by woodland, laid out in a valley leading down to the Tamar. At the head of the valley, just below some stone-walled terraces, are a medieval stew pond and a domed dovecote that once provided meat and fish for the community here, and hidden in the woods and set along the river are further reminders of the way the Cotehele estate once operated and of the one-time importance of river traffic.

ABOVE LEFT Cotehele is an atmospheric place of small dark rooms, worn stone steps and massive wooden doors, with glimpses of the lushly planted garden from casement windows.

Cotehele Quay, described in 1819 as 'a very large and commodious quay with a most desirable situation on the river', lies a quarter of a mile (0.4 kilometre) downstream. Clustered round the quay is a group of impressive old grey stone buildings, one of which houses an exhibition telling the story of the local shipping industry. At the end of the nineteenth century, when strawberries and other soft fruit from growers in the valley were taken over the river to Bere Alston station on the new Plymouth–Tavistock line, the quays would have been regularly visited by the sailing barges that plied the river, one of the last of which, *Shamrock*, is berthed here. Earlier in the century there had been shipments of ore from mines in the wooded Danescombe Valley upstream, the sites of which are now marked by grassy humps and some old mine buildings. These mines, at their peak in 1844–70, were just some of the many which exploited rich sources of copper and arsenic along the Tamar Valley.

The buildings of Cotehele Quay seem too tranquil for this industrial past, but hidden in the woodland across a reedy inlet to one side are the remains of a row of huge lime kilns, now romantically shrouded in greenery but once a source of lethal fumes. A path from here leads through woodland up the tributary valley of the River Morden to another picturesque group of estate buildings, including a three-storey eighteenth-century mill powered by an overshot wheel. This is now in working order and produces stoneground wholemeal flour that is sold in the National Trust shop. Here, too, are a wheelwright's shop, with a lathe driven by a huge flywheel, a forge where charcoal smoulders gently in the hearth, a saddler's shop filled with harness, lengths of chain and stirrups, and a sawpit and carpenter's shop.

Above the house, beyond a sloping daffodil meadow, is a building of a different kind. Set in a field is a triangular tower with granite pinnacles and dummy Gothic windows that gives the illusion, from only a short distance away, of being much more substantial than it is and was perhaps built to celebrate the visit of King George III and Queen Charlotte in August 1789. Panoramic views from the top look west to Kit Hill and east to Dartmoor, and in the valley below are the graceful arches of the Calstock Viaduct. This beautiful structure was built to carry the new railway opened in 1908, whose advent killed the river traffic.

ABOVE The ancient manor house of Cotehele, built round three courtyards, is approached through a battlemented gatehouse tower that was part of early sixteenth-century improvements to the medieval building.
OPPOSITE The east wing of Cotehele has beautiful views over the valley garden to the River Tamar.

Coughton Court

Warwickshire
2 miles (3.2 kilometres) north
of Alcester on the east side
of the A435

Only an expanse of grass separates Coughton Court from the main Studley to Alcester road, giving passing motorists a memorable view of the great Tudor gatehouse dominating the entrance facade. Dating from the early years of Henry VIII's reign, when even in remote countryside on the southern fringes of the Forest of Arden men could at last build to please themselves rather than to protect their property, the gatehouse is a glittering glass lantern, with the stone tracery and gleaming panes of a two-storeyed oriel window stretching the width of the two upper floors. Though Sir George Throckmorton thought it prudent to surround his new house with a moat, this may also have been regarded as a status symbol rather than purely as a means of defence. Less showy Tudor ranges flank two sides of the courtyard beyond the gatehouse, their domestic gabled facades and half-timbered upper storeys a direct contrast to the stone splendour of the gatehouse and a foil for a formal garden planted with white roses in box-edged beds. Lawns framed by avenues of pollarded limes stretch away from the open east side of the court, past two sunken gardens, towards the little River Arrow and peaceful wooded countryside beyond.

The Throckmortons, whose descendants live here still, first came to Coughton Court in 1409 and much of the fascination of the house derives from its continued association with this prominent Roman Catholic family. Increasingly prosperous during the fifteenth and sixteenth centuries, they were to pay a high price for their faith during the reign of Elizabeth I and the years that followed, when Roman Catholicism was associated with treason. In 1584 Francis Throckmorton was executed for his part in a plot to depose Elizabeth and replace her with Mary Queen of Scots. Francis's cousin, Thomas, was more circumspect. Although he lent Coughton to the conspirators in the Gunpowder Plot, he took care to be absent on the night of 5 November 1605 when a small group waited anxiously for news in one of the gatehouse rooms.

Like Baddesley Clinton only a few miles to the north-east (*see* p.36), Coughton was a refuge for recusants. Mass continued to be celebrated here and priests were concealed in

ABOVE The magnificent Tudor gatehouse at Coughton Court, with a beautiful double-storeyed oriel window lighting the upper floors, is one of the finest of its kind in England.

RIGHT The drawing room, where de Largillière's portrait of the 4th Baronet hangs over the fireplace, is lit by the great oriel window.

ingenious hiding places, among them a compartment above the newel stair in the north-east turret, discovered only in 1858, that was furnished with a bed and a folding leather altar. Another reminder of these times is the painted canvas hanging in the room above the hide that displays the arms of all the Catholic gentry who were imprisoned for recusancy during Elizabeth's reign. Other religious memorabilia include a magnificent early sixteenth-century cope of purple velvet embroidered in gold.

Staunchly Royalist during the Civil War, the Throckmortons' loyalty was tested when the house was besieged and occupied by Parliamentary troops in 1643, the rising ground where the Roundhead army placed their guns only too visible in the view west from the top of the gatehouse tower. Two generations later the entire east side of the courtyard was destroyed when Coughton was sacked by a Protestant mob running wild after the flight of James II and it was never subsequently rebuilt. A number of mementoes in the house, including a linen shift that belonged to Mary Queen of Scots in the year she was beheaded and locks of hair from the Old and Young Pretenders, reflect the Throckmortons' allegiance to the Stuart cause.

In later years, partly as a result of prudent marriages, the family fortunes revived. The stone-built Gothick wings on either side of the gatehouse were added in the 1780s by Sir Robert, 4th Baronet, who embarked on an extensive refurbishment of the house when already an old man and who probably also filled in the moat. Sir Robert, whose portrait by Largillière presides over the drawing room, was responsible for the delicate Gothick entrance hall, which he created out of the ground floor of the gatehouse, and for the elegant classical staircase, which is now hung with a magnificent array of early family portraits. Like the Catholic memorabilia and other contents, many of these paintings were brought to Coughton when grander family properties elsewhere were disposed of. There is some fine furniture, including a set of late seventeenth-century walnut-veneered Dutch chairs and a cabinet of the same date with a mirrored recess that was used to hold the Host, while the tapestry bedroom is hung with eighteenth-century pastels of the family, most of them by William Hoare of Bath.

A mid-Victorian Roman Catholic chapel close to the house is one of the family's last building ventures. House and chapel stand cheek by jowl with the ancient parish church just to the south in a group that is an enduring reminder of the divisions bred by religion.

Cragside

Northumberland
13 miles (20.9 kilometres) south-west of Alnwick on the B6341 and 16 miles (26 kilometres) north of Morpeth via the A697

When the inventor and industrialist William Armstrong visited Rothbury in 1863 as a break from the unrelenting pressures of his factory on the River Tyne, he decided to purchase what he could of the secluded Debdon Valley where he had so often wandered as a boy during family holidays. Four years earlier he had seen the army adopt the new gun he had developed after the poor British performance in the Crimean War and, as a result, his prosperous engineering firm was being gradually transformed into a vast industrial concern. Once primarily concerned with hydraulic machines, by the late nineteenth century Armstrong's was an international arms manufacturer, rivalled only by Krupps of Germany.

A couple of watercolours showing tall chimneys belching smoke over factory buildings ranged along the Tyne are the only direct reminders of the works that financed the rambling house set high above a ravine on the Debdon burn, with a jumble of gables, soaring chimneys, mullioned windows and half-timbering framed against a wooded hillside. But there are other pointers to the inventive mind of the man who built it. This was the earliest house in the world to be lit by hydroelectricity and water was also used to power a saw-mill, a revolutionary hydraulic lift and even a kitchen spit.

Armstrong's activities are reflected too in the gradual transformation of Cragside, which was originally built, in 1864–6, as a modest weekend retreat. Shortly after the completion of this first building, Armstrong engaged the distinguished architect Richard Norman Shaw, who over the next 15 years turned the house into a country mansion and enriched it with some of his most original work. Shaw's

LEFT Cragside, dramatically set on a steep wooded hillside, was designed as a romantic assemblage of stone-mullioned windows, gables, half-timbering and soaring chimneystacks.
BELOW James Ramsay's portrait of William Armstrong, painted when he was studying law, as his father wanted, hangs over the fireplace in the study.

grandest rooms were designed for important overseas clients. The King of Siam, the Shah of Persia and the Crown Prince of Afghanistan all slept in the monumental black walnut bed, with solemn owls carved on the end posts and a massive half-tester which Shaw created for the guest chambers. No doubt they appreciated the plumbed-in washstand and the sunken bath in an alcove in the dressing room next door. A long top-lit gallery with a wooden barrel ceiling leading from the Owl Suite was once hung with the best of Armstrong's Victorian paintings. These were mostly sold after his death, but pictures and sculpture are still set against the deep-red walls, and at the far end is Shaw's *tour de force*, the drawing room completed for a royal visit in 1884. The top-lit cavernous interior is dominated by W.R. Lethaby's Renaissance-style carved marble chimney-piece, with veining in the stone round the fireplace suggesting running water. Inglenooks with red leather settees are set on either side and white lamps hang in clusters from the ceiling like bunches of snowdrops.

The little rooms of the original lodge and Shaw's early additions for the family are quite different in character. His beautiful and unusual library with magnificent views of the glen is perhaps the most harmonious room in the house, the warm reds and browns of the furnishings setting off brilliant-blue tiles and onyx panels framing the fireplace and glowing enamelled electric lamps along the low bookcases.

Armstrong alone seems to have been responsible for Cragside's wildly romantic setting, for which the hillside was blasted to expose craggy rock formations and over 688 hectares (1,700 acres) of pleasure grounds created by planting millions of conifers, rhododendrons and alpines on what were originally bare slopes. A pinetum was established in the valley and on the steep slope below the house, like an expanse of scree above the burn, is a huge rock garden, planted with heathers, alpines and shrubs. On a south-facing slope on the other side of the valley, reached across Armstrong's steel footbridge and up a steep path from the stream, is a formal terraced garden with ferneries, a fruit house and a display of Victorian carpet bedding. An intricate network of paths snakes across the estate, with dramatic views to the Cheviots from the higher routes, and a scenic drive takes in the lakes over 100 metres (340 feet) above the house which were used to feed the hydroelectric turbine.

Croft Castle and Parkland

Herefordshire
5 miles (8 kilometres) north-west of Leominster, 9 miles (14.4 kilometres) south-west of Ludlow

This engaging house, with slender corner towers and rough stone walls, has a long history. Dating back to a time when this glorious country on the Welsh borders was insecure and torn by rebellion, the shell of the house is the four-square castle round a central courtyard which the Croft family, who came here from Normandy some years before the Conquest, built to defend their property. Much modified since, Croft was massively remodelled in the eighteenth century and features from various periods contribute to its present picturesque appearance. In the centre of the entrance front, Georgian bays with playful Gothick sash windows frame a mock-Jacobean castellated porch, added in 1913. The approach is through what appears to be a medieval archway, but this too was a more recent addition, probably built in the 1790s.

The country house takes over inside. Thomas Farnolls Pritchard, the Shrewsbury architect who designed the world's first iron bridge at Coalbrookdale, was responsible for the light-hearted Gothick interiors introduced in 1765, his pointed arches in white plaster on a coffee background on the stairs strongly reminiscent of a row of church windows. Even the stair balustrade looks ecclesiastical: column clusters forming the newel posts are miniature versions of those that might support the vaulting of a nave. Rare and valuable furniture in the same style includes a set of Gothick chairs in dark oak in the long gallery that would be suitable props for a dramatisation of Mary Shelley's *Frankenstein* or Horace Walpole's *The Castle of Otranto*. T.F. Pritchard also had a hand in the similarly striking but quite different decoration of the Blue Room, where *trompe-l'oeil* gold rosettes stud blue Jacobean panelling. Family portraits hang in almost every room, including a beautiful study by Gainsborough of Elizabeth Cowper, wife of Sir Archer Croft, the colouring all brown and red, and works by Lawrence and Philip de Laszlo. Crofts also dominate the little church of rough local stone set just east of the house. The most memorable of the many family memorials here is an early sixteenth-century altar tomb to Sir Richard and Dame Eleanor Croft, with realistic effigies showing the couple in extreme old age.

ABOVE Many members of the Croft family, who came to this beautiful place before the Conquest, are commemorated in the tiny medieval and Tudor church that lies close by the castle.

Thickly wooded parkland surrounds the castle, as it has done for centuries, the great avenues for which Croft is famous including a line of Spanish chestnuts, in which some of the trees may be 350 years old, stretching about half a mile (0.8 kilometre) to the west, and oaks and beeches flanking the long entrance drive. An ancient lime avenue that once shadowed the chestnuts has now been replanted. While most of the park escaped the attentions of an improver of the 'Capability' Brown school, the late eighteenth-century landscaping of Fish Pool Valley in the Picturesque mode was a direct reaction to his ideas. This little steep-sided glen planted with mixed deciduous and evergreen trees has a dramatic wilderness quality, which is in perfect accord with the castle's Gothick interiors. Another notable feature of the estate is the Iron Age hill-fort of Croft Ambrey, set on a ridge a mile (1.6 kilometres) north of the house.

RIGHT The elegant staircase hall at Croft Castle, with its delicate Gothick plasterwork, was created by T.F. Pritchard in the 1760s when he remodelled the interior of the house.

Croome

Worcestershire
9 miles (14 kilometres) south of
Worcester and east of the A38 and
M5, 6 miles (10 kilometres) west
of Pershore

Inheriting Croome Court and the surrounding estate in 1751, when he was only 30, the cultivated and wealthy George William, 6th Earl of Coventry set about transforming both the existing 1640s house, which he was determined to remodel as a fashionable Neo-classical mansion, and its surroundings. The two young men he engaged to realise his ambitions, Lancelot 'Capability' Brown, who came to Croome in 1752 at the age of 35, and Robert Adam, who was first commissioned by the earl in 1760, when he was 32, had yet to emerge as the leading designers of their day, but their work at Croome is totally characteristic. In his decorative schemes for the house, Adam designed everything, from the plasterwork, mirrors and marble chimneypieces to much of the furniture, while Brown's landscaping of the park, the first he was to create in a naturalistic style, employed all the devices for which he would become well known, from the artificial river which winds past the court to a pleasingly irregular lake and the artfully placed clumps of trees and shelter belts to the classical eye-catchers in the pleasure grounds round the lake and the borrowing of the wider landscape, with which the park seems to merge. This is a design on an epic scale in which the house plays an integral part, both as a grandstand for admiring the landscape and as a focus for the views from a network of meandering paths and drives.

Brown, whose only previous experience had been as head gardener at Stowe, was first engaged to remodel the house, although it is likely that the gentleman-architect Sanderson Miller, who was a friend of the earl and had recommended Brown, also had a hand in the design. In the 1790s, after both Brown and Adam had died, the earl employed the renowned architect James Wyatt to remodel some of the existing garden buildings and add other decorative features, among them statues made out of Coade stone and a distant eye-catcher like a fragment of a medieval castle.

The Coventrys owned Croome for another 250 years, but in 1948 the house and the land immediately around it were sold and in the years that followed the court became, successively, a Catholic school, a centre for the International Society of Krishna Consciousness and, briefly, a conference venue and a private house. The lake silted up, weeds and shrubs invaded the pleasure grounds, garden buildings fell into disrepair and much of Brown's park was ploughed up and his plantations ravaged by Dutch elm disease. In 1996, with the help of the Heritage Lottery Fund and Royal Sun Alliance, the National Trust acquired the pleasure grounds and park and has re-created Brown's grand design, incidentally providing visitors with a unique opportunity to see what his landscapes would have looked like while the planting was still immature. Since 2007, when the newly formed Croome House Trust bought the court and leased it to the National Trust, house and park have been reunited.

The court, and a sizeable red-brick service wing also designed by Brown, is first seen from above, across the great sweep of grass which leads down from a ridge to the east. The central two-storey block with a balustraded roofline was built on the foundations of the existing house, but Brown added on a giant Ionic portico on the south front, with a wide flight of steps guarded by sphinxes giving access to the park, and also extended the house at both ends, marking each corner with a large three-storey turret. All is in warm Bath stone, but the

BELOW Croome Court was remodelled in a fashionable Neo-classical idiom in the mid-eighteenth century, but the massive chimneys are those of the earlier, 1640s house.

effect is heavy rather than elegant, particularly as the chimneys of the old house, which Brown retained, form a massive wall across the roof. The Gothic church of St Mary Magdalen (not National Trust), which Brown designed up on the ridge in the late 1750s to replace a medieval building close by the house, is a more successful composition, its great west tower standing high above the valley. Adam was responsible for the delicate Gothic plasterwork, intricately carved pulpit and other furnishings in the light and airy interior. This was his first commission for George William, and the earl was so pleased he engaged Adam to finish off and refurnish the interior of the house.

The 1640s building lives on in the basement, and here too there are intriguing traces – a fragment of window, cambered brickwork that may once have paved a courtyard – of what may have been a Tudor house on this site. A procession of grand, unfurnished reception rooms fills the principal floor above. From the stone-floored entrance hall, with its pre-Adam Palladian decoration, double doors give onto the saloon filling the centre of the south front. Rising to a high coved ceiling and warmed by two marble fireplaces, this is the room where George III, Queen Charlotte and three of their daughters were given dinner in July 1768, their visit a reflection of how famous the Croome landscape, the first of its kind, had become. A huge painting of a horse and groom, with a race in progress behind them, almost fills the east wall. Dating from 1680–1710, and possibly the work of John Wootton, this massive canvas used to hang on the main staircase and has been loaned back to the house.

Alas, the fittings of Adam's tapestry room off the saloon, including his delicate ceiling and carved chimneypiece, are now in the Metropolitan Museum, New York, and the mahogany bookcases that he designed for the earl's library are in the Victoria and Albert Museum. The long gallery running down the west front, with a great bay window looking towards the pleasure grounds, has lost the statues of Greek goddesses by John Cheere which once filled the niches on the interior wall, but the plasterwork ceiling, designed by Adam and

executed by Joseph Rose, is still here, as are two of the three grisaille panels painted for the room and the marble chimneypiece decorated with lifesize nymphs carved by Joseph Wilton. Although the contents were disposed of in 1948, many of the most significant pieces, such as the window seats made for the gallery, were retained by the Croome Heritage Trust so it may be possible in the future to return objects and paintings to the rooms from which they came. The lost fittings, some of which disappeared from the house in the years after 1948, are another matter. Some surprising colour schemes, such as the gilding of the plasterwork in the saloon and the multi-coloured treatment of the dining-room decoration, were the work of the Hare Krishna movement.

The garden buildings, now largely restored, are essentially unchanged. Adam designed the pedimented, temple-like greenhouse of 1760, which was used to display tender exotics, and he was probably also responsible for the classical pavilion built on an island in the lake in 1776–8. Brown's domed rotunda, built in 1754–7 on the ridge above the house, with stuccowork by Francesco Vasalli, is still shaded by some of the cedars that were planted to shelter it in the mid-eighteenth century, and his grotto, a curving wall of tumbled stone blocks, is still a feature of the path round the lake. And, for the energetic, there are longer walks beyond the park to visit the distant eye-catchers with which Wyatt enriched the landscape.

RIGHT These griffins are on one of the Coade stone plaques that decorate the little pavilion on the island in the lake.

Dinefwr

Carmarthenshire
On the western edge of Llandeilo,
off the A483

At the western end of the Black Mountains, in the broad green valley of the River Tywi, an extensive and beautiful eighteenth-century landscape surrounds a tall, four-square house, with turrets at each corner. Newton House, former seat of the Rice family, Barons Dynevor, dates from the mid-seventeenth century but was remodelled in *c.*1770 by George Rice and his wife Cecil Talbot, who added playful corner turrets and the crenellated parapet, and again in 1856–7, when the 4th Baron Dynevor enlarged the turrets, added other features and refaced the house in stone. The baron commissioned plans from the local architect Richard Kyrke Penson, but it seems these were not used and the designer of the alterations is not known. The main facade, with Gothic arches over the windows, an Italianate *porte-cochère* and tall pyramidal roofs crowning the angle turrets, suggests a cross between a Venetian palazzo and a French chateau, while the garden side of the house is embellished with an arcade and a first-floor conservatory.

The original contents were dispersed in 1976, when the house was sold, but many period features remain and rooms have been re-created by the National Trust as they might have been in the Edwardian era. Ornamental plasterwork of 1660 adorns the sunny drawing room and the inner hall, hung with family portraits, still has what appears to be a seventeenth-century stair, with sturdy oak balusters. There is a show of Rice family portraits in the dining room, which is where the household gathered for prayers, and there are stunning views down the valley from the conservatory at the head of the stairs. Two intriguing arrow-loop windows in the ale cellar in the basement, where there is a full range of service rooms, may be survivals from a medieval building on this site. There are also some interesting paintings of the house as it was in the later seventeenth and early eighteenth century, showing the barns that are now incorporated in the service courtyard.

The ruins of a former castle (owned by the Wildlife Trust of South and West Wales) overlooking the valley reflect Dinefwr's and the Rice family's involvement in the early history of Wales. This stronghold, rebuilt in stone some time in the twelfth century, was the capital of Deheubarth, one of the three ancient kingdoms of Wales and seat of the great Rhys ap Gruffydd, ancestor of Henry Tudor and sponsor of the first recorded eisteddfod, held in 1176. Rhys was anglicised to Rice in 1547, following the return of family lands confiscated sixteen years earlier because of a trumped-up charge of conspiracy against Henry VII.

The naturalistic park, landscaped by George and Cecil Rice with some advice from 'Capability' Brown, who visited Dinefwr in 1775, stretches down to the banks of the Tywi. Mature oak woodland includes descendants of the ancient wildwood that was enclosed for a medieval deer-park. There are still fallow deer beneath the trees and the Trust has reintroduced Dinefwr's distinctive white cattle, a feature of the park for at least 700 years until the herd was dispersed in 1976, at the same time as financial difficulties forced the sale of the house and the home farm. With the help of local authorities and other organisations, the Trust acquired the park in the 1980s, Newton House in 1990 and, most recently, the former service courtyard.

BELOW At the heart of Dinefwr Park, an extensive eighteenth-century landscape in the Tywi valley, is Newton House, dating from the 1660s but much altered since.
ABOVE LEFT The Italianate arcade and conservatory on the garden side of the house.

Downhill Demesne and Hezlett House

Co. Londonderry
1 mile (1.6 kilometres) west
of Castlerock and 5 miles
(8 kilometres) west of Coleraine
on the A2 Coleraine–Downhill
coast road

The wild and beautiful Ulster coast, with broom, ling and blaeberry heath clothing cliffs of limestone and basalt that stand high above the Atlantic, was where the remarkable Frederick Augustus Hervey, Bishop of Derry and later 4th Earl of Bristol, chose to site his house. The construction of the mansion began in about 1775, and the bleak moorland round about was transformed into a landscape park, 'a green carpet sprinkled with white clover', as the bishop described it in an invitation to his friend, the agriculturalist and travel writer Arthur Young. Thousands of deciduous and evergreen trees were planted.

The bishop's obsession with circular buildings, which reached its full flowering at Ickworth in Suffolk (*see* p.176), was heralded at Downhill. Perched right on the edge of the cliffs to the north of the house is the little Mussenden Temple, a domed rotunda crowned with a huge urn and with twelve Corinthian columns ringing the facade. The design, which was based on the Temple of Vesta at Tivoli, had been suggested to the earl-bishop by James Wyatt, although the long-suffering Irish architect Michael Shanahan, who had overseen the construction of the house, again executed the plans for his difficult client. The little building was named after the bishop's attractive cousin, Mrs Frideswide Mussenden, who died shortly before it was completed in 1785, and it was fitted out as a library. Here Frederick could study undisturbed, the silence broken only by the screaming of the gulls, by the ceaseless roar of the waves breaking on the rocks below and by the Atlantic gales, which sometimes threaten to tear the building from its roots. In the late twentieth century, the temple was increasingly at risk from cliff erosion and in 1997 the National Trust carried out a major stabilisation programme to prevent the building being lost to the sea.

Downhill itself is now only a shell, a bleak ruin in the middle of the estate, but the eighteenth-century landscape park survives. From the grand triumphal arch forming the Bishop's Gate on the Coleraine road, a path leads north to the coast along the steep wooded valley known as Black Glen,

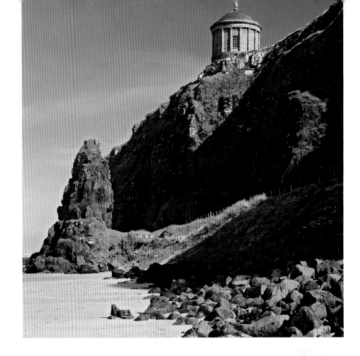

ABOVE Mussenden Temple, perched right on the edge of the cliffs, was built by the eccentric Bishop of Derry, who retreated here to study.

emerging on the edge of the cliffs. The Mussenden Temple stands a little to the west and there are glorious views beyond over Lough Foyle to the coast of Donegal. On the edge of the woods framing the view south from the house, another triumphal arch on a pedestal is the remains of the mausoleum Frederick erected in memory of his brilliant eldest brother George, Ambassador to Madrid and Turin, Lord Lieutenant of Ireland and Lord Privy Seal.

About 1½ miles (2.4 kilometres) south-east of Downhill, set back from the coast road at the Liffock crossroads, is a long, low, one-storey cottage with a thatched roof known as Hezlett House. Despite its Georgian sash windows, this cottage is one of the few dwellings of its kind in Ireland dating from before the eighteenth century. Probably built as a parsonage for the rector of Dunboe in 1691, it was acquired by Isaac Hezlett, a prosperous Presbyterian farmer, a century later and his descendants continued to live here for another 200 years.

Apart from its age, Hezlett House is also unusual for its cruck construction, involving a frame of curved lengths of wood stretching from the floor to the ridge of the roof. Relatively common in buildings of the same date in Cumbria, this technique is rare in Northern Ireland. The tiny cottage rooms, including a womb-like kitchen painted deep red, are furnished with some eighteenth-century pieces, and one room has been left open to the roof to display the carpenters' work.

Dudmaston Estate

Shropshire
At Quatt, 4 miles (6.4 kilometres) south-east of Bridgnorth on the A442

Looking west over the River Severn to the Clee Hills, Dudmaston lies close to some of the most beautiful countryside in Britain. Built for Sir Thomas Wolryche in the late seventeenth century, it is an unpretentious four-square house attributed to Francis Smith of Warwick, with some later alterations. Sir Thomas's line died out in the eighteenth century, but descendants of his sister Anne, who took the name Wolryche-Whitmore, continued to live here. Today, the small-scale intimate family rooms display the collections and decorative taste of Sir George Labouchere and his wife, Rachel Hamilton-Russell, who inherited the property from her uncle, Geoffrey Wolryche-Whitmore, in 1966. Sir George was responsible for the unusual assemblage of twentieth-century painting and sculpture, while Lady Labouchere introduced historic art and furniture.

Lady Labouchere's interest in botanical art, continuing a long family tradition, is shown in the collection of works by such great exponents as Pierre-Joseph Redouté (1759–1840), P. Reinagle (1749–1833), G.D. Ehret (1708–70) and W.H. Fitch (1817–92). Formal studies by these masters and glowing flower canvases by the eighteenth-century Dutch painter Jan Van Os in the library contrast with the fresh, fluid approach adopted by Mary Grierson (1912–2012), who was the official botanical artist at Kew for 12 years. A similar love of nature is revealed in the displays of photographs and drawings by the naturalist Frances Pitt (1888–1964), who lived in this area all her life and was a close friend of the Wolryche-Whitmore family. A notebook in her neat writing meticulously records her finds.

Two rooms devoted to twentieth-century painting and sculpture, including abstracts by Ben Nicholson, sculptures by Henry Moore and Barbara Hepworth, and some rather forbidding Spanish paintings acquired by Sir George while he was Ambassador in Madrid, set a more sombre tone. Apart from flashes of red and yellow from two Poliakoffs and Alan Davie's still-life in red, green and orange, colours are muted: grey and black, green and brown. Chinese porcelain and French furniture are also fruits of years in the diplomatic service, as are some of Lady Labouchere's delightful topographic watercolours, which include pictures of

ABOVE These decorative gates, commissioned by Sir George and Rachel Labouchere in 1993 to mark their golden wedding, echo the display of modern art and sculpture at Dudmaston.

Barcelona, Bruges, India and China, among them Edward Lear's tiny study of the gardens of Government House, Calcutta, and William Alexander's cameo of a smoking Chinaman, as well as atmospheric English landscapes and local views of Bridgnorth and Shrewsbury.

Associations of a different kind are reflected in the gallery devoted to the connection between Lady Labouchere and the

Darbys of Coalbrookdale, cradle of the Industrial Revolution. By a strange coincidence, Dudmaston is also linked with the modern microchip revolution, as Charles Babbage, the father of the computer, married a daughter of the house in 1814 and spent much time here.

The great oaks and cedars on the terraced lawns stretching down to the lake known as the Big Pool on the garden side of the house are reminders of another pioneer, Geoffrey Wolryche-Whitmore, whose enlightened approach to forestry on the estate in the first half of the twentieth century earned him a national reputation.

BELOW A room at Dudmaston displays the Laboucheres' collection of twentieth-century British and French art, including Barry Flanagan's 'Boxing Hares' and works by Henry Moore and Jean Dubuffet.

Dunham Massey

Cheshire
3 miles (4.8 kilometres) south-west
of Altrincham, off the A56

Dunham Massey reflects long occupation by the Booth and Grey families and the gradual enlargement and rebuilding of the Elizabethan and Jacobean core. A finely crafted mechanical model of the solar system, showing how the six known planets moved round the Sun (Uranus and Neptune were yet to be discovered), is the centrepiece of the library that was created for George Booth, 2nd Earl of Warrington, as part of extensive remodelling of the house by the obscure John Norris in the early eighteenth century. The earl's cipher appears on many of the faded bindings in the oak bookcases and over the fireplace is a dramatic, in-depth carving of the Crucifixion by the young Grinling Gibbons, who based it on a painting by Tintoretto and set his agonised figures in a tranquil floral border.

Apart from the south front, with its sash windows and Edwardian dormers, the exterior of Dunham Massey is much as George Booth left it, an attractive red-brick building, long and low, set round two courtyards and still protected by the medieval moat that embraced the earlier house. The sombre, low-ceilinged, oak-lined chapel and the magnificent collection of Huguenot silver are both reflections of the Booth family's ardent Protestantism. The glittering display now set out in the Rose Room includes a wine cistern made in 1701 by Philip Rollos, who created handles in the form of the wild boars of the Booth crest.

Dunham Massey's exceptional Edwardian interiors were commissioned by William Grey, 9th Earl of Stamford, whose family acquired the estate through the marriage of George Booth's daughter, Mary, to the 4th Earl. With advice from the connoisseur and furniture historian Percy Macquoid, and the outstanding firm of Morant & Co., decorators to Edward VII, the 9th Earl and his wife created rooms that rival the appeal of those from 200 years earlier. In their long saloon with a bay window arching out into the garden, Grey family portraits hang against deep-green walls suggested by Macquoid, who also advised dyeing the two mossy Donegal carpets and reupholstering the fine early eighteenth-century walnut chairs, from the same period as the magnificent walnut chests on show elsewhere in the house, to match the room. Yellow damask curtains hanging at the long sash windows give the

ABOVE The early eighteenth-century brick south front of Dunham Massey was substantially remodelled in 1905, when the elaborate stone centrepiece and dormer windows were added.

final touch in a colour scheme that could well have been created for Bunthorne in Gilbert and Sullivan's *Patience*. The 9th Earl also commissioned J. Compton Hall to create an elaborate neo-Jacobean entrance front loosely based on Sudbury (*see* p.307).

A remarkable series of early views of Dunham Massey, recording its gradual transformation from 1696 to c.1750, hang in the great gallery and here, too, is Guercino's early seventeenth-century *Mars, Venus and Cupid, with Saturn as Time*, possibly purchased by the 2nd Earl of Warrington. The young 5th Earl of Stamford, when on his Grand Tour, arranged for the two huge caricatures of his travels by Thomas Patch which hang in the early eighteenth-century tearoom. Commissioned as light relief from the serious study of Italian art and culture, they are an irreverent look at the earl and his friends.

A courtyard beside the house contains the kitchens and other domestic offices and there is an Elizabethan watermill beyond the eighteenth-century stables. A delightful gabled building of warm red brick with mullioned windows, the mill is the only visible survival from the time of Sir George Booth, 1st Baronet. Originally used for grinding corn, in *c*.1860 it was refitted as a saw-mill and estate workshop. The overshot waterwheel is fed from a continuation of the lake in front of the house and the Victorian machinery, including a big frame saw for cutting up trees known as the Dunham Ripper, is all in working order.

An ancient deer-park surrounding the house is enclosed by the 2nd Earl's high brick wall and still shaded by trees he established, some of which form a series of radiating avenues. Yews and oaks on the lawns to the east of the house were part of an informal Victorian and Edwardian layout, which has now been re-established and enhanced, with beds of rhododendrons and azaleas and a water garden along the stream feeding the moat. A curious mound just north-west of the house may be the remains of a Norman motte.

BELOW Fine walnut chairs, part of a set of 42 in the house, surround the George III table in Dunham Massey's dining room.

Dunster Castle

Somerset
In Dunster, 3 miles (4.8 kilometres) south-east of Minehead on the A396, just off the A39

A few miles east of Minehead, a ridge of the Brendon Hills reaches almost to the Bristol Channel, ending in a steep-sided outlier. This natural defensive site was chosen by the Norman William de Mohun for his castle. Besieged for 160 days by Cromwell's troops in the Civil War, Dunster was considered a major threat to the Commonwealth and the regime ordered its complete destruction, sparing only the Jacobean mansion, by the local stonemason William Arnold, which had been built within the walls. Although little trace of the medieval defences survives, Dunster still looks like a castle, with a tangle of towers and battlements rising romantically from the thickly wooded hill. Largely a nineteenth-century vision of what a castle should be, this is a house masquerading as a stronghold, created by Anthony Salvin in 1868–72 for George Fownes Luttrell, whose family had lived here since 1405. Salvin kept the Jacobean mansion, grafting on towers and battlements and remodelling much of the interior.

A steep approach from the village clustered below the tor leads to the fifteenth-century gatehouse. Beyond, a thirteenth-century gateway, the oldest surviving feature of the castle, gives access to what was once the lower ward. Across it, the north facade of the house is dominated by Salvin's great four-storey tower, with an octagonal staircase turret, complete with authentic medieval arrow loops, rising above it. The nineteenth-century work blends so well with the Jacobean walls to the right that only details in the New Red sandstone masonry show where one ends and the other begins. Two of the finest features of the interior were commissioned by Colonel Francis Luttrell in the late seventeenth century. He was responsible for the fine oak staircase with naked cherubs and dogs racing through a thick acanthus undergrowth carved on the panels of the balustrade. The work is cunningly dated by the fact that one of the beasts leaps over a clutch of Charles II silver shillings from the 1683–4 issue. The carving is of a very high standard, comparable with that on the staircase at Sudbury Hall (see p.307), and it may be that the distinguished Edward Pierce, who was engaged at Sudbury, also worked here. Craftsmanship of similar quality is displayed in the plasterwork ceiling in the dining room, also dating from the

BELOW The row of bells in the servants' corridor at Dunster includes one for a room named after Charles II, who is said to have slept at the castle when he came to the West Country as Prince of Wales in 1645.

1680s, where a thick encrustation of flowers and foliage almost conceals the creatures hidden in the design. Here a cherub shoots a deer with a bow and arrow; there a winged horse bursts from a blossom. A spider's web of plaster in the hall, the only original Jacobean ceiling to escape remodelling, looks down on an allegorical portrait of Sir John Luttrell, dated 1550, in which he is shown emerging half naked from a stormy sea while sailors abandon a foundering ship behind him. Less enigmatic but equally striking is the set of seventeenth-century painted leather hangings illustrating the story of Antony and Cleopatra which fills Salvin's gallery, the curiously expressionless faces and wooden horses redeemed by the brilliant, glittering colours produced by painting on silver foil.

A deliciously cool Victorian conservatory, a leafy extension of the airy, pale-green drawing room, leads out onto a sheltered south-facing terrace. Although the tor is exposed to westerly winds, the mild maritime climate allows tender plants and shrubs to grow here. Steep paths curling round the hill below the castle are lined with fuchsias and hydrangeas, there is a grove of strawberry trees and huge conifers tower above willows, camellias, rhododendrons and moisture-loving plants along the River Avril in the depths of the valley. A path following the river round the base of the tor leads to Dunster water-mill and an eighteenth-century bridge over the water. There has been a mill on this site since medieval times, but the present building, which has been restored to working order, dates largely from 1779–82.

The grassy platform which was the site of the Norman keep and many rooms in the castle has magnificent views over the surrounding countryside, where a patchwork of small hedged fields rolling away to the hills of Exmoor still looks very much as it is depicted in a set of early eighteenth-century scenes. To the north, the tower of the village church is echoed in the folly on Conygar Hill, with the blue of the Bristol Channel beyond.

ABOVE Dunster was once a Norman stronghold, but the romantically towered and battlemented castle seen today is a largely nineteenth-century creation.

Dyrham Park

Gloucestershire
8 miles (12.8 kilometres) north
of Bath, 12 miles (19.3 kilometres)
east of Bristol

After recording the burial of John Wynter in 1688, the local rector drew a thick line across the page. He knew it was the end of an era. Two years previously John's only surviving child, his 36-year-old daughter Mary, had married William Blathwayt, a rising civil servant, and by the end of the century this energetic self-made man had totally transformed the Tudor manor his wife inherited, creating this great mansion set beneath a spur of the Cotswolds. Despite his loyalty to James II in the Glorious Revolution, a rare fluency in Dutch coupled with an unusual gift for administration recommended Blathwayt to William III, for whom he acted as Secretary of State from 1692–1702.

Rebuilt in stages between 1692 and 1705, as and when money was available, Dyrham's contrasting facades reflect Blathwayt's rising fortunes. The earlier west front, with glorious views over the countryside towards Bristol, is an attractive building crowned with a balustrade. Low, one-storey wings, one of which forms a covered passage to the medieval village church, embrace a courtyard terrace. An Italianate double stairway descends from the terrace to a great sweep of grass, and the facade as a whole has continental overtones, as if its architect, the shadowy Frenchman S. Hauduroy, was planning a grand Parisian town house.

By the time Blathwayt constructed the east front with its state apartments, he was important enough to obtain the services of William Talman, Wren's deputy and rival, whose grand baroque facade is proudly surmounted by the Blathwayt eagle. The monumental orangery that extends the range to the south, successfully obscuring the service quarters in the view from the hill above the house, is also Talman's.

The elaborate formal Dutch water garden that once surrounded this palatial mansion has long disappeared. In its place is Charles Harcourt-Masters's beautiful late eighteenth-century park, with groves and clumps of beeches, chestnuts and cedars spilling down the hillsides. But the interior still reflects the taste for Dutch fashions inspired by the new king, which Blathwayt would have had ample opportunity to see at first hand. In Talman's entrance hall bird paintings by Melchior d'Hondecoeter hang against embossed leather

bought in The Hague. Door locks and hinges in the Balcony Room, where the carved panelling was originally painted to resemble marble, are engraved with tulips and daffodils, and characteristic blue and white Delftware, including two impressive pyramidal flower vases intended for the display of prize blooms, is seen throughout the house. Sumptuous crimson and yellow velvet hangings adorning the state bed in the Damask Bedchamber are typical of the rich fabrics and textiles with which Dyrham was once furnished. And then there are the paintings. Cool Dutch interiors, soft land- and

BELOW This vast state bed was made in *c.*1704 in the fashionable Anglo-Dutch style for Blathwayt's new apartments along Dyrham's east front.

seascapes and serene still lifes, including works by Abraham Storck, David Teniers the Younger and Samuel van Hoogstraeten, feature throughout the house. One of Hoogstraeten's perspective paintings shows a view through an unmistakably Dutch interior, with tiled floors leading to a distant room, where a chair is set by a glowing fire. This painting, like others at Dyrham, came from the London home of Thomas Povey, Blathwayt's uncle, where Pepys, who was a frequent guest, much admired it, and the glazed bookcases in the hall, one of which also came from Povey's home (the other is a copy), are almost identical to those made for Pepys in 1666.

The Hoogstraeten painting was bought back, together with the furniture and other pictures, by Colonel George William Blathwayt, who inherited Dyrham in 1844 after the contents had been dispersed. As part of his scheme to save the house, for which he took out a huge loan, he modernised the servants' quarters set round two courtyards behind the orangery, creating a suite of early Victorian rooms arranged either side of a long passage. Here are the bakehouse, kitchen, wet and dry larders and tenants' hall, where the most important estate tenants dined on rent days. A delicious dairy, with marble shelves and a stone fountain to keep it cool, is lined with blue and brown Delft tiles that were probably re-used from the 1698 domestic offices.

BELOW By the time William Blathwayt built Dyrham's east front, he was in a position to engage William Talman, the king's architect, who designed a grand baroque facade crowned by the Blathwayt eagle.

East Riddlesden Hall

West Yorkshire
1 mile (1.6 kilometres) north-east of Keighley on the south side of the B6265, on the north bank of the River Aire and close to the Leeds and Liverpool Canal

Although W.S. Gilbert is said to have based the Bad Baronets in *Ruddigore* on the Murgatroyds of East Riddlesden, it seems the family does not entirely deserve its dubious reputation. Certainly the rich clothier James Murgatroyd, who bought the estate in 1638, was a respected local figure, and it is he who was largely responsible for the present house, set on a bluff above the River Aire. The unusual entrance front is dominated by a striking castellated and pinnacled two-storey porch, with classical columns framing the doorway and with an ecclesiastical rose window at the level of the first floor. To the left stretch the mullioned windows and gabled facades of the square main block of the house, while to the right a great hall that was probably also built by Murgatroyd forms a link to the remains of another substantial wing. Pedimented windows and other classical details on the one surviving facade of this part of the house are the work of Edmund Starkie, James Murgatroyd's great-grandson, who seems to have remodelled the original medieval hall in the 1690s.

Absentee owners from the beginning of the nineteenth century ensured that this fine example of a seventeenth-century Yorkshire manor survived unaltered, although most of the 'Starkie' wing was demolished in 1905 and none of the original contents remains. Virtually empty when it was saved from dereliction by the Briggs brothers of Keighley in 1934 and given to the National Trust, East Riddlesden has been completely refurnished. The panelled family rooms are now filled with locally made period oak pieces, among them a carved and canopied early seventeenth-century cupboard in the dining room, said to be the one described by Emily Brontë in the opening pages of *Wuthering Heights*, and a magnificent oak settle in the drawing room. A late sixteenth-century copper curfew for keeping in the embers of a fire overnight, a grain chest and a shepherd's chair designed with a hutch for a lamb or a dog under the seat are among a number of rare and intriguing objects in the house, and there are also displays of pewter, Dutch and oriental porcelain and some seventeenth-century stumpwork.

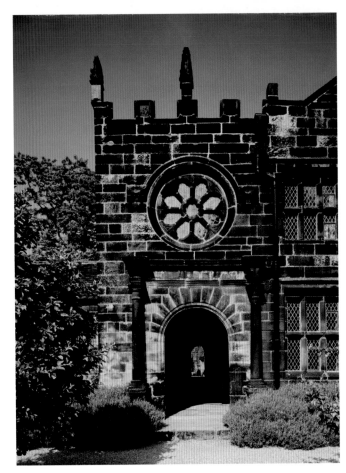

ABOVE The striking two-storey porch on the garden front of East Riddlesden Hall has a doorway flanked by Doric columns and a fine rose window lighting the little room above.

The great stone barn in front of the house, one of two shielding the hall from the sprawl of Keighley, is said to be the finest in the north of England. Tradition has it that this is a medieval barn incorporating later masonry from either nearby Kirkstall Abbey or Dalton Priory, and that the present external stone cladding was added by James Murgatroyd, but it is more likely that the whole building was constructed in the seventeenth century. The fish-pond, across which visitors get their first view of the hall, is associated with the ghost of a woman in white, a lady of the manor who drowned here when she was thrown from her horse. Among several other apparitions said to be connected with East Riddlesden is the shadowy figure known as the Grey Lady, reputed to have been shut up in her room to starve to death by her sadistic husband after she had been discovered with her lover.

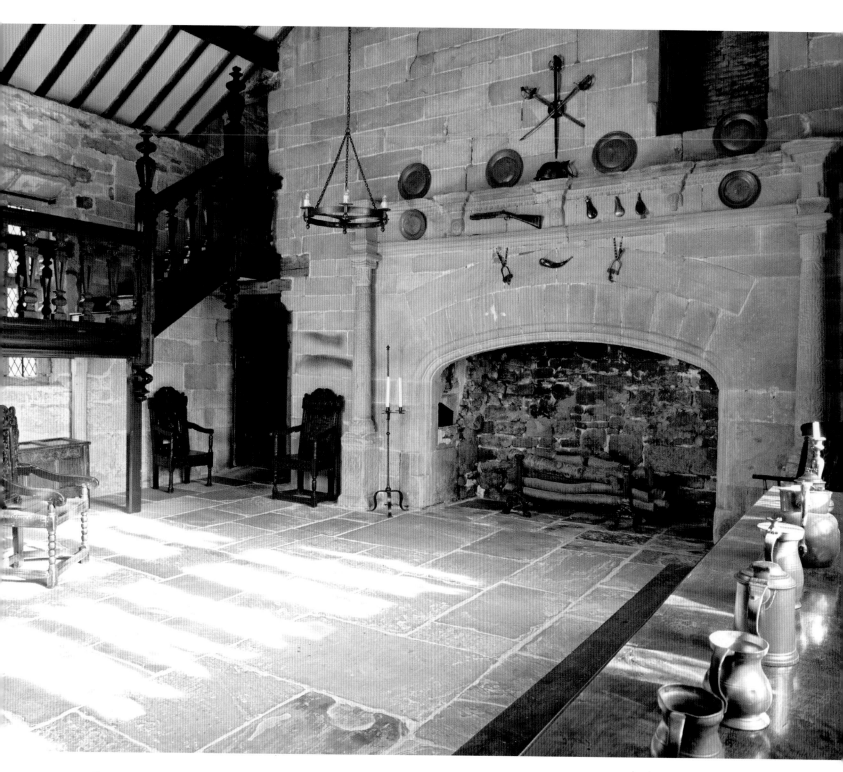

ABOVE The impressive great hall at East Riddlesden Hall, with its carved stone fireplace and period oak furniture, would have been used for receiving visitors in the seventeenth century.

Erddig

Wrexham
2 miles (3.2 kilometres) south
of Wrexham

Visitors to Erddig are given a sense of the country house as a functioning community. Instead of being welcomed at the front door, they are taken through the extensive and atmospheric complex of eighteenth- and nineteenth-century brick outbuildings that formed the estate yards. Here, tools and equipment give a unique picture of how these households and their lands were nurtured day by day. Saws hang on the walls of the pit where timber was cut into manageable widths, the tools in the blacksmith's shop are the very ones that were used to repair the fine eighteenth-century ironwork screen in the formal garden, and the dry laundry sports a mangle in which clothes were pressed using the weight of a box of stones. Similarly, the tour of the house includes the spacious, airy rooms on the attic floor where the servants slept.

Judging by the staff portraits in the servants' hall, which go back to the 1790s, life was agreeable here. One of the housemaids is depicted at the age of 87 and the 75-year-old estate carpenter looks spry enough to wield the axe he carries over his shoulder. Sadly, what was thought to be a portrait of the black coachboy who was at Erddig in the early eighteenth century now appears to be a later fabrication.

The tradition of recording the servants seems to have been started by Philip Yorke I, who inherited the house in 1767 from his great-uncle, the successful London lawyer John Meller. Philip I was also responsible for commissioning James Wyatt to re-face the west front, which had been badly damaged by the westerly gales and driving rain which are a regular feature of the weather here. The rather severe Neo-classical composition of the 1770s on this side of the house contrasts with the warm brickwork of the garden front, where the original late seventeenth-century central block is flanked by wings added by Meller in 1721–4. The length of the facade

BELOW Erddig's rather severe, stone-faced west front, the result of remodelling in the late eighteenth century. is a complete contrast to the warm brickwork on the other side of the house (above right).

ABOVE A formal parterre below Erddig's east front sets off the warm red brick of this façade, where a change in the colour of the walling marks the wings that were added to the house in 1721–4.
RIGHT The painted seventeenth-century panelling in the white bedroom came from a manor on the estate that was partly burnt down in 1886.

and the uniform sash windows give this front the look of a row of town houses.

After the architecturally modest exterior, Meller's superb furniture and rich textiles are a surprise, his sets of silvered and walnut chairs and ornate looking-glasses all having been obtained from leading London cabinet-makers. Goblin-like masks smiling wickedly at each other across the head of the pier glass in the saloon are by the same hand as the carved and gilded birds on the tester of the sumptuous state bed, their exotic plumage echoed by a flock of diminutive painted companions, flashes of brilliant peacock-blue suggesting kingfishers on the wing. More birds perch in the borders of the summery Soho tapestries made for the principal bedroom.

Philip I created the library that now displays his passionate antiquarianism as well as his great-uncle's legal tomes, and he was also responsible for the delightful Chinese wallpaper in the room next to the chapel, with handpainted cameos showing oriental labourers at work. Betty Ratcliffe, companion and maid to Philip I's mother, made the extraordinary Chinese pagoda decorated with mother-of-pearl and the other model buildings in the oak-panelled gallery.

Philip I's concern for the past also led him to preserve the then old-fashioned garden. Although William Emes was employed to landscape the park between 1766 and 1781, contributing the unusual circular waterfall known as the Cup and Saucer, the hanging beech woods and picturesque walks, Philip deliberately retained the formal layout near the house,

the essential features of which, such as the enclosing walls, date from 1718–32. With the aid of a bird's-eye view engraved by Thomas Badeslade in 1740, the garden has been reconstructed as it was in the early eighteenth century and is a rare example of a design of the period.

A long gravel path stretching away from the east front, its line emphasised by a double avenue of pleached limes, provides a strong central focus, which is continued by a canal. A decorative wrought-iron screen closes the vista at the far end and magnificent mature limes shade the water. To the north, apple trees planted in blocks mirror the orderly rows shown on the engraving. Plums, pears, peaches and apricots, most of them varieties listed as growing here in 1718, are trained on the walls, and there are old varieties of daffodils and narcissus in the borders below. A Victorian parterre immediately in front of the house is perfectly in tune with the formal eighteenth-century layout.

Farnborough Hall

Oxfordshire
6 miles (9.6 kilometres) north of
Banbury, ½ mile (0.8 kilometre)
west of the A423

This honey-coloured stone house, home of the Holbech family for over 300 years, looks out over a well-wooded patchwork of fields and hedgerows to the scarp of Edgehill and the Malvern Hills beyond. It is still largely as created between 1745 and 1750 by William Holbech, who needed a setting for the sculpture and art he had collected on a protracted Grand Tour. Probably with help from his close friend, the gentleman-architect Sanderson Miller, who lived only a few miles away, Holbech remodelled the old manor house acquired by his grandfather, adding long facades with sash windows, pedimented doorways and a roofline balustrade to the earlier classical west front commissioned by his father. The result is harmonious, but there are some amateur touches too, such as floor-level bedroom windows.

The front door opens straight into the Italianate hall. Busts of Roman emperors and of goddesses from classical mythology look down on visitors from their niches high in the walls, there is magnificent rococo plasterwork on the ceiling by the Yorkshireman William Perritt and a copy of a view of Rome by Panini over the fireplace. This fine interior is a prelude to the outstanding decoration in the sunny former saloon, now a family-sized dining room, which was designed specially to house four large canvases of Venice by Canaletto and two of Rome by Panini (now replaced by copies). Here, sinuous, three-dimensional rococo plasterwork, standing out white against the blue walls, clamours for attention. A cornucopia bursts with fruit and flowers over the wall mirror between the windows, a fully strung violin and guns, bows and arrows reflect William's musical and sporting interests, and little dogs with upturned noses are profiled on the plasterwork picture frames set into the walls. The ceiling decoration, white on white, is similarly arresting. Although

ABOVE LEFT The pedimented classical doorway in the 1740s entrance front.
LEFT The south and west fronts of Farnborough Hall look over the eighteenth-century park.
RIGHT Farnborough's entrance hall has a fine rococo plasterwork ceiling and classical busts in niches set round the room.

also by Perritt, whose bill for the room survives, some of the plaster detailing, such as the foliage curling over the mirror as if embracing it, suggests the work of Roberts of Oxford, or even the hand of the Italian Francesco Vassali. The late seventeenth-century garland of fruit and flowers ringing the domed skylight above the stairs is also very fine, each plaster blossom, grape and pomegranate fashioned individually.

The south front surveys a stretch of grass and trees bordering a long ornamental lake, one of two in the eighteenth-century landscape park. To the south-east William's striking grass terrace stretches three-quarters of a mile (1.2 kilometres) along a ridge high above the valley, its smooth sward, hedged with bushy laurel, wide enough for two carriages to pass with ease and adorned with what are probably Sanderson Miller's eye-catchers. A little pedimented temple, its Ionic columns pleasingly weathered, is almost hidden by trees. Further along the terrace, a curving stone staircase gives access to the upper room in a two-storey domed pavilion, where rococo plasterwork picked out in white against blue echoes the craftsmanship in the house. Perhaps the Italian prisoners treated at the military hospital set up here during the Second World War, who inscribed their names on the obelisk at the end of the terrace, appreciated the panoramic view, now, alas, spoiled by the routing of the M40 through the Warmington Valley below the house.

Felbrigg Hall, Gardens and Estate

Norfolk
Near Felbrigg village, 2 miles (3.2 kilometres) south-west of Cromer, off the A148 Holt Road

In 1738 William Windham II, accompanied by his multi-talented tutor Benjamin Stillingfleet, whose sartorial habits are the origin of the term 'bluestocking', set off on a protracted five-year Grand Tour. As soon as William succeeded to Felbrigg in 1749, he asked James Paine to remodel part of the interior to provide a suitable setting for the paintings he had acquired, some of the best of which now hang in the intimate Cabinet Room in the west wing. Here small Dutch and Italian canvases, including 26 delightful gouaches by Giovanni Battista Busiri, are set three deep on crimson damask, displayed in frames that William commissioned and in a carefully balanced arrangement which he worked out. The young William also acquired Samuel Scott's panoramic *Old London Bridge* and the companion piece of the Tower of London, both of which may have been painted for their present positions in the drawing room, and the huge canvas by William van der Velde showing a battle at sea in 1673.

Paine's sumptuous and beautiful eighteenth-century interiors, with some flowing rococo plasterwork by Joseph Rose the Elder, lie within a largely seventeenth-century building that was the work of William's great-grandfather, Thomas Windham, a descendant of the wealthy merchant who had purchased the estate in 1459, and his son William Windham I. Thomas was responsible for Felbrigg's haunting Jacobean entrance front, the plaster-covered brick and flint with stone dressings of which it is built now attractively weathered and lichened. A projecting central porch, with classical columns supporting nothing framing the front door, rises the height of the house; a huge mullioned window incorporating fragments of English and continental stained glass lights the great hall to the left of the porch; and banks of octagonal brick chimneys rise from the roof. Most striking are the huge stone letters carved into the parapet crowning the façade, which spell out the inscription GLORIA DEO IN EXCELSIS. This balanced composition is almost certainly the work of Robert Lyminge of Blickling (*see* p.57).

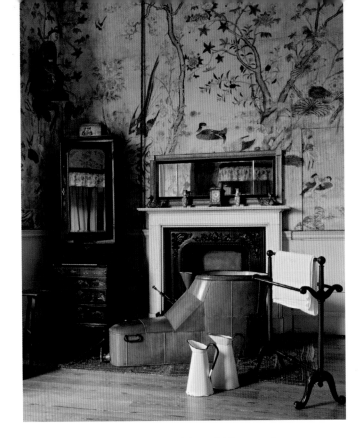

ABOVE One of the bedrooms is hung with beautiful Chinese wallpaper, decorated with silver pheasants and birds of paradise.
OPPOSITE Weathering has enhanced the appeal of Felbrigg Hall's glorious Jacobean entrance front, with Doric columns framing the doorway and carved heraldic beasts along the parapet.

Paine's Gothick library, with pinnacled cluster columns between the bookcases, was intended to complement this Jacobean work. The exceptional collection now housed here, which was started by William Windham II, owes much to his politician son, whose friendship with Dr Johnson is commemorated in books once owned by the learned lexicographer.

Although William Windham I was building only 50 years later than his father, a mid-century revolution in architectural styles resulted in an extraordinary contrast between the two phases of work. Walking round the house, there is an abrupt transition from the romantic Jacobean front to the ordered classicism of the late seventeenth-century west wing designed by William Samwell, with its sash windows and hipped roof. This austere exterior hides ornate plasterwork that is probably by the celebrated Edward Goudge, who is best known for his work at Belton (*see* p.49). Peaches, pears, grapes, apricots,

lemons and other fruits moulded in sharp relief on the drawing-room ceiling are accompanied by lovingly detailed depictions of pheasants, partridges, woodcock and plover. More birds dart and perch amidst lotuses and peonies on the eighteenth-century Chinese wallpaper in one of the bedrooms, the relatively sombre plumage of a couple of ducks floating companionably on a pond contrasting with the brilliant-red tail feathers of a bird of paradise.

Birds also feature in the walled garden set on a gentle south-facing slope to the north of the drive, where a peacock weathervane crowns the octagonal brick dovecote at one end. Undulating parkland, studded with stands of mature woodland, comes right up to the front of the house. Thousands of trees – beeches, sycamores, oaks and maples – date from the time of William Windham I, who laid the foundations of the Great Wood which shelters the house from biting winds off the North Sea only 2 miles (3.2 kilometres) away. His work was continued by his son with advice from the improver Nathaniel Kent and possibly also from Humphry Repton, and was taken up again by the last squire of Felbrigg, who planted some 200,000 trees and formed the V-shaped rides commemorating VE day in Victory Wood. Memorials of a different kind, monuments to generations of Windhams, including some fine brasses, fill the little flint church in the park, all that remains of the village that once stood here.

ABOVE The great hall was remodelled in a heavy Jacobethan style in c.1840, when the carved oak pedestal table was probably made for the room.
OPPOSITE Serene Fenton House, with rows of elegant sash windows and a pediment marking the entrance front, is one of the most pleasing of Hampstead's many late seventeenth-century houses.

Fenton House and Garden

London
In Hampstead, on the west side of Hampstead Grove

Hidden away in a leafy road just off busy Heath Street, this charming William and Mary house with its secluded walled garden is an oasis of peace and tranquillity. A square two-storey building, with dormers in the steeply pitched roof and tall chimney-stacks, Fenton House is both one of the earliest and one of the architecturally most pleasing of the many mellow brick houses built in Hampstead in the late seventeenth century, when mineral springs on the slopes of the hill attracted London merchants and lesser gentry to what was then a village in the country. A pediment crowning the south facade marks what was once the entrance front, from which a gravel path leads to an elaborate iron gate on Holly Hill. Records on the house are patchy, but it seems to have been built, in c.1686, by William Eades, the son of a bricklayer, and it is called after the Baltic merchant who owned the property by 1793.

Intimate rooms on two floors, most of them panelled and one still retaining its original closet, just a few feet across, for a close-stool, now display the outstanding assemblage of furniture, pictures, needlework and eighteenth-century porcelain bequeathed to the National Trust, together with the house, by Lady Binning, who lived here from 1936 until her death in 1952. Lady Binning inherited much of the collection from her uncle, the connoisseur and collector George Salting, who made important bequests to the Victoria and Albert Musuem, National Gallery and British Museum, and from her mother Millicent Salting, who was George's sister-in-law, but Lady Binning also made acquisitions herself.

Mostly shown in glass-fronted cabinets, the porcelain includes an exquisite Meissen gold-ground tea and coffee service and ornamental pieces from a number of major German factories. There are two sets of Seasons from the short-lived Bristol and Plymouth works, Winter in one being represented by an old bearded man leaning on a stick, a bundle of faggots under his arm, while a wall of the sunny bedroom where Lady Binnings slept, now furnished and decorated as it was in 1950, is filled with the blue and white Chinese porcelain that was to inspire the colouring of Delft pottery.

The pictures, including a delightful array of seventeenth-century embroidery pieces hanging in a little upstairs room, animal paintings by Sartorius and works by William Nicholson on loan from the family of the late T.W. Bacon, were recently augmented by a bequest from the actor Peter Barkworth, who left 55 works to Fenton House on his death in 2006. Featuring oil paintings by the Camden Town group and sea- and landscapes in pencil and watercolour, this collection now hangs throughout the house, with many works brightening the tiny attic rooms. There is Charles Ginner's night-time view of nearby Flask Walk, where Peter Barkworth lived, works by Walter Sickert and Duncan Grant and a distant view of Rye, rising like an island from Romney Marsh, by James Bolivar Manson, who painted it while on holiday with Lucien Pissarro. Two pictures by Constable include one of his characteristic cloud studies.

The individuality of the house also comes from the early keyboard instruments that stand in nearly every room and fill the little attics, brass hinges gleaming on polished cases. Originally formed by the late Major Benton Fletcher, the collection includes harpsichords by the two most prominent makers in London in the later eighteenth century, Jacob Kirckman and Burkat Shudi, as well as earlier continental and English harpsichords and spinets. A virginal dated 1664 by Robert Hatley of London could have been the instrument Pepys saw being rescued by boat from the Great Fire on 2 September 1666. Most of the instruments are kept in working order and a tour of the house may be accompanied by the sound of distant playing.

From a balcony reached through one of the attic rooms visitors can look down on the sheltered walled garden on the north side of the house, with its raised terrace walks, clipped holly and yew and little apple orchard, and out over the rooftops of Hampstead and the spire of Christchurch to the distant outlines of city skyscrapers.

Florence Court

Co. Fermanagh
8 miles (12.8 kilometres)
south-west of Enniskillen, via the
A4 and the A32 Swanlinbar road

South of Lough Erne, the border between the Irish Republic and Northern Ireland runs across the wild and dramatic Cuilcagh mountains. These lonely hills were the backdrop for Sir John Cole's early eighteenth-century house, which he chose to build on a site 8 miles (12.8 kilometres) from Enniskillen, where the family had been established since 1607. His building, probably little more than a hunting lodge, has long been replaced, but the name he gave it, which was that of his wife, lives on. And it was Florence Cole's considerable fortune that enabled their son John, 1st Lord Mount Florence, to build much more grandly than his father.

The 1st Lord's dignified house, dating from the 1750s, now forms the heart of Florence Court. Seven bays wide and three storeys high, it is built of rendered brick with stone dressings and crowned by a parapet. Delightful baroque details enliven the entrance front, giving the house an archaic touch. On the garden facade, a projecting bay window lighting the staircase stretches the height of the building, with three massive scallop shells marking the top. Open colonnades with round-headed arches leading to one-storey pavilions on either side of the central block were added in 1771, probably to designs by Davis Ducart, the Sardinian-born architect, by William Willoughby Cole, later 1st Earl of Enniskillen.

The house was extensively restored by the National Trust after a fire in 1955, in which many family portraits were lost. The main feature of the interior is the riotous rococo plasterwork attributed to Robert West, the talented Dublin stuccadore. In the dining room thick encrustations of acanthus foliage swirl round the central motif, where an eagle with outstretched wings is surrounded by puffing cherubs representing the four winds. Tendrils of foliage hang over the border of the design, as if new young fronds are outgrowing the frame. The acanthus theme is repeated on the staircase, where three panels filled with fluid foliage are set either side of the well. A donation of family portraits, a set of large landscapes of the area and other pieces belonging to the Enniskillen family, such as an eighteenth-century Italian specimen table, together with fine Irish furniture acquired by the Trust, such as the marquetry desk prominently decorated with scallop shells in the study, have helped to re-create the atmosphere of a great Irish country house.

The extensive service rooms in the basement, including a stone-flagged kitchen with a fire-proof ceiling like a huge umbrella, look out onto cobbled courtyards on either side of the house, one a coach yard, the other housing a dairy, laundry, drying rooms and other essential facilities. A saw-mill down the lane to the south is powered by an overshot Victorian waterwheel. To the north is a walled garden with an extensive clematis- and wisteria-hung pergola.

The surrounding park, first laid out in the eighteenth century, was improved by the Irish landscape gardener John Sutherland for the 2nd Earl, who planted many of the trees and the rhododendrons and magnolias below the house. Here, too, are examples of the graceful Florence Court weeping beech and of the Irish yew (*Taxus baccata* 'Fastigiata'), a freak plant discovered at Florence Court in 1767, which can only be reproduced from cuttings.

BELOW The main block of Florence Court, built in the 1750s, was extended with open colonnades and pavilions in 1771.

Fountains Abbey and Studley Royal

North Yorkshire
2 miles (3.2 kilometres) west
of Ripon, off the B6265 to
Pateley Bridge

The ruins of Fountains Abbey lie hidden in the valley of the River Skell, framed by steep wooded slopes. The approach from the west follows a narrow lane past the mellow stonework of the late Elizabethan Fountains Hall, which was partly built with material from the abbey ruins. The hall's symmetrical, many-windowed facade, with a deeply recessed central bay and projecting towers at both ends, has echoes of Hardwick Hall (*see* p.161), and Robert Smythson, who designed Hardwick, may also have been involved here. Classical columns and delightful carved figures flank the porch and there is an impressive carved chimneypiece in the Great Chamber, with a panel depicting the Judgement of Solomon.

Beyond the hall, and the monastic water-mill, the lane suddenly opens out into a grassy court in front of the monastery. Ahead, the west end of the abbey church, with the outline of a huge window above the west door, is dwarfed by Abbot Marmaduke Huby's great tower projecting from the north side of the nave. Almost 53 metres (172 feet) high, the tower is so tall that it can be seen from far away peering over the rim of the valley. To the right stretches the west range, as impressively long as Huby's tower is tall and extending over the Skell at one end. All is built of the greyish sandstone that outcrops just beside the abbey.

Fountains is the largest abbey in England and has survived remarkably complete, probably because it was too remote to be turned into a country house or extensively plundered for building stone after its dissolution in 1539. The impressive remains, centred on the cloister at the heart of the abbey, contain many telling reminders of the daily life and routines of the community that lived here for 400 years. Worn stone steps on the south side of the cloister once led up to the long dormitory where the monks slept and the room beside the stair still has the two great fireplaces where a wood fire was kept burning from November to Easter, so the monks had somewhere they could warm themselves. Stone benches by the refectory door once held the basins where the community could wash their hands before meals, drying them on towels from a cupboard built into the arched recess that can still be seen on the wall of the warming room. The stone supports for the tables in the refectory itself still protrude from the grassy floor, and a flight of steps built into the thickness of the wall leads up to the pulpit where devotional works were read to the brothers while they ate.

A group of idealistic monks who had rebelled against the relaxed atmosphere of their parent Benedictine house founded St Mary of Fountains in 1132 as a pioneering Cistercian community. The austere and simple lifestyle of the early days is reflected in the unadorned architecture of the oldest parts of the abbey, such as the huge tree-trunk pillars supporting the cathedral-like nave. But the very success of the community was to lead to the relaxation of the principles that had made it great. With the aid of lay brothers, who vastly outnumbered the monks themselves, the abbey eventually controlled huge estates stretching west into the Lake District and north to

ABOVE LEFT This little classical temple in the water garden was designed as a cool garden house on the shady side of the valley.
BELOW The rhythmic stone vaulting of the west range of the abbey.

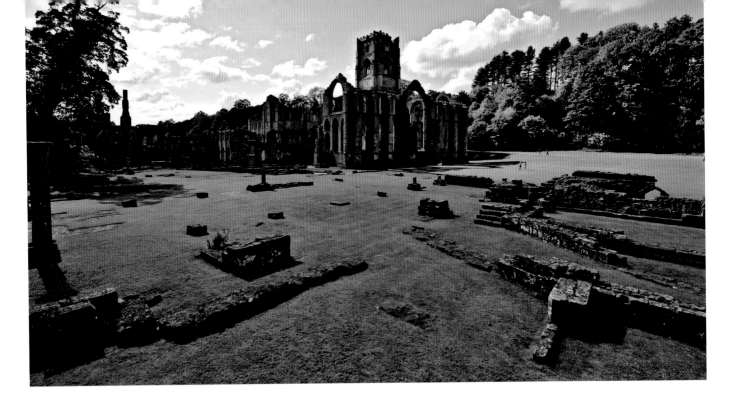

Teesside, the source of the wealth that made it one of the richest religious houses in Britain by the mid-thirteenth century. Wool merchants who came to Yorkshire from Flanders and Italy were accommodated in self-contained suites in the guest houses that can still be seen on Abbey Green.

This prosperity financed later building, such as the early thirteenth-century Chapel of the Nine Altars at the east end of the church, with its soaring Perpendicular window. But the greatest monument to earthly concerns, Marmaduke Huby's tower, was added in the community's final decades. A prodigy tower in the spirit of Sissinghurst or Tattershall (*see* pp.291 and 312), Huby's creation, erected to his personal glory, was in direct contravention of early Cistercian practice. A magnificent example of the strength of religious faith, Fountains is also a monument to lost ideals.

Downstream from the abbey is the eighteenth-century water garden of Studley Royal whose creator, John Aislabie, retired here in 1720 after involvement in the South Sea Bubble brought his political career to an abrupt end. Mirror-like ponds on the valley floor reflect classical statues and a Tuscan temple and walks threading the wooded slopes on either side give vistas to a Gothic tower and other eye-catchers. Most memorably, from a high-level path through the trees there is a sudden view up a sweep of grass-framed water to the abbey ruins. The serenity of this part of the garden contrasts with a wilder landscape downstream, beyond a lake fed by the Skell. Here Aislabie's son William enhanced the natural drama of a gorge-like section of the river and planted beech woods to create an early example of a Picturesque landscape.

Running down to the valley of the Skell is an extensive deer park where another spectacular building was an addition of the late nineteenth century. Silhouetted on the skyline at the end of a lime avenue which climbs slowly from gates on the eastern side of the park is the Gothic church of St Mary the Virgin, with a spire soaring above the trees. Built for the 1st Marquess and Marchioness of Ripon from 1871–8, this is a *tour de force* by William Burges. The exterior is relatively restrained but the interior is a riot of colour and rich carving in wood and stone. Angelic musicians set against a gilded background throng the sanctuary, the choir-stalls are carved with multi-coloured parrots, the organ case masquerades as a medieval house, complete with spiral staircase, and there is stained glass illustrating the Book of Revelation.

This sumptuous example of High Victorian taste adds to the richness and variety of what is overall an exceptional property, now designated a World Heritage site.

Gawthorpe Hall

Lancashire
On the eastern outskirts of Padiham; ½ mile (1.2 kilometres) drive to the house on the north of the A671

Set on the edge of the Pennines, with peaceful views to distant hills, Gawthorpe seems magically detached from the urban sprawl along the Burnley road out of Padiham by which it is approached. It is a compact three-storey Elizabethan house, with three projecting bays on the entrance front, a glittering grid of mullioned windows and a staircase tower rising above the roof and giving wide views over the country around. The building of the house was supervised by the mason Anthony Whithead, but the design, which has strong similarities with that of Hardwick Hall (*see* p.161) and Wollaton in Nottinghamshire, has been attributed to the talented Robert Smythson.

Gawthorpe had been the home of the Shuttleworth family for some 200 years before the present house was started in 1600, financed by the fortune of the Elizabethan barrister Sir Richard Shuttleworth. Inside, original Jacobean ceilings and woodwork set off the nineteenth-century restoration by Sir Charles Barry, architect of the Houses of Parliament (*see also* p.98 and 184), who also made some changes to the exterior, such as raising the height of the prospect tower. He and his collaborators, A.W.N. Pugin and J.G. Crace, were employed in 1850–2 by Sir James Kay-Shuttleworth, the great Victorian reformer, who had married the heiress to the property. Barry also laid out an Elizabethan-style formal garden, part of which still overlooks the River Calder on the north.

The interior has an atmosphere of crowded opulence. In the richly furnished drawing room, startling green curtains and settees upholstered in velvet are combined with a striking carpet strongly coloured in blue and red. Photographs in ornate silver frames clutter the rare octagonal table made by Pugin and Crace. Potted ferns on pedestals, fringed table covers and a florid pink and blue Italian glass chandelier complete the effect. With the addition of a few cobwebs, it would be a perfect setting for Miss Havisham. The Jacobean frieze, with ornate three-dimensional plasterwork in which mermaids and other half-human creatures are entwined amongst writhing foliage, adds to the overall restlessness.

The long gallery running the length of the south front on the second floor is equally evocative and still has the feel of a place where people came for exercise in inclement weather. Decorated with original plasterwork, it is hung with portraits of early seventeenth-century society figures. These pictures and many others in the house, including a rather unflattering depiction of Charles II's mistress, the Duchess of Cleveland, are on loan from the National Portrait Gallery. Several rooms on the first floor contain an exhibition of needlework, embroideries and costumes assembled by the Hon. Rachel Kay-Shuttleworth, the last of the family to live here. This unparalleled collection displays a wide range of needlework techniques: beautifully embroidered waistcoats, smocks, christening robes, quilts and many other pieces. The work is largely of the eighteenth and nineteenth centuries but also includes some charming modern samplers. This delightful verse, dated 1961, is embroidered with a border of seashells and mischievous fish: 'I wish I were a fish/In the Aegean Sea/Instead of which, here is my niche/In London, being me.'

BELOW A fine oriel window on Gawthorpe Hall's east front lights one end of the long gallery stretching across the top of the house.

George Inn

London
In Southwark, on the east side of Borough High Street, near London Bridge Station

A rather uninviting arch off Borough High Street leads into a courtyard flanked by the one surviving wing of a seventeenth-century inn. Looking down into the yard from the galleries fronting the first and second storeys, it is possible to imagine the noise and excitement when The George was a major terminus for stagecoaches to all parts of England in the eighteenth and nineteenth centuries. It is now the last galleried inn in London, but several similar staging-posts once stood nearby, among them The Tabard, where Chaucer set the beginning of his *Canterbury Tales*.

The George was built in 1677 on the site of a much older hostelry that had been destroyed by fire the year before.

Originally it enclosed three sides of the yard, but two wings were pulled down in 1889. A strong period atmosphere survives inside: the coffee room lined with private drinking compartments, the bar with an open fireplace and the panelled dining room all conjure up the kind of establishment described by Dickens, who certainly knew The George as he mentions it in *Little Dorrit*. Even today the open galleries are the only way to reach rooms on the first and second floors.

Although it is no longer possible to stay here, The George is still very much an inn. Occasional performances of Shakespeare's plays foster the legend that the bard himself once acted in the courtyard.

BELOW In the days when stagecoaches set out from London to all parts of England, the George was just one of several inns in Southwark that catered for this traffic.

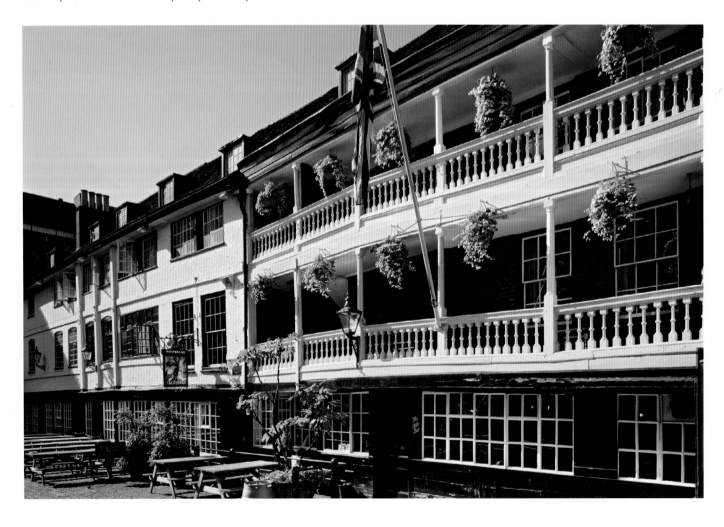

Gibside

Tyne & Wear
6 miles (9.6 kilometres)
south-west of Gateshead,
20 miles (32 kilometres) north of
Durham between Rowlands Gill
and Burnopfield

This atmospheric property in the leafy Derwent Valley is at its best at dusk, when the urns set along the roof of the chapel and the central dome are silhouetted against the dying sun. From the chapel, a wide avenue of ancient oaks runs just under half a mile (0.8 kilometre) along the side of the valley towards a great Tuscan column that rises over 40 metres (140 feet) from the wooded hill at the far end. A statue of Liberty crowns the column. These features are part of an eighteenth-century layout, now being restored, in which formal avenues and a series of garden buildings designed as focal points were set in a more natural wooded landscape.

The Gibside estate came into the Bowes family in the early eighteenth century and it was George Bowes, a coal baron who combined good living with more intellectual pursuits, who transformed his inheritance, as funds allowed, from 1729–60. The chapel was the last building to be added to the landscape. Designed by James Paine, it was begun in 1759, the year before George Bowes died, and stands on a platform above his mausoleum. Built of creamy local sandstone, it is in the shape of a Greek cross, with a columned portico reached by a double staircase marking the entrance. The interior has early nineteenth-century furnishings of the highest quality.

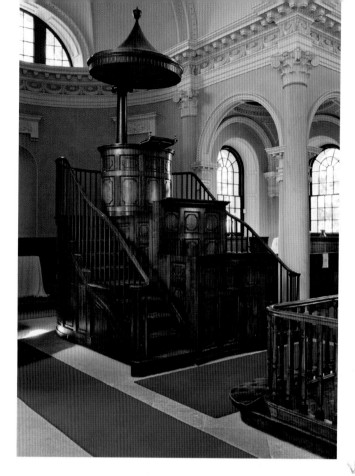

ABOVE The magnificent three-decker pulpit, made of cherrywood.
BELOW LEFT Gibside Chapel was begun in 1759 but was not finished until over 50 years later, when the elegant plasterwork was added.

A splendid three-tier mahogany pulpit stands behind the altar, its umbrella-like sounding board perched on an Ionic column ensuring that the preacher's message reached those seated below. On either side elliptical cherrywood pews for servants and visitors fill the semicircular apses in the arms of the cross and there are box pews for the owner, agent and chaplain.

The stables and banqueting hall by Daniel Garrett also survive, the former with a grand Palladian facade, the latter in Gothick style, set high to enjoy prospects over the estate, but the monumental orangery added by Mary Eleanor Bowes, George's daughter, is now a ruin and the rambling seventeenth-century hall set on a shelf above the Derwent is just a shell.

As George's only child, Mary Eleanor had inherited a fortune and was married, for her money, by John Lyon, 9th Earl of Strathmore, who changed his name to Bowes-Lyon to secure his prize. The late Queen Mother, daughter of the 14th Earl, sometimes came to Gibside as a child from the Strathmores' house near Barnard Castle for a picnic in the park.

Godolphin

Cornwall
Between Hayle and Helston, off
a zigzag road from Godolphin
Cross to Townshend

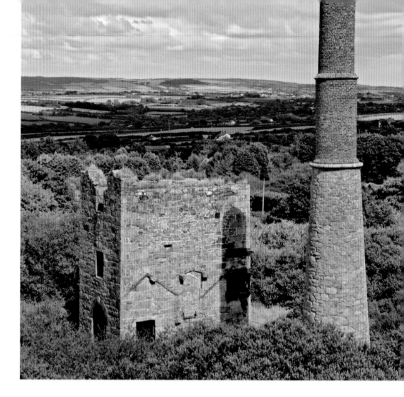

The Godolphin estate lies deep in Cornwall, in a well-wooded landscape of small fields, scattered settlements and twisting lanes, and with a sense of the sea near at hand. At its heart, beneath the cone of Godolphin Hill and shielded by woodland along the Hayle River, is this magical Tudor and Jacobean house, one of the most atmospheric places in the West Country. Low, two-storey ranges, lit by stone-mullioned windows and built of local granite like the field walls and stiles on the estate, are set round three sides of a grassy courtyard. What was the great hall range on the south side, with an arched porch giving onto the court, is now a romantic ruin and a second courtyard that once lay beyond it was demolished in the early nineteenth century.

The Godolphin family, who were living on this site from the twelfth century, grew rich on the mining of rich seams of tin and copper on the estate and, through judicious marriages and loyal service to the Crown, gradually secured their position as one of the leading families of Cornwall, emerging as players on the national stage from the reign of Henry VIII. The old king, diseased and failing, knighted William Godolphin after the successful siege of Boulogne in 1544 and Francis Godolphin, who inherited in 1575, was the first of a line of Godolphins to be governor of the Scilly Isles, which were held for the king in the Civil War. As the family's status grew, so the house was enlarged, becoming the largest and grandest in Cornwall in the seventeenth century. This was the high point. By the time Sidney Godolphin, the 1st Earl, became Queen Anne's First Lord of the Treasury in the early eighteenth century, the family had a London house and their old Cornish seat, increasingly neglected, slowly decayed, becoming a run-down farmhouse. Godolphin was lovingly restored by Sydney Schofield, son of the American landscape painter Elmer Schofield, and his wife Mary, who came here in 1937. The National Trust bought the estate from the

Schofields in 2000, and in 2007 the house and garden were also acquired.

Weathered, lichen-spotted stone and mossy cobbles add to the appeal of this exceptional place. Across what was once a walled forecourt, eight stocky Tuscan columns of carved granite form a long colonnade in the centre of the north-facing entrance front. This Italianate loggia, an exceptionally sophisticated feature for its date in this part of the country and separated only by a screen wall from an identical colonnade looking onto the courtyard, was added in the 1630s, together with the rooms above, when the house was remodelled for the last time by Sir Francis Godolphin II. A cultured and sophisticated man, whose brother was the poet Sidney Godolphin, Sir Francis would have moved in court circles and been aware of the new Italianate architecture, typified by Inigo Jones's Banqueting House, appearing in London. The lead drainwater heads on this front carry the double-headed eagle of the Godolphin arms and the leaping dolphin of the family crest, and a Tudor arch closed with original massive oak doors that was incorporated in the seventeenth-century work leads through into the courtyard.

The interior is a succession of light, airy rooms, the most glorious being the long chamber with windows on both sides that runs above the colonnade. A room that was used by William Godolphin IV, friend of the diarists Pepys and Evelyn, still has its 1630s decorative frieze, original pine floorboards, and enchanting blue and white seventeenth-century Delft tiles featuring mythical beasts round the fireplace. The closet off, now a bathroom, was probably William's library and study. Seventeenth-century improvement also accounts for the lofty chamber in the west range with large mullioned windows looking onto the courtyard. Known as the King's Room, this is where the future Charles II is said to have rested when he was fleeing to the Scilly Isles and France in 1646 after his crushing defeat at the Battle of Naseby in 1645. The high coved ceiling has pendants of what may be Jacobean plasterwork and a richly carved oak overmantel on the south wall is thought to commemorate the wedding of William Godolphin III and Thomasine Sydney in 1604. Once in the hall, it was moved to this room in the nineteenth century when the hall was demolished. The earliest parts of the house, dating from the 1470s, are in the east wing, where rich linenfold panelling and carved ceiling beams in one of the intimate rooms are embellishments of 1537.

Godolphin came to the Trust without any contents and, although now a holiday let, has been sympathetically furnished with pieces that, like the refectory table in the dining room, of 1750–1830, suit the spirit of the house. There are a couple of Godolphin family portraits and striking paintings of Cornish fishermen by Walter Schofield, who used one of the rooms in the west range as his studio. A squint big enough to take a musket covering the entrance is a reminder of Cornwall's former lawlessness and of the Godolphins' support for Charles I in the Civil War, the expense of which probably prevented Sir Francis from completing the updating of his house.

A sixteenth-century stable block with a rough cobbled floor sits beside the house, while to the east are the skeletal remains of a compartmental fourteenth-century garden, with raised walks and the depressions of former fishponds. In the woodland along the river and up on the hill are the pits, gullies, spoil heaps and other remains of mining in the nineteenth century, now romantically deserted and overgrown.

FAR LEFT These decorative columns are part of the richly carved overmantel in the King's Room.
LEFT This romantically ruined engine house and three-tiered stack on the hill above the house are among many reminders of the tin and copper mines which made the family rich.
BELOW Atmospheric Godolphin House, where a range of Elizabethan stables frames one side of the King's Garden.

Great Chalfield Manor

Wiltshire
3 miles (4.8 kilometres)
south-west of Melksham, via
Broughton Gifford Common

When Thomas Tropnell rebuilt his manor between 1467 and 1480, England was still torn apart by the Wars of the Roses and no one could feel secure. His new courtyard house was approached through a defensible fourteenth-century gatehouse and encircled by a curtain wall and a moat. Visitors coming to the porch could be assessed through a squint from the parlour (now hidden behind panelling), and a little wicket in the ancient oak front door admits only one at a time.

There is still a medieval gatehouse, a moat and the remains of the curtain wall, but seeing the house today, so peacefully set in the countryside only a few miles from Bath, it is difficult to connect it with the troubled times in which it was built. The honey-coloured stone, gabled facades and mullioned windows give it the look of a Cotswold manor and there are delightful stone carvings of griffins holding the Tropnell arms and soldiers in fifteenth-century armour crowning the gables on the entrance front. Across what was the outer courtyard, at right-angles to the house, is a little fourteenth-century church, which Tropnell enhanced with a bellcote and spire.

Inside, a traditional great hall, lit by windows high in the walls, rises to what would have been a richly painted ceiling, and arched openings lead to the fine first-floor rooms in the gabled blocks on either side. Both have charming oriel windows, the beautiful semicircular example in the family's

BELOW At the back of the house, the garden slopes down to an arm of the moat that was dug to protect the manor in the Middle Ages.
ABOVE RIGHT The hall at Great Chalfield Manor is hung with seventeenth-century Antwerp tapestries.

solar being marked by a crown of decorative tracery on the exterior. This room looks out on the little church and from here, too, ladies could watch proceedings in the hall through two of the curious stone masks with cut-away eyes that hang in the room below – one a king with ass's ears, another a bishop in his mitre, the third a laughing face. Another curiosity is the mural painting in the dining room, showing a man with five fingers on each hand. This painting may depict Thomas Tropnell himself, a 'perilous, covetous man'.

The house as it is seen today reflects Sir Harold Brakspear's restoration in 1905–12 for the Fuller family after about two centuries of neglect and disrepair, during which both the east and south wings that once closed the inner courtyard were demolished (although the foundations of the latter can still be seen in the garden). Sir Harold's sensitive and scholarly reconstruction used drawings made by Pugin's pupil Thomas Larkin Walker in 1836, when the manor was already in a ruinous state. The Fullers were also responsible for introducing the period furniture, Flemish tapestries and eastern carpets that now enhance the house. Since its restoration, Great Chalfield has again been the hub of a rural estate that includes home farms, woodland, labourers' cottages and its own parish church. Little has changed on the land, where field names and boundaries are still as they are shown on a map of 1794.

Greenway

Devon
Greenway Road, Galmpton, on the east bank of the River Dart off the A379.

One of the most successful and prolific authors of all time, outsold only by Shakespeare, is Agatha Christie (1890–1976). As well as producing a library of ingenious detective stories and a number of other books, she also wrote several plays, one of which, *The Mousetrap*, has been running continuously on the London stage for over 60 years. It seems appropriate that this exceptional woman, who knew how to conjure up suspense and mystery, should have fallen for this romantic and atmospheric place overlooking the magical Dart estuary. A luxuriant woodland garden, developed over the last 200 years and filled with many rare and tender plants and specimen trees, surrounds the house and plunges steeply to the water, adding greatly to Greenway's individual charm. On the other side of the river is the little village of Dittisham, from which ferries cross to the quay below the property, and there are spectacular views over the water and down the estuary to Dartmouth.

Although there was a late sixteenth-century Tudor mansion here, home to several generations of the adventuring Gilberts of Compton Castle (*see* p.105), the central block of the present white Georgian house was built, by an unknown architect, for the merchant adventurer Roope Harris Roope in 1771 on a site in front of the old Greenway Court. A tall stuccoed building, with an array of sash windows looking west over the river and a hipped roof, the house is tucked into the slope at the top of the garden. One-storey wings fronted by colonnaded porticoes on either side of the main block were added in 1815 by James Marwood Elton, whose father, another merchant adventurer, had bought the property in 1791.

Dame Agatha, whose childhood home in Torquay lies just a few miles away, bought Greenway with her second husband, the archaeologist Max Mallowan, as a holiday home in 1938, employing the young Guilford Bell to demolish a billiard-

LEFT Agatha hung French ivory-framed mirrors above the bookcases in her bedroom.

room wing that had been added in the later nineteenth century and make other alterations. Their daughter Rosalind Hicks and her husband Anthony lived here from 1978 and in 2000 Rosalind and Anthony, together with Rosalind's son Matthew Prichard, gifted the property, with its shield of surrounding woodland and farmland, to the National Trust. The garden has been open since 2003 and the house, which came to the Trust with all its contents, opened in 2009.

Shown as it was when a holiday home in the 1950s and '60s, Greenway is a most attractive house, with light, well-proportioned rooms, their cream decoration being one of Guilford Bell's improvements, and a sense of comfort and serenity. Apart from some de-cluttering by the Trust, the furnishings are largely as recorded in the 1942 inventory and there are displays of family portraits and photographs and the kind of belongings that make a house feel lived in, from Anthony Hicks's hats to golf clubs, walking sticks and soft toys. All the family were great collectors and every table, chest and mantelpiece and every glass-fronted cabinet is used to display their rather individual treasures, among them ceramics, pocket watches, boxes made of scrolled paper and Tunbridgeware. Large built-in cupboards in what was originally the housekeeper's sitting room are stuffed full of further items, including modern studio glass and the Mallowans' collection of silver.

In the drawing room filling the west wing, a sofa and deep armchairs are set invitingly round the fire, as the family had it. This is where Agatha Christie used to read the manuscript of her latest thriller to family and friends, asking them to guess who the murderer in the story might be; she wrote letters at the mahogany bureau and played the boudoir grand that sits in a corner of the room. A portrait of Agatha aged 4, painted by Douglas Connah in 1894, hangs in the room next door, and the doll she is shown clutching sits on the chair below. Upstairs, the writer's bedroom, with its large walk-in closet and display of *papier-mâché* furniture, is largely unchanged, and a striking black and gold kimono here is the one being worn by her mother in a photograph downstairs. An adjoining room is now devoted to Max Mallowan's excavations in

ABOVE Greenway is an attractive Georgian house set high above the Dart estuary, with magical views over the river and downstream towards Dartmouth.

Mesopotamia, with a display of miniature pottery heads and other finds. A haughty ceramic camel dating from the Tang dynasty (AD618–906) was a present from Max to Agatha and other pieces in the house came from her childhood home.

Another aspect of Greeenway's history comes through in the library, where an unusual frieze dates from the Second World War when the 10th Flotilla of the US Coastguard was based in the house and Greenway was caught up in the preparations for D-Day. Painted by Lt Marshall Lee in 1943 in what was the officers' bar, the frieze depicts incidents in the flotilla's war, such as the hard-fought invasion of Sicily; a final tableau shows the house half-hidden in trees high above the Dart, with a naval vessel in the deep-water anchorage below.

A stable block tucked away to the north-west of the house, still with some original stalls and loose-boxes, also dates from the eighteenth century, but a bell tower and clock were additions of the 1850s. Down on the river, in leafy seclusion, is a substantial two-storey late Georgian boathouse. The lower level is a bathing room, which fills with salt water at high tide, while above, with a balcony overlooking the Dart, is a roomy saloon, complete with fireplace. This is where Agatha Christie set the murder of Marlene Tucker in *Dead Man's Folly*, thus bringing the place she loved into her writing.

In keeping with Greenway's history as a much-loved retreat for Agatha and her family, the top of the house has been turned into a spacious holiday apartment.

Greys Court

Oxfordshire
3 miles (4.8 kilometres) west
of Henley-on-Thames, east
of the B481

This picturesque assemblage of old buildings set on a peaceful wooded hillside was caught up in one of the most notorious murders of the seventeenth century. When the poet Sir Thomas Overbury died in the Tower of London in 1613 in mysterious circumstances, James I's favourite, Robert Carr, Earl of Somerset, and his beautiful wife, Frances Howard, were found guilty of poisoning him. Reprieved by the king, the two were confined at Greys Court, the home of William Knollys, whose wife was Frances's sister.

There could be few more enchanting prisons. The modest brick, flint and stone Tudor house of the Knollyses, with some eighteenth-century improvements, is set within the courtyard of the medieval manor of the de Greys, who gave the property its name. The gabled east front of the house, its mellow pink and grey walls half obscured by climbing plants, looks across a sweep of grass to two fourteenth-century towers, one now ruined, but the other, the Great Tower, still looking as it did when Edward III granted the 1st Lord de Grey a licence to

BELOW The modest late sixteenth-century house at Greys Court, built of a pleasing mix of brick, flint and stone, with the castellated bay window of the elegant drawing room added in c.1750 protruding to the north.

crenellate in 1347. The foundations of two gatehouses and the walls of two courtyards appear as outlines in the grass in dry summers. Inside the house, intimate family rooms include an elegant classical drawing room, created in about 1750, where there is some exceptional plasterwork on the walls and ceiling that may be by Roberts of Oxford and where a fine marble chimneypiece replaced a sixteenth-century one in stone; the so-called school room, which also has elaborate plasterwork; and a kitchen with massive beams that appears to have survived from the medieval house.

There is late seventeenth-century and early eighteenth-century English furniture in mahogany, walnut and oak, and two large Swiss chests and sixteenth- and seventeenth-century Swiss stained glass in the window that lights the pine staircase reflect the fact that in 1937 Greys Court was bought by Sir Felix and Lady Brunner, and now contains pieces from the collection of Swiss artefacts that were bought by Sir Felix's grandfather, the Brunners being an ancient Swiss family. Lady Brunner's theatrical background is reflected in portraits of her grandfather, the great Sir Henry Irving, and other Irving relatives and the view of the house from the north-west that hangs over the drawing-room fireplace was painted for her in 1993 by James Lynch. The Brunner family gave Greys Court to the National Trust in 1969.

A group of brick outbuildings to the south of the house includes an early Tudor wheelhouse with a massive donkey wheel. The largest still surviving in Britain, the donkey wheel raised water 61 metres (200 feet) from an ancient well and was used until 1914.

Across the grass from the house, the romantic ruins of the medieval fortifications form the skeleton of an enchanting garden. Ancient flint walls form the backdrop to a rose garden, planted with old-fashioned species, a White Garden against the Great Tower and a wisteria arbour, flowering profusely from craggy and monstrous stems that form a woody canopy above visitors' heads. An opening in the wall of an ornamental kitchen garden leads out to the maze centred on an armillary sphere that was added in 1981, its brick paths symbolising the journey through life. Where the garden is small-scale and inward looking, the grassy court in front of the house gives uninterrupted views south over the ha-ha and across a deep, tree-framed fold of the Chilterns.

Gunby Hall

Lincolnshire
2½ miles (4 kilometres) north-west of Burgh-le-Marsh, 7 miles (11.2 kilometres) west of Skegness on the south side of the A158

Gunby lies at the southern tip of the Lincolnshire Wolds, only 10 miles (16 kilometres) from the North Sea. This is one of the most remote corners of England, a countryside of scattered villages and hamlets and of great vistas across rich arable, criss-crossed by a network of drainage dykes in the fen country around the Wash. Gunby is out of place in these surroundings. Built of a warm rose-red brick with limestone dressings, this elegant oblong with a flat roofline and a broad flight of steps rising to a pedimented front door should face an identical facade across a leafy London square. It is a town house stranded in the country.

As the keystone over the front door proclaims, Gunby dates from 1700. It was commissioned by Sir William Massingberd, whose ancient Lincolnshire family had risen from the ranks of the yeomanry in the early Middle Ages to a baronetcy by the time of Sir Henry Massingberd in the seventeenth century, helped on their way by judicious marriages. When the last baronet died only 20 years after the house was built, the property and the name descended through the female line.

The warm panelled rooms are filled with fine old paintings, furniture and china, most of which have been in the family for generations. Among the treasures is Sir Joshua Reynolds's portrait of Bennet Langton, whose son Peregrine married the heiress to the estate in 1784 and who was a lifelong friend of Dr Johnson. This association brought Gunby a very rare autographed copy of the first edition of Boswell's biography, one of only six known to have survived and the only one in England. Bennet was also on close terms with Reynolds, whose sympathetic portrait shows his friend in relaxed pose, with long unpowdered hair falling in curls over his shoulders.

Tennyson, who was born at Somersby only a few miles away, knew the house too and it may have been Gunby that inspired the autographed lines that now hang in the front hall, with their reference to 'a haunt of ancient peace'. The book-lined library, which was destroyed in 1926 when the wall between it and the hall was demolished and the books dispersed around the house, has been re-created by the National Trust, its shelves filled with volumes acquired by the Massingberds over many generations.

The gardens are another of Gunby's attractions, the present layout dating largely from the early years of the twentieth century. Lawns dotted with ornamental trees sweep round the house and there are two old walled gardens, planted with traditional English vegetables, fruit and flowers. A square brick pigeon-house crowned by a weather vane pre-dates the present hall, as do various outbuildings.

The extensive wooded estate, crossed by a network of paths, incorporates some fifteen farms and a stretch of disused

ABOVE Gunby's brick facades are echoed in the mellow brick walls of the garden.

railway line. The property also includes the remote Monksthorpe Chapel, near the little place of the same name. Dating from the late seventeenth century, and still looking like the barn it once was, the chapel was used by local baptists who needed a secluded place of worship during the years when dissenters were persecuted. It has its original baptismal pool.

Ham House

Surrey
On the south bank of the
River Thames, west of the
A307, at Petersham

Ruthless ambition created this red-brick palace beside the River Thames, with its principal rooms still furnished in the style of Charles II's court. Elizabeth, Countess of Dysart, was not content with the Jacobean house she inherited from her father, William Murray, 1st Earl of Dysart, despite the improvements he made in 1637–9. A second marriage gave her the opportunity to spend lavishly on remodelling. Even before the death of her first husband, the countess's name was being linked to the high-flying Earl of Lauderdale, a member of Charles II's cabal ministry. When his wife conveniently died, the two were married. In the same year, 1672, the earl received a dukedom, and the couple set out to mark their position with new building. He was at the height of his power; she, it was said, with complete ascendancy over him. The haughty, rather unattractive couple confidently surveying the world from Lely's portrait in the round gallery clearly deserved each other and together they produced one of the most lavishly appointed houses of their day.

Externally, Ham is sober enough. A long three-storey block of a house with tall chimneys, it is enlivened on the entrance front with two projecting wings, each of which incorporates a short colonnade, and with sixteen busts set in niches at the level of the first floor. More busts are set round the brick wall enclosing the forecourt. There were once wings on the south front too, but these were engulfed when the Lauderdales doubled the size of Ham by building new apartments along this side of the house. The new rooms were given sash windows, which had only recently been invented, but these were designed to blend with the Jacobean casements.

Inside, there are few traces of the interiors created in 1610 for Sir Thomas Vavasour, Knight Marshal to James I, for whom Ham was built, but several rooms still display the taste of Elizabeth's father, which reflects the period love of rich effect. Bronzing picks out martial details – a drum, armour,

RIGHT The early seventeenth-century Green Closet is a rare survival of the intimate rooms that were designed for the display of small paintings and miniatures.
OPPOSITE The north front of Ham House.

a cannon with a pile of shot – on the carved and pierced panels of his great staircase and on the baskets of fruit crowning the newel posts. The stairs lead to the sequence of first-floor state rooms created by William Murray along the north front. His great dining room is now the gallery above the hall. Beyond lie his tapestry-hung drawing room and his refurbished long gallery, the first with original plasterwork, woodwork and marble chimneypiece, the second lined with gilded panelling divided by Ionic pilasters which the earl added to the Jacobean room.

Portraits in sumptuous gold frames line the gallery, among them several works by Lely and the portrait that Charles I gave to William Murray, who was one of his most loyal supporters. A rare survival is the intimate Green Closet off the gallery, where some 60 miniatures and small paintings framed in ebony and gilt are hung closely on brilliant green damask. Many of the pictures, which include miniatures by Nicholas Hilliard and Isaac Oliver, were hanging here in the seventeenth century. The ceiling paintings of cupids, nymphs and satyrs, in tempera, are by Franz Cleyn, who was principal designer for the Mortlake tapestry works.

Along the south front, arranged over two floors, are the apartments created by the Lauderdales. On the first floor, the long gallery leads into a suite of three rooms fitted out for Charles II's queen, Catherine of Braganza, in 1673. Although partly refurnished in the eighteenth century by the duchess's great-great-grandson, the 4th Earl of Dysart, many of the

extravagant original fittings remain. There are hangings of silk damask and velvet, fire-irons ornamented with silver, intricate parquet floors and a carved wooden garland of subtle craftsmanship. Most of the seventeenth-century decor survives in the intimate closet at the end of the suite, which is still hung with winter hangings of 'crimson and gould stuff bordered with green and gould stuff' and has a baroque ceiling painting by Antonio Verrio, who had worked extensively for Charles II. More paintings by Verrio in the overblown style favoured at the time, such as a group of maidens representing the arts, also adorn the private closets in the two suites of rooms that the Lauderdales created for themselves on the ground floor of the south front. Here the flavour is more mixed. The Duchess's closet, where she would have retired for privacy, or to talk to her closest friends, shows the white crackled teapot that brewed her precious tea; and survivals of the original decorative scheme include inset sea paintings by William van der Velde (in his rooms) and bird paintings by Francis Barlow (in hers). But her bedroom has had to be re-created as it might have appeared, and what was the duke's bedchamber has the 1740s furnishing scheme of the 4th Earl, who turned it into a drawing room. Flemish tapestries have an elegant French flavour, gilded chairs and sofas upholstered in gold silk have X-frames in the style of William Kent, and a new carpet woven for the room, based on archive material, has been designed to pick up the strong blues and pinks in the tapestries.

The spirit of the house extends into the garden, where the formal seventeenth-century layout, in which the garden was devised as a series of contrasting compartments, has been re-created. The south front looks over a broad terrace to a lawn divided into eight uniform square plats and beyond to the wilderness. Looking from a distance like a well-ordered wood, this too has an architectural plan. Grassy walks lined by hornbeam hedges radiate from a central clearing, dividing the wilderness into a series of small enclosures, four of which contain little summerhouses. East of the house, a secluded knot garden is flanked by the cool green tunnels of hornbeam alleys and a period kitchen garden has been restored in front

of the wisteria-hung seventeenth-century orangery to the west. Outhouses include the eighteenth-century dairy, with marble shelves carried on cast-iron cow's legs, and the late seventeenth-century slate-floored still house, where soaps, sweet-scented waters and ointments were prepared. Close by, down one of the avenues that lead the eye beyond the garden, is the Thames and the little ferry from Twickenham, which has for centuries brought visitors across the water.

Hanbury Hall

Worcestershire
4½ miles (7.2 kilometres) east of Droitwich, 1 mile (1.6 kilometres) north of the B4090; 6 miles (9.6 kilometres) south of Bromsgrove, east of the M5

James Thornhill was at the height of his career when Thomas Vernon, a successful barrister, commissioned him to decorate the staircase of his new house in 1710. Although his work for St Paul's Cathedral was still in the future, Thornhill had completed the Sabine Room at Chatsworth in Derbyshire and was halfway through his magnificent Painted Hall at Greenwich. Like this masterpiece, the Hanbury staircase is exuberantly baroque, with mythological scenes, most of them taken from Homer's *Iliad*, framed between classical columns on the walls and a host of deities set among clouds looking down from above. In the long hall below, where a bust of Vernon stands over the fireplace, the subtle monochrome ceiling, probably by one of Thornhill's assistants, matches the quality of the master's work, with musical instruments and agricultural tools representing the seasons of the year separated by *trompe-l'oeil* domes and shells.

Vernon's square red-brick house, begun *c.*1700 and probably designed by a local mason, is a typical example of Restoration domestic architecture, with dormers in the hipped roof and a central cupola. Pavilions in the French or Dutch style project from all four corners. The design of the striking pedimented entrance facade, with a central bay set between Corinthian columns and decorated with flowing carving, may have been influenced by the treatment of a grand house such as Thoresby Hall in Nottinghamshire, which had been remodelled in the 1680s for the Duke of Kingston. An unusual detached long gallery has two ornate Jacobean overmantels made up of carved woodwork brought from elsewhere. Domed gazebos at the corners of the entrance court are Victorian.

BELOW The sitting room, with its Neo-classical marble chimneypiece, is now furnished to evoke Hanbury in the 1920s.
BELOW RIGHT The forge scene on the great staircase shows a suit of armour being made for Achilles to render him invulnerable.

Hanbury's original contents were mostly sold in 1790 after the dissipation of the family fortunes during the disastrous marriage between Emma Vernon and Henry Cecil, later Lord Exeter. Some family pieces, such as the two Dutch marquestry chests of drawers in the Blue Bedroom, have returned in recent years and all the portraits, including works by Reynolds, Kneller and John Vanderbank, are now back in the house, hanging in the hall and dining room. Generally, most of the interiors, including a sitting room in the idiom of the 1920s, have been re-created, but a flavour of the early eighteenth century comes through in a panelled bedroom and dressing room, the latter still with its original corner chimneypiece. And in the smoking room at the back of the house, once Thomas Vernon's office, a painting of Hanbury commissioned by Bowater Vernon, Thomas's heir, from John Wootton, shows the house in the setting of its early eighteenth-century landscape, with long avenues of trees stretching into the distance.

Nearby hangs a bird's-eye view of the estate in 1732 by Joseph Dougharty showing both the avenues and Vernon's compartmental formal garden, both part of a grand design by George London. Later changes destroyed all but remnants of London's layout but, using this bird's-eye view and surviving plans, the avenues have now been replanted and the garden, with its sunken parterre, grove, wilderness, bowling green and fruit garden, re- created. A handsome orangery was a mid-eighteenth-century addition to the design.

BELOW Serene Hanbury Hall, built of brick with stone dressings and finished off with a little cupola, is typical of the architecture of Restoration England.

The Hardmans' House (Mr Hardman's Photographic Studio)

Merseyside
59 Rodney Street, Liverpool

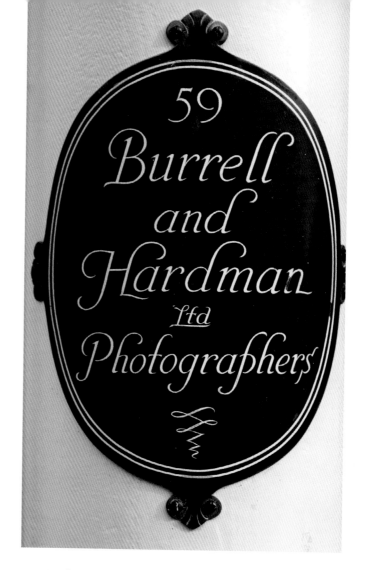

ABOVE Hardman always kept the name of the original business, although his friend and partner Kenneth Burrell left Liverpool in 1929.

This substantial Georgian terrace house, with a long garden behind, was for years both home and workplace of Edward Chambré Hardman (1898–1988), Liverpool's leading portrait photographer from the 1920s to the 1960s. In the era before informal poses became fashionable and every family had the equipment to produce their own photographs, there was a demand for formal portraits that was met by commercial studios. Hardman catered for this market, photographing anyone who was anyone in Liverpool as well as a stream of distinguished visitors, among them Ivor Novello and Margot Fonteyn. He was also a skilled landscape photographer, capturing the Liverpool of his day and more distant places and countrysides. Working in the pictorial tradition, with much use of soft focus, re-touching and other manipulative devices, Hardman created images that are moody and atmospheric. Many of them are now also of documentary interest. He never set out to make a record of the changes in the city around him, but his evocative images of the now-vanished Liverpool shipbuilding industry, such as photographs showing the use of wooden scaffolding in the yards, and of other aspects of the urban scene, are of great historical value. His achievements were fully recognised in his lifetime: he was one of only four photographers to receive a special medal to mark the London Salon's Golden Jubilee in 1959, and he was awarded an Honorary Fellowship of the Royal Photographic Society in 1980.

Hardman was born in southern Ireland and, following the example of his father, who was a keen amateur photographer, began taking photographs seriously as a child, winning his first competition at the age of 14. After serving in the army in India from 1917–22, he decided to set up a photographic studio with a fellow officer, Kenneth Burrell, who seems to have been of value largely for his social connections and was not involved in the day-to-day running of the business (initially based in Bold Street). Soon, anyone of any pretensions or importance in the area was being photographed by Burrell & Hardman and Hardman began a series of portraits of actors appearing at the Liverpool Playhouse, among them, over the years, Richard Todd, Robert Donat, Patricia Routledge, Michael Redgrave and Beryl Bainbridge. With his future wife Margaret, who had joined the studio as an employee and whom he eventually married in 1932, he set off by train and bicycle into the countryside to photograph landscapes, many of which were commissioned as covers for *Cheshire Life* or the back page of the *Daily Post*.

The business prospered. Hardman opened a second studio in Chester and in 1948 moved to Rodney Street. But little more than a decade later the tide turned. With demand for formally posed portraits declining, he worked less and less, becoming virtually a recluse after Margaret died in 1970. On his death, the house and its contents passed to the E.C. Hardman Trust, which in turn gave everything to the National Trust in 2001.

Still as it was when the Hardmans lived and worked here, 59 Rodney Street is a complete example of a period photographic studio and is full of furnishings and ephemera from the 1930s, '40s and '50s. At the front of the house are the clients' waiting room and changing room and Hardman's studio, the latter fully equipped with backdrops, cameras, lights, props and even drawers of toys to entertain younger sitters. Three darkrooms and areas for printing, cutting and

mounting were where Hardman manipulated and finished his images, and the Hardmans themselves lived in the cramped and relatively frugal quarters at the back. Some of the furniture is in the style of Sir Gordon Russell, who was a pioneer of the Modern Movement in English furniture design, and there is a strong period feel, with many everyday items, such as tins of food and packets of soap and silk stockings, in the condition in which they were purchased over 50 years ago.

Hardwick Hall

Derbyshire
6½ miles (10.4 kilometres)
west of Mansfield, 9 ½ miles
(15.2 kilometres) south-east
of Chesterfield

This cathedral of a house stands tall and proud on the top of a windswept hill, its distinctive, many-towered outline lifting the spirits of those hurtling past on the M1. As the huge stone initials set along the roofline proclaim, this is the house of Elizabeth Shrewsbury, better known as Bess of Hardwick, the formidable and ambitious squire's daughter who rose from relatively humble beginnings to become one of the richest and best-connected people in Elizabethan England.

By the time Hardwick was begun, Bess was already approaching 70 and had four marriages behind her, each of which had advanced her social position and increased her wealth. Her last husband was George Talbot, 6th Earl of Shrewsbury, the head of the oldest, grandest and richest family in England. By 1583, when she bought the family estate from her brother James, she and Shrewsbury were estranged and Bess initially embarked on remodelling the manor house where she had been born, the romantic ruins of which (in the guardianship of English Heritage) still crown the crest of the ridge just to the south-west of the New Hall. Although built piecemeal, on a cramped and awkward site, this first venture was in many ways a trial run for what was to come, incorporating features, such as the enormous windows lighting the Great Chambers on the top floor, which Bess would use again. This house was still unfinished when, in 1590, Bess's situation was transformed by the earl's death. It is possible the foundations for the New Hall had already been laid a few weeks before, but now Bess had the funds to fully finance her new project. Whereas the Old Hall had been produced piecemeal, the New Hall rose on virgin land and was designed as one by Robert Smythson, the most original of Elizabethan architects. It is a prodigy house, in a class of its own, but it was never large enough for all Bess's household. Even after the new building was finished, in 1597, servants and guests were still accommodated in the Old Hall.

Both houses are built of limestone quarried from just down the hill, but whereas the gabled and irregular outlines of the Old Hall reflect the remodelling of an existing building, the profile of the New Hall is clean and symmetrical. Windows that become progressively larger up the house enhance the strong vertical thrust of the six towers, giving Hardwick the appearance of a glittering glass lantern. Inside, a broad, tapestry-hung stone staircase, to the same innovatory design as one in the Old Hall, weaves its way majestically to the state apartments lit by huge windows on the third floor. These rooms are still very much as Bess left them. Her High Great Chamber for the reception and entertainment of important guests was designed round the tapestries that still hang here, purchased new in 1587. The goddess Diana with her court on the three-dimensional plaster frieze above was intended as a tribute to Elizabeth I, whom Bess always hoped would visit Hardwick (she never did).

A tapestry-hung door leads into the atmospheric long gallery, where some of the 80 pictures covering the walls were here in Bess's time. Portraying royalty, family, friends and patrons – evidence of her good connections – they include three of Bess's husbands and a glittering representation of the queen herself, her famous red hair piled high and her dress decorated with sea creatures and birds and studded with pearls. Here, too, is a memorable painting of the philosopher Thomas Hobbes, tutor to Bess's grandson, the 2nd Earl of Devonshire. Hobbes is shown just a few years before he died at Hardwick in 1679, toothless in extreme old age.

Elizabethan tapestries and paintings are complemented by an important collection of embroideries dating from 1570–1640, many of which were worked on by Bess herself and which include pictorial wall hangings made out of a patchwork of velvets and silks and exquisite cushion covers worked in cross stitch. There is also some exceptional original furniture, such as the eglantine table in the High Great Chamber, inlaid with a mosaic of musical instruments, playing cards and board games, even the setting of a four-part

ABOVE Many of the embroideries at Hardwick, such as this red velvet panel, are decorated with Bess's ES monogram, standing for Elizabeth of Shrewsbury.

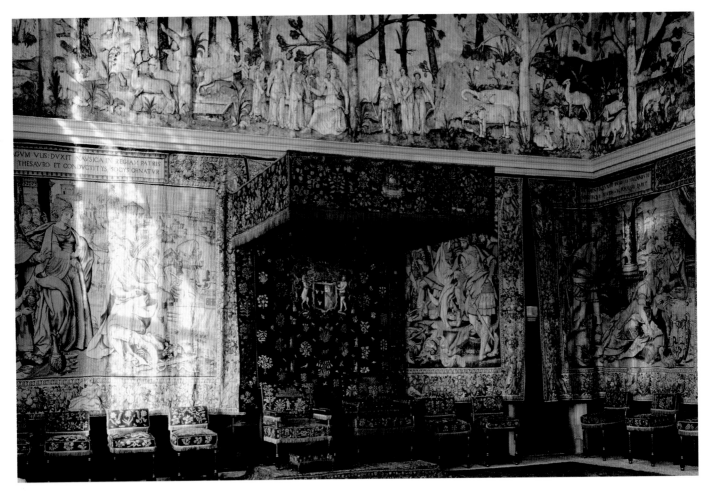

motet, that was probably made to celebrate Bess's marriage to the Earl of Shrewsbury in 1568, and, in the adjoining room, an inlaid walnut table that is carried on carvings of sea dogs and tortoises.

Hardwick's unique character owes much to the 6th Duke of Devonshire, who inherited in 1811 and deliberately enhanced the antiquarian atmosphere of the house, promoting the legend that Mary Queen of Scots stayed here and filling it with additional furniture, paintings and tapestries from his other properties, particularly from Chatsworth some 15 miles (24 kilometres) to the west.

Formal gardens to the south were laid out in the late nineteenth century. One section is a herb garden, another is a pear orchard and there are colourful herbaceous borders. A little Elizabethan banqueting house was used as a smoking room by the 6th Duke's private orchestra, who were forbidden

to smoke in the Hall itself. Buildings grouped round a stableyard beyond the garden include a smithy that existed in Bess's time, and a great barn (now the restaurant) and ox-house (now the shop) that date back to the early seventeenth century. Grain threshed in the barn would have been taken to be ground at the mill at Stainsby, in the northern part of the estate, where the present building, of 1849–50, has an iron water-wheel and other machinery that is stll in working order.

The 800-hectare (1,990-acre) estate embraces two different landscapes. At the back of the hall, a formal stretch of grass focused on a central basin looks out across the flat, partly cultivated land on the limestone plateau east of the house. To the west is the oak-wooded, hillier terrain of the former deer-park, with a series of fishponds and a partly restored duck decoy. Now a country park, it is grazed by rare breeds of cattle and sheep.

ABOVE LEFT The High Great Chamber at Hardwick, with tapestries that were bought new by Bess hanging below the exceptional painted plaster frieze, is a virtually unchanged Elizabethan interior.

ABOVE With its six towers, advancing and receding bays and great array of glass, Hardwick is the most theatrical and dramatic of Elizabethan houses, standing tall on a windswept hill.

Hardy Country

Dorset
Hardy's Birthplace is at Higher Bockhampton, 3 miles (4.8 kilometres) north-east of Dorchester, ½ mile (0.8 kilometre) south of the A35; Max Gate is 1 mile (1.6 kilometres) south-east of Dorchester, off the A352

The Wessex of Thomas Hardy's imagination, which gives such a strong sense of place to all his novels, was rooted in the countryside of Dorset and the towns and villages set in a tapestry of lush valleys, untamed heath and open downland that he had known since childhood. The market town of Dorchester, which would be thinly disguised as Casterbridge, was the centre of both his real and fictional worlds. Just a couple of miles outside the town is the secluded and picturesque cottage where the poet and novelist was born, in the bedroom at the top of the stairs, in 1840, his hold on life so tenuous that he was at first thought to be dead. Here Hardy grew up, walking 6 miles (9.6 kilometres) to school in Dorchester and back every day. Although he set off for London in 1862 to work as an architect, he returned five years later to live with his parents while he practised locally, continuing to write in the little upstairs room with a window looking west to the monument on Black Down, 10 miles (16 kilometres) away.

OPPOSITE This delightful cottage, of cob and thatch, is where the poet and novelist Thomas Hardy grew up, drawing inspiration for his writing from the people and landscapes around him.
RIGHT The house Thomas Hardy designed for himself and built outside Dorchester, just a few miles from the cottage where he was born, is an unremarkable, red-brick suburban villa.

The cottage dates from 1800, when his family settled here. With its deep thatched roof, casement windows and cob walls covered in roses, honeysuckle and japonica, it is everyone's idea of what a cottage should look like. The sheltered old-fashioned garden, crowded with pansies, lupins, lavender, day lilies, pinks, marigolds and a host of other plants, is as Hardy would have known it.

Many of the places and incidents Hardy describes so vividly are drawn from his life here. The cottage itself appears in *Under the Greenwood Tree*, in which the villagers' dance is set in the parlour to the left of the porch; the description of the musicians ousted by the new-fangled organ in Mellstock church echoes what happened in Stinsford church nearby, where Hardy's grandfather, father and uncle used to play the violin and cello for services; and Hardy used Egdon Heath behind the cottage, now largely tamed but once a wild and desolate expanse of bracken, heather and gorse stretching almost to the coast, as the setting for *The Return of the Native*.

In 1874, with the success of *Far From the Madding Crowd*, the fourth of his novels, Hardy took the decision to devote himself totally to writing and this was also the year in which he finally left the cottage for his troubled marriage to Emma Gifford. For several years the couple moved restlessly from one place to another, a period during which Hardy produced only one major work, but in 1885 they returned to Dorchester to live in the angular red-brick villa on the south-eastern edge of town which Hardy had designed for himself and where he lived until his death, in 1928. In his study at Max Gate he wrote *Tess of the d'Urbervilles*, *Jude the Obscure* and *The Mayor of Casterbridge*, as well as the moving poetry rooted in the disintegration of his marriage and Emma's death, in 1912 (two years later, in 1914, he married Florence Dugdale). In his last years, a stream of literary visitors came to the house, among them T.E. Lawrence, whose Clouds Hill (*see* p.100) was nearby, W.B. Yeats, Robert Louis Stevenson and Virginia Woolf. There are several pieces of Hardy's furniture in the house although not, alas, his study, which was reconstructed in Dorchester County Museum, and there is a fine view, but, unlike the cottage, this is not an appealing place, its rooms shadowed by the trees Hardy planted to protect his privacy. Tellingly, Hardy went back to Stinsford church from Max Gate and his heart is buried in the churchyard.

Hatchlands Park

Surrey
East of East Clandon, north of the
A246 Guildford–Leatherhead road

In the late 1750s Edward Boscawen, second son of the 1st Viscount Falmouth and Admiral of the Blue, used prize money from victories over the French in the Seven Years War to finance a new house. The architect of his square red-brick Georgian mansion, probably Stiff Leadbetter, ingeniously designed it with seven different floor levels. Looking at the house from the south-west, three storeys on the west front change mysteriously into two on the south. Sadly, the admiral did not live to enjoy his new mansion, dying only a year or so after he and his wife moved in.

Hatchlands contains the earliest recorded decoration in an English country house by Robert Adam, who was engaged in 1758, just after he had returned from his Grand Tour. Appropriately, his plaster ceilings in the saloon and library have nautical themes, the motifs used ranging from mermaids, dolphins and seahorses to drums, cannon and anchors. At the end of the century Joseph Bonomi made alterations to the staircase and the garden entrance, and a hundred years later Sir Reginald Blomfield added the music

ABOVE Hatchlands Park, with a little pediment marking the entrance front, was built in the 1750s for Admiral Boscawen.
BELOW LEFT The grandiose music room at Hatchlands, where recitals are given, was an addition of c.1903 in the style of the late seventeenth century by the architect Reginald Blomfield.

room in seventeenth-century style for Stuart Rendel, who was at one time a managing partner in London of Sir William Armstrong's engineering firm (*see* Cragside, p.115) and became Lord Rendel of Hatchlands.

Apart from a few pieces from the Rendel collection, such as the eighteenth-century gilt pier tables in the saloon, Adam's interiors are now complemented by pictures, furniture and keyboard instruments lent by the collector and musician Mr Alec Cobbe, who is the National Trust's tenant at Hatchlands. Red silk panels in the saloon set off works by Carlo Dolci, Rubens, Frederick de Moucheron and a rare sixteenth-century altarpiece by the Florentine Alessandro Allori, and a number of portraits in the house include canvases by Gainsborough, Wright of Derby, Angelica Kauffmann and Hoppner. Among the collection of keyboard instruments by European makers from the period *c.*1750–1840 are an Erard pianoforte reputedly made for Marie Antoinette, one of the few French harpsichords to escape destruction in the years after the Revolution, and a very rare quadruple-strung piano by Conrad Graf, one of only three known such instruments by this maker. The collection is maintained for performance and visitors may be lucky enough to hear the distant sound of music by Mozart, Couperin or Schubert.

High Cross House

Devon
At Dartington, off the A385/A384
to Totnes

The Dartington estate, set in the lush green countryside of south Devon, surrounds a great medieval courtyard house (not National Trust) dating from the fourteenth century. Bought in a ruinous state by the philanthropists Leonard and Dorothy Elmhirst in 1925, and lovingly restored, the hall became the focus for the pioneering and progressive co-educational school which the Elmhirsts founded here in 1926, and for which, in the 1930s, they commissioned a number of significant modernist buildings by the Swiss-born architect William Lescaze, who had studied in Zurich under the pioneering modernist Paul Moser before moving to the United States. High Cross House, which is managed by the National Trust for the Dartington Hall Trust, was both the first of these and one of the earliest essays in the international modernist style in England (*see also* The Homewood, p.172).

Set on a steeply sloping site beside the narrow lane running up to the old hall, High Cross House is an angular and geometric flat-roofed building, like an arrangement of boxes, with bands of metal casement windows and rendered brick facades that are partly white, partly a vivid sky-blue. One curved wall, its lines followed by a long strip of glass, provides counterpoint on the garden elevation. The house was built in 1931–2 for Bill Curry, the school's new headmaster, and it was through Curry, who had known Lescaze in America and who persuaded the Elmhirsts of the importance of giving children the experience of the new, that Lescaze got the job. The sizeable interior, spread over two floors, has the same clean lines as the exterior and another show of strong colour in the intense yellow of the hall and western wall of the staircase. Empty for several years after the school closed in 1987, and now without most of the furniture that was specially designed for it, the house was restored in the 1990s when part of the ground floor was turned into gallery space.

Lescaze's aesthetic comes through in the absence of mouldings, the concealed up-lighting and a play with levels, in the gleaming chrome handrail of the staircase and the flushed plywood doors in their smooth steel frames; his 'design for living' in such useful features as the capacious built-in wardrobes, in African walnut and pear, provided for the family

bedrooms and the lavish provision of bathrooms. The kitchen, now an empty space, has lost the state-of-the-art labour-saving gadgets with which it was fitted out, but the adjoining dining room has a copy of the original table, in American cherrywood, and the chairs designed for the house by the Dutch Bauhaus architect Mies van der Rohe, and there are sofas by Lescaze in the sitting room. A two-car garage, now exhibition space, was fitted into the slope of the hill and there was accommodation, and a separate entrance, for servants, showing Mr Curry's lifestyle was of its time. Most striking is the way the house looks outwards, embracing the garden and the countryside beyond through walls of glass. From the generous terraces provided at bedroom level and from the roof above there are panoramic views south-east over the valley of the Dart and north to the heights of Dartmoor.

Originally created to show the Elmhirsts' collection of early twentieth-century art, the exhibition spaces are now devoted to changing displays of contemporary art, including works by local artists.

BELOW The garden facade, showing the one curved wall and the rooftop sun terrace.

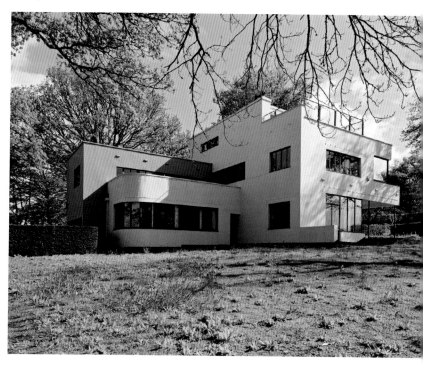

Hill Top

Cumbria
At Near Sawrey, behind the Tower Bank Arms

The young Beatrix Potter met virtually nobody and went almost nowhere. The one bright spot in a stifling existence with her domineering parents in London was the annual family holiday, in her early years to houses in Scotland, but from 1882, when she was 16, to the Lake District. These brief episodes, and the freedom they brought, fuelled a longing for the country which emerged in meticulously observed watercolours of wild creatures and plants and in the beginnings of the animal fantasies that have delighted children and adults for over a century.

Beatrix's purchase of this small, largely seventeenth-century farmhouse in 1905 was a momentous step. Presented to her parents as nothing more than a good investment (which it was), to their lonely 39-year-old daughter the rough stone building with a view over Sawrey to the fells beyond represented the possibility of escape from an increasingly dreary and unchanging regime. Although she was only able to snatch weeks here in the eight years that followed, this period was to see her best work, with the production of thirteen of the stories in which rabbits, mice, squirrels, hedgehogs and other creatures become humans in miniature, all of them illustrated with Beatrix's charming and individual paintings.

Anyone who has read these nursery classics will recognise Hill Top and its well-furnished, homely rooms, filled with accumulated clutter. The long sloping garden flanking the steep path to the house, with rows of vegetables on one side and a medley of traditional flowers on the other, is still as it appears in *The Tale of Tom Kitten* and *Pigling Bland*. The old-fashioned kitchen range with a black kettle bubbling away strikes a reassuring note in several animal holes and burrows, the nineteenth-century dresser is featured in *The Tale of Samuel Whiskers*, and the grandfather clock with a cheerful sun on its face was the model for the one in *The Tailor of Gloucester*. Peter Rabbit's red-spotted handkerchief and the doll's house food – dishes of oranges and pears and a large ham – stolen by Hunca Munca and Tom Thumb are in one of the upstairs rooms. Some grander pieces of furniture, striking an unexpected note, were acquired after Beatrix's mother died, and one of the bedrooms is hung with her brother Bertram's landscape paintings.

For the last 30 years of her life, during which she was contentedly married to William Heelis, a local solicitor, Beatrix lived as a prosperous farmer in the nearby Castle Cottage (not open), reserving Hill Top, which was kept unchanged, for those times when she wished to be alone with her memories. During this period, she became increasingly concerned about the conservation of the fells and began to buy land to save it from being broken up or developed. In 1895 her friend Canon Rawnsley founded the National Trust and her substantial landholdings, with their farmhouses and cottages, came to the Trust on the death of her husband in 1945.

BELOW The young Beatrix Potter with Spot the spaniel, one of the many family pets which she drew and painted from an early age and which fed her later animal creations.
OPPOSITE Hill Top, the small farmhouse in the Lake District which Beatrix Potter bought in 1905 and which is featured in many of her stories, is approached through a long, richly planted cottage garden.

Hinton Ampner

Hampshire
On the A272, 1 mile (1.6 kilometres) west of Bramdean village, 8 miles (12.8 kilometres) east of Winchester

Ralph Dutton, the 8th and last Lord Sherborne, was a man born long after his time. A true connoisseur, with a wide-ranging knowledge of architecture, interior decoration and gardening, and with the income to indulge his tastes, he would have been in his element in Georgian England. Given the very different world of the twentieth century, his achievements were remarkable. Inheriting a large Victorian mansion at Hinton Ampner, he remodelled it in 1936–9 to create a pleasing neo-Georgian house in warm red brick that would be a suitable setting for a distinguished collection of furniture, *objets* and paintings. A disastrous fire on 3 April 1960 almost completely destroyed the house and most of its contents. Undaunted, Ralph Dutton immediately set about rebuilding and refurnishing as beautifully as before.

Everything in the house has been chosen and placed to fulfil an overall vision. The elegant drawing room facing east and south, with a classical screen partitioning the northern end and opulent gold and sea-green wallpaper and curtains, is particularly pleasing. The furnishings are indicative of Ralph Dutton's taste. An inlaid English cabinet of about 1800 and a giltwood side table with a top of white marble and bluejohn that was once in Lord Curzon's house in Carlton House Terrace reveal his love of hardstones; so, too, do the marble roundels and sleeping putto and the porphyry chimneypiece and bust of Augustus Caesar, part of a collection of porphyry of which Ralph Dutton was particularly fond, in the hall.

Similarly, a landscape by Locatelli hanging above the cabinet in the drawing room and canvases by Pellegrini in the hall show Lord Sherborne's appreciation of Italian seventeenth- and eighteenth-century painting and of Venetian art in particular. Two disturbing pictures by Fuseli hang in Ralph Dutton's intimate sitting room, where almost everything was saved from the fire. Some pieces were purchased on his travels abroad, others acquired at auction, from dealers, or from houses that had been or were being demolished. Two marble fireplaces and three doors came from Robert Adam's Adelphi Terrace, which was destroyed, and the dining room has a reproduction of a plaster ceiling, with inset paintings, which Adam designed for a house in Berkeley Square.

The house is built near the top of a rise with the ground falling away gently to the south, a magnificent site that Ralph Dutton used to full advantage. As well as designing an individual formal garden, with long grassy walks and strategically placed eye-catchers, he also moulded a muddle of hedgerows and scattered trees beyond the garden into a carefully composed landscape park to create an idyllic foreground to views over unspoilt chalk countryside. A peaceful orchard marks the site of a Tudor manor that lay to the north of the present house and was demolished in the late eighteenth century.

OPPOSITE In remodelling the 'hideous' house he had inherited, Ralph Dutton set out to create a Georgian manor house, rebuilding again when fire destroyed his new home in 1960.
BELOW The comfortable library at Hinton Ampner, lined with the fine collection of books which Ralph Dutton put together after the fire, is furnished with Regency pieces and a Savonnerie carpet of c.1800.

The Homewood

Surrey
Portsmouth Road, Esher

Just outside Esher, set in a 2.8-hectare (7-acre) landscaped garden, is this striking and unusual country house. From the garden, it appears as a long white box on stilts, with an almost unbroken wall of glass lighting the first floor and open terraces either end. Inside, it is airy and spacious, with panoramic views of the garden and sliding glass doors leading onto a balcony. Completed in 1938, when the Modern Movement in Britain was still very much in its infancy, it is an early and important example of a house built under the influence of the continental avant-garde, in particular Le Corbusier and Mies van der Rohe (*see also* High Cross House, p.167). It was designed, for his parents, by the young Patrick Gwynne (1913–2003), who started working on the house when he was only 24. Gwynne had begun his architectural training with John Coleridge, a former assistant of Sir Edwin Lutyens, but, inspired by what was happening on the Continent, he had joined the practice of the pioneering modernist Wells Coates, where he was introduced to new construction techniques, using reinforced concrete, and cutting-edge design. By the time he started on The Homewood he had also seen key modernist buildings abroad and had studied Le Corbusier's iconic Villa Savoie, outside Paris, which was a major influence on his thinking.

For his parents, who took the courageous decision to entrust the building of the new house to their son, Gwynne combined modernist architecture with a concern for living that was to be a hallmark of all his residential work. The house is built of reinforced concrete with a flat roof and consists of two

OPPOSITE From the garden, the house looks like a white box on stilts, with a wall of glass lighting the main living area on the first floor.
ABOVE LEFT The Homewood was designed both for entertaining and for everyday living, with a cosy arrangement round the sitting-room fireplace for intimate evenings.
ABOVE RIGHT Gwynne's huge picture windows bring the garden into the house.

unequal wings joined to a central block. One wing holds the bedrooms; the other, staff quarters and service areas. There is a dramatic spiral staircase, lit from below by a sunken spotlight. As at the Villa Savoie, the main living area is on the first floor and is carried by slender columns and lit by huge windows looking onto the garden. Although uncompromisingly modern, the house is based on a classical system of proportions and has a pleasing sense of order and harmony.

The sophisticated interior shows Gwynne's attention to detail and materials. The living room is a multi-purpose space for relaxation and entertaining. The maple floor is sprung for dancing and doors to the dining room and balcony beyond can be pushed back to create one huge room. Sliding doors in an interior wall hide a drinks cabinet and gramophone, a drop-leg table swivels out to serve as a bar, and food can be passed through a hatch from the kitchen. For more private living, there is a cosy arrangement round the fireplace and two loungers placed by the window give views over the garden.

Stylish finishes include a wall of Levanto marble and tiny Murano glass wall tiles lining the hall. Gwynne also designed much of the furniture, including a writing desk that doubles as a drawing board and the Chinese lacquered book table, and there are many imaginative and witty touches, among them the round table in the dining room that has been provided with a central well for holding flowers or a low light.

The house owes much to its leafy setting, which was initially landscaped by Gwynne's father, and there is an oval pool designed by the young Denys Lasdun, with whom Gwynne worked at Wells Coates.

The Homewood was Gwynne's first independent commission. Returning to Esher after service with the RAF in the Second World War, Gwynne went on to design a series of private houses for distinguished clients, among them Charles Forte and Laurence Harvey, as well as a number of larger projects, such as the glass and concrete extension to the Gothic Theatre Royal in York and the Serpentine Restaurant in London's Hyde Park, where he used glass lavishly to give the impression that diners were eating al fresco. He continued to live at The Homewood after his parents died and in 1999 gave the house with the majority of its contents and the garden to the National Trust.

Hughenden

Buckinghamshire
1½ miles (2.4 kilometres) north of
High Wycombe, on the west side
of the Great Missenden road

The six years of Tory government from 1874 saw some of the greatest successes enjoyed by any ministry of Queen Victoria's reign, including progressive social reforms and an imperialist foreign policy that gained the queen the title of Empress of India. These achievements owed much to the vision, skill and persuasive passion of the Prime Minister, Benjamin Disraeli, who was already 70 when the new parliament began. His greatest international triumph, which earned him the admiration of Bismarck, was at the Congress of Berlin in 1878, where Disraeli's diplomatic skills were largely responsible for a settlement that checked Russian expansionism, one of the key issues of the day. A writer as well as a politician, his radical domestic policies had been foreshadowed some 30 years earlier in his political novels, *Coningsby* and *Sybil*, which were concerned with the condition of the rural and urban poor.

Disraeli had acquired Hughenden in 1848, the year after his election as MP for Buckingham and the year before he became leader of the Conservative Party. At a time when political power was largely in the hands of the landed aristocracy, he had increasingly felt the need for an estate to bolster his political ambitions, but he had only been able to make the purchase with the help of Lord Bentinck and his brothers, who loaned two-thirds of the sum involved. The grandson of an Italian Jew who had come to England looking for work, Disraeli had little in the way of financial resources himself.

Disraeli and his wife Mary Anne, twelve years his senior, lived at Hughenden until their deaths, in 1881 and 1872 respectively. The plain, three-storey Georgian house they acquired was gothicised with the help of Edward Buckton Lamb, who has been described as one of the most perverse and original architects of his day. Stucco was removed to reveal the blue and red brickwork behind, stepped battlements

and pinnacles were added and the interior was enhanced with plaster vaulting and grained woodwork. Because of alterations by Disraeli's nephew Coningsby, who inherited the house, and the sale of some of the contents, Hughenden is no longer as the Disraelis had it, but the richly coloured High Victorian interiors reproduce some of their decorative schemes, such as the deep red walls of the hall and staircase, and portraits that were here in Disraeli's day, of friends and those Disraeli admired, as well as of close family, and original furnishings can be seen in almost every room.

Francis Grant's likeness of the great man, painted in 1852, presides over what is now the library, where wall-to-ceiling shelves hold works by Disraeli's father, the novelist and poet Isaac D'Israeli, as well as by Disraeli himself. A marble foot on the desk is a copy of Mary Anne's left foot and two plaster statuettes on the mantelpiece, one depicting the faithful John Brown, were a gift from Queen Victoria, who became genuinely fond of Disraeli. The sombre, north-facing dining room is where Victoria was treated to lunch in 1877, the legs of her chair cut down so her feet could reach the floor. Upstairs, the Disraelis' sunny, south-facing bedroom, all yellow and white, has been re-created with the help of the 1881 inventory and the study where he conducted a lively correspondence and worked on his last three novels is largely as he left it. Watercolour portraits of his parents hang over the mantelpiece, the black-edged notepaper that he always used after his wife's death lies ready on his desk and his red dispatch box is to hand.

Hughenden stands high above a steep Chiltern valley, looking out over parkland and ancient woods. An obelisk on a near hillside, erected by Mary Anne in 1852 in memory of Disraeli's father, would have reminded him of the two people who influenced him most and his writings show how he loved this place, valuing the solitude and escape it offered. Disraeli never let political ambition destroy his humanity and he was the only premier other than Melbourne to be honoured with a visit from the queen.

In recent years, Hughenden's vital secret role in the Second World War has come to light. Requisitioned by the Air Ministry in 1941 and renamed Hillside, the house was used to produce maps for night-time bombing missions, among them

ABOVE Disraeli turned the arcade on Hughenden's entrance front into a conservatory and filled it with 'marble vases, busts, ferns and flowers'.
OPPOSITE, TOP This portrait of Disraeli by Sir Francis Grant, painted in 1852, hangs in the library.
OPPOSITE, BOTTOM When the Disraelis came to Hughenden in 1848, they set about giving the house a fashionable Gothic flavour and inserted ribbed and vaulted plaster ceilings in several of the rooms.

the Dam Busters raid and the operation to sink the battleship *Tirpitz*. A hundred people were stationed in the house, and the maps they produced were dispatched at night in trucks that were kept in the stable yard. A basement room is now devoted to this riveting period in Hughenden's history and Disraeli's ice-house in the grounds, where the maps were photographed, has been fitted out to evoke its wartime role. A vast air-raid shelter carved out of the hill below for the use of those working here has been colonised by bats.

Ickworth

Suffolk
In Horringer, 3 miles
(4.8 kilometres) south-west of
Bury St Edmunds on the west side
of the A143

Frederick Augustus Hervey, 4th Earl of Bristol, must rank as one of the Church's more remarkable bishops. Appointed to the see of Derry, the richest in Ireland, in 1768 when only 38, his sympathy with both Roman Catholics and Presbyterians made him enormously popular, despite a sometimes light-hearted approach to his duties which once led him to organise a curates' race along the sands at Downhill (*see* p.121), rewarding the winners with vacant benefices.

A large income coupled with an inherited fortune allowed the 4th Earl to embark on extensive foreign tours, now commemorated in Hotels Bristol all over the Continent, during which he amassed the works of art he intended to display in his new house on the family's Suffolk estate.

Ickworth is as grandiose and flamboyant as its creator. A larger version of the 4th Earl's earlier house at Ballyscullion, it was inspired, like the little Mussenden Temple at Downhill, by the circular Belle Isle on an island in Windermere. A huge domed rotunda decorated with classical columns and terracotta friezes is linked by curving corridors to rectangular wings, the whole building stretching some 183 metres (600 feet) from end to end. But Frederick was never to see his house completed. Work on Ickworth began in 1795 to the designs of the Italian architect Mario Asprucci the Younger, but came to a halt on the 4th Earl's death from gout in an outhouse in Italy in 1803 (from where his body was shipped back to England, labelled as an antique statue). Tragically, the bishop had had his magnificent collection appropriated by Napoleonic troops in Rome in 1798.

The 4th Earl's ambitious plans were realised by his son, created 1st Marquess of Bristol in 1826. The superb paintings, porcelain and furniture now displayed here largely represent the slow accumulation of several generations of Herveys, who have owned the estate since the mid-fifteenth century. Many followed brilliant political careers, as did Frederick's gifted eldest brother George, the 2nd Earl, who acquired gilt furniture and paintings while he was on diplomatic postings to Turin and Madrid. It was the 1st Earl, Frederick's grandfather, another prominent politician, who bought the early eighteenth-century Huguenot pieces among the silver displayed in the Museum Room, the relatively restrained hand of Paul de Lamerie contrasting with more ornate rococo Italian work. One case here is devoted to a shoal of silver fish, some designed as ornamental pendants, others as scent containers, their realistic, scaly forms including a whale and a swordfish as well as more mundane species. The landing outside is used to show some of the fan collection acquired by Geraldine Anson, who married the 3rd Marquess.

The 1st Marquess housed the bulk of the collection in the grand state rooms in the rotunda rather than in the wings, as his father had intended. The largest room in the house is the hemispherical library across the south front, notable for its rare late seventeenth- and early eighteenth-century political periodicals and ornamented with busts of Pitt, Canning, Fox and Liverpool and Benjamin West's portrayal of the death of General Wolfe, which the artist painted specially for the Earl-Bishop. Hogarth's *Holland House Group* in the Smoking Room, showing Frederick's father, Lord Hervey, in the centre of a group of friends that includes the 3rd Duke of Marlborough, is one of a number of outstanding portraits in the house. A painting of a grave little boy with two greyhounds and a huge mastiff at his feet is Velázquez's study of the Infante Balthasar Carlos, son of Philip IV of Spain, and there is a full-length canvas by Gainsborough of the colourful Augustus John Hervey, Vice Admiral of the Blue, who briefly succeeded as 3rd Earl between his two brothers. It seems this philanderer deserved his wife, Elizabeth Chudleigh, whose bigamous marriage with the Duke of Kingston in 1769 gave rise to one of the most famous scandals of the eighteenth century. Quite different in character is the charming self-portrait by Madame Vigée Lebrun, commissioned by the Earl-Bishop in Naples in 1791, the artist's severe black dress setting off a vivacious face crowned with a mop of curly hair that is loosely caught up in a white handkerchief. The most extraordinary exhibit is Flaxman's marble group, *The Fury of Athamas*, based on a scene from Ovid's *Metamorphoses*, which dominates the staircase hall. Commissioned by the 4th Earl, Athamas is here shown holding his young son over his shoulder by an ankle, about to dash him to death. A second child clings to their mother, terrified.

From the 1st Marquess's orangery, the only part of the west

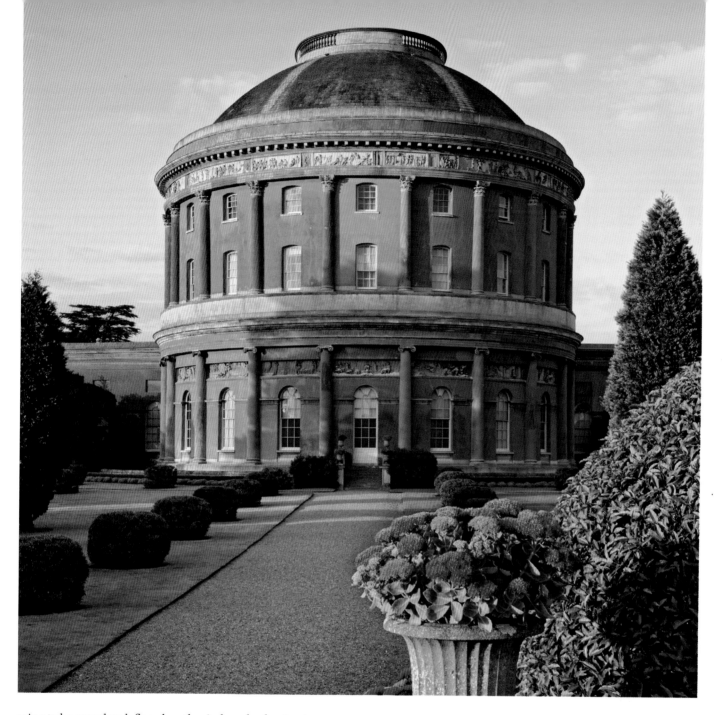

wing to be completed, floor-length windows lead out onto a terrace looking south over the heavily wooded garden, where tall cypresses, yews, evergreen oak and box create the illusion of an Italian landscape. Artfully contrived vistas give enticing glimpses of the rotunda. From the long raised terrace walk beyond the trees, created in *c*.1870 to shield the garden, there is a sweeping panorama over clumps of mature beeches and oaks in the park, many of them probably planted by

ABOVE The rotunda as seen from the garden. Asprucci's designs for Ickworth, sent from Italy, were executed by Francis Sandys, who simplified them.

'Capability' Brown for the 2nd Earl. In the foreground, partly hidden in a dip, is Ickworth church, while an obelisk just visible above a wooded ridge on the far horizon was erected by the people of Derry in affectionate memory of their bishop.

Ightham Mote

Kent
6 miles (9.6 kilometres) east of
Sevenoaks, off the A25, and
2½ miles (4 kilometres) south
of Ightham, off the A227

A steep path from the car park leads down to this magical house set in a deep, wooded valley in the Kentish Weald, its walls rising sheer from a surrounding moat. Half-timbered upper storeys project from the facade here and there, a little hump-backed stone bridge crosses the water to an old wooden door, and the roofline is a medley of steeply pitched gables, massive brick chimneys and moss-stained tiles. Ducks paddle about beneath the walls.

Built round three courtyards and dating originally from the 1320s, Ightham Mote has retained its medieval appearance, despite many later alterations, because additions were piecemeal, were always made using local oak and Kentish ragstone and were sympathetic to the ancient building. The great hall filling one side of the cobbled main courtyard was the core of the early house and still has its early fourteenth-century timber roof. Tudor improvements, when the house was owned by the courtier Richard Clement, account for the armorial glass inserted as a tribute to Henry VIII in the great window of the hall. The Tudor rose and the pomegranate of Catherine of Aragon, the king's first wife, which appear both here and on richly carved oak bargeboards facing onto the courtyard, must have been in place well before Henry cast Catherine aside and married Anne Boleyn in 1533, a ceremony at which Richard Clement officiated.

Sir Richard Clement was also responsible for decorating the long, half-timbered room on the first floor that is now a chapel, but was probably originally designed as a grand guest chamber. Its arched barrel roof is exuberantly painted, again in honour of Henry and Catherine, with vividly coloured badges and emblems in red, orange, green and white representing the royal houses of England, Spain and France. The colours have faded now, but it is easy to imagine how glowing they must once have been. The room appears to have become a chapel in the 1630s and seems to have been fitted out gradually, resulting in a beautiful array of fine woodwork – linenfold panelling, a richly carved pulpit, choir stalls and pews – of various dates. There is sixteenth-century stained glass in the windows and a remarkable late fifteenth-century oak door at the west end.

Across a landing from the chapel is the drawing room and a startling change in atmosphere and style. The room is dominated by a monumental Jacobean fireplace decorated with carved Saracen heads and painted in black and gold, and is lit by an eighteenth-century Venetian window. The walls are covered in hand-painted Chinese wallpaper of c.1800 and the room as a whole has a distinctly exotic flavour, although, as in the rest of the house, the furniture, with the exception of a few pieces, has been added since 1951, when the original contents were sold.

The drawing room fills one end of the early fourteenth-century west range. On the other side of a central gatehouse tower are the simply furnished bedroom and dressing room that were used by Charles Henry Robinson, the American bachelor who bought Ightham Mote in 1953, having spotted a sale advertisement in a back number of *Country Life*, and gave it to the National Trust in 1985. The library, with its alcove bookshelves, is also as he had it. His desk sits in one of the alcoves and the pictures include drawings of his house in Maine.

An extensive lawn stretches up the combe north of the house, its regular outlines marking the site of a medieval stewpond that was once fed by the stream that now tumbles over a cascade and crosses the grass to fill the moat and a lake below the house. A raised walk fringing the lawn leads to another lake hidden in the trees beyond. Near the house a long border is crowded with traditional English flowers and there is a paved Fountain Garden. This consciously old-fashioned garden, based on a medieval layout, reflects the late nineteenth-century's romantic view of the Middle Ages and also the influence of William Morris's Arts and Crafts movement (*see also* Red House, p.271). There are romantic views of the house from walks through the woodland and always there is the constant sound of running water, like soothing background music.

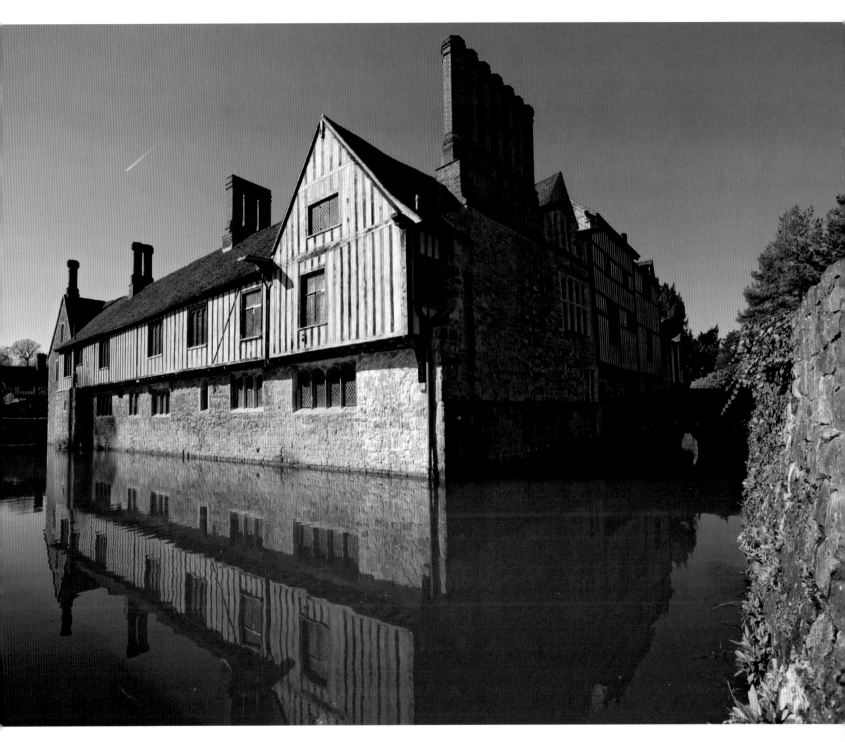

OPPOSITE A half-timbered range overlooking the cobbled courtyard at the heart of Ightham Mote has bargeboards carved with the emblems of Henry VIII and his first wife, Catherine of Aragon.
ABOVE The south front of the house dates from the late fifteenth or early sixteenth century, but the upper storey was given its attractive 'Tudor' studding only in c.1904.

Kedleston Hall

Derbyshire
3 miles (4.8 kilometres) north
of Derby, easily reached and
signposted from the A38
Derby bypass

No one could describe this grand Neo-classical palace as homely. But then, it was always intended as a show place. On the impressive entrance front, looking north over a sweep of open pasture, a massive pedimented portico adorned with classical sculpture rises the full height of the three-storey central block. To either side are substantial rectangular pavilions, linked to the main building by curved corridors. A tower peeping above the west pavilion flags a medieval church, all that remains of the village swept away when the landscape park was created.

Sir Nathaniel Curzon, later 1st Lord Scarsdale, began the house in 1759, only a year after he had inherited the estate. A cultivated man who was interested in the arts, he saw it as a setting for his paintings and sculpture, a collection that was on view to visitors from the day the house was built. The formal reception rooms and guest suite filling the central block were never intended to be used except for the entertainment of important visitors. The family lived in one pavilion; the kitchen and domestic offices were in the other.

Although work began under the direction of Matthew Brettingham and James Paine, by 1760 these two architects had been superseded by the young Robert Adam, recently returned from Rome, who transformed his predecessors' rather conventional designs. Adam's monumental Marble Hall, with ten alabaster columns like tree-trunks on both sides and classical statues in niches along the walls, is top-lit to suggest the open courtyard of a Roman villa. The adjoining rotunda known as the Saloon, its coffered dome rising to a height of 19 metres (62 feet), was based on the Pantheon in Rome, one of the most admired buildings of classical antiquity. To either side lie formal reception rooms, Adam's hand evident in virtually every detail of their decoration. Delicate plaster ceilings were executed by the Yorkshireman Joseph Rose, paintings were grouped and hung according to Adam's schemes – plaster frames built into the walls in some rooms ensure his arrangements have survived – and the furniture, some of it by Adam, some designed by the London cabinetmaker John Linnell, some with inputs from both men, picks up on decorative themes. In the State Withdrawing

ABOVE Robert Adam designed a dramatic portico resembling a Greek temple for Kedleston's north front, with a windowless facade ornamented with lead figures in niches and carved stone medallions as a backdrop to the columns.

Room, carved and gilded dolphins, merfolk and sea nymphs on the four great sofas echo nautical touches in the ceiling. Made by Linnell, they are based on an Adam design, but one that Linnell radically altered.

The paintings hanging double-banked in all the principal rooms, including a number of epic canvases such as

ABOVE In the Music Room, Adam took great care over the arrangement of the paintings, many of which hang in his fitted plaster frames.

Benedetto Luti's *Cain and Abel* or Salomon Koninck's *Daniel before Nebuchadnezzar*, illustrate Lord Curzon's taste for seventeenth-century Italian and Dutch art. Family portraits dating back to the sixteenth century adorn the guest apartments, among them a charming study by Nathaniel Hone showing the 1st Lord Scarsdale walking in the grounds with his wife. Thomas Barber's portrayal of the elderly Mrs Garnett, the housekeeper who took Boswell and Dr Johnson round Kedleston in 1777, is also memorable.

Bluejohn vases and ornaments are part of a notable collection of this prized Derbyshire stone, and Kedleston was further enriched in the early twentieth century by Marquess Curzon of Kedleston, who acquired Indian and oriental artefacts during travels in Asia and while he was Viceroy of India from 1899 to 1905. In his will, the marquess left half the collection to the Victoria and Albert museum. The other half, on show in the house, is dominated by the peacock dress that was worn by Lady Curzon, its pattern of glistening peacock feathers created by embroidering cloth of gold with metal thread and jewels.

The long drive from the great arched gateway of Adam's north lodge runs through his idealised landscape park, with its carefully placed clumps of trees and a chain of serpentine lakes crossed by a three-arched stone bridge. Adam also designed the fishing pavilion on the upper lake, a Venetian window facing north over the water enabling ladies to cast a line into the pool below while being shielded from the sun.

To the south of the house, a broad open lawn bounded by a ha-ha marks the eighteenth-century informal garden and there are uninterrupted views across the park beyond as it rises gently to a belt of trees. A hexagonal summerhouse and orangery were both designed by George Richardson in the late eighteenth century and a pair of gates leads into a winding 3-mile (4.8-kilometre) circuit of the park, with views back towards the house from the section following the wooded skyline.

Killerton

Devon
On the west side of the B3181,
formerly the A38,
Exeter–Cullompton road

Below the steep wooded slopes of Killerton Clump, the highest point for miles around, is the sprawling, two-storey house of the Acland family. Later additions mask the plain Georgian block that was built in 1778–9 for Sir Thomas Dyke Acland, 7th Baronet, by the architect John Johnson to replace an Elizabethan house on more or less the same site. This house was only intended to be a temporary residence while a grandiose mansion by the much more fashionable James Wyatt was built on the hill, but Wyatt's plans never got further than the drawing board, and Johnson's modest building ended up being considerably expanded in the early nineteenth century and again in Edwardian times. At the foot of the drive are his magnificent stone stables, with an elegant cupola rising over the pedimented archway leading into the courtyard. Another Sir Thomas, the 10th Baronet, was responsible for the Victorian Norman Revival chapel by C.R. Cockerell to the north of the stables. This was built to supersede the tiny Elizabethan building on the other side of the hill that is almost all that remains of a former Acland seat at Columbjohn.

Killerton's interiors, much altered over the years and as unpretentious as the exterior, reflect domestic life and country living between the First and Second World Wars. A music room in the centre of the house, lit by a window bay added in the 1820s, was the main focus of family activities. Music by Samuel Sebastian Wesley on the chamber organ that dominates the room is dedicated to the wife of the 10th Baronet, who took lessons from Wesley when he was organist of Exeter Cathedral. Dinner in the dining room on the west front, looking onto the garden, was always eaten in evening dress, with bare arms for the ladies however cold the weather and a place near the fire for the most privileged. The room is decorated with Johnson's eighteenth-century plaster frieze and with two terracotta roundels by the Danish sculptor Bertel Thorvaldsen, and it is hung with family portraits celebrating the 6th Baronet's advantageous marriage, to the heiress Cecily Wroth, in 1721. Wooden columns frame a connecting door to the library, where the books now include some of those that belonged to the Rev. Sabine Baring-Gould (1834–1924), the larger-than-life parson of

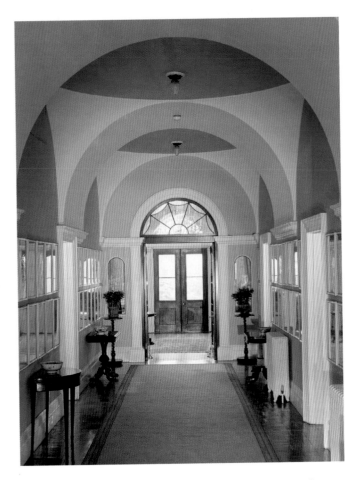

ABOVE The elegant corridor leading to Killerton's original front door, on the south side of the house, has eighteenth-century fanlights designed by John Johnson and is little changed.

the Devon village of Lewtrenchard, best known for his hymn 'Onward Christian Soldiers'. In a corner of the room is a set of false book-backs with fanciful titles.

A massive Edwardian staircase leads to the second floor and the rooms used to display the costume collection of Paulise de Bush, who rescued many eighteenth- and nineteenth-century items from a house in Berkshire during the Second World War. The changing displays feature carefully composed tableaux to show the life and society of the day.

Sir Thomas Dyke Acland, who built the Georgian house, also engaged the young John Veitch – he was not yet 21 – to lay out the grounds. Veitch, who went on to become one of the greatest nurserymen and landscape designers of his day and

ABOVE The modest Georgian house which forms the core of Killerton (right) was greatly extended in the 1820s by Sir Thomas Acland, who built new rooms for his children with direct access to the garden.

had a life-long association with Killerton, planted an arboretum on the slopes of Killerton Clump with paths climbing ever upwards through the trees and a beech walk following the contours of the hill.

The 10th Baronet, who presided over Killerton from his coming of age in 1808 and who did so much to create this exceptional place, is remembered by the granite cross that stands high up on the western edge of the garden and which was erected by 40 of his friends in 1873.

Killerton sits at the centre of an extensive estate in the fertile valleys of the Clyst and Culm. A mix of farmland and sizeable areas of woodland, it also includes the villages of Broadclyst and Budlake. There are many traditional buildings, among them Marker's Cottage in Broadclyst, a small cob and thatch house dating back to the fifteenth century which has a contemporary cob summerhouse and some mid-sixteenth-century paintings on a wooden screen. A few minutes' walk away, on the River Clyst, is the working Clyston Mill, probably built in the early nineteenth century but occupying an ancient site, and half a mile (0.8 kilometre) north up the B3181 is Budlake village, where a small thatched cottage still has its 1950s Post Office Room.

Kingston Lacy

Dorset
On the B3082
Wimborne–Blandford road,
1½ miles (2.4 kilometres)
west of Wimborne

Home of the Bankes family from 1663, when Sir Ralph Bankes built a house here to replace the earlier seat at Corfe Castle (*see* p.106), ruined in the Civil War, Kingston Lacy is a monument to the eccentric and original William John Bankes (1786–1855), friend of Byron. With the aid of Sir Charles Barry, architect of the Houses of Parliament, William transformed the house into an Italianate palazzo and filled it with paintings and other works of art he had acquired during his extensive travels in the Mediterranean. But he had little opportunity to enjoy what he

had created. In 1841 he was accused of behaving indecently with a soldier in a London park and he fled to Italy, where he spent the rest of his life. Nevertheless, although unlikely ever to see his house again, this extraordinary man continued to concern himself with its furnishing and decoration.

Kingston Lacy still retains the shape of the double-pile Restoration mansion built by Sir Roger Pratt for Ralph Bankes, but has been much altered. The hipped roof, pierced by prominent dormers, is crowned with a balustrade and cupola by Barry and his tall chimneys at each corner give the house the look of an upturned footstool. On the south front, Barry's broad Italianate terrace sweeps right across the facade, with central steps flanked by urns and guarded by lions descending to a lawn dotted with Venetian well-heads. His impressive marble staircase leading up to the principal rooms on the first floor is also of Italian inspiration. Bronze figures set in niches in the airy loggia on the half-landing include a depiction of brave Lady Mary Bankes, who twice defended Corfe Castle for Charles I in the Civil War. She is shown holding the key of the castle, the actual keys to which are displayed over the fireplace in the library.

No traces of Roger Pratt's house survive inside, but some rooms still remain from R.F. Brettingham's remodelling in the 1780s for Henry Bankes. The painted ceiling by Cornelius Dixon in the saloon arches over the room like elaborate wrapping paper, delicate curves and spirals of foliage echoing the rich floral borders on the opulent Savonnerie carpet. The paintings hanging two and three deep include Rubens's portraits of Maria Pallavicino and Maria Grimaldi that were acquired by William: one encased in her gleaming wedding-dress like an exotic beetle, the other pictured with her dwarf. The library, with a fine collection of leather-bound books dating from the mid-seventeenth century, is also largely as designed by Brettingham. Now returned to the layout and decorative scheme shown in a photograph of 1904, this room is dominated by a ceiling painting by Guido Reni that William Bankes acquired from a palazzo in Bologna in 1840. Executed in 1599, the painting illustrates the description of the first day in Genesis, when the darkness was separated from the light, and is a rare example of Reni's early work. Taken down from the ceiling when the National Trust took over Kingston Lacy in 1981, this fragile painting, one of the most significant in the house, was stripped of nineteenth-century retouching and painstakingly restored in 2007.

More recently, in 2010, a vast mythical painting by Tintoretto was restored and put on display for the first time in the dining room. Painted in 1570–9, it was probably acquired by Bankes from a Venetian palazzo and, like the Guido Reni, has been in store since 1981. Sebastiano del Piombo's unfinished *The Judgement of Solomon*, which hangs nearby, was painted about 50 years earlier and was probably also intended for a Venetian setting.

While the dining-room panelling dates from the late nineteenth century, the adjoining Spanish Room is as William created it, with works he procured during his travels in Spain at the time of the Peninsular War set against gilded leather hangings and seen beneath a sumptuous coffered ceiling, thought to be one of those Scamozzi added to the Palazzo Contarini on the Grand Canal in Venice. Papal power and splendour shine through Velázquez's portrait of Cardinal Massimi, clothed here in peacock blue.

A naturalistic late eighteenth-century landscape park, dotted with mature trees and grazed by North Devon cattle, surrounds the house. The Edwardian garden restored by the Trust includes a brightly coloured parterre to the west of the house and a Victorian fernery to the east. A cedar walk lined with trees planted by visiting notables, including the Duke of Wellington, leads to the lime avenue and an arboretum beyond. A pink granite obelisk, one of four in the garden, was brought here by William Bankes from a temple on the Nile.

Kingston Lacy is also the centre of an extensive agricultural estate in the valley of the River Stour. Including some fourteen farms and parts of the villages of Shapwick and Pamphill, this is a historic rural landscape, dotted with earthworks and rich in vernacular buildings. White Mill, a substantial brick and tile corn-mill on the Stour, was largely rebuilt in 1776 but is probably on the site of one of the eight mills recorded on the river in Domesday Book. It still has its original and now very rare elm and applewood machinery.

LEFT The east front of Kingston Lacy looks out over a formal Dutch garden, with balls of golden yew, which was laid out in 1899.
RIGHT The upper flight of Barry's grand marble staircase linking the principal floors turns round a copy of a Roman marble candelabrum.

Knightshayes

Devon
2 miles north of Tiverton
on the A396

The drunken mob that destroyed his Leicestershire factory on 28 June 1816 prompted the young John Heathcoat to move his revolutionary new lace-making machines to the safety of Devon, where he set up his works in one of the Tiverton mills left empty by the decline of the wool industry. The profits from what was to become the largest lace factory in the world enabled his grandson, John Heathcoat-Amory, the 1st Baronet, to purchase the Knightshayes estate and to build the idiosyncratic Gothic house that overlooks the little town in the valley below. Dating from 1869 to 1874, it is a singular place. Built of dark-red Hensley stone, the house rises forbiddingly from the terraces to the right of the drive in a frontage of pointed gables, large mullioned windows and prominent gargoyles.

A rare example of the domestic architecture of William Burges, the High Victorian medievalist who is much better known for his churches, such as the masterpiece at Studley Royal (*see* p.141), this rather dour exterior was planned to conceal interiors of exceptional richness. Although Burges's designs were mostly rejected by his client, who thought them too extreme, the schemes produced by his more conventional replacement, John Diblee Crace, were by no means subdued and, too bold and colourful for Sir John's taste, were largely covered up in later years. Where possible, the National Trust has sought to restore the nineteenth-century work. Maxims by Robert Burns in bold gold lettering run round the frieze in the dining room, where rich red and green wallpaper designed by Crace complements the dark half-panelling. Above is a

LEFT The Gothic south front of Knightshayes, with its gables and gargoyles and an oriel window tucked into an angle of the facade, looks over formal terraced gardens on this side of the house.
ABOVE RIGHT The boudoir ceiling, with its zodiac roundels, was repainted in 1981 by Ian Cairnie, who based his work closely on a scheme by Crace.
RIGHT A portrait of Alexandra Seymour, Lady Heathcoat Amory, who gave Knightshayes to the Trust, hangs over the fireplace in the boudoir.

beamed and painted ceiling supported on corbels carved with creatures from the Devon countryside: a badger, a fox and an otter with a fish. The medievalism of the hall, with its Gothic arches, gallery, timber vault and whimsical carvings, is even more striking. This was the only room to be completed largely as Burges planned, and he also designed the painted bookcase with panels by Burne-Jones and Rossetti that stands here and is on loan from the Ashmolean Museum in Oxford. Recently, too, a bedroom has been decorated on the basis of his original drawings and shows clearly the richness of his planned interiors. A wide painted frieze filled with birds perched on stylised branches echoes a motif used by Burges at his London house and a golden bed and painted cabinets, all on loan from the Victoria and Albert Museum, were also made to his designs.

The drawing room and morning room, both of which have boldly painted, compartmental ceilings, are hung with the nucleus of the art collection acquired in the years after the Second World War, when Knightshayes became a convalescent home for American airmen, by the 3rd Baronet (1894–1972) and his wife, the former golfing champion Joyce Wethered, whom Sir John had married in 1937. Vivid red poppies like a scarlet splash on the wall are one of two flower pictures attributed to Constable, a misty river scene in Picardy by Richard Parkes Bonington is complemented by a copy of a Turner seascape, and a Madonna and Child by Matteo di Giovanni is one of a number of early religious works. The original fireplace having been lost, the restored nineteenth-century decoration in the drawing room is now set off by a massive carved marble chimneypiece which was designed by Burges for Worcester College, Oxford, where it remained until 1966, and which the college has given to the Trust.

Although based on a nineteenth-century design by Edward Kemp, the garden owes much to the 3rd Baronet and his wife, who greatly enlarged it, creating the extensive woodland garden, and made it one of the finest in the county. A formal layout near the house includes a water-lily pool in a battlemented yew enclosure and a topiary hunt on the hedges framing the lawn to the south, one of the pursuing hounds shown gathering itself to leap a leafy obstacle. West of the house, a little valley has a show of daffodils in spring, and there is a large walled kitchen garden, with unique stepped walls, which was designed by Burges.

Knole

Kent
At the south end of Sevenoaks,
just east of the A225

A sudden opening between the buildings lining the main A225 through Sevenoaks signals the unpretentious gateway to Knole. The drive from this modest entrance emerges unexpectedly into the glorious park surrounding the house, scored with deep valleys, planted with ancient oaks, beeches and chestnuts, and grazed by herds of fallow and sika deer. As the road breasts a rise, there is a view of what looks like a compact hilltop town, with rabbit-cropped turf running almost up to the walls and a jumble of chimneys, gables, battlements and red-tiled roofs rising behind.

Sprawled round several courtyards like an Oxford college, Knole could house the retinue of a medieval prince. The main ranges are of rough Kentish ragstone, but hidden away in some of the minor courts are half-timbered facades, like those that can be seen in a hundred villages round about. Inside, in contrast to the rather plain and rugged exterior, are furnishings and decoration of great richness and rarity.

The core of Knole was built by Thomas Bourchier, Archbishop of Canterbury, between 1456 and his death in

1486, when he bequeathed it to the see of Canterbury. Three more archbishops enjoyed and improved the splendid residence Bourchier had created before Archbishop Cranmer was forced to give it to Henry VIII in 1538. By this time, Knole had been enlarged by the addition of an outer courtyard with a turreted gatehouse, but it seems the covetous king spent little or no time here. Knole was later held briefly by Elizabeth I's favourite, the Earl of Leicester, but by 1605 the freehold of the house and estate had been acquired by the late queen's cousin Thomas Sackville, the 1st Earl of Dorset, who had also been Elizabeth I's Lord Treasurer (a post to which he was

ABOVE Knole's Spangle Bedroom takes its name from the sequins on the bed hangings, now blackened but once silver, and is lined with fine Jacobean panelling and seventeenth-century Brussels tapestries.
OPPOSITE Knole's long west front looking over the park, with its massive brick chimneystacks and turreted gatehouse, probably dates from the late 1400s, although the curved gables were later embellishments.

reappointed by James I), and the earl's descendants, later Dukes of Dorset and then Lords Sackville, have lived here ever since. The 1st Earl transformed Knole, turning the medieval and Tudor palace into a Renaissance mansion. He employed James I's master plasterer, Richard Dungan, and, probably, the king's master carpenter, William Portington, to create the Jacobean ceiling and intricate carved screen in the great hall, and he established a series of state apartments on the first floor, each with its own long gallery, connecting them to the hall with a grand staircase decorated in grisaille.

All this remains, and in the late seventeenth century, after depredations during the Civil War, when Knole and its lands were seized and the contents largely sold, the house was filled with an outstanding collection of seventeenth-century furniture and textiles by the 6th Earl. As Lord Chamberlain to William III, the earl was entitled to take away discarded furnishings from the royal palaces and he also enriched Knole with the furniture acquired by his grandfather, the Earl of Middlesex, who was Master of the Great Wardrobe to James I. As a result, Knole's galleries and bedchambers are filled with state beds, tapestries, chairs and stools that would once have adorned the palaces of Whitehall, Hampton Court and Kensington. Blue damask chairs in the Brown Gallery are stamped WP for Whitehall Palace, brass locks in the Cartoon Gallery carry William III's monogram, and a state bed hung with watery green Genoa velvet that was made for James II may have been the one in which the king spent his last night in Whitehall Palace, on 17 December 1688, before fleeing to

exile in France. Some of the rarest and finest pieces are displayed in the King's Room. A silver looking-glass, table and candlestands shine brilliantly in simulated candlelight, drawing the eye away from the magnificent great bed with its cloth of silver and gold and matching chairs and stools.

In the late eighteenth century, Knole was enriched again by the cultivated and handsome 3rd Duke, who added a notable picture collection of his own to the many paintings already in the house, among them portraits by Mytens, Dobson and Van Dyck from the early seventeenth century and John Wootton's panoramic landscape in the great hall, showing the 1st Duke and his retinue arriving at Dover Castle in 1728, its period frame adorned with two prominent Sackville leopards. The 3rd Duke acquired a number of Old Masters and patronised English painters of his day, in particular his close friend Joshua Reynolds, whose many canvases at Knole, most of them hung two deep in the Crimson Drawing Room, include a self-portrait, which Reynolds gave to the duke, and likenesses of Samuel Johnson and the playwright and poet Oliver Goldsmith and of the Duke's Chinese page. In an age when great houses all over the country were being remodelled in the newly fashionable classical style, the 3rd Duke also stands out for his appreciation of the ancient mansion he had inherited, which he did not alter and, less exceptionally, for his long relationship with the Italian dancer Giovanna Baccelli, who is immortalised in a plaster statue at the foot of the grand staircase, where her nude form, introduced at one time as that of 'a close friend of the family', reclines provocatively on a couple of tasselled plaster cushions.

This remarkable house is still much as it was in the 3rd Duke's day and has something to fascinate in every corner. Even the drainpipes have ornate leadwork heads, some in the form of a tiny castle, each one subtly individual. And each gable on the entrance front is crowned with a carved Sackville leopard. A major programme of building and conservation work that started in 2012 has closed parts of the house, but visitors can see newly opened rooms and work in progress.

LEFT Knole's Brown Gallery is hung with a set of sixteenth- and early seventeenth-century portraits showing famous people of the age and lined with chairs and stools acquired from royal palaces by the 6th Earl.
ABOVE RIGHT Shell-backed chairs dating from the 1630s in the Stone Gallery are painted with the lion of the Talbots, who lived at Lacock for centuries.

Lacock Abbey, Fox Talbot Museum and Village

Wiltshire
3 miles (4.8 kilometres) south of Chippenham, just east of the A350

This romantic house, with ranges of golden stone set round a grassy court, lies in a leafy pastoral setting beside the River Avon. Twisted Tudor chimneys break the roofline and a prominent octagonal tower juts out at one corner. This unusual and evocative place has a history going back almost 800 years, with many echoes of the nunnery for Augustinian canonesses founded in 1232 by the redoubtable Ela, Countess of Salisbury, in memory of her husband William Longespee. At its suppression by Henry VIII's commissioners in 1539, the nunnery was acquired by the duplicitous and self-seeking William Sharington, a rather unattractive man who seems to have behaved with more than the usual dishonesty in his public life, but who showed both sensitivity and imagination in converting his purchase into a house. Although he demolished the abbey church, the outlines of which are now marked by long grass in the south lawn, Sharington kept many of the nunnery's original rooms and also incorporated innovative Renaissance features that were rare in England at this date. Beautiful fifteenth-century cloisters, with carved bosses punctuating the stone vaulting, still frame the court at the heart of the house. The daughters of well-to-do families who formed the community sunned themselves on the stone seats set into the walls or stretched out their hands to the blaze in the great fireplace preserved in the warming room, one of a set of fine, mostly stone-vaulted thirteenth-century chambers, including the sacristy and chapter house, opening onto the east cloister walk. The ghost of the nunnery is also evident in the thirteenth-century vaulted undercroft in the west range, part of which became the servants' hall; in a huge blocked medieval fireplace in the kitchen; in wall-paintings of St Christopher and the crucifixion of St Andrew in the chaplains' room; and in the Brown Gallery, which Sharington created out of part of the refectory and where original corbels still support the roof, although this is now hidden by the ceiling.

The wide Stone Gallery which Sharington fashioned from part of the nuns' dormitory to give views over his formal garden on the east side of the house is still much as he left it, lit by largely Tudor windows and with a delicately carved classical chimneypiece. More Renaissance features adorn Sir William's three-storey octagonal tower, where a narrow angled passage leads to a high-ceilinged chamber on the first floor. A place where Sharington could keep important papers and display precious objects, this tiny cupboard of a room, possibly the only one of its kind surviving in England, was both a strong-room and an early equivalent of the *studiolo* of an Italian Renaissance prince, where books and treasured works of art would be kept. It is almost filled by an elaborate octagonal stone table supported on the shoulders of four satyrs and carved with the scorpions of the Sharington crest, their vicious tails and matchstick legs also recognisable in pendants studding the vaulted ceiling. This exceptional stone carving may be the work of John Chapman, who worked for Henry VIII, or by a foreign craftsman from the Tudor court. There is another stone table in the room above (not shown). Filling the top of the tower and only accessible from the roof, this was a banqueting house where Sharington would have entertained his guests, Sir John Thynne of Longleat among them. His scorpions appear again on the Tudor tiles which have been re-used in a Georgian stewing range in the kitchen.

The newest architectural fashions were again introduced to Lacock in the middle of the eighteenth century, when John Ivory Talbot, a descendant of Sharington's niece, made extensive changes to the house and grounds. Sanderson Miller's Gothick hall, commissioned in 1753 and completed in 1755, is entered by a prominent double flight of steps on the west front. Below the painted heraldic ceiling, decorative niches with pinnacled canopies are filled with terracotta figures made in 1755–6 by the Austrian sculptor Victor Alexander Sederbach, whose strange company, two nuns, a bishop, a knight and a grisly skeleton among them, is dominated by Ela in heroic pose over the fireplace, a bird perching on her outstretched left arm. The adjoining dining room was also remodelled by John Ivory Talbot, in 1751–2, but here, in contrast to the drama next door, the decoration is coolly classical.

In the lovely South Gallery hung with family portraits, including a painting of Sir William dressed in black with a long, red beard, a brown, indistinct photograph placed by one of the oriel windows shows the bare outlines of the lattice panes. This blurred print was produced from a tiny negative, the world's first, made in 1835 by the pioneer photographer William Henry Fox Talbot, who inherited the estate as a baby in 1800. Although he did not come to live at Lacock until 1827, introducing the oriel windows in the South Gallery in c.1830, he conducted many of his early experiments at the abbey. The earliest photograph was taken by Joseph Niépce in 1826, but Fox Talbot was responsible for inventing the negative–positive process which paved the way for the development of modern photography.

The ground floor of the converted barn at the abbey gates is devoted to this exceptional man's life and work, displaying the skeletal forms of leaves and flowers captured in early experiments as well as portraits of his family and life at Lacock. Fox Talbot's achievements in other areas are also recorded, from his translation of the cuneiform inscriptions discovered in 1847 at the palaces of the Assyrian kings in what is now Iraq to his work on microscopy, demonstrated by magnified insect

wings and plant sections. Also a prominent mathematician and astronomer and a Fellow of the Royal Society, Fox Talbot's scientific interests were accompanied by an appreciation of the artistic possibilities of photography, as clearly illustrated by his plates in *The Pencil of Nature* (1844–6), the first book to include photographs. The museum also exhibits examples of the work of other pioneers in this field, such as Daguerre, Niépce and Wedgwood, and early photographic equipment.

Beyond the Fox Talbot museum is the village of Lacock, now a picturesque assemblage of well-preserved buildings from the fourteenth to the late eighteenth century and primarily a tourist attraction, much used for filming period dramas, but for hundreds of years a busy and prosperous place. There has been a permanent settlement here since Saxon times and probably even earlier, but the present layout, with four main streets forming a square, dates from the thirteenth century, when a planned village was established for workers on the abbey estates. Its inhabitants grew rich on the medieval wool industry and the weekly market initiated by Ela. Lacock was ideally placed for both, being within a day's journey of prime grazing lands on the Cotswolds and Marlborough Downs and a staging-post on the road linking centres of the wool trade in the West Country. There was also access to the sea via the River Avon, which meanders past to the east. At its height in the late Middle Ages, Lacock's continued prosperity after the decline of the wool trade owed much to its position on a through route between Marlborough and Bristol, which brought wealth to the village and travellers to fill its many inns until the mid-eighteenth century. From then onwards Lacock stood still. Lack of development in the nineteenth century, when many nearby settlements expanded rapidly, was largely due to the Talbot family, who ensured no railway lines came too near the village. Lacock fossilised, resulting in one of the most pleasing and individual places in England.

Reflecting the village's origins, the irregular terraces that line the streets are all built on narrow medieval house plots running back from the frontages. There are timber-framed buildings with mullioned windows and jettied upper storeys, seventeenth-century stone cottages and elegant Georgian brick mansions, such as the two examples dated 1719 and 1779 in East Street, but many of the apparently later buildings are older than they look and were originally timber-framed.

Lichen and moss encrust stone-slated roofs and gables, and dormers add to the pleasingly varied street facades.

Of the numerous inns, the timber-framed Angel in Church Street retains its medieval layout and the passage through which horses would be led to the yard behind, while the George in West Street has an original dog-powered spit. A magnificent fourteenth-century tithe barn would once have stored rent paid to the abbey in the form of corn, hides and fleeces. Standing slightly apart is the battlemented and pinnacled church of St Cyriac. Largely rebuilt when the village was at its most prosperous in the fifteenth century, it contains the grandiose Renaissance tomb of Sir William Sharington. A narrow lane leads from the church to the eighteenth-century packhorse bridge over the Bide Brook and to the Avon beyond, where a medieval bridge crosses the river.

Fox Talbot's granddaughter Matilda gave the abbey and the village to the National Trust in 1944, and members of the Talbot family continued to live in the abbey until 2011.

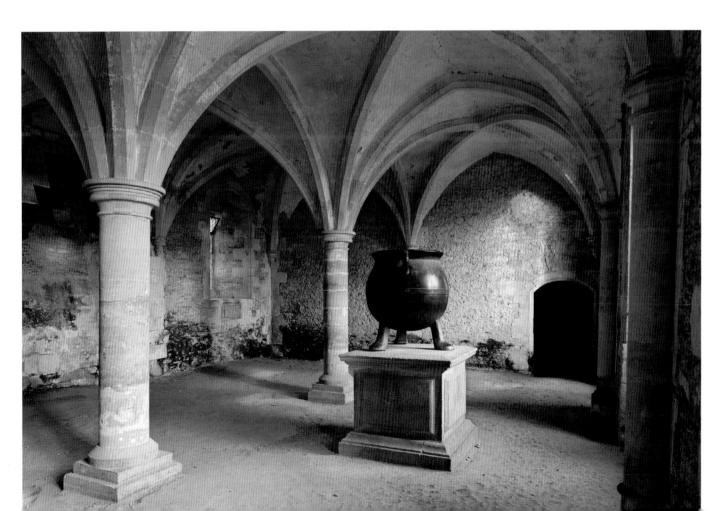

Lamb House

East Sussex
In West Street, Rye, facing
the west end of the church

In 1726 a fearful storm drove the ship carrying George I from Hanover to England ashore on the sands fringing the estuary of the River Rother, 2 miles (3.2 kilometres) from Rye. James Lamb, mayor of the prosperous little town, escorted the king to his house and offered him his bed, although his wife was heavily pregnant and in fact gave birth to a son that night. Heavy snow kept the king in Rye for three days and the Lambs, whose ignorance of German matched the king's lack of English, were rewarded with a silver bowl and 100 guineas as christening presents for their infant, who had the king as his godfather. The modest brick-fronted house that bears Lamb's name, one of the many delightful buildings lining Rye's cobbled streets, had been completed just two years earlier.

Some 200 years later the house was connected with another outstanding character, in this case the American novelist and critic Henry James, who bought it for £2,000 in 1900. Already in late middle age and well established in both Europe and America, James was to reach the height of his powers here. It was at Rye that he wrote his three greatest novels, *The Ambassadors*, *The Wings of the Dove* and *The Golden Bowl*, dictating them in a sonorous voice to his secretary in the garden pavilion in summer and in a small, sunny study in winter. Here, too, he entertained a stream of other established literary figures, including H.G. Wells, Ford Madox Ford, Rudyard Kipling, Max Beerbohm and Edith Wharton.

Remarkably, after James's death in 1916, Lamb House became the home of three other novelists, the brothers A.C. and E.F. Benson and, later, Rumer Godden. They too found the tranquil atmosphere conducive, with the neighbourhood and society of Rye clearly inspiring E.F. Benson's *Mapp and Lucia* novels.

Since 1950, when Lamb House came to the National Trust without any contents, the Trust has been gradually retrieving items connected with Henry James and a collection of his books is now on show in the morning room.

The tiny walled garden, much loved by those who have lived here, contains a rich variety of plants. Sadly, the eighteenth-century garden room, with a bay window looking down the street, was destroyed by a German bomb in 1940.

LEFT Lamb House, a modest Georgian building tucked away on the corner of a cobbled street in the delightful little town of Rye, has been lived in and visited by a stream of literary figures.

Lanhydrock

Cornwall
2½ miles (4 kilometres) south-east
of Bodmin, overlooking the valley
of the River Fowey

Lanhydrock is lost in a long Victorian afternoon. No one is at work in the cool, tiled dairy, or in the huge stone-flagged kitchen, and buckets and brushes are lined up in the housemaids' closet ready for the next day. No sound comes from the extensive servants' quarters, where a pair of black boots stands neatly by a bed and the footman's livery lies ready to wear, while in the nursery wing all is still. Pipes lie waiting in the masculine confines of the smoking room and the dining-room table is laid for ten, the menu already handwritten in French. The period feeling is so strong that it would be no surprise to meet a scurrying maid with a tray or to hear the Robartes family and their guests, or their nine children, coming in from the garden.

Lanhydrock's interiors vividly evoke gracious living in the 1890s. The house itself, with three battlemented ranges of silver-grey granite set round a courtyard and mullioned windows, is much older, but was largely rebuilt at the end of the nineteenth century after a disastrous fire in 1881. Although, to avoid the risk of another fire, no gas or electricity was installed, the designs by Richard Coad, a local architect who had trained in London, incorporated the latest comforts and conveniences, such as the massive radiators featured in almost every room. The hill behind the house was cut away to accommodate a full range of service rooms and a steam generator in the cellar powered the jets for scouring greasy pots in the scullery and a range of equipment in the airy, high-ceilinged kitchen, where butterscotch walls reflect the late nineteenth-century colour scheme. Ice was brought by train from Plymouth for the ice chests in the pantry and spring water from the hill above the house was channelled along runnels in the slate and marble slabs in the dairy where jellies and custards were put to stand.

At the same time, as he was instructed, Coad restored the Jacobean exterior of the rather old-fashioned house built here by Sir Richard Robartes and his son between 1630 and 1642, his new work merging beautifully with the one wing that was not extensively damaged in the flames. An enchanting detached gatehouse still stands at the head of a beech and sycamore avenue leading away across the park, as it has done

ABOVE In the dairy, spring water from the hill above the house was channelled along runnels in the marble and slate slabs to keep butter, cheeses and puddings cool.

since the seventeenth century, and obelisks crowning this little architectural conceit are echoed by more on the main building and on the low wall enclosing formal gardens around the house.

Only the north wing, which survived the fire intact, gives a flavour of the original interiors. A sunny 35.5-metre (116-foot) gallery running the length of the second floor and lit by windows on both sides suggests what might have been lost. The barrel ceiling arching overhead is covered with magical plasterwork dating from just before the outbreak of the Civil War. Although the 24 panels illustrating incidents from the Old Testament take centre stage, the delightful creatures surrounding them are far more memorable, furry porcupines, bears, armadillos and peacocks rubbing shoulders with

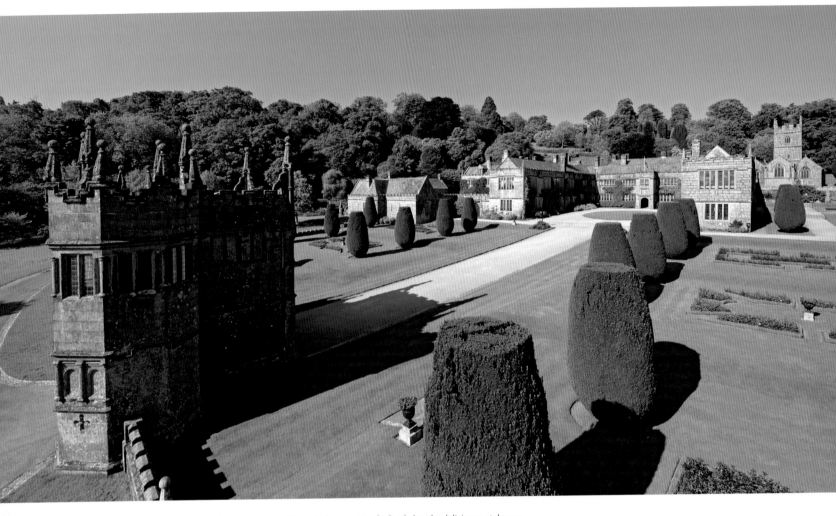

ABOVE A disastrous fire in 1881 destroyed most of the main house at Lanhydrock, but the delicious gatehouse, built in 1651 as a hunting lodge from which to watch the pursuit of deer, was untouched.

mythical beasts, such as dragons and centaurs. The gallery is hung with portraits, including works by Thomas Hudson, who was a West Country painter, and George Romney, and this room houses an exceptional collection of early books dating from 1590 to 1700, among them a four-volume atlas of 1694 with delicate watercolour maps showing the Cornish landholdings of the 2nd Earl of Radnor.

Like Coad's interiors, Lanhydrock's garden reflects Victorian taste. In front of the house, clipped yew marks the corners of six geometric shapes planted with roses in George Gilbert Scott's formal layout of 1857 and more yew studs his intricate parterre beside the north wing, bedded out twice a

year. Beyond the obelisks and castellations of the surrounding parapet, a large informal garden dating from the 1860s covers the steep slopes rising above the house. Winding paths through shrubs and trees, including exceptional displays of large Himalayan magnolias, rhododendrons and camellias, lead ever upwards, past the well used by the monks of St Petroc's Priory at Bodmin, who held Lanhydrock before the Dissolution, and the strong spring feeding the stream that runs down the slope. Vistas over the house and the wooded valley of the Fowey culminate in magnificent views from the broad terrace walk at the top of the garden and there is a network of paths across the wood- and parkland of the estate.

Lavenham Guildhall

Suffolk
Market Place, Lavenham

The medieval town of Lavenham, with streets of crooked half-timbered houses and a glorious late fifteenth-century church, is a monument to the prosperity brought by the Suffolk cloth industry, at its height in the fifteenth and early sixteenth centuries. Apart from the church, one of the finest buildings is the guildhall, which is prominently sited in the little market square. Traditional timber-framing, its exuberant carving now heavily weathered, is limewashed to a pleasing silvery-grey, the upper floor is jettied out over the lower and both are lit with oriel windows. An ornate two-storey porch projects into the square and the building as a whole rests on a brick plinth, which deepens as the ground slopes away behind.

The hall was built in about 1510 by the Guild of Corpus Christi, one of four religious and social guilds in the town. Less than 20 years later, when Henry VIII turned against the Roman Catholic Church, the guild was dissolved, and the guildhall was subsequently used as a town hall, prison and workhouse before being restored in 1887. The former meeting rooms of the guild, with moulded ceiling timbers and a floor of ancient oak, are at street level. The warren of small rooms above (probably let as storage to cloth merchants) now houses a local history museum. Mostly devoted to the cloth industry that made Lavenham so rich, displays here include the range of colours, from pale blue to black, which can be obtained from woad and a model of the tenter frames on which cloth was stretched to dry. The most unusual exhibit is a mummified cat that had been placed in a nearby roof to ward off evil spirits.

Dye plants in the walled garden were used in the production of medieval cloth. There is also a restored nineteenth-century lock-up and mortuary and a Newsham fire engine, thought to be the oldest in East Anglia.

RIGHT The wealth created by the Suffolk cloth industry in the fifteenth and early sixteenth centuries financed many buildings in Lavenham, among them the fine half-timbered guildhall in the market square.

Levant Mines and Engines

Cornwall
On the west coast near St Just, at Pool, 2 miles (3.2 kilometres) west of Redruth on either side of the A3047, and other locations

The tall outlines of ruined engine houses standing high on windswept moorland or perched on lonely cliff-top sites are romantic reminders of the great days of the Cornish mining industry in the mid-nineteenth century.

At the height of the boom, the population of the county almost doubled as newcomers flooded in to provide the manpower needed for the extraction of rich sources of tin, copper and china clay. Now only the china-clay quarries remain open, but the technology refined here in Victorian times was exported all over the world, from South America to Australia.

The key to the growth of the Cornish mining industry was the expiry of the patent on the Boulton and Watt steam engine in 1800. Developed in the coal-rich areas of the north, where fuel efficiency was not the prime consideration, this engine was expensive to run in the south-west, where all coal had to be brought over the sea from Wales. The moment restrictions were removed, Cornish engineers – in particular Richard Trevithick (1771–1833), the first to realise the potential of high-pressure steam – set about producing more efficient engines, leading to the establishment of a number of great engine-building firms, such as Holman's of Camborne and Harvey's of Hayle. Necessity was the mother of invention, giving Cornwall the lead in mining technology that it was to hold for half a century.

The National Trust owns several survivals from this great chapter in Cornish history, most of them now included in the new Cornish Mining World Heritage Site. On the Penwith peninsula in the far west, a rich mining coast is centred on St Just. At the Levant mine about 2 miles (3.2 kilometres) north of the little town is the oldest surviving beam engine in Cornwall, sited in a tiny engine house right on the cliff edge.

Once again being worked by steam, this machinery was designed by Francis Michell, a member of the engineering Michell family, and was built by Harvey's in 1840. Even more spectacular are the engine houses at Botallack, which cling to the rocks just out of reach of the pounding Atlantic. This whole mining coast, with Botallack and Kenidjack at its heart, has been the focus of considerable restoration and stabilisation by the National Trust in recent years.

At the East Pool and Agar mine, straddling the A3047 east of Cambourne, is the largest of the great beam engines left in Cornwall, commissioned from Harvey's in 1891 and put to work pumping out water here in 1925. With a gleaming cylinder 2 metres (7 feet) in diameter and a huge beam weighing some 52 tons, this monster could lift 2,000 litres (450 gallons) of water a minute from a depth of 518 metres (1,700 feet). The 1853 engine designed by a pupil of Trevithick at South Crofty tin and arsenic mine about a mile (1.6 kilometres) to the south-west could operate at even greater depths, raising 1,500 litres (340 gallons) a minute from some 610 metres (2,000 feet).

A working example of the rotative engines normally used for lifting men and materials survives at the East Pool mine, where F.W. Michell's 1887 engine made by Holman's is now powered by electricity. Also at East Pool is the Industrial Discovery Centre, which gives an overview of Cornish mining and sets it in context.

There are a number of other empty engine houses in the Trust's care, some in situations as dramatic as those of Penwith. Wheal Prosper dominates the cliff above Porthcew Cove, while Towanroath engine house at Chapel Porth is perched on a ledge high above the sea. Equally romantic is Wheal Betsy, set on lonely Black Down on the west edge of Dartmoor, its tall chimney a conspicuous sight from the A386 to Okehampton. Richard Trevithick's whitewashed thatched cottage at Lower Penponds, Camborne, from where he departed for the silver mines of Peru in 1816, also belongs to the Trust.

OPPOSITE Mining for tin on the north Cornish coast in the nineteenth century has left a legacy of impressive buildings, among them Towanroath engine house, built in 1872 on a dramatic site high above the sea. The pumping engine housed here kept Wheal Coates mine, further up the hill, free of water.

Lindisfarne Castle

Northumberland
On Holy Island, 6 miles
(9.6 kilometres) east of
the A1, across the causeway

Accessible only by a causeway that is submerged for several hours at high tide, Holy Island feels like a place apart, a visit here like an adventure into the unknown. The castle is set on a dolerite crag at the far end of the island, its stone walls continuing the lines of the rock as if rising naturally from it. A cobbled approach curves steeply up the face of the crag to the entrance high above, a precipitous drop on one side, a cliff-like wall on the other. With spectacular views south to Bamburgh Castle and east over the water to the Farne Islands, this is an entrancingly romantic place, even when lashed by the winter gales that can sweep in from the North Sea.

Created in 1903 by the young Edwin Lutyens out of the shell of an originally Tudor fort, Lindisfarne's small rooms look backwards rather than forwards. There are Norman-style pillars, huge fireplaces, deeply recessed mullioned windows and rounded stone arches, and the castle's very individual charm is enhanced by the varied materials and floor levels that are characteristic of Lutyens. Herringbone brick floors are juxtaposed with stone, timber and slate. Some rooms are austerely whitewashed; in others, such as the dark drawing room in the bowels of the building, where massively thick vaults arching overhead once protected the castle's magazine, the stone is left bare. With the exception of the kitchen, where a high-backed settle and armchairs are grouped round the leaded range, none of the rooms could be described as cosy, although carved English and Flemish oak furniture, blue and white Delftware and richly coloured carpets give a feel of seventeenth-century Dutch interiors.

The old fort would probably have been left to quiet decay if Edward Hudson, the founder of *Country Life*, had not happened upon it on a visit to the island and employed Lutyens to turn it into a summer retreat. Hudson was a hospitable man who loved to entertain: a cello and music stand in the long upper gallery recall the many house parties he hosted at the castle, when the celebrated cellist Madame Suggia used to play for her fellow guests.

A little walled garden lies on a south-facing slope to the north of the crag that is sheltered from the worst of the weather. The original planting scheme designed by Gertrude Jekyll, flowering in a mass of purple, grey, pink and burnt-orange in high summer, has been faithfully re-created.

LEFT Although Lindisfarne Castle's rooms are small and intimate, the use of much bare stone and slate and of Norman-style pillars gives the interior of the house an austere atmosphere.
BELOW The castle is romantically set on Holy Island off the Northumbrian coast.

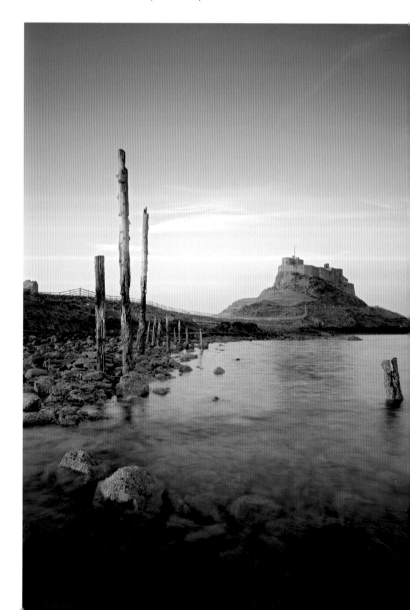

Little Moreton Hall

Cheshire
4 miles (6.4 kilometres) south-west
of Congleton, on the east side of
the A34 Newcastle road

The prosperous Moretons of Little Moreton Hall were gentleman farmers who profited, like many others, from the opportunities to acquire land after the Black Death, when there was a dramatic decline in population, and from the sale of former monastic property after the Dissolution of the Monasteries. Between the mid-fifteenth century, when the house was begun, and *c.*1580, when it was complete, they doubled the size of their estates. As the family grew richer, they enlarged their timber-framed, moated manor house, building additions that gradually embraced a central courtyard. Most striking is the south wing, erected in the 1560s. Whereas most of the hall is of two storeys, this range rises to a third floor, which is filled with a magnificent long gallery. Probably added as an afterthought while building was in progress, the gallery perches top-heavily on the house like a stranded Noah's Ark and has pulled the supporting timbers out of shape, so that the building lurches drunkenly. A charming projecting gatehouse links this range to the bridge over the moat.

Apart from three pieces, all the original furniture has disappeared and rooms are shown unfurnished. Nothing distracts from the quality of the building itself. Constructed in an age when wood was plentiful and half-timbered houses were common in the West Midlands and Welsh Marches, Little Moreton Hall is still exceptional. It seems to have been devised to display the full range of the joiner's and carpenter's art, with timbers arranged in a huge variety of patterns to glorious effect. The confidence and pride of the carpenter who carried out work in 1559 is proclaimed in the inscription he left on one of the prominent bay windows built for William Moreton II: 'Rycharde Dale Carpeder made thies windovs by the grac of god.' The leaded windows are similarly unusual, with glazing patterns varying from room to room and even window to window. This craftsmanship in wood and glass, a testament to the ingenuity and skill of Tudor workmen, gives Little Moreton Hall its unique character.

The interior is a corridor-less warren, with one room leading into another and four staircases linking different levels. Some rooms are little more than cupboards and plainly

ABOVE The decorative timber framing which covers every façade of Little Moreton Hall is arranged in a great variety of patterns, most of them set within square panels.

decorated; others are much grander, with fine chimneypieces and panelling. There is a simple chapel, to which worshippers are still summoned on Sundays by a bell in the courtyard. Texts from the Bible painted on the chancel walls were probably added in *c.*1580 at the same time as the decoration of the parlour, where a frieze crowning the elaborate painted panelling, the whole composition a rare example of sixteenth-century painted decoration, illustrates the story of Susannah and the Elders, a favourite Protestant theme. Characters are shown in contemporary Elizabethan dress, the blues and reds of their costumes still fresh and bright. In the long gallery, where the massive weight of the roof is taken by huge curved beams morticed and tenoned into the rafters, plasterwork picked out in orange and green at either end of the room depicts the virtues of hard work and the power of knowledge over superstition. A hedge of hornbeam, holly, thorn and honeysuckle edges the moat, enclosing a lawn planted with fruit trees and a reconstruction of an Elizabethan knot garden, with box-edged compartments filled with gravel. Two prominent mounds were probably vantage points for surveying the surrounding countryside.

Llanerchaeron

Ceredigion
Off the A482, 2½ miles
(4 kilometres) south-east of
Aberaeron

Just inland from Cardigan Bay and the sea, in the pastoral wooded valley of the Afon Aeron, is a rare survival of the small gentry estates that were such a mainstay of the economy of rural Wales in the eighteenth and nineteenth centuries. In the same family for ten generations, Llanerchaeron reflects a self-sufficient, country-oriented way of life that has largely vanished. By 1700, it had passed to the Lewis family and it was Colonel William Lewis, soon after he inherited in 1789, who commissioned the young John Nash to replace a mid-seventeenth-century house. Nash, who had retreated to Wales to recover from bankruptcy and was turning out a number of villas for the Welsh gentry at this period, incorporated the existing building in his plans and set the new house to take full advantage of views across the park. It is a charming mix of the conservative and the unexpected. The plain, well-proportioned late Georgian exterior, with stuccoed walls and a slate roof, is unexceptional, but Nash included decorative oval rooms on the first floor and a dramatic top-lit staircase, and there is subtle detailing, such as in the design of the plaster friezes, each of which is different.

The interior still has a sense of the family. Stuffed fish and woodcock, and an array of fox and otter heads, reflect their passion for hunting. The drawing room, with its ebonised cabinets and chairs by a late nineteenth-century Manchester cabinet-maker, is hung with family photographs and portraits, one a pastel by Lawrence of Colonel William, and the books in the library, assembled since 1918 when many of the contents of the house were sold, reflect their interest in the outdoors. Upstairs, one of the oval rooms is a boudoir with deliciously feminine plasterwork, the other a dressing room. Both have curved doors and a niche in each corner and the dressing room still has the mahogany cupboard and chest of drawers that were made for it in the eighteenth century.

A bell corridor flanked by the butler's pantry and the original light and airy kitchen leads to Nash's elegant service courtyard, ringed by a slate-slabbed walkway that is sheltered by deeply overhanging eaves. Eighteenth-century fittings still survive, among them solid slate cream pans in the dairy and original cheese presses. Beyond the courtyard is the detached, stone-walled billiard room that was built in 1843 and which was designed with a prominent lantern in the centre of the roof to give an even light on the billiard table beneath.

The surrounding park was landscaped in the spirit of the Picturesque, with gothicised cottages. A church beside the drive was used as an eye-catcher in the views from the house and the now-abandoned track of the railway to Aberaeron, which the family encouraged, runs through the park. The family's sporting lifestyle comes through again in the home farm, where the buildings round the yard, mostly contemporary with the house, include kennels for otter hounds and elegant stables. Their importance in the local economy is seen in the little church, where estate employees once filled 40 of the 60 seats.

House, gardens and grounds have been restored by the National Trust. Vegetables, fruit and herbs are grown in the two walled gardens and the estate is run as an organic farm. There are extensive walks across the park and estate.

BELOW Nash ornamented the ground floor of his entrance front with two elegant windows, but the one on the left is a fake, inserted to preserve the symmetry of the facade.

Lodge Park

Gloucestershire
3 miles (4.8 kilometres) south-east
of Northleach, across the A40
from Sherborne village

On the open Cotswold plateau east of Cheltenham is a unique survival of a finely wrought building set in a sporting landscape. Commanding sweeping views south and east towards the Thames Valley is an exquisite Jacobean hunting lodge, its main facade positively crammed with architectural detail. Pedimented windows set shoulder to shoulder across the first floor carry bearded and moustachioed heads, there are exaggerated quoins, shell-headed niches and a columned portico supporting a wide balcony, and a massive classical chimneystack breaks the balustraded roofline.

This compact architectural caprice, more box than house, was built to overlook a broad grassy track edged with dry-stone walls that still runs over a mile (1.6 kilometres) south from the A40. From the roof and balcony of the lodge, the well-to-do would watch and bet on dogs chasing fallow deer along the course, which finished at a shallow ditch in front of the house. The lodge was built in the 1630s for Sir John 'Crump' Dutton, a characterful hunchback who seems to have weathered the Civil War by keeping a foot in both camps. The interior had just two large rooms, one on each floor, above a basement kitchen, with a grand staircase to take the company up to the Great Room opening onto the balcony. Here they ate and watched the hunt, or went on up to the viewing platform on the roof. The designer is unknown, but the local mason-architect Valentine Strong may well have directed the work, drawing some of the detail from pattern books that illustrated the kind of Italianate features favoured by Inigo Jones. Crump had created a deer-park too, but in the early eighteenth century the lodge was made the focus of a landscape by Charles Bridgeman, who planted wooded enclosures for the deer, artful clumps of trees and a double lime avenue (now replanted) leading away behind the house.

ABOVE RIGHT Although isolated on the windswept Cotswold plateau, Lodge Park, built in the 1630s, has a main facade that is crammed with innovative Italianate detail in the latest fashion of the day.

RIGHT The Great Room at Lodge Park, designed for entertaining visitors, opens onto a wide balcony where guests enjoyed a grandstand view of deer coursing on a track in front of the house.

At about the same time as Bridgeman's landscaping, the lodge was refurbished, probably to a scheme devised by William Kent. In later years, it was converted into estate cottages and, in the nineteenth century, when the gate lodges were added, turned into a house. The National Trust has returned it, as far as possible, to its original configuration, with a reconstructed Jacobean-style oak staircase leading to the Great Room and a lively modern version, carved by masons of the Hereford Cathedral workshop, of the great hooded fireplace that was once here and which was moved to Sherborne House in the nineteenth century. There is a show of Dutton portraits on the walls. In the hall downstairs there are two of the side tables that were made for the lodge in c.1730 and an atmospheric landscape by George Lambert depicts the open, well-wooded countryside of the 1740s, without the regular stone-walled fields that now dominate the view from the roof.

Lodge Park is part of the 1,677-hectare (4,144-acre) Sherborne estate. Straddling the A40 and the serene Windrush Valley, this largely agricultural holding includes much former parkland and most of Sherborne village. Strung out along the valley, this is a charming collection of nineteenth-century, estate-built cottages in a Cotswold vernacular style, with gabled stone-tiled roofs and stone-mullioned windows. All are south-facing, with gardens separating them from the road. The big house, seat of the family since the sixteenth century, was sold away in 1970, and the 7th Lord and Lady Sherborne lived at the lodge, where the fortune she had inherited from her father, the Canadian multi-millionaire Sir James Hamet Dunn, financed a colourful lifestyle. On the 7th Lord's death in 1982, the Sherborne estate came to the Trust; the peerage, which dates from 1784, died with the 7th Lord's cousin, Ralph Dutton of Hinton Ampner (see p.170).

Lyme Park, House and Garden

Cheshire
On the south side of the A6;
6½ miles (10.4 kilometres)
south-east of Stockport, entrance
on the western outskirts of Disley

Used to the blinding sun and hard shadows of his homeland, the Venetian architect Giacomo Leoni must have found it hard to contend with the grey skies and misty distances of the bleak Peak moors at Lyme when Peter Legh engaged him to remodel his largely Elizabethan mansion in 1725. As at Clandon (see p.92), Leoni responded by bringing a touch of Italy to the English countryside.

The courtyard of the Tudor house was ringed by shady arcades and given a double flight of steps rising to the pedimented entrance, as if it were the *cortile* of a grand *palazzo*. The Mediterranean effect was later enhanced by the addition of a marble pavement and an Italian Renaissance well-head. The long south front is entirely Leoni. Built of rose-tinted stone, it is dominated by a classical portico extending the full height of the house. Giant lead figures of Venus, Neptune and Pan set along the pediment stare at their reflection in the lake below and six bays separated by pilasters stretch away on either side. Something of the grand Elizabethan house survives on the north, where a towering Tudor gateway leads into Leoni's courtyard.

Despite much later remodelling, two Elizabethan interiors survive: a light and airy panelled long gallery hung with seventeenth- and early eighteenth-century portraits and a richly panelled Tudor drawing room. In the eighteenth century, although he was primarily involved with the exterior of the house, Leoni also created some internal spaces, of which his oak-panelled saloon, lit by windows looking over the park through the columns of his portico and adorned with a gilded rococo ceiling, has all the elegance of the period. Pale three-dimensional limewood carvings decorating the panelling were introduced from elsewhere in the house by Lewis Wyatt, in an entirely sympathetic idiom, in the early nineteenth century. One of these realistic compositions, which are traditionally attributed to Grinling Gibbons, cunningly intertwines an artist's palette and brushes, a partly folded chart and navigation instruments. In another, a beautifully embroidered lace handkerchief falls in naturalistic folds.

OPPOSITE The Venetian architect Giacomo Leoni, who was commissioned to remodel Lyme Park in the 1720s, was responsible for the Italianate south front, with its massive Ionic portico overlooking the lake.

A full-length portrait of the Black Prince in Leoni's grand classical entrance hall is a vivid reminder that the land of Lyme was won for the Legh family in 1346 on the battlefields of France. Lyme was to remain the home of the Leghs for 600 years and many other aspects of the family history are reflected in the contents. A copy of Velázquez's *Las Meninas* portrays the celebrated mastiffs that were bred here until the twentieth century and were traditionally presented as royal gifts to the courts of Europe. The ancient Greek sculptures in the library, one of the interiors fashioned by Wyatt, were excavated in the early nineteenth century by the intrepid Thomas Legh, whose portrait in oriental costume enlivens the

staircase. His grandest find, a stele of Melisto and Epigenes of *c*.350BC, has pride of place over the fireplace, but the little tombstone of the same date in the window bay, commemorating a mother and her newborn babe, is more memorable. A tragedy of a different kind is recalled in the Stag Parlour, where faded red covers on the Chippendale chairs were reputedly made from the cloak Charles I wore on the scaffold. In the late twentieth century the house was enriched by the magnificent collection of seventeenth- and eighteenth-century bracket and longcase clocks acquired by Sir Francis Legh, who was born at Lyme in 1919, the earliest of them an instrument by Ahasuerus Fromanteel of 1658, which

ABOVE The attractive long gallery at Lyme Park, with its fine Jacobean oak panelling and seventeenth- and early eighteenth-century family portraits, dates from the building of the Elizabethan house but has been altered since.

was one of the first pendulum mechanisms ever produced. Five clocks by the outstanding London maker Thomas Tompion from the collection of Mr M.H. Vivian are now also on display. Most recently, the rare illuminated Missal that was printed for William Caxton in 1487, and probably acquired by Sir Piers Legh V on publication or soon afterwards, has been bought back for the house.

There has been a garden on this unpromising site, carved out of moorland, since the seventeenth century. But the present layout and planting are essentially Victorian and owe much to William John Legh, 1st Lord Newton, who inherited in 1857 and took advice from the garden writer and theorist Edward Kemp. A sweep of grass running down to a naturalistic lake below the terrace on the south front and the informal semi-wild area along the deep ravine carved by the stream feeding the lake contrast with a series of formal gardens with massed bedding, one of which is overlooked by an orangery designed by Lewis Wyatt.

From the south terrace there are views across the lake to Lyme's medieval deer-park, 9 miles (14.4 kilometres) in circumference and already walled in Elizabethan times. Set dramatically on a windswept ridge high above the grazing herds broods Lyme Cage, its stark outlines relieved by little domed turrets at each corner. Probably built to designs by Leoni as a hunting tower and banqueting house, it was modified in the early nineteenth century by Lewis Wyatt. This arresting eye-catcher is the building that approaching visitors see first.

Lytes Cary Manor

Somerset
1 mile (1.6 kilometres) north of the
Ilchester bypass on the A303

This enchanting manor house built of warm local limestone and set round a courtyard in the depths of rural Somerset bears the name of the family who lived here for 400 years, from the fourteenth to the eighteenth century. Rounded topiary yews line the flagged path leading to the entrance, where the swan of the Lyte family, wings half raised, crowns the gable of the porch. To the left is the oldest feature of Lytes Cary, the simple little chapel built by Peter Lyte in *c*.1343, attached to the house but only accessible from the outside. Family coats of arms in red, white and yellow stand out prominently on the painted frieze added in 1631 that enlivens the whitewashed interior and there is some medieval stained glass in the windows.

Although the appearance of the house today owes much to Sir Walter and Flora Jenner, who acquired it in a dilapidated state in 1907 and lovingly restored it, rebuilding the north and west ranges in an unobtrusive late seventeenth-century style and filling the rooms with appropriate furniture and china, Lytes Cary has a feeling of great age, of a place that has grown out of its surroundings. The Tudor great hall between the porch and the chapel, with a little oriel off it where the family would eat in privacy away from their servants and retainers, rises the full height of the house to an open timber roof with carved angels on the ends of the rafters. On show in the hall is a copy of Henry Lyte's *Niewe Herball*, first published in 1578, which was translated from the work of the renowned Flemish herbalist Dodoens and dedicated to Queen Elizabeth I. Subsequently known as the *Lytes Herbal*, it was still being reprinted in 1678. Henry would have enjoyed the splendid plaster ceiling in the great chamber on the floor above, added by his father in the 1530s, the interlaced hexagons and diamonds studded with armorial bosses heralding Elizabethan plasterwork of a generation later. This room also has a fine interior porch covered in linenfold panelling and crested with trefoils.

Neglected after the departure of the Lytes in 1755, the house was being used to store cider and farm equipment when the Jenners bought it. The medieval and Tudor core is shown as Walter and Flora had it, furnished with high-quality

ABOVE With the exception of the eighteenth-century farmhouse wing to the right, the east front of Lytes Cary, with the traceried window of the little chapel on the far left, is medieval and Tudor.

seventeenth- and early eighteenth-century oak pieces and with fabrics in authentically medieval browns, olives and muted reds. Seat covers and panels decorated with vaguely Elizabethan embroidery are the work of Walter's sister-in-law, Nora Jenner, who, with her husband Leopold, Walter's brother, had bought the similarly neglected Avebury Manor (*see* p.33) in 1902.

Sir Walter and Flora also laid out the beautiful compartmental garden, with clipped yew hedges enclosing a series of outdoor rooms. A vivid mixed border punctuated with urns set between buttresses of yew leads to a long raised walk overlooking an orchard planted with the crab apples, medlars and quinces that the Elizabethans loved. Other yew compartments frame smoothly mown lawns and a fountain pool.

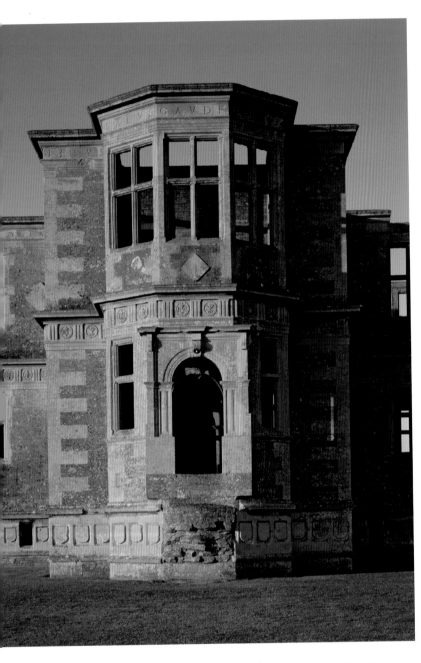

Lyveden New Bield

Northamptonshire
4 miles (6.4 kilometres)
south-west of Oundle via
the A427, 3 miles (4.8 kilometres)
east of Brigstock

This compelling, roofless architectural shell, finely built of local limestone and with large mullioned and transomed windows staring sightless over an empty rolling landscape of woods and meadows, was begun in 1594 but never completed. The creation of the individual and staunchly Catholic Sir Thomas Tresham, who was probably his own designer, it was intended partly as a garden lodge for Tresham's manor house in the valley below, and partly as a place of retreat and secret worship. Designed to be habitable, with a well-equipped basement kitchen and room for a small library, it is also an intriguing reflection of the Elizabethan love of riddles and devices and of Tresham's ardent Catholicism. Built in the shape of a symmetrical, equal-armed cross, it is conceived as a play on symbolic numbers. The number five, as in the five-sided bay windows at the end of each arm, refers to Christ's wounds on the Cross, seven alludes to the instruments of the passion, which are carved on the lodge, and the number three, as in the fragmentary remains of an 81-letter inscription running round the first floor, refers both to the Trinity and to the three-leaved clover of the Tresham emblem.

Work on the lodge proceeded slowly, partly because Tresham, although totally loyal to Queen Elizabeth, who knighted him in 1575, suffered greatly for his beliefs. After 1581, when the Catholic threat to England was at its greatest, he was fined heavily as an example to others and was frequently arrested. Although he continued to direct operations from prison, it is not surprising that the lodge was unfinished at his death, in 1605.

To link lodge and manor, Sir Thomas devised an elaborate formal garden, with moats, prospect mounds and a raised terrace walk, much of which has recently been re-created from the remaining bumps and watery hollows. Extending over some 6 hectares (15 acres), and one of the oldest surviving layouts in Britain, this too was symbolic, and probably included an allegorical labyrinth within the moated area. Tresham may have intended that the lodge would act as a viewing platform from which the garden could be admired. A formal orchard on the slopes of the valley has been replanted with fruit trees listed in Tresham's papers.

ABOVE A grand classical doorway, designed to be reached up a flight of steps, marks the main entrance to the garden lodge. If the house had been finished, the bay above would have been part of the best bedchamber.

Melford Hall

Suffolk
In Long Melford on the west side of the A134, 14 miles (22.5 kilometres) south of Bury St Edmunds, 3 miles (4.8 kilometres) north of Sudbury

Set into the high brick wall bordering Long Melford's village green is a delicious octagonal banqueting house, with finials rising like brick fingers at every angle and from all eight gables. This giant doll's house, probably a survival from an early seventeenth-century formal garden, faces along a grassy terrace – the former bowling-green – to one of the most satisfying Tudor houses in East Anglia.

Looking east over the park, its back towards the village, is a U-shaped mansion of mellow pink brick, with two long gabled wings flanking the courtyard on the entrance front. A dramatic array of soaring chimneystacks and fanciful turrets crowned with onion domes breaks the roofline and there is also a two-storey Renaissance-style porch decorated with fluted pilasters. Although neither the builder nor the date of building is certain, the hall probably dates largely from the early sixteenth century, when the abbot of the great Benedictine house of St Edmundsbury (now known as Bury St Edmunds) enjoyed the estate as his private domain. By the Dissolution it had passed to Sir William Cordell, a shrewd and upwardly mobile lawyer, who at first leased the hall but was granted the property outright by Queen Mary in 1534. Despite subsequent alterations, such as the removal of the gatehouse range that once enclosed the courtyard, the disappearance of part of the moat, and the insertion of some early eighteenth-century sash windows, the exterior is still very much as Queen Elizabeth I must have seen it when she was entertained lavishly here in 1578. The interior was substantially altered twice, first in the 1730s, when the principal rooms were given fashionable rococo decoration, and again in the nineteenth century, when Thomas Hopper injected Regency touches in a Greek Revival style.

The house was ransacked during the Civil War, when looters left the cellars knee-deep in beer, and suffered a

ABOVE When the north wing of the Hall was rebuilt after being gutted by fire in 1942, it was redecorated in Scandinavian style, with white walls and uncarpeted floors, reflecting the taste of Lady Ulla.

LEFT The staircase in the north wing of Melford Hall has three balusters to a tread, each carved to a different pattern, and other fine decorative detail.

devastating fire in 1942, which destroyed most of the rococo decoration, but recovery from both disasters was swift and there are still echoes of the Cordells, who were here for 250 years, and a strong sense of the seafaring Parker family, notable for producing no fewer than three admirals, who bought the hall, with most of its furnishings, in 1786. Although transformed by Hopper, who introduced the grand processional staircase, the panelled great hall still has its Tudor shape and is hung with a collection of seventeenth-century portraits. The old oak furniture, which also seems so fitting, was introduced by the antiquarian Sir William Parker, 9th Baronet, in the late nineteenth century. Also here is the survey of the estate that Sir William Cordell commissioned in 1580; every field is named and the long strip of the village green with the church at one end is clearly shown.

Hopper was also responsible for the splendid Regency Library with its curved oak bookshelves, florid Greek couches and armchairs appropriately decorated with owls. Paintings by

Dominic Serres of historic naval engagements fought by the 5th Baronet, Vice Admiral Sir Hyde Parker, and his second son, also an admiral, line the library walls, one of the most memorable showing fireships drifting on the tide towards a British fleet on the Hudson River during the American War of Independence. The 5th Baronet, who ran away from school to join the merchant navy and worked his way up through the ranks to become the most technically skilled admiral of his day, appears as a larger-than-life figure in a portrait by Romney in the little octagon off the main library, and this exceptional man was also responsible for much of the Chinese porcelain displayed in the house, which he took as prize booty from a Spanish galleon laden with gold and precious things that he captured in 1762. Twenty-one years later, aged 70, the 5th Baronet set sail from Rio de Janeiro to take up the East Indies command, but his ship was never seen again; with him on board was his grandson Harry, who was only 14 years old.

A dining room in the part of the house that was damaged by the fire was decorated in Scandinavian style, with cool white walls and a polished stone floor, by Ulla, the Danish wife of the 11th Baronet, and the house also has connections with Beatrix Potter, whose cousin married the 10th Baronet. Some of the illustrations for *Jeremy Fisher* were sketched at the hall's old fish ponds and on show is the room where she slept, her menagerie of animals being accommodated in an adjoining turret, and the model of Jemima Puddleduck, neatly dressed in a blue poke bonnet, which she gave to the Hyde Parker children.

Lawns studded with domes of box and planted with specimen trees set off the mellow brickwork of the west front and are framed by an undulating crinkle-crankle wall on one side and by the bowling-green terrace on the other. The north arm of the moat is now a sunken garden by the terrace but the west arm still runs along the village green, past some intriguing topiary figures outside the garden wall.

Mompesson House

Wiltshire
In Salisbury, on the north side of
Choristers' Green in the Cathedral
Close, near High Street Gate

Salisbury's leafy cathedral close, bordered by an array of dignified old houses, seems the perfect setting for Anthony Trollope's Barsetshire novels. Mrs Proudie, the bishop's domineering wife in *Barchester Towers*, would certainly have been at home in Mompesson House, with its beautiful sash-windowed Queen Anne facade rising to a hipped roof. In early summer, two white magnolias soften the grey Chilmark limestone that faces the house. Inside, elegant airy rooms with eighteenth-century plasterwork and marble chimneypieces look over the close towards the cathedral spire soaring above the rooftops.

The house was built in 1701 by Charles Mompesson, MP for Old Sarum, but the sumptuous stucco decoration by an unknown hand was commissioned by his brother-in-law and heir Charles Longueville, son of the patron and literary executor of the poet Samuel Butler. The most spectacular plasterwork is in the staircase hall, where the bold and florid design includes flowers, fruit, satyrs' masks and the head of King Midas with ass's ears. In the Green Room an eagle with outspread wings crouches in the middle of the ceiling, ready to pounce.

Later residents have also left their mark. Cool seascapes in an upstairs corridor and a scene of peaceful domesticity hanging on the stairs are among several watercolours by Barbara Townsend, one of the three daughters of George Barnard Townsend, a local solicitor who came to Mompesson in the mid-nineteenth century. Living on here until her death at the age of 96 in 1939, Barbara became a legend in the close, continuing to sketch and paint right up to the end of her life, a tiny figure wrapped in layers of shawls, scarves and veils. Coming to the National Trust without any contents in 1975, Mompesson has been refurnished with pieces appropriate to its Georgian heyday and now displays the Turnbull collection of over 370 English eighteenth-century glasses and eighteenth-century English porcelain figures from the William Bessemer Wright collection.

The high wall of the close, partly built with material from Old Sarum, bounds the secluded garden at the back of the house, where a wisteria- and honeysuckle-covered pergola provides welcome shade on hot summer afternoons. The old privy is hidden behind a tree in one corner.

RIGHT The beautiful Queen Anne facade of Mompesson House, looking onto the cathedral close at Salisbury, is built of grey Chilmark limestone and is half-smothered by two venerable magnolias.

Monk's House

East Sussex
4 miles (6.4 kilometres)
south-east of Lewes, off the former
A275 (now the C7) in Rodmell
village, near the church

This modest weather-boarded house at the far end of Rodmell village was the home of one of the most innovative novelists of the twentieth century. By 1919, when Virginia Woolf and her husband Leonard bought the property as a retreat from London life, Virginia's first two novels had been completed, but the experimental work that was to establish her reputation, in particular *To the Lighthouse*, *The Waves* and *Mrs Dalloway*, was still in the future. Two years earlier, at their house in Richmond, she and Leonard had founded the Hogarth Press, whose outstanding list, including the first published works of T.S. Eliot, was to make a major contribution to literary life. Ten miles (16 kilometres) or so across the South Downs stood Charleston, where Virginia's sister Vanessa, the gifted painter, had set up house with her art-critic husband Clive Bell and the artist Duncan Grant.

Although there are only echoes of Virginia at Monk's House, the rooms are full of reminders of the talented circle in which she moved. Painted furniture by her sister and Duncan Grant in a post-Impressionist style includes a table

and chairs in the sitting room: muted abstract designs in brown, blue and olive-green are relieved by a panel of peaches on the back of each chair. Books are piled on one of Duncan's tile-topped tables and a formidable portrait of Einstein in old age, his face only half-lit, is one of a number of telling photographs. China on the mantelpiece was decorated by Duncan Grant, Vanessa Bell and her son Quentin, and their work also fills the top half of the dresser in the tiny kitchen.

Every room is hung with paintings by the family circle, including Italian and Sussex landscapes and tranquil still-lifes, apples or a jug of flowers, by Vanessa, as well as some of her distinctive portraits, one of them a haunting likeness of her sister. Flowering potted plants might have come from the heated greenhouses where Leonard nurtured the begonias, lilies and gloxinias with which he filled the house. A gurgling fish tank behind the sitting-room door recalls his habit of looking after ailing fish from the garden ponds, and the dogs' blue pottery water bowl is still in its place.

In these modest rooms the Woolfs entertained some of the best-known literary and artistic figures of the day, among them Vita Sackville-West, Maynard Keynes, Lytton Strachey, E.M. Forster, David Garnett and Roger Fry. A black Chinese silk shawl embroidered in pink and green that is casually thrown over a chair in Virginia's sunny bedroom at the east end of the house was a present from Lady Ottoline Morrell. Many visitors were members of the Bloomsbury Group, which Virginia and Vanessa had founded with their brother Thoby Stephen and which was to give the sisters an influence far beyond their own work.

Near the house, where low flint walls are the remains of a piggery, informal cottagey plantings spill over brick paths and sculpture decoration includes a cast of Stephen Tomlin's unfinished bust of Virginia, modelled in 1931. The garden continues into grass and trees; there is a dewpond and orchard and the lawn where the Woolfs played bowls. Here the view opens out, and from the weather-boarded garden house where Virginia wrote there is a wide panorama east towards the River Ouse and a spur of the South Downs beyond. The huge battered table at which she sat and her distinctive blue paper are still here and there is also a display of her photographs, accompanied by quotations from her diaries and letters.

OPPOSITE This weather-boarded shed, where Virginia Woolf wrote, was built specially for her at the end of the garden at Monk's House in 1934 and still has the blue writing paper she liked on her desk.

ABOVE Virginia Woolf loved her sunny bedroom at the east end of Monk's House, from which she could look out on the garden, and which has tiles decorated by her sister Vanessa round the fireplace.

Montacute House

Somerset
In Montacute village, 4 miles (6.4 kilometres) west of Yeovil, on the south side of the A3088, 3 miles (4.8 kilometres) east of the A303

Montacute invites the kind of elaborate compliment paid by one sixteenth-century visitor, who thought the fronting stone terrace superior to St Mark's Square in Venice. Probably finished by 1601, it is a tall and confident H-shaped Elizabethan house of local honey-brown Ham stone, with a huge display of glittering glass. Designed by a local stonemason, the gifted William Arnold (*see also* Dunster Castle, p.126), it was built for Sir Edward Phelips, an upwardly mobile lawyer who would become Master of the Rolls and Chancellor to the Household of Prince Henry, Charles I's ill-fated elder brother.

Long facades facing east and west rise three storeys to a roofline fretted with delicate chimneys, parapets and pinnacles and adorned with curved Flemish gables. Classical details on the entrance front, such as the nine curiously lumpy statues in Roman dress, betray the influence of the Renaissance, slowly filtering north from its beginnings in Italy. The other side of the house is even more engaging. Here stonework from nearby Clifton Maybank, a splendid sixteenth-century mansion that was partly dismantled in 1786, ornaments the two-storey front grafted on between the existing wings in the late eighteenth century. The roofline parapet is crowded with heraldic beasts on pedestals, the shadows cast by these decorative features and by the advancing and retreating wall surfaces giving the house a sculptural quality. Montacute's fantasy outline is continued in the spiky balustrade and the two delightful Elizabethan pavilions topped with obelisks that border the entrance court.

Although hardly any of the original contents survived the decline in the Phelipses' fortunes, which led to Montacute being put up for sale in 1929, fine furniture and tapestries from the Sir Malcolm Stewart bequest give the rooms an authentic atmosphere. In the medieval-style great hall the

LEFT The local honey-coloured limestone of which Montacute is built is now attractively weathered and lichened.
ABOVE Montacute's east front, with ornate Flemish gables on the projecting wings, is set off by a balustraded forecourt of the same date as the house, ornamented with stone lanterns and obelisks.
OPPOSITE Early seventeenth-century plasterwork in the great hall shows a village drama, in which a man is punished after his wife caught him drinking when he should have been minding the baby.

early morning sun casts richly coloured pools through the heraldic glass in the east-facing windows. Phelips family portraits hang above the original panelling and an elaborate stone screen with columns framing rusticated arches runs across one end. Rams' heads with extravagant curling horns are carved on the capitals of the columns. A rare early seventeenth-century plaster panel on the north wall gives a tableau of rural life: a hen-pecked husband caught by his wife drawing beer from a barrel rather than attending to the baby is punished by being paraded round the village astride a pole.

A rich collection of hangings includes a fine fifteenth-century French *millefleurs* tapestry showing a knight on horseback against a beautifully detailed carpet of flowers, and the importance of domestic needlework in past centuries is shown in a changing display of samplers from the collection formed by Dr Douglas Goodhart, which ranges in date from 1609 to the twentieth century. The room where Lord Curzon slept when he leased Montacute in the early twentieth century has an ingenious bath concealed in a Jacobean-style cupboard

and the former great chamber, with its majestic carved chimneypiece, the finest in the house, has the only original furniture, a set of six early eighteenth-century walnut cane-back armchairs.

A magnificent long gallery, the largest surviving Elizabethan example in Britain, runs over 50 metres (170 feet) down the length of the third floor. Used for entertaining important guests and for exercise in inclement weather, the gallery is hung with Tudor and Jacobean paintings from the National Portrait Gallery that echo the portraits of family and notables that would once have hung here. A set of stiff kings and queens like a pack of playing cards contrasts with more realistic works, such as the delightful picture showing Robert

Carey, 1st Earl of Monmouth, with his family, the five adults posed as if in a photograph, or the portraits of the handsome, curly-headed Robert Sidney, 1st Earl of Leicester (1563–1626), and of little Henry, Prince of Wales (1594–1612), the child's creamy pallor emphasised by his rich crimson dress. There are panoramic views from the two great oriel windows, framed by orange trees in pots, at either end of the gallery.

Although now incorporating both nineteenth- and twentieth-century features and planting schemes, the extensive garden still follows the outlines of the original layout. The oriel window at the north end of the long gallery looks down on a formal rectangle of trees and grass which lies on the site of the Elizabethan garden. Raised walks framing the sunken lawn with its nineteenth-century balustraded pond probably date from when the house was built and a border of shrub roses under the retaining wall includes species in cultivation in the sixteenth century. The cedar lawn, with an arcaded garden house to which Lord Curzon may have added the Elizabethan facade, lies on the site of an old orchard.

An avenue of mature cedars, beeches and limes, fronted by clipped Irish yew, frames the west drive created in 1851–2, its lines continued in the wide grassy ride edged with limes which stretches away across the park to the east.

Moseley Old Hall

West Midlands
4 miles (6.4 kilometres) north of Wolverhampton; south of the M54 between the A449 and the A460

In the early hours of 8 September 1651, five days after his defeat at the Battle of Worcester, Charles II in the guise of a woodcutter came through the gate at the end of the Nut Alley and moved silently up the flagged path leading to the back of the house. Waiting in the dark outside were Thomas Whitgreave, the owner of Moseley, and his chaplain, John Huddlestone. The king was escorted through the heavily studded back door and, by the light of a candle, directed up the narrow stairs to the priest's room, now known as the King's Room.

Here he sat sipping a glass of wine while his sore feet were soothed, watching the firelight playing over the hangings of the four-poster bed where he was to spend his first night in comfort since the battle. Here, too, he was shown the hiding place, too small for a man to stand, which was concealed under a trapdoor in the cupboard to the right of the fireplace. Here Charles crouched when the Parliamentarians came to the house two days later. The night after this unwelcome visit, the king mounted a horse brought to the orchard stile and rode away, disguised as a serving man, on the first leg of his long and hazardous journey to safety on the Continent.

Visitors retrace Charles's route on that fateful night 350 years ago when the Stuart cause was nearly lost. Although the half-timbered Elizabethan house that the king would have seen was faced in brick in 1870 and the mullioned windows have been replaced by casements, Moseley still has its tall Elizabethan chimneys, much of the original panelling and timber framing survives inside the house, and seventeenth-century oak furniture, including the bed on which Charles slept, and contemporary portraits of the king and those who helped him, all contribute to an authentic atmosphere, miraculously not destroyed by noise from the nearby M54. Standing at the window of Whitgreave's study over the front porch, as he and the king did, it is possible to imagine that the remnants of the defeated Stuart army will shortly appear, straggling up the lane on their long walk back to Scotland. Mementoes of those perilous days include a proclamation of 10 September 1651, offering a £1,000 reward for the capture of the king, and Charles II's letter of thanks to Jane Lane, who accompanied him when he rode away from Moseley.

The house is now surrounded by a reconstructed seventeenth-century garden. In the elaborate knot garden, based on a design of 1640, box hedges outline a geometrical pattern like a horizontal wrought-iron screen, each compartment filled with coloured gravels and stones and some studded with box spheres. The orchard has been planted with old varieties of fruit trees; quinces, mulberries and medlars frame the path from the Nut Alley, and more box hedges embrace a little herb garden. Perhaps the king saw a similar garden from the chapel windows when John Huddlestone took him to visit the oratory in the attic, now adorned with an eighteenth-century painted barrel ceiling. Charles was certainly to remember Moseley, giving Thomas Whitgreave a pension of £200 a year on his restoration in 1660 and summoning Huddlestone to administer the last rites of the Catholic Church when he lay dying in 1685.

BELOW Moseley Old Hall is where the young Charles II, on the run from the Parliamentarians, was sheltered for two days after the devastating defeat of his army at Worcester in 1651.

Mottisfont

Hampshire
4½ miles (7.2 kilometres)
north-west of Romsey, ¾ mile
(1.2 kilometres) west of the A3057

Those lucky enough to acquire monastic houses at the time of the Dissolution in the 1530s were then faced with the problem of transforming them into domestic residences. Most chose to adapt the monks' living quarters, but a few ambitious men sought to incorporate the church itself into their conversions. One such was William Lord Sandys, Lord Chamberlain to Henry VIII, who was granted the priory of Mottisfont in exchange for the villages of Chelsea and Paddington and whose descendants were to move here from The Vyne (*see* p.334) after the Civil War. The north front of his Tudor house, built of silvery stone, runs the full length of what was the nave of the church, ending in the truncated crossing tower. The outline of the arch leading to the north transept shows clearly on the wall of the tower. Original mullions survive on the ground floor, but sash windows were inserted above as part of extensive Georgian alterations. These also account for the eighteenth-century stone balls crowning the medieval buttresses, transforming them into ornamental pilasters.

The cultured world of the 1740s is far more pronounced on the south side, where an elegant red-brick Georgian facade with a central pediment is framed by two shallow bayed wings stepped out from the main body of the house. Three storeys here, in contrast to two on the north, reflect the sloping site.

Few traces of the Tudor interior escaped the Georgian remodelling, but the ghost of the priory emerges in the atmospheric early thirteenth-century cellarium, where columns of Caen stone, now partly buried, support a vaulted roof. The most individual feature of the house, the Whistler Room over the cellarium, is a much later addition. This enchanting drawing room takes its name from Rex Whistler's elaborate *trompe-l'oeil* murals, imitating Gothick plasterwork, which he painted in 1938–9, after the completion of his mammoth work at Plas Newydd (*see* p.258). More theatrical backdrop than room decoration, Whistler's work includes the illusion of a smoking urn and of a paint pot abandoned high on a cornice. At Mottisfont Whistler had also been commissioned to design the furniture, but he never returned from the Second World War to complete his assignment.

Whistler's sketches for the drawing-room murals, and some idyllic landscapes that were offered as an alternative decorative scheme, are now part of an exceptional assemblage of late nineteenth- and twentieth-century art shown in the house. Apart from the Whistler drawings, these are all from the collection of the artist Derek Hill (1916–2000), whose friend Mrs Gilbert Russell gave Mottisfont to the National Trust. Hung in the library, morning room, entrance hall and west corridor, the pictures, many of them drawings, pastels or gouaches, are by artists who inspired Hill in his own work or who reflect his interest in his contemporaries. There are representative works by Bonnard, Vuillard, Seurat, Corot and Degas, but most of the names shown here are British, with several paintings by Hill's former students at the British School in Rome, where he was art director in the 1950s. On the whole, these are intimate pieces, ranging from a drawing of a surgical operation by Barbara Hepworth, a gouache by Graham Sutherland and a gentle portrait of his sister Gwen by Augustus John to studies of trees, leaves and pears. A number of landscapes include many works by Hill himself, among them scenes from the west of Ireland, where the artist had a house in Co. Donegal, and Italian landscapes that were captured when he was living near Florence on the estate of the art historian Bernard Berenson. Further twentieth-century works and contemporary art are shown in changing exhibitions in the light and airy gallery on the top floor of the house.

Lying low on sweeping lawns by the River Test, the abbey is the centrepiece of beautiful wooded gardens. Many of the mature walnuts, sycamores, Spanish chestnuts, beeches and cedars for which the property is now famous were part of the eighteenth-century grounds, but some are even older. A little Gothick summerhouse also dates from the eighteenth century and incorporates medieval floor tiles and a corbel from the priory.

OPPOSITE The medieval priory that was established at Mottisfont in 1201 emerges most clearly in the cellarium, where columns of Caen stone, now partly below floor level, support a fine vaulted roof. RIGHT A former entrance hall at Mottisfont Abbey was decorated in 1938–9 by Rex Whistler, whose *trompe l'oeil* fantasy, set off by the rich green velvet curtains, includes trophy panels painted in grisaille.

Mr and Mrs Gilbert Russell, who came to Mottisfont in 1934, introduced features designed by Geoffrey Jellicoe and, later, Norah Lindsay, among them the paved octagon surrounded by clipped yew and the box- and lavender-edged parterre. There is also a magnolia garden and a beech circle, and two walled gardens contain Mottisfont's renowned collection of roses. On the far side of the grounds, crystal-clear water still gushes from the spring that attracted the Austin canons to this sheltered spot nearly 800 years ago.

BELOW Although the south front of Mottisfont Abbey largely dates from the 1740s, the house incorporates the remains of a medieval priory, the cloister of which was on the site of the box parterre.

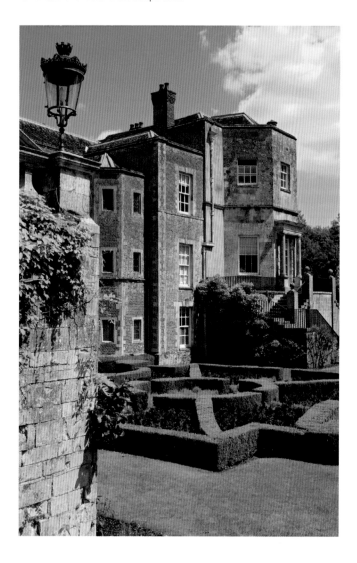

Mount Grace Priory

North Yorkshire
6 miles (9.6 kilometres) north-east of Northallerton, ½ mile (0.8 kilometre) east of the A19 and ½ mile (0.8 kilometre) south of its junction with the A172

The simplicity and austerity of this little Carthusian priory on the edge of the wooded Cleveland Hills is far removed from the splendour of Fountains, which is only some 20 miles (32 kilometres) to the south (*see* p.141). Whereas the remains of the Cistercian house speak of an increasing relaxation of the principles on which it was founded, Mount Grace reflects the pursuit of asceticism, untouched by worldly concerns. The Carthusians were more hermits than monks, living apart from each other as well as in isolation from what went on outside the priory walls. Whereas other orders ate, prayed and slept together, each Carthusian was mostly alone in his cell, to which meals were brought.

The main feature of Mount Grace is an extensive grass cloister, measuring some 82 metres (270 feet) on its longest side. Ranged around it, and along one side of an outer court, are the remains of the stone-built, four-roomed cells where the little community – there is provision for only 21 monks – spent long hours in prayer and contemplation and in copying out devotional works. Most of the cells still show the hatch through which food was served from the cloister, the right-angled bend ensuring that monk and server did not see one another. And each monk had his own walled garden, some 6 metres (20 feet) square, with his own garderobe at the far end. Perhaps some of the community allowed themselves to sit here and doze in the sun on warm summer afternoons. On the north side of the cloister is the diminutive church, a plain, simple building that was rarely used except on Sundays and feast days, its little battlemented and pinnacled tower a telling contrast to Marmaduke Huby's soaring monument at Fountains Abbey.

But although Mount Grace turned its back on the world, the community was not averse to modern conveniences. Arched recesses still visible in the cloister walls of some cells once held taps fed from a spring just outside the priory. Another spring was channelled to flush the drain serving the garderobes, some of which still project from the garden walls on the north side of the precinct.

ABOVE The ruins of Mount Grace Priory, set against the wooded Cleveland hills, include the remains of the little church where the Carthusian monks gathered only on Sundays and feast days.

Mount Grace was founded in 1398 by Thomas de Holland, Duke of Surrey and Earl of Kent, and is one of only nine Charterhouses established in England, most of them part of the great Carthusian expansion between 1343 and 1414. It was surrendered quietly to Henry VIII's commissioners in December 1539, and more than a century passed before the range housing the priory's guest accommodation and kitchens was converted into the long gabled house with a projecting two-storey porch (not open) which is now a feature of the site.

On the north side of the cloister the reconstructed cell, like a tiny two-storeyed cottage, dates from the early twentieth century, the fireplace in its living room suggesting a degree of comfort in winter. For those who chose to live like hermits here, physical privation was probably not the major burden of the regime. The cells outlined on the grass would have been a spiritual sanctuary for the strong and resolute, but a prison for those who found they could not live with themselves or began to doubt their faith.

Mount Stewart

Co. Down
15 miles (24 kilometres) east of
Belfast on the A20
Newtownards–Portaferry road,
5 miles (8 kilometres) south-east
of Newtownards

This long, low house looking south over Strangford Lough is associated with two exceptional men, the architect James 'Athenian' Stuart and the politician Viscount Castlereagh, but it is alive with the spirit of Edith, Lady Londonderry, the vivacious and brilliant wife of the 7th Marquess, who redecorated and furnished most of the house between the First and Second World Wars.

The main block, built of dark grey local stone and with a huge classical portico looking onto the balustraded entrance court, was designed in the mid-1830s, to replace the original eighteenth-century house, by the renowned Irish architect William Vitruvius Morrison for the 3rd Marquess of Londonderry. Morrison's grandiose octagonal hall, lit from above by a huge dome and with a black-and-white chequered floor and classical statues framed by Ionic pillars, fills the centre of the house. A bust immortalises the linen merchant Alexander Stewart, the 3rd Marquess's grandfather, who acquired the estate in 1744, while the rust-coloured early eighteenth-century Chinese dinner service displayed here was inherited by Stewart's wife, whose brother was Governor of Bombay. Morrison's vast drawing room divided by screens of green Ionic columns is similarly imposing and gave Lady Londonderry just the setting she needed for her lavish entertaining.

George Dance's west wing, created for the 1st Marquess in the early nineteenth century and built of the same grey stone as the later work, has a lighter and more intimate touch. The delightful music room, the least changed of his interiors, has an inlaid floor by John Ferguson, with a scalloped octagon of oak and mahogany surrounded by radiating boards of mellow bog fir enclosing a central motif like a Catherine wheel. Delicate plasterwork on the ceiling reflects the design. Double doors lead into Dance's elegant staircase hall, which is dominated by George Stubbs's intriguing painting of the racehorse Hambletonian. Stubbs shows the horse after his

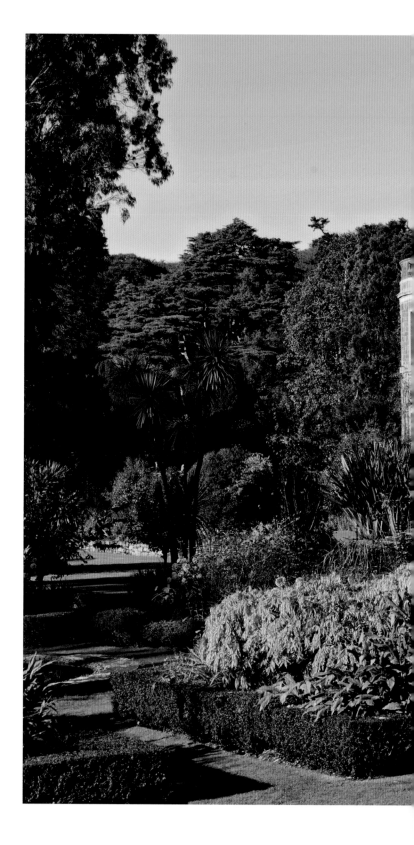

RIGHT Mount Stewart's long south front is punctuated by a pedimented loggia and looks over part of the formal gardens laid out round the house.

win at Newmarket in 1799, a race in which the artist felt the animal had been driven too hard. Hambletonian is depicted in an impossible pose, standing on his two left legs, his groom's right arm stretched like elastic over his neck.

The principal bedrooms called after European cities (Rome, Moscow, even Sebastopol), the mementoes in the Castlereagh Room and Empire chairs used by delegates to the Congress of Vienna in 1815, including those occupied by Wellington and Talleyrand, recall the proud and austere 2nd Marquess, Foreign Secretary for ten years, who died so tragically by his own hand in 1822, misunderstood by the nation to which he had devoted his life. The main architect of the Act of 1801 that united Great Britain and Ireland until the creation of Eire in 1921, Castlereagh went on to play a major role in the war against Napoleon and in the Congress of Vienna that concluded it, regarded as the world's first summit. It is a measure of Castlereagh's achievement that the European boundaries established at this time were to endure until the start of the First World War.

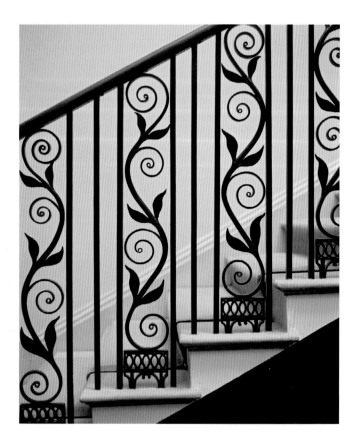

The 6th and 7th Marquesses also followed prominent political careers, and both Edward VII and the future George VI were entertained at Mount Stewart. As Secretary of State for Air from 1931 to 1935, the 7th Marquess promoted the Hurricane and Spitfire fighter planes, which were to prove so crucial in the Battle of Britain in 1940, and introduced legislation to establish air corridors. And in the late 1930s he made several private visits to Germany to meet Hitler and other Nazi leaders in an effort to promote Anglo-German understanding.

Leading politicians, among them Sir Arthur Balfour, Harold Macmillan and Ramsay MacDonald, featured at the celebrated house parties that Lady Edith gave in the interwar years. Her flamboyant 1920s decor, the backdrop for these glittering occasions, survives in most of the principal rooms. Salmon-pink walls in Morrison's drawing room set off a green grand piano and comfortable chairs and sofas are spread invitingly on the pink Aubusson carpets. Subdued low-level lighting comes from lamps of every description, some made out of classical urns, others once altar candlesticks. Chinese tea caddies converted into lamp stands, chinoiserie screens and other oriental pieces were brought back from a trip to China in 1912.

Two chairs in this room and the friendly stone animals sitting on a terrace on the south front, four plump dodos, a grinning dinosaur, a hedgehog and a frog among them, recall the Ark Club, formed from those who attended Lady Londonderry's gatherings for political and military figures at the family's London house during the First World War. Members of the club, all of whom were given the name of some exotic creature, included Sir Arthur Balfour (the albatross), Winston Churchill (the warlock), and Lord Hailsham (the wild boar). Appropriately, Lady Londonderry was Circe the Sorceress.

This legendary beauty, whose charm is if anything enhanced by the drab khaki uniform she is wearing in the

LEFT George Dance's staircase hall in Mount Stewart's west wing is the finest interior in the house, with a delicate cast-iron balustrade supporting the mahogany handrail of the stairs.
OPPOSITE The first-floor room in the Temple of the Winds, which was designed as a banqueting house, has an exquisite marquetry floor that echoes the plasterwork of the ceiling.

portrait showing her as head of the Women's Legion, was also largely responsible for Mount Stewart's enchanting 31.5-hectare (78-acre) garden, which flourishes with subtropical luxuriance in the temperate climate of the Ards peninsula.

Many of the tender trees and shrubs cultivated here are rarely seen elsewhere in the British Isles and there is a notable collection of evergreens and other species from the Southern Hemisphere. Around the house a formal garden is laid out as a series of varied outdoor rooms. An Italian garden, with steps descending to fountain pools, was designed by Lady Londonderry and is enhanced by imaginative statuary, including mischievous monkeys and winged dragons perched on columns. The more intimate sunken garden to the west of the house is based on a design by Gertrude Jekyll, with rose-hung pergolas and scalloped beds, and the secluded, shady Mairi Garden laid out in the shape of a Tudor rose recalls Lady Mairi Bury, the 7th Marquess's daughter, who gave Mount Stewart and many of its contents, together with an endowment, to the National Trust in 1976.

Away from the house the planting is informal, with magnificent trees, shrubs and herbaceous plants lining the walks round the lake created by the 3rd Marquess, part of a nineteenth-century layout which Lady Londonderry embellished. Conical roofs glimpsed above the trees on the summit of the wooded hill beyond the lake mark the Londonderrys' burial ground, Tir Nan Og, which contains the graves of the 7th Marquess and his wife.

The octagonal Temple of the Winds, on a prominent knoll in the woods to the south of the house, is a replica, like its counterpart at Shugborough (*see* p.287), of the Tower of the Winds in ancient Athens and the only building in Ireland by the pioneering Neo-classical architect James 'Athenian' Stuart. Erected by the 1st Marquess between 1782 and 1785, it was designed as an eye-catcher and banqueting house. The sumptuously decorated upper room has another star-like marquetry floor by John Ferguson, the design again echoed in plaster on the ceiling, and a dew-drop chandelier hangs from the central medallion. On the floor below, long sash windows can be lowered into the basement to give an uninterrupted view over the island-studded waters of Strangford Lough to the prominent silhouette of Scrabo Tower on the north shore, built in memory of the 3rd Marquess.

Mr Straw's House

Nottinghamshire
5–7 Blyth Grove, Worksop

This bay-fronted, three-storey Edwardian villa is like a thousand other red-brick suburban semis built for well-to-do tradesmen and professionals in the early years of the twentieth century. But the Straw brothers – William and Walter – who lived here for 50 years were anything but ordinary. Perhaps never quite recovering from the deaths of their parents, William and Florence, in the 1930s, and maybe naturally reclusive and conservative, they preserved the house as it was when their father and mother were alive, ignoring modern conveniences, such as central heating and the telephone, and the advent of radio and television.

Today, 5–7 Blyth Grove is partly a shrine to William senior and Florence, partly a uniquely well-preserved example of interwar middle-class living. Completely refurbished before the family moved in, in 1923, the house boasts dark 1920s wallpapers with decorative Sanderson borders, doors and other woodwork painted to simulate oak, and period carpets and lino. Furnishings are heavy, the rooms cluttered, with the parents' belongings still in their customary places. William senior's coats and hats still hang in the hall, and in William and Florence's bedroom, where the brass bedstead is covered with newspaper to keep off the dust, the dressing-table still has the box for William's detachable collars and drawers of personal belongings, such as the blue sunglasses Florence wore on her annual holiday in Scarborough. The period detail even includes trade calendars advertising the grocery business that William built up, and an unheated, starkly functional 1920s bathroom. The kitchen, where bread was baked every Saturday night, is similarly uninviting, although the brothers did put in a 1950s gas stove.

The boys seem to have fitted in round their parents' space, living largely in the south-facing dining room, one of only two rooms where a fire was regularly lit in cold weather, and, in William junior's case, sleeping in a small atticky bedroom at the top of the house. An ordered routine, unchanged for 40 years, included the Sunday outing to church, where the brothers always sat in the same pew, and the Sunday afternoon walk into town to inspect their grocery store and other property, while every weekday, after the shop closed, Walter would call in at his cousin's house over the road to listen to the 6 o'clock news on the radio. Both brothers liked to work in the little garden, which still has its outside privy. It seems William, who read English at university and taught for some years in London, was the dominant personality, resisting innovation and refusing to let Walter bring the car he bought in the 1960s to the house. It was William, too, who became the custodian of Blyth Grove, leaving notes around the place to record details about the family and its possessions. But he was by no means unworldly. Savings from his teacher's salary were invested in Marks & Spencer shares, worth over £150,000 at his death in 1990.

BELOW The Edwardian villa where William and Walter Straw lived for fifty years, preserving the house as it was when their parents were alive, still has William senior's coats and hats hanging in the hall.

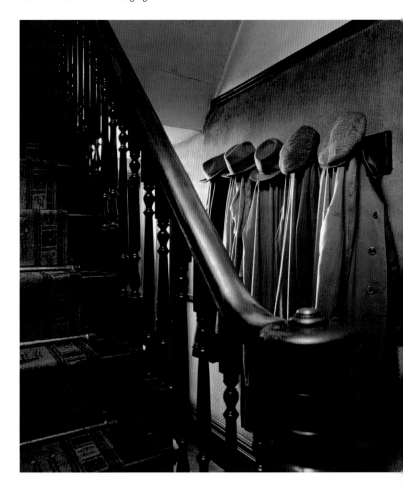

Needles Old and New Batteries

Isle of Wight
West of Freshwater Bay and
Alum Bay

The threat of a French invasion in 1858, fuelled by Lord Palmerston's aggressively nationalistic foreign policy, threw Britain into a panic, not least because the coastal defences, little changed since the time of the Battle of Trafalgar in 1805, were clearly inadequate. This magnificently sited little fort, set 76 metres (250 feet) above the sea on the far western point of the Isle of Wight, was one of the new artillery works built to guard the approaches to the Solent and the major naval base at Portsmouth.

A walk of about a mile (1.6 kilometres) across the downs leads to the dagger-shaped headland, with precipitous chalk cliffs falling to the jagged outlines of the Needles, where the fort was built. On the other side of a ditch cut to protect the landward approaches is the only entrance, a massive archway dated 1862. A tunnel-like passage emerges in the parade ground, where five semicircular gun emplacements, two of them now mounted with guns rescued from the sea by the National Trust in 1983, face west and north. Built into the rock are underground chambers for storing gunpowder, shells and cartridges: the ingenious arrangements that allowed candles or oil-burning lanterns to be used without danger of igniting the powder and the system of ventilation ducts that kept the ammunition dry can still be seen. From the parade ground another tunnel leads out to the look-out positioned on the very tip of the headland, where a searchlight was set up in 1899. The views are breathtaking: down onto the points of the Needles, with their wheeling colonies of cormorants and seagulls, and across the bay to the mainland, where the outline of Hurst Castle marks the western arm of the Solent. Just up the hill, on the site of the original Needles lighthouse, are the remains of the Needles New Battery, built in 1893–5 and finally closed in 1954 when the guns were scrapped.

Although the Needles batteries saw little active service, they have played an important role in military history. A massive iron ring in the parade ground of the Old Battery marks the site of the world's first anti-aircraft gun, set up here in 1913. And in 1956 the headland was the engine-testing site for the Black Knight rocket, subsequently launched at Woomera in Australia.

BELOW From the look-out on the very tip of the headland, there are spectacular views of the Needles and of the mainland over the water.

Newark Park

Gloucestershire
1½ miles (2.4 kilometres)
north-east of Wotton-under-Edge,
1½ miles (2.4 kilometres) south
of the junction of the A4135 and
the B4058

This unusual, atmospheric house stands high on a spur of the Cotswolds looking south over steep wooded slopes plunging to the valley of the River Severn. Buttresses, battlements and Georgian sash windows added by James Wyatt in the 1790s only partly disguise the modest four-storey Tudor hunting lodge built by Sir Nicholas Poyntz in *c.*1550. His romantic dragon weathervane, its long coiled tail silhouetted against the sky, still surmounts the building. Like his father and grandfather before him, Sir Nicholas was prominent at court, becoming Groom of the Bedchamber to Henry VIII after 1539. His hunting lodge was built on monastic land which had formerly belonged to the Abbey of Kingswood in the vale below and which was granted to him by the king after the monastery was dissolved. Some materials from the former abbey were incorporated in Newark.

The Tudor building emerges most strongly on the east, where Wyatt's sympathetic hand did not destroy original features. Although Sir Nicholas's architect is unknown, this tall, symmetrical facade, with huge mullioned and transomed

BELOW The delightful porch on the south front of Newark Park is one of the gothic touches added by James Wyatt in c.1810.

windows lighting the upper floors, reflects the sophisticated world of the court rather than local building styles, and suggests something of the Elizabethan prodigy houses that were to follow at the end of the century. A prominent three-light oriel projects from the centre of the building and a pedimented doorway flanked by Doric columns is a remarkably pure Renaissance feature for its date. The two top floors were originally banqueting rooms, from which Sir Nicholas and his guests would have enjoyed wide views over the deer-park around the house and the wooded countryside beyond.

Internally, Wyatt left the lodge more or less as it was and Tudor fireplaces still warm some of the rooms in this part of the house, but he remodelled a second block added in the late seventeenth century, introducing Neo-classical interiors. More Doric columns divide the unusual hall he inserted between the two parts of the building, his frieze of sheep's skulls perhaps intended to recall the wool trade which brought wealth to this area in the Middle Ages.

Formal axial gardens to the north and east were laid out by Mr Robert Parsons, the Texan architect who rented the house from 1970 to 1994 and began to restore it, but there are still remnants of the wild bulb garden and rock gardens created in the late nineteenth century on the slopes below the lodge.

Nostell Priory and Parkland

West Yorkshire
On the A638 out of Wakefield
towards Doncaster

Sir Rowland Winn, 4th Baronet, commissioned two houses at Nostell in the mid-eighteenth century. One of them, a classical building only a few feet high, stands at the foot of the south staircase of the priory. Like the similarly fine dolls' house at Uppark (*see* p.330), it is fully furnished in period style, and was built to delight an adult as much as to enchant a child. Marble chimneypieces are copied from plates in James Gibbs's *Book of Architecture* of 1728, carved mouldings and cornices in the principal rooms are picked out in gilt, and the furnishings are accurate in every detail. Little figures representing the family are looked after by servants in the Winn livery of grey and yellow, and there is even a glass mouse under the kitchen table. If family tradition is correct, this minor masterpiece was the work of two young men closely associated with Rowland Winn's new mansion: James Paine, who executed and modified the plans of the gentleman-architect Colonel James Moyser; and the cabinetmaker Thomas Chippendale, both then still in their teens.

The estate had been acquired by the Winns, a family of London merchants, in 1650, ten years before a baronetcy was granted by Charles II, and has been held by the family ever since. The present house, built to the north of an earlier building formed out of the old priory, was created over 50 years, beginning in 1735, with a strong contrast between James Paine's rococo decoration for Sir Rowland and the more severe classical designs of his successor, Robert Adam, later to oust Paine again at Kedleston (*see* p.180), for Sir Rowland's son. Fine interiors include paintings by Antonio Zucchi that are among his earliest work in England, plasterwork by Joseph Rose the Younger and furniture by Chippendale.

Because only one of Adam's planned extensions to Paine's pedimented classical house was ever completed, the exterior of the priory is pleasingly asymmetrical. Adam was also responsible for lifting the main entrance facade by adding the substantial terrace reached by two flights of gracefully curving

steps. Inside, however, it is Paine's rooms that are the more flamboyant. Adam's beautiful hall is a serenely graceful room, with Rose's delicate plasterwork picked out against a subtly darker background. The library, decorated with nine stylised classical paintings by Zucchi and with the Winn family's important collection of books housed in the pedimented bookcases, is dominated by a superb desk by Chippendale. The outstanding book collection overflows into the billiard room next door, where an intriguing longcase clock is an early piece by the young John Harrison, who made the mechanism for the clock almost entirely out of wood. The son of the estate carpenter at Nostell, Harrison went on to make his name by inventing the first timepiece that was accurate enough to enable seamen to determine their longitude, for which he received a reward of £20,000.

Adam's restrained treatments only serve to heighten the opulence of Paine's rooms. Zucchi's playful cherubs in the elaborate panels over the doors in the dining room and the plaster frieze of vines and satyrs' masks suggest an appreciation of the good things in life. Paine was also responsible for the splendid ceiling in what is now the state bedchamber, with its trio of music-making cherubs, but the exquisite Chinese paper, with brightly coloured birds of all sizes and varieties perching on branches laden with flowers and foliage, was chosen by Chippendale to complement his rich green and gold lacquer furniture, among his most unusual work.

Fine paintings hang throughout the house, among them a copy of Holbein's group portrait of Thomas More and his family that was painted by Rowland Lockey in 1592, a characteristic landscape by Pieter Breughel the Younger, with a procession of diminutive figures accompanying Christ on his way to Calvary (recently saved by public appeal and support from the Art Fund and National Heritage Memorial Fund), and a self-portrait of 1791 by Angelica Kauffmann, in which she portrays, in classical symbolism, her decision to abandon a promising operatic career in favour of painting.

ABOVE The austere east front of Nostell Priory, with the projecting portico of Robert Adam's family wing at the north end and with Adam's steps leading to the first floor.
OPPOSITE The plasterer Joseph Rose the Younger and the decorative painter Antonio Zucchi executed Adam's delicate ceiling designs.

The house is set off by a pastoral landscape that still has traces of Stephen Switzer's formal design of 1730 for the 4th Baronet, but which was developed in a more naturalistic style over the next hundred years. The main view from the house looks across a sweep of grass to a lake and the little hump-backed bridge built in 1761 to carry the main Wakefield to Doncaster road. A Gothick menagerie that was probably designed by Paine but has additions by Adam stands in the pleasure grounds to the west of the lake and Adam designed three lodges for the 5th Baronet, one of which is in the form of a pyramid.

Nuffield Place

Oxfordshire
On the A4130 between Wallingford
and Henley-on-Thames

The little village of Nuffield sits at the western edge of the Chilterns, where the hills fall away towards the Thames. Surrounded by trees on the edge of the village is the unpretentious and comfortable house where the industrialist and philanthropist William Morris, 1st Lord Nuffield, lived for 30 years. A self-made man who left school at 15, Morris, who started in business by repairing and building bicycles, made his fortune by producing one of the first affordable family cars. His prototype model was designed in 1912, when Morris was in his mid-30s, but it was only after the First World War, when he applied the kind of streamlined manufacturing techniques developed in America to the mass production of cars at his Cowley works in Oxford, that output took off and vehicles could be sold at prices that a wide sector of the population could afford. By 1925 the factory was producing 56,000 cars a year, owning one was no longer the preserve of the very rich and Morris was well on the way to becoming one of the wealthiest men in the world.

William and his wife Elizabeth bought Nuffield Place in 1932, the year before Morris became Lord Nuffield. Designed by Oswald Milne (*see* Coleton Fishacre, p.102), a pupil of Lutyens, as an L-shaped building of red and grey brick, the house was built in 1914 as a country retreat for the shipping magnate Sir John Bowring Wimble. Alterations by Lord Nuffield, in particular the addition of a capacious billiard room, have blurred the original lines, but the many-windowed facades looking onto the garden, with their deep eaves, tall chimneys breaking the sweep of the tiled roof and grey shutters, show the character of Milne's work.

The interior is essentially as it was when Lord Nuffield died in 1963, with furnishings that reflect a certain kind of 1930s taste, and a strong sense of William Morris the man and of the couple's lifestyle. Apart, perhaps, from the billiard room, with its Art Deco burr walnut cocktail cabinet, there is nothing showy here, although the reproduction furniture that was made for the Nuffields in the 1920s and '30s, much of it by the local firm Cecil A. Halliday of Oxford, and the richly coloured oriental rugs, are all of the highest quality. A love of the historic and traditional comes through in the limed oak panelling lining the hall and first-floor landing and in the copies of antique pieces, among them a 'Tudor' oak food cupboard made of genuinely old timber in the dining room and a high-backed carved settle in the hall. The table in the dining room, also made by Hallidays, is laid for dinner with the Nuffields' striking blue bohemian glass, but, except when entertaining, William and Elizabeth preferred to sit in the much more modest room next door, Scottie dog at their feet. A television cabinet tucked away in one corner, with a period wireless perched on top, was bought in 1955.

Lord Nuffield's love of things mechanical comes through in the four longcase clocks in the hall, which he kept in perfect working order, in the automatic match dispensers in the drawing room and, above all, in the vast built-in tool cupboard, crammed with screwdrivers, spanners, saws and an array of other useful items, from materials for repairing shoes to coils of wire, in his bedroom. The carpet here is patched together and there is a tangle of flex round the reading light rigged up over the bed. In summer, Lord Nuffield often slept in the little room next door, created out of a balcony on the corner of the house, where a long window gives a panoramic

ABOVE Lord Nuffield used to ride this exercise horse, which was made for him in Oxford.
OPPOSITE The attractive west front of Nuffield Place, with grey shutters framing the windows, deep eaves and a sundial set into the brickwork.
RIGHT Lord Nuffield rigged up the reading light over the bed in his bedroom and kept the many clocks in working order.

view north-west over the Thames valley to Wittenham Clumps on the other side of the river.

Rooms are hung with flower paintings, prints or watercolours of Oxford, and there is one portrait of the great man, painted by Henry Gates in 1931, but there are no fine works of art here. Lord Nuffield was the ultimate philanthropist, preferring to use his fortune to benefit others rather than to spend lavishly on himself. An ultra-violet sun lamp like those he provided for night workers in his factories in the Second World War and a huge iron lung like the

hundreds he provided for hospitals throughout the Commonwealth reflect his particular interest in health and medicine. In 1937 he founded Nuffield College in Oxford, but by far the most important of his many benefactions was the gift of £10 million for the setting up of the Nuffield Foundation for medical, scientific and educational research in 1943. At his death, the house and estate passed to Nuffield College and in 2011 the college gave the house and some of the land to the National Trust.

Nunnington Hall

North Yorkshire
In Ryedale, 4½ miles
(7.2 kilometres) south-east of
Helmsley on the A170
Helmsley–Pickering road; 1½ miles
(2.4 kilometres) north of the B1257
Malton–Helmsley road

For much of its history, this tranquil house on the banks of the River Rye was a secondary residence, lived in by stewards or tenants of influential men rather than being in the mainstream itself. One grandee was William Parr, brother of Catherine, Henry VIII's sixth queen, who forfeited Nunnington to the Crown in 1553 when he unwisely supported the plan to put Lady Jane Grey on the throne. Another was Robert Huicke, physician to Henry VIII, Edward VI and Elizabeth I, who told the queen she would never have children. The earliest parts of the present building, visible on the west front, are Elizabethan, dating from Parr's time. The house was much improved and extended by the Norcliffe family, who lived at Nunnington in the early seventeenth century, but when Parliamentary troops billeted here during the Civil War badly damaged the hall, Thomas Norcliffe, after first removing various desirable fittings, gave up the lease.

Richard, 1st Viscount Preston, who inherited Nunnington from his great-uncle in 1685, restored and remodelled the hall, largely creating the house as it is today. A convert to Rome, Lord Preston was Master of the Wardrobe to James II and one of five peers entrusted with the government of the country when James fled in 1688. Apprehended on the fishing boat he had hoped would bear James triumphantly back to England, Preston was taken to the Tower of London and saved from execution only by the pleadings of his youngest daughter Susannah. Stripped of his offices and disgraced, he returned to Yorkshire, where he died a few years later.

Preston is traditionally attributed with Nunnington's finest architectural feature: the long, two-storeyed south front with projecting gables at either end. Unusually, two central doors stand one above the other, with a charming wrought-iron balcony round the upper one, and the whole composition appears both welcoming and refined.

Inside, the house is cosily elegant, its panelled rooms filled with period furniture, tapestries and porcelain collected by the last owner. The grandest room is Preston's oak hall, with its elaborate chimneypiece supporting his coat of arms joined

with those of his wife and a three-arched classical screen leading to the great oak and pine staircase climbing round three sides of a well. Preston emerges again in the two large ceiling canvases, curiously depicting various family coats of arms against a cloudy sky, that he commissioned for a small upstairs room, and in the little oratory adjoining a bedroom in the west wing, a reminder of his adopted Roman Catholicism and of the family's continued recusancy in the eighteenth century. Part of the attic above now houses the Carlisle

Collection of Miniature Rooms, fully furnished in different period styles.

The delightful walled garden to the south of the house is a rare survival from the seventeenth century, which still bears traces of the original formal layout. A rusticated stone gateway inserted in the south wall in the 1920s marks the site of the *clairvoyée*, a railing on a low wall extending the view beyond the garden, which is shown on a rough sketch by Samuel Buck of *c*.1720. A lawn is flanked by rectangles of spring-flowering

meadows and an orchard is planted with old varieties of fruit trees. Eccentrically individual arches and gates through which the garden is approached have bold rustication in a French style that Lord Preston may have seen when he was Ambassador to France for Charles II.

Nymans

West Sussex
On the B2114 at Handcross,
4½ miles (7.2 kilometres) south
of Crawley, just off the M23/A23
London–Brighton road

The enchanting compartmental garden set high in the Sussex Weald that was devised and nurtured by three generations of the Messel family is laid out round an apparently ancient house. Now largely a picturesque ruin, with climbers smothering the buttressed walls, mullioned windows that are now glassless and empty and roofless gable ends, this romantic backdrop is all that remains of the southern side of a pastiche Tudor manor that was built here in 1928 by Leonard Messel, whose father Ludwig created the original garden.

Ludwig and his wife, who had come to Nymans in 1890, had commissioned the architect Sir Ernest George to enlarge an existing early nineteenth-century villa, which was given an Italianate tower, a huge conservatory and other improvements, such as a billiard room. Leonard and his wife Maud, who took over Nymans in 1916, longed to live in a West Country manor and they engaged Norman Evill and subsequently Sir Walter Tapper to transform the existing building into a convincing reproduction of a medieval and Tudor house. Then, in February 1947, in the middle of an exceptionally hard winter, the house caught fire and, the standpipes being frozen, the flames could not be brought under control until water was pumped up from a pond at the bottom of the park. The whole southern side of the building, with the great hall and other principal rooms, was gutted and almost all the contents, including a valuable collection of botanical books, lost. Although damaged, the north and west parts of the house survived, and the family rooms were re-created in a more intimate setting with furniture salvaged from the fire and other pieces that were brought down to Sussex after the Messels' London house was sold. Miraculously, much of the planting on the south front also withstood the flames, including the great *Magnolia grandiflora* that now smothers the end of the ruined great hall.

After Leonard's death in 1953 and that of his wife in 1960, Nymans became the home of their daughter Anne and her second husband, the 6th Earl of Rosse, who did much to nurture and enrich the garden. The house is shown as the countess had it, with many echoes of her brother, the theatre designer Oliver Messel, and of her son by her first marriage, the photographer Lord Snowdon, who advised on the arrangement of the rooms. A door in the ruined wing opens into a long, wide, low-ceilinged corridor, more hall than passage, which links the main rooms in the range beyond. Arched openings reveal a comfortable sitting room, with a Broadwood grand piano covered in family photographs at one end, and the little book room, where the television that belonged to Oliver Messel has been given curtains and a proscenium arch, as if it were a theatre. There are irregular Tudor stone flags in the hall, heavy arched wooden doors, great fireplaces and other period touches, some of them, such as a narrow archway, survivals from a genuinely ancient house on this site, the scant remains of which were embraced by the villa; others, such as a timber partition, which came from a barn, brought here from other medieval buildings. The atmosphere of antiquity is enhanced by the Messels' collection of tapestries and seventeenth-century furniture and by a Flemish panel painting of Christ blessing the children, with figures in robes of luminous scarlet. These pieces are mixed with many twentieth-century touches, among them Norman Evill's drawing of the house, a sketch of the actress Merle Oberon by Oliver Messel and a dramatic self-portrait by Lord Snowdon. This last is among another show of family photographs in the comfortable library, complete with drinks trolley, at the end of the passage. The countess, who died in 1992, used to write here at the desk under the window that looks out onto the little stone-walled court on the west side of the house, with a delicious octagonal dovecote in one corner.

OPPOSITE The romantic Tudor-style ruins at Nymans, with the traceried windows of the great hall on the right, are smothered in climbers, some of which survived the fire which gutted the house in 1947.

Ormesby Hall

Middlesbrough
3 miles (4.8 kilometres)
south-east of Middlesbrough,
west of the A171

ABOVE Ormesby Hall was designed in a severe Palladian style that was popular in North Yorkshire in the mid-eighteenth century.
BELOW Ormesby Hall's service wing to the east of the main house, which contains this fully equipped Victorian laundry, was formed out of the earlier Jacobean house of *c.*1600.

Sir James Pennyman, 6th Baronet, and his aunt Dorothy were clearly people of taste. Although 'Wicked Sir James', a spendthrift in the best eighteenth-century manner, ran through the fortune he inherited in 1770 in eight years, he spent his wealth on enlarging the Ormesby estate and enriching the house his aunt had built some 30 years earlier. Unfortunately, he was then obliged to surrender the property to the bailiffs.

Probably completed by 1743, Ormesby was designed by an unknown architect in a characteristically plain Palladian style then popular in North Yorkshire. The rather severe outlines of the tall three-storey main block rising to a hipped roof are relieved only by a heavy cornice and pediments on the two main facades. Projecting porches were Victorian additions.

A two-storey service wing on the east was formed out of the earlier Jacobean house, thought to have been built in about 1600, its low facades an interesting contrast to the later building. Although most of the original features of the service wing have been lost, one fine ornamented Jacobean doorway has survived, with the crest granted to James Pennyman in 1599 proudly displayed on the coat of arms above.

The interior of the main block is a complete contrast. Ormesby is not at all grand but the most talented of local craftsmen were employed to create the rich plaster decoration and woodwork that are such a feature of the house. Ionic columns screening both ends of the hall and Palladian motifs here and in the library are of Dorothy's time, but Sir James introduced the delicate Adamesque ceilings attributed to Carr of York in the drawing room and dining room, where the silver cup he presented to Northallerton racecourse now stands proudly on the sideboard. Plain family rooms on the first floor contrast with some decorated guest rooms on the north side, one adorned with carved festoons of fruit and foliage. These rooms are served by a notable panelled gallery, essentially a glorified landing, which runs across the house. Some of the finest eighteenth-century carving at Ormesby is on the sumptuous pedimented doorcases here, with subtle variations in the design indicating the status of the chamber beyond.

The house is now filled with Regency and Victorian furniture, and a number of family portraits reflect the generations of Pennymans who continued to live at Ormesby despite the 6th Baronet's extravagance. Sir James's dignified stables crowned with a cupola, probably also designed by Carr of York, are now let to the mounted police.

A small rose garden and mixed beds and borders, some planted in cottage-garden style, set off the house. A holly walk shows off fancy-leaved varieties, and naturalised spring bulbs carpet the woodland towards the church, where William Lawson, author of several gardening books, was vicar in the early seventeenth century.

Osterley Park

Middlesex
Just north of Osterley station,
on the western outskirts of
London (Piccadilly tube line)

This grand Neo-classical villa was created in the mid-eighteenth century out of a mansion built by Sir Thomas Gresham, Chancellor of the Exchequer to Elizabeth I. The ghost of the sixteenth-century courtyard house still lingers on in Osterley's square plan, with three ranges of warm red brick looking onto a central courtyard. But the delightful corner turrets crowned with cupolas, somewhat reminiscent of those at Blickling (see p.57), are later additions, there is nothing Elizabethan about the sash windows and balustraded roofline, and on the fourth side of the courtyard, where once there would have been another range, a wide flight of steps leads up to a magnificent double portico stretching between the wings. The courtyard itself is raised, to give direct access to the principal rooms on the first floor.

Although there were alterations to Gresham's mansion in the late seventeenth and early eighteenth centuries, the house was transformed from 1761 by Robert Adam, who spent 20 years working on Osterley. Statues of Greek deities standing in niches and 'antique' vases on pedestals in Adam's cool grey and white entrance hall introduce the classical theme of the house. In the airy library, paintings depicting the world of ancient Greece and Rome by Antonio Zucchi are set into plaster frames built into the walls above the pilastered and pedimented bookcases. Marquetry furniture attributed to John Linnell includes a pedestal desk inlaid with trophies representing the arts, and there is a delicate Adam ceiling. Close by is an eating room arranged in the eighteenth-century way, with the chairs against the walls and no large central

BELOW Adam's dramatic double portico at Osterley forms a grand entrance to the house.

table. The kitchen in the basement below, where five servants were employed in the mid-eighteenth century, was originally set in the opposite corner of the house, so diners were not disturbed by noise and cooking smells.

Adam also designed the three rooms that form the state apartment on the south front. One of his most ambitious pieces of furniture, a domed eight-poster bed, dominates the state bedroom, but the most original decorative scheme is in the Etruscan dressing room, where ochre-coloured dancing figures and urns set beneath arches look as if a series of Greek vases has been flattened on the walls. In contrast, and despite its Adam ceiling, the antechamber has a French flavour. All claret and gold, it is hung with Gobelins tapestries.

Unlike most of the interiors on the principal floor, the gallery that stretches the length of the garden front has decorative features which pre-date Adam, such as the marble fireplaces carved by Joseph Wilton from a design by William Chambers, although Adam was responsible for the pea-green wallpaper, the Ionic doorcases and the four large pier-glasses, probably the work of John Linnell.

Red-brick Tudor stables just north of the house, with original staircase turrets in the angles of the building, survive largely intact, apart from some alterations to doors and windows and the addition of a clock tower in the eighteenth century. Behind are the eighteenth-century pleasure grounds, where a Doric temple and Adam's semicircular garden house are set off by lawns, serpentine gravel paths and a re-creation of a Regency flower garden. The park stretches away, with majestic cedars planted in the eighteenth century shading a lake and cattle grazing beneath the trees in the Great Meadow to the west. Despite the proximity of Heathrow and the M4, Osterley still feels like a country estate.

OPPOSITE The decoration in Adam's Etruscan dressing room at Osterley was created by Pietro Maria Borgnis, who painted the motifs on paper and then pasted them on canvas for fixing to the walls and ceiling.

Adam was employed by Francis Child, whose grandfather had purchased the estate in 1711 after rising from obscurity to found one of the first banks in England (now subsumed in the Royal Bank of Scotland). After Francis's early death at the age of 28, his brother Robert completed Osterley, but he also died prematurely, perhaps partly as a result of anxiety about his only child Sarah Anne, who eloped with the 10th Earl of Westmorland at the age of 18. When mildly rebuked by her mother, who pointed out she had better matches in mind, the high-spirited girl replied, 'A bird in the hand is worth two in the bush.' The father forgave his only child, but altered his will to leave Osterley and most of his fortune to Sarah Anne's second son, or eldest daughter, thus cutting out the Westmorland heir.

In the event, Osterley passed, through Sarah Anne's daughter, to the Earls of Jersey, and it was the 9th Earl who gave the house to the National Trust in 1949. Sadly, a collection of exceptional paintings, including works by Rubens, Van Dyck and Claude, which were displayed in the gallery were almost all destroyed in a fire while en route to the earl's new home in Jersey. The present hang in the gallery, based on loans and gifts, has been devised to conjure up the eighteenth-century arrangement and is strong on later seventeenth- and eighteenth-century Venetian painting. Some enormous eighteenth-century Chinese jars and vases spaced down the room are part of an important collection of ceramics in the home, while the Child and Jersey family silver, gold plate and other valuables, dating back to the 1740s, are shown in cabinets in the strong room in the basement, where traces of the original Tudor brickwork can still be seen in the wine and beer cellars.

Overbeck's

Devon
1½ miles (2.4 kilometres) south-west of Salcombe, signposted from Malborough and Salcombe

The rolling country of south Devon is crossed by a network of narrow, winding lanes, one of which leads steeply up from the little port of Salcombe to this elegant Edwardian house set on a slope above the sea. Like the small Victorian villa it replaced, it was for long known as Sharpitor after the prominent craggy line of rocks just offshore, but it now bears the name of Otto Overbeck, the scientist who lived here from 1928–37 and who filled the house with his collections.

Everything is laid out in some half-dozen homely rooms. Shipbuilding tools and exquisitely detailed model ships reflect Salcombe's heyday as a port in the 1870s and there is also a collection of sailors' snuffboxes and marine paintings, one of them almost certainly showing the *Phoenix*, which was built here in 1836 and which disappeared with all hands on a voyage to Barcelona, in full sail in the background.

Natural history exhibits illustrate local wildlife and British shells, birds' eggs and insects, several species among the cases of butterflies now very rare. A cabinet devoted to Otto Overbeck himself contains his popular rejuvenator, patented in 1924, which was said to inject new life into the old and tired by passing electricity through the body. Perhaps clients were also urged to consume Mr Overbeck's non-alcoholic beer, another of his many inventions. A secret room under the stairs, full of dolls and toys, has been specially created for children.

The 2.5-hectare (6-acre) garden, which enjoys the mildest of microclimates, is the most Mediterranean of those in the National Trust's care. Apart from the upper lawn around the house, most of it slopes steeply towards the sea in a series of sunny, sheltered terraces, where many rare and tender species thrive. And far below there is the constant backdrop of the sea, often speckled with little boats. Cliffs across the bay run south to the dramatic headland of Prawle Point, while inland there are views to Salcombe and up the wooded reaches of the Kingsbridge estuary.

BELOW From the garden of Overbeck's, set high on the cliffs above Salcombe on the coast of south Devon, there are panoramic views up the wooded Kingsbridge estuary, where the water is speckled with sailing boats in summer.

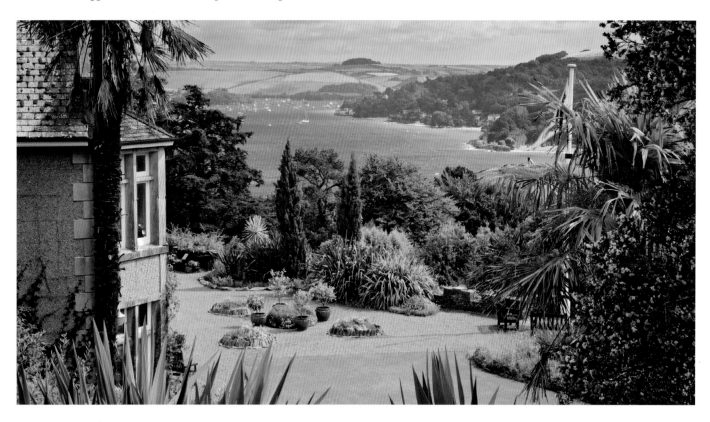

Owletts

Kent
1 mile (1.6 kilometres) south of
the A2, at the west end of village
of Cobham, at the junction of roads
from Dartford and Sole Street

This red-brick, two-storey Charles II house, with dormer windows peering over the parapet added in 1754 and a steeply pitched, hipped roof, was built for a prosperous Kentish farmer, Bonham Hayes. His initials and those of his wife Elizabeth are cut into the bricks of the tall chimneys and also figure prominently in the bold plasterwork over the staircase. The finest original feature of the interior and very unusual in such a modest house, this decorative stucco, probably created by Italian craftsmen, features realistic three-dimensional flowers and fruit and carries the date of the work, 1684, as well as the Hayes's initials.

A bird-bath formed of Corinthian capitals from the old Bank of England recalls the architect Sir Herbert Baker, who was born at Owletts in 1862 and gave the house, with much of its contents, to the National Trust in 1938, a few years before he died. Known today for his imperial London buildings – India House, South Africa House and the Bank of England – and for his collaboration with Sir Edwin Lutyens in the design of New Delhi, Sir Herbert also had a successful early career in South Africa, where he built Groote Schuur for Cecil Rhodes in 1890. He made a number of different improvements to Owletts, in particular adding an extension to the library, and was largely responsible for creating the present historic atmosphere by, for example, stripping the paint off original pine doors and lining the dining room with cedar panelling.

The contents reflect the architect's travels and talents. Sir Herbert's carved dining room chairs are delightfully decorated with creatures symbolising the family and the house, a Dutch grandfather clock and chest were brought back from Cape Town and there is a memorable strip cartoon of his journey from Delhi to Owletts, with an early frame showing Sir Herbert and Lutyens together on an elephant. The living room is hung with several watercolours by Sir Herbert, but the most prominent feature here is the blue and gold wall-clock which shows the time in the countries that once composed the Empire.

This airy, sunny room looks onto the garden, where broad lawns and a tennis court emphasise that this is a family place. Figs and peaches ripening above neat rows of vegetables in the walled garden to the east of the house recall the dangling grapes in the plasterwork over the stairs.

LEFT This attractive, red-brick Carolean house was the home of the architect Sir Herbert Baker, who was born here in 1862.

Oxburgh Hall

Norfolk
At Oxburgh, 7 miles
(11.2 kilometres) south-west of
Swaffham, on the south side
of the Stoke Ferry road

This romantic moated house is set on what was once an island in the East Anglian fen. The land around is now criss-crossed with drainage dykes and cultivated, but when Edward IV gave Sir Edmund Bedingfeld licence to build his fortified manor house at Oxburgh in 1482, the site was on a promontory in the marsh. Apart from a brief period in 1951–2, when Oxburgh was sold and then bought back and given to the National Trust, Bedingfelds have lived here ever since, the gradual impoverishment of the estate that resulted from their adherence to the Catholic faith also ensuring that the house survived unaltered through the sixteenth and seventeenth centuries.

Even in this remote corner of England, Sir Edmund was more concerned with display and comfort than defence. The best-preserved part of his fifteenth-century courtyard house is a piece of early Tudor showmanship: a seven-storey gatehouse with battlemented turrets and stone-mullioned windows rising sheer from the moat. Flemish-style stepped gables and twisted terracotta chimneys on the brick ranges to either side, which contribute so much to the romantic character of the place, seem to be all of a piece; in fact they were added by J.C. Buckler as part of extensive restoration in the mid-nineteenth century for Sir Henry Paston-Bedingfeld, the 6th Baronet. Buckler was also responsible for the beautiful oriel window that fills two storeys of his convincingly medieval battlemented tower at the end of the east range.

The interior of the house includes both Tudor survivals and atmospheric Victorian rooms. The brick-walled King's Room in the gatehouse tower, warmed by a great fireplace, was where Henry VII slept when he came to Oxburgh in 1487. A priest's hole in the floor of a former garderobe off this room is an evocative reminder of the family's religious sympathies. Oxburgh's most prized possession, needlework by Mary Queen of Scots, is displayed in a darkened room nearby. Her rich embroidery, set onto green velvet, is mostly devoted to delightful depictions of a wide assortment of beasts, birds and fishes ranging from the unicorn to the garden snail. Wrought by the queen while she was in the custody of the Earl of Shrewsbury after her flight to England, these enchanting pieces are very rare illustrations of her skill.

The nineteenth-century interiors, with designs by J.C. Buckler and J.D. Crace, are among the best examples of Catholic High Victorian taste in Britain. Crace's heraldic ceiling in the drawing room incorporates delicately painted foliage and flowers in blue, pink and green. More heraldic devices – crimson fleurs-de-lis – are woven into the carpet of the low-ceilinged library, picking up the red in the flock wallpaper. A neo-Tudor fireplace dominating this room has a carved overmantel made up of medieval fragments from continental churches, including some delicate fan vaulting.

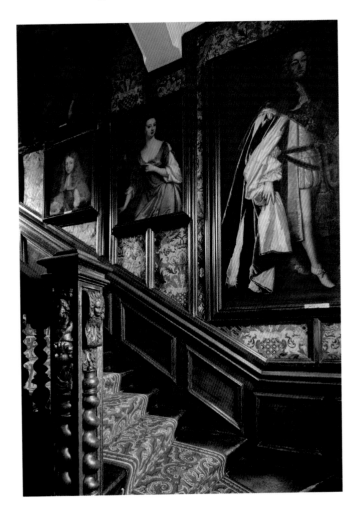

LEFT In c.1830 the west staircase was hung with early eighteenth-century embossed and painted leather to set off the paintings.
RIGHT Oxburgh is a medieval moated house of great charm that has been enhanced by late nineteenth-century alterations.

The small dining room is another rich Victorian interior, still looking exactly as it did in a watercolour of the early 1850s, the dark lustre of the panelling and of the elaborate sideboard with its crest of writhing birds relieved by vivid blue, orange and red tiles round the fireplace.

In the chapel, which was built in 1836 for the 6th Baronet, Victorian and medieval craftsmanship are again combined. The heraldic glass in the south window, dominated by a great red Bedingfeld eagle, was commissioned from Thomas Willement, but the splendid altarpiece is crowned by a sixteenth-century painted and carved triptych purchased by the Bedingfelds in Bruges in about 1860.

Apart from the nineteenth-century Wilderness Walk to the west of the chapel and mown grass around the moat, most of the garden lies to the east of the house, where Buckler's tower looks out over a florid French-style parterre flowering in swirls of blue and yellow. A yew hedge beyond the parterre fronts a colourful herbaceous border. Behind is the fanciful, turreted wall of the Victorian kitchen garden, now planted as a formal orchard with climbers on the walls.

Packwood House

Warwickshire
2 miles (3.2 kilometres) east of Hockley Heath on the A3400, 11 miles (17.7 kilometres) south-east of central Birmingham

This tall, many-gabled house looking over a grassy forecourt was built in the late sixteenth century for John Fetherston, a prosperous yeoman farmer. The original timber-framing has now largely been rebuilt in brick and rendered over, but the house still has its massive Elizabethan chimneystacks and there is an array of mullioned casement windows and a delightful red-brick stable block at right-angles to the house that was added by another John Fetherston in *c*.1670. Never a prominent or county family, the Fetherstons, it seems, lived quietly here, although they were caught up in the Civil War, apparently offering shelter and succour as seemed expedient. Cromwell's general, Henry Ireton, slept here the night before the Battle of Edgehill in 1642 and there is a family tradition that Charles II was given food and drink at Packwood after his defeat at Worcester in 1651.

When it was sold by the last of the Fetherstons in the later nineteenth century, the house had been greatly altered, with sash windows replacing the original casements and other 'improvements'. In 1905, when it was sold again, it was also much in need of repair. The buyer was the wealthy industrialist Alfred Ash, a genial man who owned a string of racehorses and is said to have viewed life 'from the sunny side – and from the interior of a gorgeous Rolls-Royce'. His son, Graham Baron Ash, a connoisseur and collector, used his father's fortune to restore the house in the 1920s and 1930s, sweeping away Georgian and Victorian alterations and painstakingly acquiring features that would give Packwood a period feel, rescuing leaded casements, floors, beams and chimneypieces from other old buildings. To complete his romantic vision of how a Tudor house should be, he also added the splendid long gallery and fashioned the great hall, complete with oriel window, out of an existing barn, leaving the room open to the original rustic timber roof. He filled Packwood with period furnishings, including fine Jacobean panelling and an exceptional collection of tapestries, such as the seventeenth-century Brussels hanging depicting a cool terraced garden with splashing fountains and urns filled with orange trees. A long oak refectory table in the great hall and a Charles II oak cupboard inlaid with mother of pearl in the

dining room are two of the many pieces that Baron Ash bought from the Ferrers family, whose moated manor house, Baddesley Clinton, is just 2 miles (3.2 kilometres) away (*see* p.36) and who, in the 1930s, were much in need of funds.

The house Graham Baron Ash created is as contrived and self-concious as a work of art. The garden, too, is a showpiece. On the south side of the house, across a large sunken lawn, brick steps lead up to a terrace walk and the exceptional topiary garden where a throng of mature clipped yews, most rising well above the heads of visitors, is said to represent the Sermon on the Mount. At the far end of the garden, a mound is crowned by a single yew tree; twelve more, similarly massive, are crowded below. These, representing the Master and his disciples, were part of the seventeenth-century garden, but many of the multitude dotting the smoothly mown grass below, each tree characterised by its own lumps and slants, were planted in the mid-nineteenth century.

A sunken garden in front of the house, also dating from the seventeenth century, has brick gazebos at each corner, one ingeniously designed so that its fireplace can be used to warm fruit trees growing on an adjacent wall. There are yew-hedged enclosures, walls and steps of mellow brick, wrought-iron gates, some with glimpses into the park, and a vivid herbaceous border.

BELOW Although originally Elizabethan, and still boasting massive period chimneystacks, Packwood House is largely a creation of the 1920s and '30s and represents an idealised vision of a Tudor manor house.
OPPOSITE At Packwood, Graham Baron Ash created a great hall out of a former barn, using the hayrack to make a balustrade for the gallery at one end and hanging fine tapestries on the walls.

Paycocke's

Essex
On the south side of the A120
West Street, the road to Braintree,
not far from the centre of
Coggeshall, next to the Fleece Inn,
5½ miles (8.8 kilometres) east of
Braintree

The wealth generated by the East Anglian wool trade in the fifteenth and sixteenth centuries produced some of the most beautiful churches in the British Isles. It also enriched the homes of the merchants themselves, many of whom used their fortunes to build fine half-timbered houses advertising their enhanced status. Paycocke's, dating from around 1500, is a splendid example, its long brick and timber street facade, the upper floor jettied over the lower, incorporating carpentry and carved woodwork of the highest quality.

Vertical timbers limewashed a silvery-grey are set expensively close along the front of the house, with brick filling the spaces that would once have been packed with wattle and daub, the two together forming distinctive pink and white stripes. An intricately decorated wooden beam running the length of the facade beneath the five oriel windows on the first floor carries a series of delightful cameos, such as a dragon depicted upside down and a small person apparently diving into a lily. Larger, naturalistic figures frame the fine oak gates through which a carriageway leads to the back of the house. As indicated by the four family tombs in the parish church, the Paycockes were people of substance, the house John Paycocke built on the occasion of his son Thomas's marriage to Margaret Harrold (indicated by the initials TP and MP carved on both interior and exterior woodwork) standing out from its more modest neighbours along West Street.

Inside, it is clear that Paycocke's was a place of work and business as well as a home. Peg holes in the studs of the walls were once used to hold the warp thread of the looms, wool was stored in the roof space and the lengths of cloth were probably stretched out to dry in the garden. A display of Coggeshall lace includes a device that used water-filled flasks to intensify candlelight, thus allowing four lace-makers to work by the light of one candle.

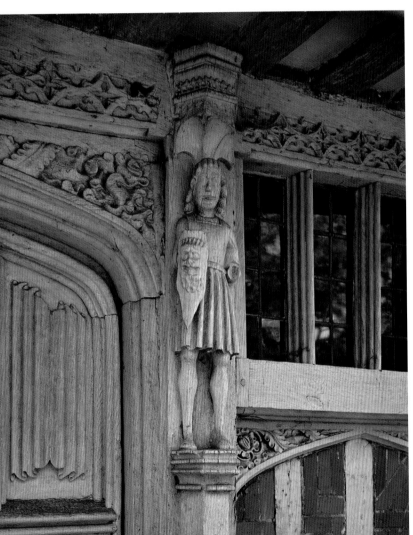

LEFT Massive doors carved with linenfold decoration and flanked by wooden figures fashioned in the frame of the gateway give access to the carriageway leading to the back of Paycocke's.
OPPOSITE Wealth from the East Anglian wool trade financed the richly decorative street facade of this medieval merchant's house, which was built by John Paycocke for his son in the early sixteenth century.

Peckover House

Cambridgeshire
On the north bank of the
River Nene, in Wisbech

Changes in the coastline of the Wash have taken Wisbech further and further from the sea. It is now some 12 miles (19.3 kilometres) away, but only 250 years ago the River Nene was navigable into the heart of the town and there was a substantial port here based on a thriving trade with the Netherlands. Although the sea traffic has long since died, imposing red-brick merchants' houses still line the river, giving this sleepy little town an elegance and importance out of all proportion to its present status. Dutch gables and hipped roofs reflect influences from across the North Sea and, as in Holland, there was a spirit of religious toleration here that fostered a substantial Quaker community in the town, many of whom, as elsewhere in East Anglia, played prominent roles in local affairs.

One such was Jonathan Peckover, who has given his name to the elegant three-storey Georgian town house on the North Brink of the Nene which he bought in 1777. Five years later, in association with the Gurneys, another leading Quaker family, he established the local bank of Gurney, Birkbeck and Peckover in a wing adjoining the house, from where the business was run for almost a century until the bank merged with Barclays in 1896. Peckovers continued to live here until the mid-twentieth century, when Alexandrina Peckover was persuaded by her nephew Alec Penrose, one of four distinguished brothers who included the artist Roland Penrose, to gift Peckover to the National Trust in 1943. Alexandrina stayed on until her death in 1948.

In contrast to the rather plain exterior, the panelled rooms have fine Georgian fireplaces and a wealth of elaborate wood- and plasterwork by local craftsmen. The decoration includes both Neo-classical motifs and more exuberant rococo features, among them the magnificently fluid carving surrounding the mirror above the drawing-room fireplace, where festoons of drapery are suspended from an eagle with outstretched wings. In recent years, the vast library that was added onto the east end of the house in 1878, and that had been denuded of its contents, has been refitted with reproductions of the original bookshelves, wallpaper and other features and filled with books.

After the built-up river frontage, the spacious walled garden, which extends behind several buildings along the Nene to the west, comes as something of a surprise. It is a surviving example of the Victorian 'gardenesque' style, in which the display of individual plants is as important as the overall effect. A spacious lawn is shaded by fine specimen trees and flanked by a bosky wilderness walk. Colourful flower beds mark a more formal area and there are spectacular climbing roses, an orangery and a cool green fern house.

LEFT The elegant entrance hall at Peckover House, with a view of the houses on the South Brink through the open front door, is furnished with a set of mahogany Sheraton chairs.
BELOW The butler's pantry at Peckover House looks out on the spacious walled garden behind the house.
OPPOSITE Peckover House is one of a number of fine eighteenth-century buildings on the banks of the Nene that reflect Wisbech's former prosperity.

Penrhyn Castle

Gwynedd
1 mile (1.6 kilometres) east of
Bangor, at Llandegai off the A5

From the long upward climb off the Bangor road there is a sudden view of Penrhyn's great four-storey keep rising above the trees, with battlemented turrets at each corner. The rest of the creeper-clad building stretches away across a bluff in an impressive array of towers, battlements and crenellations. Round-headed windows ornamented with a carved zigzag motif seem to have been lifted from a Norman church. The interior is even more dramatic, with long stone-flagged corridors, high ceilings and heavy doors and panelling. Carved stone is everywhere: surrounding arches and doors and forming bosses, corbels, friezes and capitals.

A strange population looks down from the forest of slender pillars creating blind arcades on the walls of the staircase. Each head is different. Here is a bearded wild man, there an elf with pointed ears, somewhere else a gargoyle with interlocking teeth. Look carefully and what appears to be writhing foliage becomes a contorted face. At the foot of the

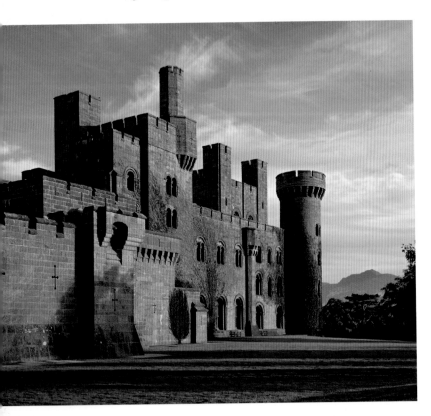

staircase, the curve of the door into the drawing room is echoed by a semicircle of carved hands around the arch. Another opening leads into the galleried great hall, where Romanesque arches soar heavenwards like the transept of a cathedral. In the evening the polished limestone flags of the floor are warmed by pools of multicoloured light from the recessed stained-glass windows.

Penrhyn is a late Georgian masterpiece, the outstanding product of a shortlived neo-Norman revival. Designed by Thomas Hopper, a fashionable architect who had been employed by the Prince Regent to build a Gothic conservatory at Carlton House, it was commissioned in 1820 by G.H. Dawkins Pennant to replace the neo-Gothic house by Samuel Wyatt he had inherited from his uncle Richard. Whereas Richard Pennant had the benefit of a fortune made from Jamaican estates (as a result of which he strongly opposed the abolition of the slave trade), his nephew built lavishly on the profits of the Penrhyn slate quarries in Snowdonia, which were exporting over 12,000 tons a year by 1792. A slate billiard table with cluster-column legs in the library and the grotesque slate bed weighing over a ton echo the basis of his prosperity.

G.H. Dawkins Pennant seems to have allowed his architect ample funds for building the castle and also for decorating and furnishing the rooms. As a result, Penrhyn is uniquely all of a piece. In the oppressive Ebony Room, original green and red curtains and upholstery and faded red damask wall-hangings give some relief from the black ebony furniture and the black surrounds to the fireplace and doorways. Huge plantain leaves on the firescreen recall the Jamaican estates. Here, too, is Dieric Bouts's delightful painting of St Luke sketching the Virgin and Child, the arches behind the apostle framing a sylvan landscape with a walled city. In the much lighter drawing room next door, mirrors at each end reflect two immense metalwork candelabra.

The house was greatly enriched in the mid-nineteenth century by the Spanish, Italian and Dutch paintings collected by Edward Gordon Douglas, 1st Baron Penrhyn of Llandegai, including a Canaletto of the Thames at Westminster, Rembrandt's portrait of a plain, middle-aged merchant's wife, and Palma Vecchio's *Holy Family*. Lord Penrhyn's son, the 2nd Baron, commissioned the elaborate brass King's Bed for the future Edward VII when he was a guest here in 1894.

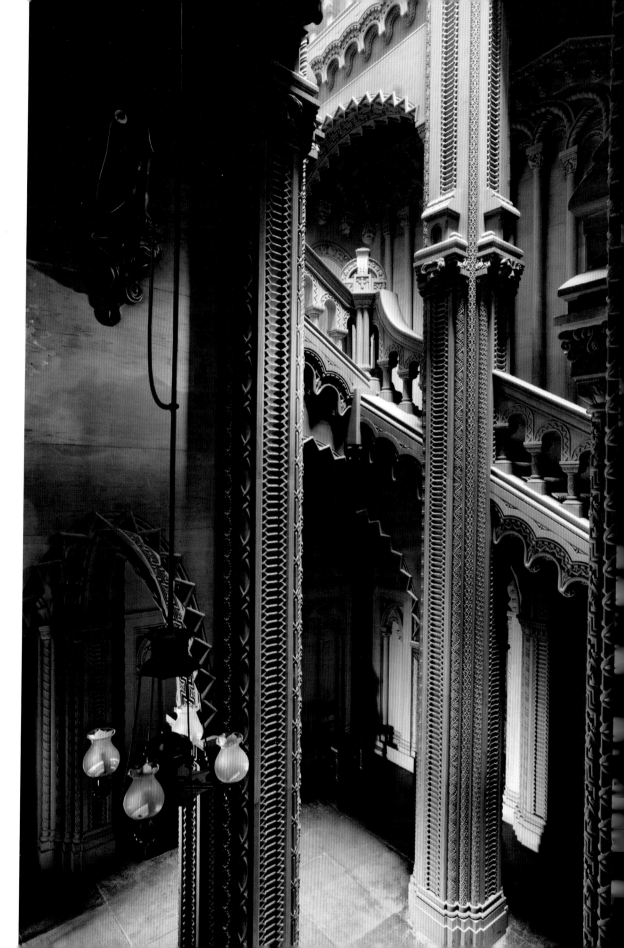

OPPOSITE Penrhyn Castle, with an impressive array of towers and battlements set against the backdrop of the Welsh mountains, is an early nineteenth-century vision of a Norman stronghold.

RIGHT The riot of carved decoration on the grand staircase is typical of the quality of stonework seen throughout Penrhyn, all of which, like the similarly impressive woodwork, was executed by local craftsmen.

This royal visit, over three days in July, saw the house staff at full stretch, required to produce gastronomic dinners of eight or nine courses and to attend to 35 house guests. At this date, Lord Penrhyn employed some 40 servants, including the men in the stables, which was by no means a lavish establishment for the period. The servants' quarters, shown as they were after rebuilding in 1868, illustrate what went into keeping the household going.

A warren of rooms giving onto an inner courtyard is centred on the kitchen, which would have been presided over by a French chef in the late nineteenth century and which still has its roasting range, pastry oven and original ash-topped table. Penrhyn slate forms cool work surfaces in the pastry room and dry larder, and tops the butter table in the dairy larder where milk, cream, butter and eggs were delivered from the home farm every morning. Fitted cupboards are stacked with fine china; candlesticks and oil lamps are ready for cleaning and trimming in the lamp room; and there are top hats for sprucing up in the brushing room. In the outer court, close to the back gate, is the Ice Tower, where a deep pit in the basement was packed with ice in the winter, some of it cut from a lake high in Snowdonia, for use in the warmer months.

Beyond the back gate is the sizeable stable block, designed for 36 horses, and with Penrhyn slate between the stalls and used for the mangers. Part is now given over to a collection of dolls from all over the world; a museum of industrial locomotives associated with the slate industry also accommodated here includes *Charles*, a saddle tank engine that once worked the railway serving the Penrhyn family's quarries, and *Fire Queen*, built in 1848 for the Padarn Railway.

The siting of Penrhyn is superb, with views south to Snowdonia and the slate quarry like a great bite out of the hills and north over Beaumaris Bay to Anglesey. A terraced walled garden sloping steeply into a valley below the castle shelters many tender shrubs and plants and includes a bog garden at the lowest level. Throughout the grounds, fine specimen trees are mixed with mature beeches and oaks and there is a ruined Gothic chapel placed as an eye-catcher on a prominent knoll. A row of headstones in the dogs' cemetery by the chapel commemorates Annette, Suzette, Wanda and other pets.

ABOVE Illustrations taken from the margins of medieval manuscripts were among the sources that inspired Penrhyn's fantastical carved decoration.

Petworth House

West Sussex
In the centre of Petworth

A luminous landscape by Turner at Petworth shows the park at sunset. Dark clumps of trees throw long shadows over the lake and in the foreground a stag stoops to drink, its antlers silhouetted against the sun-tinged water. Turner was inspired by 'Capability' Brown's masterpiece, one of the greatest man-made landscapes created in eighteenth-century Europe. This sublime wooded park, with its serpentine lake, enfolds a late seventeenth-century palace filled with an exceptional collection of works of art, including fine furniture, *objets* and sculpture as well as paintings. This great house, in a French baroque style, was the creation of the unlikeable Charles Seymour, 6th Duke of Somerset (the Proud Duke), who set about remodelling the manor house of the earls of Northumberland on his marriage to the daughter of the 11th and last earl, probably to designs by Daniel Marot. Petworth's impressive west front, over 90 metres (300 feet) long and with projecting bays at each end, has the Seymour family symbol – a pair of angel's wings – displayed over every window. Although, apart from the Grand Staircase, only two seventeenth-century interiors survive intact, these fully reflect Charles Seymour's self-importance. The major feature of the florid baroque chapel is the family pew filling the west end. Supported by classical columns, it is surmounted by carved and painted drapery on which angels bear the duke's arms and coronet to heaven. By contrast, the coldly formal marble hall with its black-and-white chequered floor must have quelled the spirits of the few thought worthy to set foot in the Proud Duke's house.

As well as remodelling the house, Charles Seymour also added to the art collection established by the earls of Northumberland, which included a series of portraits by Van Dyck and works by Titian and Elsheimer. And he commissioned Grinling Gibbons to produce the limewood carvings of flowers, foliage, birds and classical vases which now cascade down the walls of the Carved Room, and Louis Laguerre to paint the Grand Staircase.

On the Proud Duke's death, the estate passed by marriage to the Wyndham family, and it was Charles Wyndham, 2nd Earl of Egremont, who employed Brown to landscape the park. A cultivated man who had profited from the Grand Tour

and time in the diplomatic service, he was largely responsible for Petworth's collection of Italian, French and Dutch Old Masters. He also acquired the impressive array of ancient sculpture from Greece and Rome. Now of particular importance because it is one of only three such collections of the period to have survived intact, it includes the sensitive

BELOW When the grand staircase had to be rebuilt after a fire in 1714, the 6th Duke of Somerset employed Louis Laguerre to paint the walls, a commission for which Laguerre received £200.

sculptured head fashioned in the fourth century BC known as the Leconfield Aphrodite, and some good Roman portrait busts and copies of Greek originals. The 2nd Earl's son, the philanthropic and benevolent 3rd Earl, who presided over Petworth for 74 years, from 1763 to 1837, left his stamp on almost every room, enriching them with his purchases of contemporary art and sculpture, and altering and rearranging furnishings and picture hangs in the pursuit of the perfect scheme. Best known as the patron of Turner, for whom he arranged a studio at Petworth, the 3rd Earl also acquired works by Gainsborough, Reynolds, Fuseli and Zoffany. And he augmented his father's sculpture collection, for which he

BELOW Petworth's palatial west front, 97 metres (320 feet) long, was built by the 6th Duke of Somerset and designed to impress.
OPPOSITE The paintings in the north gallery are arranged as they were in the early nineteenth century, with pairs of Turner landscapes hung low down at either end of the central corridor.

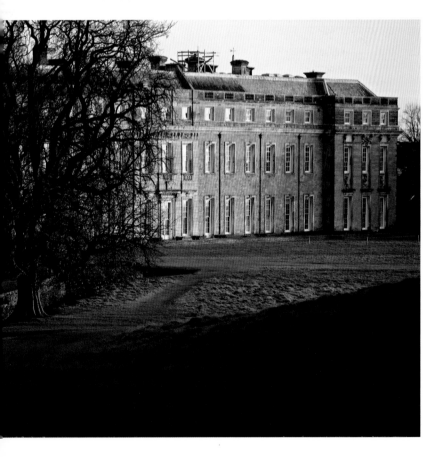

twice extended the existing gallery, with works by English contemporaries such as Sir Richard Westmacott and John Rossi and by the Irish sculptor J.E. Carew. One of the most striking pieces is the vividly fluid representation of St Michael and Satan by John Flaxman that was finished in 1826, the year in which the sculptor died. Except for the spear that St Michael is about to plunge into his grovelling adversary, this powerful work, which cost the 3rd Earl £3,500, was all carved from one piece of marble.

In spite of a family tradition that paintings should be left as the 3rd Earl had them, many changes were made to the way they were arranged by Sir Anthony Blunt, then Honorary Adviser on paintings, when Petworth came to the National Trust in 1947. In recent years, helped by generous loans of pictures from the present Lord and Lady Egremont, the Trust has re-created the spirit of the 3rd Earl's crowded and eclectic displays. In some cases it has been possible to reconstruct the hangs as recorded in watercolour gouaches painted by Turner when he was living here. Thus, on the south wall of the square dining room, a large canvas by Reynolds is now framed on three sides by columns of small paintings and crowned by a Reynolds self-portrait, just as it was some 200 years ago. Similarly, four landscapes by Turner have been returned to the Carved Room for which they were commissioned. At the same time, again with loans from Lord and Lady Egremont, additional contents have been brought in, such as the copper *batterie de cuisine* in the impressive service quarters.

Although the great storms of 1987 and 1989 brought down hundreds of trees, the park is still much as Turner painted it, with deer grazing beneath clumps of beeches, chestnuts and oaks. Trees still frame Brown's serpentine lake below the west front and crown the ridges shading imperceptibly into Sussex downland. Far in the distance on the horizon is the outline of a turreted Gothick folly, possibly designed by Sir John Soane. Brown's pleasure grounds to the north-west of the house, with serpentine paths winding through rare trees and shrubs, echo the boundaries of a vanished Elizabethan layout. A little Doric temple was probably moved here when the pleasure grounds were created, but the Ionic rotunda, perhaps designed by Matthew Brettingham, was introduced by Brown. Here, too, are some of the carved seventeenth-century urns on pedestals which the 3rd Earl placed strategically in the gardens and park.

Plas Newydd

Anglesey
1 mile (1.6 kilometres) south-west of Llanfairpwll and the A5 on the A4080, 2½ miles (4 kilometres) from the Menai Bridge, 5 miles (8 kilometres) from Bangor

'I tried repeatedly in vain ... to get some use made of my drawing.' So Rex Whistler explained his decision to join the Welsh Guards in 1940. Four years later he was dead, killed by a mortar bomb in Normandy at the age of 39. Fortunately for all who visit Plas Newydd, the house is full of works by this talented artist, who spent some of his happiest and most creative hours here. His panoramic seascape, 18 metres (58 feet) wide, fills an entire wall of the dining room. Painted on a single piece of canvas that Whistler had had specially made, it looks across the choppy waters of a harbour to an Italianate town 'bristling with spires, domes and columns' set at the foot of wild and craggy mountains, a vision that echoes Plas Newydd's own setting on the shores of the Menai Strait, with the mountains of Snowdonia rising steeply from the water on the other side.

Reproductions of Whistler's massive work never capture the sweep and scale of the composition or the wealth of detail it includes, with plentiful allusions to buildings the artist had seen on his continental travels and to the family of his patron, the 6th Marquess of Anglesey, of whom he was very fond. Every corner contains some delightful cameo. At the far end of the *trompe-l'oeil* colonnade on the left-hand side people are going about their business in a steep street running up from the water. Two women gossip; an old lady climbs slowly upwards with the help of a stick; a boy steals an apple from a tub of fruit outside a shop. A girl leaning out of an upstairs window to talk to a young man below, as if she were Juliet and he Romeo, alludes to Whistler's unrequited love for the beautiful Lady Caroline, the marquess's eldest daughter, and the artist has portrayed himself as the gardener sweeping up leaves in the colonnade.

The exhibition of Whistler's work in the room next door shows the range of his talent. Here are his illustrations for *Gulliver's Travels*, examples of costume and stage designs, bookplates and caricatures, and rebus letters he sent to the 6th Marquess's young son. Here, too, are drawings he did as a child, the horror of those inspired by the First World War heralding his own experiences some 20 years later. A painting of Lord Anglesey's family grouped informally in the music room is one of many examples of Whistler's skill at portraiture, his sensitive studies of Lady Caroline, eight years his junior, betraying his feelings for his sitter.

Whistler's mural was part of Lord Anglesey's extensive changes to Plas Newydd in the 1930s. He and his wife converted the house into one of the most comfortable of their day, following the 6th Marquess's maxim that 'every bathroom should have a bedroom', and employed Sybil Colefax to create Lady Anglesey's feminine pink and white bedroom, furnished with a white carpet, muslin curtains and bed-hangings and with a pink ribbon setting off the white bedspread. The long saloon with a view over the Menai Strait to Snowdon is also much as the 6th Marquess and his wife arranged it, with two large and comfortable settees either side of the fire and four pastoral landscapes by Ommeganck dominating the pictures.

Architecturally, Plas Newydd is intriguing. The original sixteenth-century manor built by the powerful Griffith family was substantially remodelled in the eighteenth century, most importantly in the 1790s for the 1st Earl of Uxbridge by James Wyatt and Joseph Potter of Lichfield, who produced the uncompromising mixture of classical and Gothick. There is a classical staircase leading to a screen of Doric columns on the first floor and a classical frieze by Wyatt appears boldly white against blue in the ante-room and against red in the octagon, but in the hall there is fan vaulting, with elaborate bosses at the intersection of the ribs. This stately room rising through two storeys with a gallery at one end opens into the even more splendid Gothick music room, the largest room in the house and probably on the site of the great hall of the manor.

An early artificial limb and mud-spattered Hussar trousers recall the 1st Earl's son, who was created 1st Marquess of Anglesey for his heroism at the Battle of Waterloo in 1815, where he lost a leg. He is also remarkable for the fact that he had 18 children and 73 grandchildren. Other members of the

OPPOSITE This spiral staircase at Plas Newydd leads from the Gothick hall to the comfortable bedroom fitted out in pink and white in the 1930s for the wife of the 6th Marquess.

ABOVE In this detail of the magnificent mural he painted for the house, Rex Whistler shows Neptune's trident, complete with a frond of seaweed, leaning against the central urn and his golden crown abandoned on the plinth, as if the sea-god had just come out of the water.

family gaze down from a fine array of portraits, including works by Hoppner, Romney and Lawrence and a Grand Tour painting of the 1st Earl, a rather plump young man in a salmon coat. Many of these pictures came from Beaudesert, the family's Staffordshire house that was dismantled in 1935 and which was also the source of some of the fine furniture.

Plas Newydd is first seen from above, when the path leading down from the car park suddenly reveals the Gothick west front covered in red creeper and magnolia. Sweeping lawns and mature woodland set off the house, the mix of native trees and exotics here including many fine sycamores,

beeches and oaks that predate the planting undertaken with Humphry Repton's advice. A Venetian well-head and Italianate urns in the formal terraced gardens suggest a warmer sun than that which reddens the peaks on the far side of the water in the evening.

ABOVE Plas Newydd is gloriously set above the Menai Strait, with views over the water to the mountains of Snowdonia, and has its own private harbour, built in the 1790s.
OPPOSITE Plas yn Rhiw's homely interiors are full of the belongings of the three Keating sisters, who bought this little house on the Llŷn peninsula in 1938 and lovingly restored it.

Plas yn Rhiw

Gwynedd
16 miles (25.7 kilometres) from
Pwllheli, on the south coast road
to Aberdaron

The long Llŷn peninsula, which shields Cardigan Bay from the full force of the Atlantic, is a windswept claw of craggy moorland and tiny fields. Only in the far south-east, which is protected by the tor of Mynydd-y-Graig, is there shelter enough for woodland to thrive. Plas yn Rhiw sits in this wind-shielded pocket below the hill, with views over the bay to Cadair Idris and south along the coast to Fishguard. On clear nights the lights of Aberystwyth beckon across the water. A Georgian frontage hides a much older building behind. Thick granite walls in the tiny parlour and the remains of a stone spiral staircase are survivals of a Tudor dwelling on this site. As the date stone on the front of the house proclaims, it was first extended in 1634; two wings built into the hillside, Georgian sash windows and the slate-floored Victorian verandah were additions of the early and mid-nineteenth century, turning the farmhouse into a gentleman's residence.

Plas yn Rhiw's homely interiors reflect the three forceful and indomitable Keating sisters, Eileen, Lorna and Honora, daughters of a successful Nottinghamshire architect, who bought the property in 1938 and lovingly restored it after almost 20 years of neglect. A white hat and gloves lie neatly on the patchwork quilt covering one of the simple wooden beds. A shoe rack is filled with Honora's fashionable footwear from her days in London and a successful career in the social services. Elegant Georgian chairs, fur coats and a stole speak of comfortable gentility, and an extensive collection of popular classics suggests many evenings spent listening to the old gramophone in the parlour. Gentle watercolours hanging three and four deep on the stairs, their muted colours recording local views and landmarks, recall Honora's days at the Slade and her youthful ambition to be an artist.

The little terraced garden sloping down towards the sea, with thickly planted beds framed by box hedges, dates from the 1820s. Organically managed, it is a mix of tender and exotic species and indigenous wild flora and there are bulbs in the rough meadow grass and woodland behind the house.

The sisters, who are still a legend in the neighbourhood, worked tirelessly to protect the natural beauty of the peninsula. They were often seen, wrapped up warmly, tramping the lanes to check on rubbish tips and illegal caravan sites. Fiercely outspoken in defence of their beliefs, the Keatings were personally self-effacing, little realising that the words with which they chose to honour their parents – 'there is no death while memory lives' – would serve as their own memorial.

Polesden Lacey

Surrey
5 miles (8 kilometres) north-west of Dorking, 1½ miles (2.4 kilometres) south of Great Bookham, off the A246 Leatherhead–Guildford road

Polesden Lacey is alive with the spirit of Mrs Ronald Greville, whose vivacious portrait greets visitors to the house. Those she invited to the legendary weekend parties held here from 1906 until the outbreak of the Second World War included Indian maharajahs, literary figures such as Beverley Nichols, Osbert Sitwell and Harold Nicolson, and prominent politicians. Edward VII was a close friend of the elegant society hostess, as were George V and Queen Mary, the latter often telephoning in the morning to invite herself to tea that afternoon. In 1923, the future George VI and Queen Elizabeth spent part of their honeymoon at Polesden Lacey.

Set above a deep valley on the edge of the North Downs, with views across the combe to sheep-grazed fields and hilltop woods, the house is a comfortable two-storey building sprawling round a courtyard. The white frames of generous sash windows on both floors stand out attractively against honey-coloured stucco. The flavour of the Regency villa built in the 1820s by Joseph Bonsor to the designs of Thomas Cubitt still lingers on the south front with its classical colonnade, but the house was much enlarged and the interior transformed after 1906 by Mewès and Davis, the architects of the Ritz Hotel, as an essential step in the realisation of Mrs Greville's social ambitions. Here she displayed her outstanding collection of paintings, furniture and other works of art, the nucleus of which she had inherited from her wealthy father, William McEwan, founder of the Scottish brewery that still bears his name.

The range and richness of the collection, which includes Flemish tapestries, French and English furniture, English,

continental and oriental pottery and porcelain, and European paintings from the fourteenth to the eighteenth centuries, gives Polesden Lacey its extraordinarily opulent atmosphere, vividly evoking the charmed life of the Edwardian upper classes. Some of the finest pieces were intended for very different settings. In the sumptuously decorated drawing room glittering mirrors reflect carved and gilt panelling that once adorned an Italian palace. A richly carved oak reredos in the hall, a masterpiece by Edward Pierce, was originally intended for Sir Christopher Wren's St Matthew's church just off Cheapside in London, which was demolished in 1881. From her father Mrs Greville inherited some Dutch seventeenth-century paintings, but she acquired most of the British portraits in the dining room, among them Raeburn's charming study of George and Maria Stewart as children, the little girl shown holding a rabbit in the folds of her dress, and was also largely responsible for the best of the collection shown in the corridor round the central courtyard. The pictures hanging here include several early Italian works, such as an exquisite early fourteenth-century triptych of the Madonna and Child, sixteenth-century portraits in the style of Corneille de Lyon and a number of atmospheric Dutch interiors and landscapes, among them Jacob van Ruisdael's skyscape of the Zuider Zee in which diminutive figures on the shore are dwarfed by wintry grey clouds piled overhead.

Invitation cards, scrap albums and other mementoes in the billiard room and smoking room conjure up the world in which Mrs Greville lived. The menu book records the *salade niçoise* and orange mousse on which Ramsay MacDonald dined on 17 October 1936 and the *aubergines provençales* given to the Queen of Spain the following day. The same names appear again and again in the visitors' book and the same faces recur in the photographs, statesmen and royalty, such as Grand Duke Michael of Russia and Kaiser Wilhelm II, rubbing shoulders with figures from the worlds of entertainment and literature, a memorable shot showing Mrs Greville in Hollywood with Wendy Barrie and Spencer Tracy. Upstairs, Mrs Greville's bedroom apartment runs along the south front. As yet it is unfurnished, but from here the view over the valley is even more spectacular and there is a marble bath in the bathroom.

The atmosphere of the house extends into the garden, where spacious lawns are shaded by mature beeches, cedars and limes. Although much of the layout is a twentieth-century creation, the long terraced walk is a legacy from the years when Polesden Lacey was the home of the playwright Richard Brinsley Sheridan. A series of more intimate walled and hedged enclosures to the west of the house include an iris garden and a rose garden centred on an Italianate marble well-head. Mrs Greville's garden ornaments are everywhere, from

OPPOSITE Carolus Duran's vivacious portrait of Mrs Ronald Greville, who hosted legendary weekend parties here, greets visitors from the half-landing above the hall. **ABOVE** Although the interiors were remodelled in 1906–9 for Mrs Greville, the exterior still has a flavour of the Regency villa designed by Thomas Cubitt.

the griffins on the terrace in front of the house to vases, urns and sundials and the statue of Diana on the croquet lawn. She is buried in a yew-hedged enclosure beside the rose garden.

Powis Castle

Powys
1 mile (1.6 kilometres) south of
Welshpool, signed from the A483

Some time around 1200 the Welsh princes of Powis began building their new stronghold on this splendid defensive site, a great outcrop of limestone plunging steeply to the south with panoramic views over the River Severn to the hills of Shropshire. Although long since converted to a country house, Powis still has the trappings of a castle. Seen from across the valley, a massive Norman-style keep with three projecting towers rises to a battlemented skyline. To the left, a long range flanking the entrance court was created out of the substantial curtain wall that defended the inner bailey. In front of the castle, grand baroque terraces blasted out of the rock fall to a vast expanse of lawn.

A wide flight of steps closely guarded by twin drum towers leads up from the entrance court to a Gothic archway. Here the house takes over. The front door opens into seventeenth-century grandeur and opulence and the magnificent interiors fitted out for William Herbert, 3rd Lord Powis, 1st Earl, Marquess and titular Duke. A staunch supporter of the Stuart cause, Lord Powis spent his last years in exile with James II. The most remarkable of his formal apartments, possibly designed by the gentleman-architect William Winde, is the state bedroom, which was decorated with a profusion of gilt in the 1660s and 1680s. A deep alcove is almost filled with the canopied state bed, which is adorned with rich red hangings and gilt cresting and separated from the rest of the room by a finely carved balustrade. The only one of its kind in Britain, this barrier is a direct link with the formal etiquette of Louis XIV's Versailles that was closely imitated by the British aristocracy.

OPPOSITE The Elizabethan long gallery at Powis has an original plasterwork ceiling and elm floor and is designed in the shape of a T, giving the room a subtle play of light.
BELOW Although long since converted into a country house, Powis Castle, standing high above a series of magnificent Italianate terraces, still looks like the medieval stronghold it once was.

ABOVE The Clive collection of Indian treasures displayed at Powis includes a tent of painted chintz which belonged to Tipu Sahib, Sultan of Mysore, who was defeated by the 2nd Lord Clive.

OPPOSITE Opulent interiors at Powis, such as this grand painted staircase hall, were created in the late seventeenth century for William Herbert, 3rd Lord, who died in exile in France with James II.

Velvet-covered furniture, a painted ceiling and rich tapestries contribute to the opulent effect. A huge and much more accomplished ceiling by Antonio Verrio, based on Veronese's *Apotheosis of Venice*, with an assembly of deities seated on clouds, dominates the 1st Marquess's grand staircase.

There is no hint of this pomposity in the only surviving Elizabethan interior, a beautiful T-shaped long gallery dating from Sir Edward Herbert's acquisition of the castle in 1587. Young trees and tendrils of foliage branch across the plasterwork ceiling above the rather indifferent family portraits set against early seventeenth-century *trompe-l'oeil* panelling and the polished silver sconces forming pools of light down the room. A table carries a more than life-size marble cat, crouched aggressively over the body of a snake, ears pricked as it looks back over its shoulder, teeth bared and muscles rippling beneath its fur. This remarkable ancient Roman sculpture, perhaps modelled on a wild animal, came to Powis through the marriage of the daughter of the house to

the eldest son of Clive of India in 1784. Indian curiosities acquired by the Great Nabob and his son, who was Governor of Madras, are shown in the Clive Museum that now adjoins the curiously elongated ballroom (originally almost twice as long), commissioned from T.F. Pritchard in 1775, in the range flanking the courtyard. Among the glittering exhibits are jewelled slippers that once adorned the feet of Tipu Sahib, Sultan of Mysore, a gold tiger's head from his throne, a jewelled hookah encrusted with rubies, diamonds and emeralds, and sumptuously decorated padded armour. The tone is set for this exotic display by the richly coloured mid-seventeenth-century tapestry filling one wall of the ballroom, showing an embassy to Cairo or Istanbul. A potentate on a gold couch greets the ambassador against the backdrop of an eastern city peppered with onion domes, the trees peeping over the walls conjuring up a sense of hidden gardens.

The final alterations to the castle were made for the 4th Earl of Powis in 1902–4 by G.F. Bodley, who was responsible for the Jacobethan-style panelling, plaster ceilings and other features in the dining room and oak drawing room, and for inserting mullioned windows to replace some existing sashes.

Powis's four great Italianate terraces ornamented with lead statues and urns hang over the valley below, forming a giant staircase descending the rock. Who designed them and when is unclear, but it is likely they date from the 1680s and were the inspiration of William Winde, who created the grand arcaded terrace at Cliveden (*see* p.98), with some of the work being carried out by the French gardener Adrian Duval in the early years of the eighteenth century. Clipped yews cluster closely below the castle, some lapping the terrace wall as if about to flow downhill. Rare and tender lime-tolerant plants flourishing here contrast with those planted in the wilderness laid out in the eighteenth century on the ridge across the valley, where the soil is acid and where there are panoramic views of the castle from winding wooded walks.

A wooded medieval deer-park surrounds Powis, its naturalistic contours and planting partly reflecting alterations by 'Capability' Brown's disciple William Emes, who was engaged to landscape it in 1771 and diverted a public road away from the castle. Although most of the great beeches, sycamores and limes were planted between 1800 and 1850, some of the massive oaks may be as much as 800 years old.

Quarry Bank Mill and Styal Estate

Cheshire
1½ miles (2.4 kilometres) north
of Wilmslow off the B5166, 2 miles
(3.2 kilometres) from the M56,
exit 5, 10 miles (16 kilometres)
south of Manchester

In 1769 Richard Arkwright started a revolution in the textile industry when he invented a water-powered machine that could spin cotton. In the 1780s there was another watershed when the patents protecting his invention were challenged and overthrown, opening the way for a huge expansion in factory-produced yarn. One of the first to take advantage of the new opportunities was the young Samuel Greg, who in 1780 had inherited one of the largest textile businesses in Manchester. He found a suitable site for a water-powered mill in the isolated Bollin Valley some 10 miles (16 kilometres) south of the city and had built his first mill here by 1784. As the mill prospered, it was enlarged, and a little village complete with school, shop and two chapels was built in the early nineteenth century to house the growing labour force.

This early industrial complex now lies at the centre of over 120 hectares (300 acres) of well-wooded park following the River Bollin. The surroundings seem delightfully rural, with grass and trees setting off the red-brick four-storey mill with its cupola, tall chimney and impressive rows of windows. Samuel Greg lived in the elegant white Georgian house next to the mill, and on the other side of the works is a smaller but no less comfortable residence that was inhabited by the mill manager, who controlled the flow of water powering the factory. At Quarry Bank House, where the modest rooms make clear that this was a home rather than a showplace, Samuel Greg and his family were very much part of the factory community and the mill with its soaring chimney dominates views from the ornamental garden running down to the Bollin. The upper, kitchen garden has recently also been acquired by the National Trust and is being restored. Dramatically set above a sandstone cliff with spectacular views over the valley, this garden has some of the earliest surviving cast-iron glasshouses, probably dating from the early 1820s, which were used for growing vines and peaches. Later generations of Gregs moved to a grandiose Victorian house high up on the side of the valley.

Although their approach was tempered by self-interest, the Gregs had an enlightened attitude to the care of their workers and this comes through in the design and layout of the village at Styal. Behind each red-brick cottage are the remains of a privy, a great luxury at a time when such facilities were usually shared between several families. The long gardens, now mostly given over to flowers, were once allotments in which tenants could grow their own vegetables. Some thatched, half-timbered buildings, including the impressive Oak Farm which once provided the village with fresh dairy produce, are remnants of a medieval settlement.

Close to the mill is the Apprentice House, built in 1790 to accommodate the children who then made up about a third of the workforce. By the 1830s, this double-gabled three-storey building was home to up to a hundred pauper apprentices. Brought in from workhouses, most of them were on seven-year contracts to work twelve hours a day, six days a week. Neat rows of vegetables in the organic garden, including the red-veined leaves of cottagers' kale, illustrate the traditional produce the children grew in their spare time, although their diet largely consisted of bread, milk, porridge and potatoes.

On Sundays, they went twice to church, walking across the fields to Wilmslow.

Although none of the original machinery survives, the mill has been restored as a working museum of the cotton industry. At its heart is a giant iron waterwheel, the most powerful in Britain, which drives spinning machines and looms, these and other exhibits showing how cotton was transformed, first by hand, later by machine, into spun yarn and calico cloth. The noise in the weaving shed and the lack of space round the flying machinery give some idea of what conditions must have been like during the mill's heyday, when tired children could be disfigured for life if they nodded off over their work.

OPPOSITE Quarry Bank Mill, one of the earliest purpose-built, water-powered factories in England, has been much expanded since it was first opened in 1784, but still lies in an unspoilt sylvan landscape.
BELOW The entrepreneurial Samuel Greg lived with his family in this elegant white Georgian house beside his cotton mill; later generations of the family, though, moved further away from the works.

Quebec House

Kent
At the east end of the village of Westerham, on the north side of the A25, facing the junction with the B2026 Edenbridge road

A high brick wall on a sharp corner on the road from Westerham to Sevenoaks conceals the unpretentious gabled facades of Quebec House, where James Wolfe spent the first eleven years of his life. His parents rented the house, then known as Spiers, in 1726, and James was born a year later. The house, which is sixteenth-century in origin, was subsequently extensively altered but has now been returned to its seventeenth-century appearance. Basically square, it is built of a pleasing mixture of brick and Kentish ragstone and has three distinctive gables on each facade. This is a homely, welcoming place, its character signalled by the fact that visitors ring the bell for admittance, as if paying an afternoon call.

The low-ceilinged, panelled rooms contain many mementoes of General Wolfe and his victory at Quebec in 1759, when he defeated the French by scaling the Heights of Abraham above the town but was mortally wounded in the battle. A pencil sketch of Wolfe in the Bicentenary Room was drawn by his aide-de-camp on a page torn from a pocket book while they were in the field. The curiously pointed profile,

ABOVE James Wolfe, who defeated the French at Quebec in 1759, spent the early years of his life in this modest building of brick and Kentish ragstone.

a caricaturist's dream, is easily recognisable in a number of other paintings in the house.

Wolfe's travelling canteen in a corner of the same room gives a glimpse of the comforts enjoyed by an officer on campaign in the mid-eighteenth century. Clearly the finer things in life were not entirely discarded, as the canteen contains a cruet and glass decanters as well as more mundane objects, such as a griddle and a frying-pan. Also here is the finely quilted dressing-gown in which Wolfe's body was brought back to England from Quebec. A seventeenth-century staircase leads up to a tranquil panelled drawing room on the first floor, furnished with William and Mary and Queen Anne pieces and a Broadwood square piano of 1788, and warmed by an open fire on cold afternoons. An imaginatively staged exhibition in the old coach house across the walled garden describes the Quebec campaign and its background and gives details of Wolfe's life. Three niches in the south wall of this building are thought to be bee boles where bees were kept in straw skeps, or hives, possibly to aid the pollination of fruit trees on the wall.

Red House

Kent
Red House Lane, Bexleyheath

In the midst of the sprawl of south London, behind an undulating brick wall, a tranquil, leafy garden sets off the small house in the country that the young Philip Webb designed for his friend William Morris, who was just starting out on married life. It was Webb's first commission and was finished in 1860, in what was then a gentle Kentish countryside of orchards, fields and meadows. An unpretentious L-shaped building of deep-red brick with a steep tiled roof, also startlingly red, it is part Kentish farmhouse, part sleepy French *manoir*, part medieval monastery. Gothic porches shelter heavy wooden doors, sash windows are topped off with brickwork arches, a buttress is corbelled out to carry an oriel window, and the roofline is broken by two massive brick chimneystacks, by the steep pyramidal roof with a finialled cap which marks the staircase tower, and by gables and dormers. Everything is at different levels, and the sashes are mixed with casements and round bull's-eye windows. This individual place, so different from the stuccoed villas favoured by his contemporaries, embodied Morris's yearning for a pre-industrial world and his romantic ideas about the good life and the value of hand-craftsmanship. Morris stayed here only five years, but the house and the way it was fitted out were to have an enduring influence on later approaches to domestic architecture and ideas of good taste. This was the birthplace of the Arts and Crafts movement, of which both Morris and Webb were leading figures.

When Red House was built, Morris was only in his 20s. He had met Webb during a short stint in the offices of the Gothic Revival architect G.E. Street and he had also become friendly with two of the leading figures of the Pre-Raphaelite movement, Edward Burne-Jones, whom he had met while a student at Oxford, and Dante Gabriel Rossetti. It was Rossetti who, on the look-out for models with the kind of unconventional beauty valued by the Pre-Raphaelites, had spotted Janey Burden, whom Morris married in 1859. Both Burne-Jones and Webb were closely involved in the fitting out of Red House, which was decorated with rich embroidered hangings, medieval-style stained glass and tiles and specially made furniture, designed by Webb to be both practical and in tune with Morris's vision. Weekend visitors, collected from the nearest station by horse-drawn wagon, were put to work painting ceilings and furniture and the textiles, too, were all produced in the house, to Morris's designs. In 1861, some half-dozen of these friends became the core of the firm of decorators and designers that Morris founded, and which took his romantic ideals and artist-craftsman principles to a much wider audience.

The interior, which is centred on the sturdy oak staircase set in the angle of the L, has long since lost most of the furniture made for it, but some important pieces remain, or have returned, and sympathetic later owners, in particular Ted and Doris Hollamby, who lived here for half a century, have preserved other original features and introduced Morris and Co. wallpapers and innovations in keeping with the house. Although now largely unfurnished, it is welcoming and well lit. There are abstract painted ceilings (that over the stairs darkened by smoke); richly coloured Persian carpets on the floors; exposed brick fireplaces in every room; painted

BELOW A detail from the mural in the drawing room of Red House, one of the three scenes based on a medieval romance by Froissart that Burne-Jones completed in 1860.

panelling and a selection of Morris papers in cool greens and blues, their designs shaped by the flowers growing outside in the garden. The hall, where the family and their many visitors occasionally ate, and where Morris would appear from the door to the cellar clutching several bottles of wine, still has the tall settle designed by Webb, with painted panels thought to be by Morris, and the dining room to one side is furnished with Webb's massive red dresser, topped off with a Gothic canopy, and his large oak refectory table, and is hung with an unfinished embroidery of Aphrodite designed by Morris. One of twelve originally planned for the room, of which only seven were begun, it is thought to have been worked by Bessie Burden, Morris's sister-in-law.

Two of the main rooms are upstairs. The beautiful drawing room, with a high barrel ceiling going up into the roof, has another settle, by Burne-Jones, and an oriel window looking onto the garden, with a window seat where the ladies of the house sat to work on their embroidery. One wall is covered with the Hollambys' books and there are three murals on a medieval theme by Burne-Jones, all that he completed of the proposed cycle of seven. At the end of one wing is Morris's airy L-shaped studio, lit by windows on three sides. Ted Hollamby, who worked as an architect, designed the desk that fills the bay window and there are examples of the blocks used for printing Morris wallpapers.

Webb designed the compartmental garden as a natural extension of the house, although little remains. Apples and pears trained on the house and an evocative gnarled orchard evoke the Kentish countryside that was once all around. Sadly, Morris did not enjoy his dream for very long. The demands of his work took him back to London in 1865 and he is thought never to have visited Red House again. Many of the furnishings ended up at Kelmscott Manor, the Oxfordshire farmhouse he rented with Rossetti as a country retreat, and his idealism contributed to the founding of the Society for the Protection of Ancient Buildings, which directly inspired the formation of the National Trust.

LEFT Red House, built for William Morris by his friend Philip Webb in what was then lush Kentish countryside, has a well in the garden with a tall conical roof that suggests a Kentish oast house.

Rufford Old Hall

Lancashire
7 miles (11.2 kilometres) north of Ormskirk, in the village of Rufford on the east side of the A59

Like his father, grandfather and great-grandfather before him, Sir Thomas Hesketh married an heiress. Certainly no expense was spared on the half-timbered manor house he built in *c*.1530, establishing the family seat for the next 230 years. Although only the great hall survives in its original form – the west wing being now no more than marks in the grass and the east wing having been extensively rebuilt – this impressive Tudor interior speaks eloquently of wealth and position. The hall was built for show. Some 14 metres (46 feet) long and 6.5 metres (22 feet) wide, it rises to a richly carved hammerbeam roof in which each massive timber is fretted with battlements. Angels, all but one now wingless, look down from the ends of the supporting beams and carved roof bosses display the arms of the great Lancashire families with which Hesketh was allied.

Instead of a partition separating the hall from the screens passage, as was usual in houses of this date, there is a massive, intricately carved wooden screen. Three soaring finials look as if they might have come from a pagoda. This deliberately theatrical set-piece, backed by blind quatrefoils lining the upper wall of the passage and placed within a wooden arch supported by beautifully decorated octagonal pillars, must have delighted the young William Shakespeare, who very probably spent a few months here as part of Sir Thomas's company of players in 1581. A canopy of honour curves over the far end of the room, where the lord and his guests would have sat at high table, their special status further emphasised by the great bay window that bulges out to one side. A long refectory table, richly carved oak chests, and pieces from the Hesketh collection of arms and armour add to the hall's atmosphere. The exterior is similarly fine, an impressive display of studding, quatrefoils and wood-mullioned windows greeting visitors as they come up the drive.

A Carolean wing juts out at right-angles to the medieval great hall, its symmetrical gabled facade built of warm red brick contrasting strongly with the black-and-white half-timbering. A castellated tower peering over the angle between the two ranges is a later addition, a feature of the nineteenth-century building in Tudor Gothic style that joins the great hall

to the Charles II wing and which was partly formed out of a 1720s rebuilding, using sixteenth-century timbers, of the east range. This part of the house includes a spacious drawing room stretching the full length of the first floor, which rises to an open timber roof and has a spy-hole looking down into the great hall below. As elsewhere in the house, richly carved court cupboards, spindle-backed rush-seated chairs and oak settles add to the antiquarian atmosphere, although not all are genuinely old. A show of family portraits includes Sir Godfrey Kneller's imposing likeness of the Thomas Hesketh who rebuilt the east wing and a number of landscapes are dominated by a huge canvas by the Flemish artist Gommaert van der Gracht, whose still-life is set against a distant formal garden and walled town beyond.

Throughout the house are displayed toys, household utensils, textiles and many other items from the unique Philip Ashcroft collection, which illustrates village life in pre-industrial Lancashire. Larger pieces of agricultural equipment from the collection are on show in the stables.

BELOW The hammerbeam roof in Rufford's great hall is decorated with carved angels.
OPPOSITE In 1662, a gabled three-storey wing with a datestone set into the brickwork was built at right-angles to the Tudor great-hall range.

St Michael's Mount

Cornwall
½ mile (0.8 kilometre) south
of the A394 at Marazion

The craggy island of St Michael's Mount rises from the sea off the Cornish coast like a spiny sea monster arching its back below the waves, its dramatic profile crowned by Arthurian battlements and towers. When the skies are grey and an Atlantic gale is sending breakers crashing onto the rocks, it is easy to see why the Archangel St Michael was thought to have battled with the Devil here. On still summer evenings, the island floats serenely in a crystal-clear sea.

This strange hybrid is part religious retreat, part fortress, part elegant country house. Associated with Christianity since the fifth century, when St Michael is said to have appeared to some local fishermen, it became an important place of pilgrimage in the Middle Ages, when the attraction of the saint's shrine was enhanced by the charms of the jawbone of St Appolonia of Alexander, which was said to cure toothache. A little fourteenth-century granite church built on the highest point of the island is the most important survival from the Benedictine priory that was established here in the twelfth century, daughter house of the much grander Mont St Michel, set on another rocky outcrop some 150 miles (240 kilometres) across the Channel. Two beautiful fifteenth-century rose windows light the building, the one at the west end featuring a company of angels in flowing robes.

What was probably the monastic refectory is now the impressive Chevy Chase Room, its name a reference to the prominent and unusual plaster frieze on which rabbits, boars, stags, a bear and a fox are being pursued by men with spears and guns. Some of the hunters' dogs have got away from the pack and are perched mischievously on top of the frieze. Appropriately furnished with a gleaming seventeenth-century refectory table, the room is dominated by the royal coat of arms picked out in gold and red over the fireplace, set up here in celebration of Charles II's restoration. The massive granite walls are probably those built in the twelfth century, but the arching timber roof dates from 300 years later.

The guardroom in the entry range, the garrison room embedded in the rock, an old sentry box overlooking the steep cobbled path up to the castle and gun batteries pointing out to sea recall the 200 years when the Mount was a manned fortress. It was a major link in England's defences against the Spanish Armada (a beacon lit on the church tower in 1588 heralded the approach of the fleet) and a royalist stronghold in the Civil War until the castle's surrender in 1646. The last military governor, the Parliamentarian Colonel John St Aubyn, began the conversion of the fortress into a private house and his descendants have continued to live here. Sir John St Aubyn, 3rd Baronet, transformed the ruined lady chapel into the elegant blue drawing room, where early rococo Gothic plasterwork picked out in white against the blue walls, niches filled with pink Italian vases in jasper and alabaster and fine Chippendale furniture upholstered in blue conjure up the cultivated world of Georgian England.

Far below, on the steep and exposed lower slopes of the island, is the St Aubyn family's terraced rock garden and eighteenth-century walled garden. Despite the sea gales, rare tropical and subtropical plants flourish here.

From the castle terraces there are magnificent views along the Cornish coast and inland to rolling granite moors, while far below a thread of ant-sized people crossing the causeway leading back over the sands to Marazion at low tide could be a procession of medieval pilgrims. A row of whitewashed cottages huddles above the clawlike harbour on the sheltered north side of the island, where sailing ships once loaded Cornish tin and copper for the Continent.

LEFT St Michael's Mount, set on a rocky outcrop just off the Cornish coast that is islanded by the sea at high tide, is one of the most picturesque of the Trust's properties.
OPPOSITE The paintings on the Saloon ceiling at Saltram are by Antonio Zucchi, who depicted the goddess Diana hunting in the central roundel.

Saltram

Devon
2 miles (3.2 kilometres) west of Plympton, 3 miles (4.8 kilometres) east of Plymouth city centre, between the A38 Plymouth–Exeter road and the A379 Plymouth–Kingsbridge road

Anyone who has travelled by train from Plymouth to London will know the pleasure of seeing the Saltram estate shortly after leaving the city, when the line suddenly emerges on the banks of the Plym estuary and the wooded slope of the park rises on the other side of the water. With a view over Plymouth Sound to the trees of Mount Edgcumbe, this is a perfect position for a house and the building created here lives up to its setting. Although dating back to late Tudor times, Saltram is essentially a product of the eighteenth century, the rooms with their original contents summing up all that was best about this elegant and civilised age.

The remodelling of the house was the work of John and Lady Catherine Parker, who wrapped three classical facades round the Tudor core, fragments of which are still visible in an interior courtyard, and the three-storey seventeenth-century block which John's father had purchased in 1712. Their son, John Parker, 1st Lord Boringdon, who inherited in 1768, was responsible for amassing the outstanding collection of pictures and for inviting Robert Adam to redesign some of the principal rooms. Already at work on Kedleston Hall (*see* p.180) and Osterley (*see* p.239), Adam was at the height of his career and his interiors at Saltram, in which he was responsible for almost everything, including the door handles, are exceptional examples of his style. In the great Neo-classical saloon, delicate plasterwork attributed to Joseph Rose stands out white against the eggshell blue and burnt yellow of the coved ceiling. Blue damask lines the walls, setting off the four great looking-glasses and a show of portraits, Old Masters and Old Master copies, hung as Adam intended. A magnificent Axminster carpet echoes the design of the ceiling and gilded chairs and sofas line the walls. Double doors at the north end of the room give a vista into the equally elegant dining room, originally designed as the library, where romanticised depictions of ruins and rocky landscapes set into the walls and lunette paintings in Adam's delicate plasterwork ceiling are the work of Antonio Zucchi.

Another aspect of the eighteenth century is reflected in the more intimate and relaxed morning room, where a quartet of cloud-based cherubs makes music in the rococo plaster ceiling. Paintings hang triple-banked in the fashion of the day, their gilded frames glowing against red velvet.

The picture collection is still virtually as the 1st Lord left it and includes eleven paintings by his close friend Sir Joshua Reynolds, who came from the nearby village of Plympton and regularly visited Saltram to shoot on the estate and gamble with Lord Boringdon. During their long association, Reynolds not only portrayed Lord Boringdon and his family but also advised him on his other acquisitions, among them works by Angelica Kauffmann and a number of Italian, Dutch and Flemish paintings. Characteristic history paintings and scenes from classical mythology by Kauffmann hang on the main staircase, and here too is her portrait of Reynolds. Probably commissioned by Lord Boringdon, it shows the artist in seventeenth-century dress with a bust of Michelangelo, whom Reynolds particularly revered, dimly seen behind him. On the landing above, a painting of a goggle-eyed youth in shining armour is Rubens's likeness of Vincenzo II Gonzaga, Duke of Mantua. A comfortable Regency library created by John Foulston for the 1st Earl of Morley on the south-west corner of the house has another show of portraits hanging above the bookcases, which are filled with leather-bound volumes largely dating from the time of the 1st Earl.

Other delights at Saltram are the eighteenth-century Chinese wallpaper, some of it depicting those curiously elongated figures so familiar from Japanese prints, which decorates some of the first-floor rooms, and a show of topographical watercolours by Frances Talbot, who married the 1st Earl in 1809. A light and airy late eighteenth-century kitchen looking onto a rough-walled internal courtyard has a splendid, 1,000-piece array of gleaming copper pans and moulds.

A pleasantly informal Victorian garden to the west of the house is a soothing mixture of lawns, wooded glades, shrubs and grass walks. An octagonal mid-eighteenth-century Gothic belvedere at the end of a long lime avenue was probably built by Harry Stockman, the estate's talented carpenter, as was the elegant pedimented orangery of 1775 by the house. Stockman also created the chapel nearby; adding battlements, buttresses and pointed windows to what was originally a barn. The extensive deer-park formed in the mid-eighteenth century was landscaped in the style of 'Capability' Brown, but the magnificent views depicted in William Tomkins's delightful landscapes in the garden room have been ruined by Plymouth's urban sprawl. Shelter belts planted by the National Trust help to hide this intrusive reminder of the twenty-first century, but passengers on the main Plymouth to London line can still enjoy a glimpse of the amphitheatre, a mid-eighteenth-century folly nestling in the woods above the Plym estuary.

ABOVE Saltram's Palladian west front dates from the remodelling of the rambling Tudor house in the mid-eighteenth century.
OPPOSITE Robert Adam was responsible for almost everything in the saloon at Saltram, from the carpet echoing the design of the ceiling to the hang of the paintings.

Sandham Memorial Chapel

Hampshire
4 miles (6.4 kilometres) south of Newbury, ½ mile (0.8 kilometre) east of the A34

Service in Macedonia and in a military hospital during the First World War inspired the visionary and touching paintings by Stanley Spencer that fill this chapel. These are not horrific, tortured scenes of trench warfare but cameos of everyday activities, conveying a sense of human companionship and providing a kind of modern equivalent to the 'labours of the months' seen in medieval art. Soldiers in Macedonia are shown filling their water bottles, dressing under mosquito nets, cooking breakfast in the open and picking bilberries. In the hospital they sort laundry, polish taps and make beds. Spencer's greatest work, *The Resurrection of the Soldiers*, entirely fills the altar wall. A stream of white crosses leads towards Christ seated in the middle distance, gathering crosses from the fallen in his arms. Soldiers emerge from their graves, shake hands with their comrades, clean buttons and wind puttees. Here, as throughout this powerful cycle, everyday life is touched by the immortal.

The 1920s red-brick chapel was built to Spencer's instructions by Mr and Mrs Behrend specially to house the paintings, which were created, on large seamless canvases, between 1927 and 1932. It is dedicated to Mrs Behrend's brother Lieutenant H.W. Sandham, who served in Macedonia during the First World War and died of an illness contracted there.

Scotney Castle

Kent
1½ miles (2.4 kilometres) south of Lamberhurst on the A21

The magical garden created by Edward Hussey III from 1837 in a deep valley of the Kentish Weald owes much of its charm to the romantic buildings incorporated in the design. At the top of a steep bluff overlooking the valley is a nineteenth-century vision of an Elizabethan house, all gables, tall chimneys and mullioned windows, while far below, encircled by a lake-like moat beside the River Bewl, are the ruins of a genuinely ancient castle. Flowering trees and shrubs on the slopes frame carefully contrived views over the valley and from one building to another.

In a move against the fashion of the time, which was swinging away from the naturalistic layouts that had been in vogue since the eighteenth century, Edward Hussey, who had inherited the estate from his father while still a child, created an outstandingly successful example of the Picturesque style, whose exponents promoted artfully created landscapes, ideally including a romantic building or two, which gave the illusion of the beauty of nature untamed. At Scotney, the castle was the perfect eye-catcher. In fact the remnants of a fortified house that Roger Ashburnham constructed here in *c.*1378–80 during the troubled decades of the Hundred Years War, when men of substance in this part of England lived in fear of French raids, the castle consists of a massive round tower rising from the lake-like moat, with a projecting parapet at roof level, and a ruined gatehouse. A brick Elizabethan range adjoining the tower is all that survives of sixteenth-century additions, and jagged walls with gaping windows mark the remains of a substantial seventeenth-century wing.

LEFT Looking towards the altar wall in Sandham Memorial Chapel, where a stream of white crosses leads towards the seated Christ.
ABOVE The wallpaper designed by Thomas Willement in the library at Scotney was originally brightly coloured, but has faded over the years.
OPPOSITE The new house at Scotney, built in Elizabethan style, has a huge stone-mullioned window lighting the stairs on the garden front.

Instead of living in the castle, where his father had contracted the typhoid that killed him from the drains, the young Edward, still in his 20s, built a new house in neo-Tudor style in 1837–43, for which he engaged the rising young architect Anthony Salvin, who was not much older than his client. But the shaping of its surroundings and the actual site of the house were determined with the advice of the artist and landscape gardener William Sawrey Gilpin, who was a disciple of Richard Payne Knight and Sir Uvedale Price, the leading exponents of the Picturesque style. The natural drama of the valley was enhanced by the creation of a deep quarry, from which the streaky golden sandstone for the house was obtained, and the seventeenth-century wing of the castle was partly demolished, to focus the eye on the older remains and make them seem more romantic.

The new building, the design of which took 33 meetings between architect and client to thrash out, was devised to be both picturesque and practical. The tall, many-gabled facades are enhanced by a battlemented tower like a Northumbrian pele that dominates the entrance front and by the chimneys rising above the roofline, and there are great mullioned and transomed windows lighting the stairs and filling the bays looking over the garden. There are arresting details, too, such as the lead rainwater hoppers designed by the heraldic artist Thomas Willement, who is better known for his stained glass.

The well-designed interior, with stunning views from most of the main rooms, has been little altered since it was built and still has many of Salvin's decorative schemes and several pieces of furniture that he designed for Scotney. Most recently, the new house has been the home of the architectural historian and writer Christopher Hussey, Edward Hussey III's grandson, who inherited the estate in 1952 and gave it to the National Trust. The garden has been open since his death in 1970, and the house passed to the Trust, with all its contents, on his wife Betty's death in 2006. It is being presented as a welcoming and lived-in home, as Christopher and Betty had it, and with nineteenth-century furnishings blended with twentieth-century additions. There are inviting sofas and a drinks trolley in the spacious library, where the faded Willement wallpaper and the Jacobean-style plasterwork ceiling are both original, as are the bookcases designed by Salvin. In the book-lined study next door, where Christopher

Hussey wrote his many articles for *Country Life* and other works, the ornamental ceiling features local Kentish hops, and there is more plasterwork by Salvin in the more formal dining room, where the huge buffet sideboard Salvin made for Edward Hussey III matches the richly carved panelling.

A few rooms were substantially altered by Christopher and Betty. Their sunny bedroom, with a bay window looking over the garden, was fitted with a walk-in wardrobe and en-suite bathroom in the 1950s and a restful blue and green bedroom,

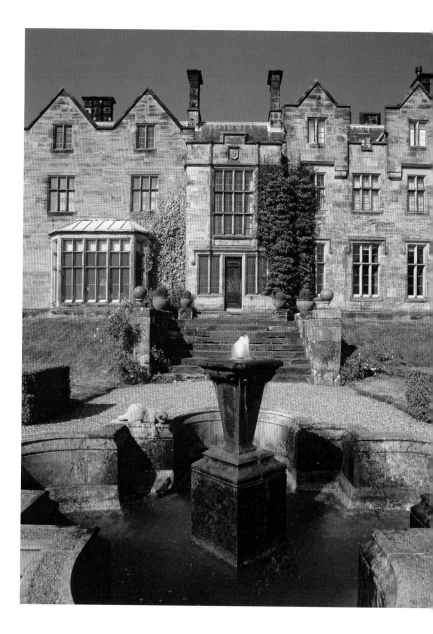

redecorated by Betty, is furnished with bamboo pieces purchased in 1951. Betty's sense of colour comes through again in the remodelled kitchen, where shelves are filled with her vibrant red and white china. The many paintings include likenesses of Christopher and Betty Hussey by their friend John Ward and views of both the new house and the old castle by John Piper, whom they also knew well, as well as family portraits, a market scene by the sixteenth-century Flemish artist Joachim Beuckelaer and a fantasy by the Italian baroque painter Faustino Bocchi, which Christopher Hussey bought while he was a student at Oxford. Most enchanting is the little room giving access to the garden, where blue and white Delftware vases are set against old Flemish panelling in the style of the seventeenth century.

One of the best views of the garden is from a semicircular bastion below the new house, which gives a vista down over the quarry and the slope of the valley, thickly planted with trees and shrubs, to the moated remains of the old castle. The only modern note in the garden, hidden away on a little isthmus in the lake, is the *Reclining Figure* by Henry Moore, a tribute to the memory of Christopher Hussey.

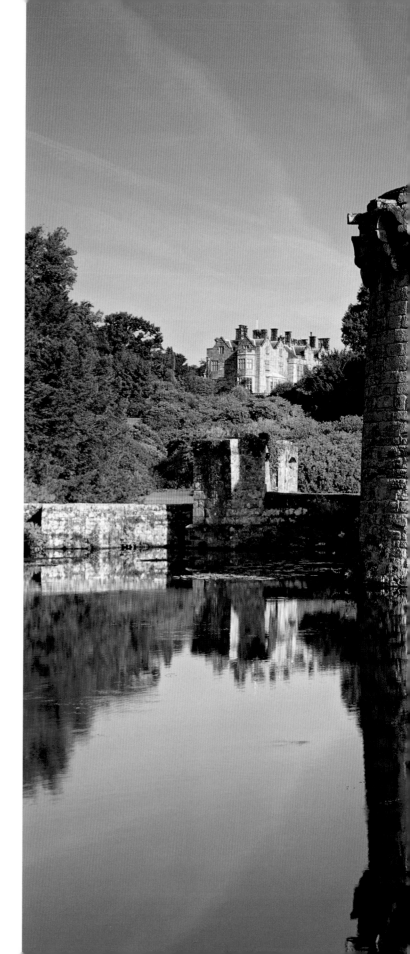

RIGHT Scotney is an outstanding example of a Picturesque landscape, with carefully contrived vistas between the old castle on the valley floor and the new house, built in neo-Tudor style in 1837–43, far above.

Seaton Delaval Hall

Northumberland
2 miles (3.2 kilometres) north of
Whitley Bay, off A190 between
Seaton Delaval and Seaton Sluice

This arresting baroque house, set less than a mile (1.6 kilometres) from the sea on a bleak and windswept coast, was designed by Sir John Vanbrugh for Admiral George Delaval and built between 1719 and c.1730. Arcaded wings framing a deep and gently sloping forecourt set off the tall and dramatic central block. Placed by Vanbrugh on a mound, like a castle keep, it is four and a half storeys high, symmetrical and detailed for theatrical effect. Huge Doric columns, supporting nothing, frame the entrance, there are massive chimneys and heavy keystones over the windows and the pedimented top storey, designed as a penthouse for the admiral's use, resembles a classical temple. Naval guns, harpoons, sea creatures and other devices carved into the stonework and the porthole windows are allusions to the admiral's career. Vanbrugh, an architect of genius and the greatest exponent of the English Baroque, was both looking back to prodigy houses such as Hardwick Hall and setting out to create 'something of the castle in the air', a play house that could also be lived in. Gutted by fire in 1822, this central block is now an architectural shell, with a dramatic Piranesian interior of huge spaces, vistas to upper levels and shafts of light. Beyond the lofty entrance hall, with fire-blackened and crumbling sculptures set into blind arcading at the level of the first floor and an original marble pavement, is the monumental saloon, 23 metres (75 feet) long and 9 metres (29 feet) wide. Running the length of the south front, this great room looks out through a grand Ionic portico to a great obelisk half a mile (0.8 kilometre) away across the former park. Slender cast-iron shafts dividing the saloon, replacements for eight stone columns destroyed in the fire, were inserted by the Newcastle architect John Dobson, who roofed the ruined building in 1860 and carried out essential restoration. Two oval stone staircases wind up through the house to either side of the hall and descend to the Stygian, stone-vaulted basement, a section of twisted iron handrail on the east stair showing how fierce the fire must have been.

Sadly, neither the admiral, who died after a fall from his horse in 1723, nor Vanbrugh, who died in 1726, lived to see the house finished, and the work was probably completed under the supervision of William Etty, Vanbrugh's clerk of works at Castle Howard in Yorkshire, which was still being built in the early 1720s. Now-vanished wings to east and west of the main house which appear in mid-eighteenth-century paintings and engravings are of uncertain date, if, indeed, they ever existed. Those flanking the forecourt were built at the same time as the central block, but not entirely to Vanbrugh's design. On the east, offering another monumental interior, spanned by vast arches of stone, are the stables, the names over the stalls – Hercules, Julius, Zephyrus, etc. – referring to beasts housed

BELOW Vanbrugh's monumental entrance hall is decorated with blind arcading and statues representing the arts, geography and astronomy.
RIGHT Seaton Delaval was designed for theatrical effect, with huge Doric columns framing the entrance, windows weighed down with heavy keystones and a penthouse like a classical temple.

here in c.1800. The west wing, originally designed as kitchen and servants' quarters, became the family's home in more recent years.

When Edward Delaval, the last of his line, died in 1814, the house passed to a nephew, Sir Jacob Henry Astley, whose main seat was at Melton Constable in Norfolk. After the fire, it was Sir Jacob's son, created 16th Lord Hastings in 1841, who employed John Dobson, although plans for fully restoring the house were never realised, leaving the shell that is seen today. The hall grounds were used for garden parties and church fêtes, and prisoners of war were housed here in the Second World War, but the family rarely came to Seaton Delaval until, in the 1950s, the 22nd Lord Hastings decided to restore the hall and make the west wing his home, furnishing the rooms with pieces from Melton Constable as well as with furniture and paintings originally in the hall. He finally settled here in 1990. What was once the kitchen, with massive pilasters supporting a high vaulted roof, is now a sitting room, with sofas ranged invitingly round the fireplace, and other rooms are in the former laundry and servants' bedrooms. Mainly eighteenth-century family portraits, among them works by John Vanderbank, Thomas Hudson and Francis Cotes, include a likeness, after Reynolds, of the profligate and philandering

Sir Francis Delaval (1727–71), the most notorious of his line, who fathered several illegitimate children and died heavily in debt. Walnut Queen Anne sofas and chairs upholstered in needlework, and two marble-topped pier tables that were once in the hall of the main block, are part of a collection of fine furniture, mostly of the eighteenth century, while a painting of Windsor Castle in c.1670 by Hendrik Danckerts was given to the Delavals by Charles II as a reward for their loyalty in the Civil War, as was a marble bust of the king attributed to Caius Gabriel Cibber. More recent family history is reflected in a sculpted head of the late Lord Hastings and in two stone sculptures from Zimbabwe, where he had a farm.

As well as restoring the fabric of the house, Lord and Lady Hastings also extended the gardens to the west of the main block, engaging James Russell to design a topiary parterre and embellishing the layouts with a fountain, urns and ornamental sculpture. On the death of both Lord Hastings and his wife in 2007, the National Trust was approached by their son, the 23rd Lord and, as a result of a major fund-raising campaign and a £6.7 million endowment from the Trust's own resources, the largest ever allocated, the house and gardens, much of the estate and the core of the collection passed to the Trust on 16 December 2009.

Shaw's Corner

Hertfordshire
At the south-west end of the
village of Ayot St Lawrence,
2 miles (3.2 kilometres) north-east
of Wheathampstead

This rather undistinguished Edwardian villa is where the Irish dramatist and critic George Bernard Shaw moved in 1906 at the age of 50, and where he enjoyed a full and fruitful old age. Apart from the museum room, which shows such gems as the Oscar that Shaw was awarded in 1938 for the screenplay for the film version of *Pygmalion*, the old-fashioned steel-rimmed spectacles he wore in his later years and his membership card for the Cyclists' Touring Club, dated 1950, the year in which he died, the house is still arranged very much as it was in his day and is filled with echoes of his individuality and genius, and of his legendary reputation. This is as Shaw intended. He wanted the house to be a 'living shrine' and deliberately bought busts, pictures and other things here from his London flat.

Shaw's collection of hats still hangs in the hall. In the study his typewriter sits waiting on the desk, with his pens to one side, and the pocket dictionaries he used for immediate reference are ranged below the window onto the garden. A little desk in the corner of the room was for his secretary, Miss Patch. One of the drawers of the filing cabinets behind where she sat carries a characteristic Shavian label: 'Keys and Contraptions'. In the drawing room next door a bronze bust by Rodin perfectly captures the craggy head, with its rather prominent nose and full beard. Shaw hardly used this room after his wife Charlotte died in 1943, preferring to sit in an armchair by the fire in the dining room after eating an early vegetarian dinner. Photographs of Gandhi, Lenin and Stalin above the dining-room fireplace reflect Shaw's socialist views and a glowing oil portrait of the great man by Augustus John dominates the room.

From here Shaw used to step out into the garden for his regular evening walks, or to bury himself in the little rotating shed where he did much of his writing, safe from interruptions, sitting in the wicker chair which is still pulled up to the table at which he worked. If visitors called, they would be told, truthfully, that Shaw was out.

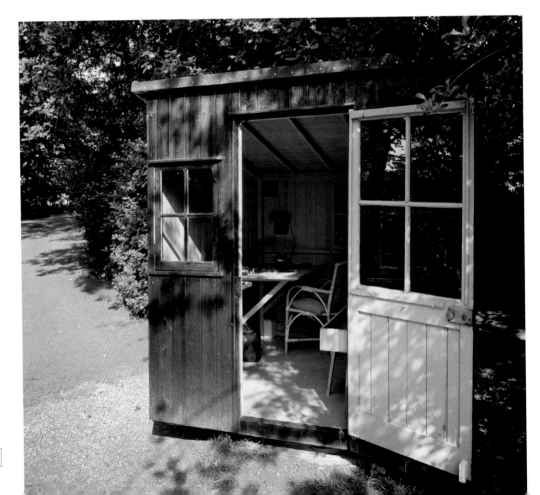

RIGHT Although the playwright George Bernard Shaw had a study in his house at Ayot St Lawrence, he liked to write in this revolving hut in the garden, where he would not be interrupted by visitors.
OPPOSITE Treasure from a Spanish galleon captured in the 1740s helped to finance the transformation of the Anson family's old seat into a substantial country house.

Shugborough Estate

Staffordshire
6 miles (9.6 kilometres) east of
Stafford on the A513 at Milford

The two Anson brothers born in the 1690s took very different paths in life. George, who went to sea at the age of 12, rose to be 1st Lord of the Admiralty and gained both fame and fortune on an epic four-year circumnavigation of the globe in the 1740s, during which he captured a treasure-laden Spanish galleon. Much of the admiral's wealth went to help his cultivated elder brother Thomas improve the three-storey, late seventeenth-century house on the banks of the River Sow which he had inherited in 1720. Among other changes and enlargements in the late 1740s and '60s, Thomas added charming domed pavilions with semicircular bay windows by Thomas Wright of Durham to frame the central block. The massive two-storey portico dominating the entrance front was a later addition, part of Samuel Wyatt's alterations for the 1st Viscount Anson at the end of the century that obliterated much of the earlier work. Similarly, Wyatt was responsible for the central bow on the garden facade, and for the verandahs on either side fronting the links to the pavilions, which he extended.

Thomas Anson was a leading spirit of the Society of Dilettanti, which promoted the art of classical antiquity, and this interest in the ancient world comes through in the interiors that survive from his time. Six huge, Piranesi-like paintings of classical ruins by Nicholas Thomas Dall strike a sombre note in the dining room, distracting the eye from Vassalli's arresting rococo plasterwork gently curving overhead, with medallion heads representing Egyptian and Greek deities. In Thomas Wright's low-ceilinged library, with a shallow arch set on Ionic columns dividing the room, marble busts set along the bookcases include a number of antique sculptures, among them likenesses of Plato and Hercules, as well as delightful nineteenth-century portraits of various members of the family, one of whom is depicted holding a rabbit.

Neo-classical motifs also mark Wyatt's interiors. Giant yellow scagliola columns punctuate the walls of his curiously elongated saloon, their reflections in the pier glasses on the end wall making the room seem even larger than it is. Joseph Rose the Younger's coved ceiling in Wyatt's impressive Red Drawing Room is decorated with delicate compositions reminiscent of a Wedgwood vase. This room also displays the few paintings that remain from Thomas Anson's once renowned picture collection, most of which was dispersed, with the rest of the contents, in the 1842 sale precipitated by the extravagance of the 2nd Viscount, created 1st Earl of Lichfield. Among them is a Murillo-inspired *Immaculate Conception*, a late work by Meléndez, painter to Philip V of Spain, and two paintings that were thought to be by Guido Reni (sadly, they are not) and which were bought back at the sale. A number of pictures connected with the estate have also survived, including two portraits of Corsican goats. Noble-looking beasts with corkscrew horns, these were part of a herd of this rare breed that was established by Thomas Anson. Some fine eighteenth-century French furniture in the principal rooms was acquired by the 2nd Earl when he set about rescuing the house in the 1850s.

A gold repeater, a snuffbox made of wood from one of his ships, Spanish coins and his commission from George III are among several mementoes of the gallant admiral. One of his officers designed the little Chinese house by the Sow, set off by a pagoda tree and other oriental shrubs, but the rococo plaster ceiling and Chinese painted mirrors that once adorned it are now in the house, complementing the oriental porcelain and other chinoiserie acquired by the brothers.

The apartments lived in by the Lichfield family, which have been private since the National Trust took over the house in 1966, are now gradually being opened following the death in 2005 of the 5th Earl, the society photographer Patrick Lichfield. Situated mostly on the upper floors, these more intimate and lived-in spaces contrast with the grandeur elsewhere and show Shugborough in a different light. They are also full of mementoes of the 5th Earl and his glittering 40-year career, during which he immortalised iconic figures of the sixties such as Mick Jagger and Joanna Lumley, caused a stir by photographing the singer Marsha Hunt in the nude, and also took memorable images of his royal relatives (he was the Queen's cousin), among them shots of the exiled Duke and

Duchess of Windsor and the official photographs of the wedding of the Prince of Wales and Lady Diana Spencer in 1981.

In the kitchen, which was fitted out in the late 1970s, a cupboard door is covered with business cards, and jams made from fruit grown on the estate, which Lichfield particularly enjoyed, are lined up on the windowsill of the light and airy circular breakfast room. Some of his most personal belongings, such as his spectacles and the boots and helmet he wore to ride his motorbike, are in the green sitting room, and here too is the collar of his dog Drum, beside the chair in which the 5th Earl used to sit. The bathrooms still have early twentieth-century plumbing and the elegant boudoir has the only hand-painted ceiling in the house and original 1794 wallpaper inlaid with silver leaf. Treasures on display, some brought out of storage and being shown for the first time, others on loan, include a collection of enamelled and gilded jardinières and urns that are said to have come from the Summer Palace in Peking.

And then there are the photographs. Some of them, as in the green sitting room, are of close family, others are of celebrities, among them some images taken on the Shugborough estate which have not been seen before. Also on show is Lichfield's studio from Oxford Gardens in west London, which has been faithfully reconstructed with his cameras and other equipment.

Formal terraced gardens lead down to the Sow, where the family's arboretum on an island in the river, formerly private, is now accessible. Thomas Wright's Picturesque ruin on the banks of the Sow, a crumbling array of columns and walls topped by the statue of a druid, is outclassed by the classical monuments based on buildings in ancient Athens in the park that Thomas Anson commissioned from James 'Athenian' Stuart. A triumphal arch stalks across the grass on a rise above the drive like a creature from outer space. Two pedimented porches with fluted columns project from the octagonal Tower of the Winds in the valley below and a shady knoll is crowned with the Lantern of Demosthenes, a cluster of columns topped by three dolphins supporting a tripod and bowl. No later development dulls the impact of these re-creations, only a gentle roar and tremors in the ground betraying the presence of the Stafford to Stoke railway line buried in a tunnel beneath the triumphal arch.

RIGHT The Red Drawing Room at Shugborough, the most impressive room in the house, was created in 1794 and is hung with the remains of a once-renowned picture collection, most of which was sold in 1842.

OPPOSITE A number of classical features in the grounds of Shugborough include this Doric temple attributed to James Stuart that was probably designed as the entrance to the kitchen garden.

Shute Barton

Devon
3 miles (4.8 kilometres) south-west of Axminster, 2 miles
(3.2 kilometres) north of Colyton
on the Honiton–Colyton road

Set on a wooded hill above the Axe valley a few miles from the Devon coast, Shute Barton is a rare survival of an unfortified medieval manor. As the arresting castellated gatehouse on the road suggests, the L-shaped building here now is a remnant of a once much larger house, most of which was pulled down in the late eighteenth century to provide stone for the grand Palladian mansion on the hill. What was left, originally the service quarters, became a farmhouse.

The two surviving ranges, battlemented and gargoyled and built of stone rubble and flint with ashlar dressings, frame the north and east sides of a tiny cobbled courtyard, with a stair

turret in the angle between the wings. An array of mullioned and transomed windows includes two pairs of original trefoil-headed lights, but there are also some sashes and other indications of a complex history of alteration and improvement, such as blocked openings and windows inserted in earlier apertures. On the south side of the court is the original gatehouse, now just giving access to the farmyard but once leading through to an extensive outer court with stabling, barns and staff accommodation.

The earliest parts of the building are in the east range. A sixteenth-century doorway from the inner court leads into the original stone-flagged kitchen, one end of which is filled with an enormous fireplace, over 6.5 metres (22 feet) wide. On a floor inserted over the kitchen, which was once much loftier, is an elegant, panelled seventeenth-century room, now part of a holiday apartment, and at the top of the house, reached by the newel stair in the angle turret, are the original servants' quarters, now a spacious chamber extending over most of the third floor and open to a medieval timber roof. There is a garderobe closet to one side of the fireplace.

Despite many vicissitudes, including the confiscation of the Shute estates during the Wars of the Roses, and involvement in the mid-sixteenth-century plot to put Lady Jane Grey on the throne, which led to the loss of the lands for a second time, descendants of Lord William Bonville, who built the fifteenth-century manor, have continued to be associated with the house. A few years after it was confiscated from the Greys, to whom Shute had passed by marriage, the estate was sold back to another descendant of the Bonvilles, Sir William Pole, in 1560 and it was he who built the delicious gatehouse. The Poles were loyal to the king in the Civil War and suffered as a result, but their fortunes revived in the eighteenth century when Sir John William de la Pole, a close friend of the Prince Regent, succeeded in vastly increasing the size of the estate and built the new house on the hill; the future George IV was entertained there in 1789. Another branch of the family inherited the serenely beautiful Antony (see p.18), in Cornwall, which had been the home of the Carews for centuries, prompting a change of name to Pole Carew, and it was Sir John Carew Pole (he altered his name again on succeeding to the Shute baronetcy) who gave Shute to the National Trust in 1959 and Antony in 1961. Pole Carews live in the house still.

Sissinghurst

Kent

2 miles (3.2 kilometres) north-east of Cranbrook, 1 mile (1.6 kilometres) east of Sissinghurst village on the A262

The lovely garden set high on a Wealden ridge owes much of its charm to the Tudor buildings of mellow pink brick around which it was created and which form a romantic backdrop to the planting. These evocative remains are all that survive of the great Tudor and Elizabethan courtyard house of the Baker family, who came to Sissinghurst in c.1490. There is also the ghost of an older manor here, its site marked by an orchard framed by three arms of a medieval moat.

Visitors approach Sissinghurst through a gabled archway crowned by three slender chimneys that was built in c.1535 by the high-flying Sir John Baker, who rose to be Chancellor of the Exchequer and made the family rich. The long ranges to either side, originally used for stabling and servants' lodgings, may be Sir John's too. Beyond, across a grassy court, rises the brick prospect tower that forms the focal point of the garden. Four storeys tall, with slender octagonal turrets, this glorified gatehouse was built by Sir Richard Baker in 1560–70 as part of a wholesale reconstruction of his father's house and once led into a courtyard lined by tall, gabled ranges. Elizabeth I, who stayed here for three days in 1573, would have ridden through Sir John's archway to be greeted by Sir Richard under the tower. A fragment of the Elizabethan mansion is now a cottage in the garden and there is a little sixteenth-century building where the family's private chaplain may have lived.

From the mid-seventeenth century, when the Baker family lost much of their wealth in the Civil War, Sissinghurst went into a long decline and was largely pulled down in 1764. Despite 200 years of neglect and decay, the evocative remains inspired the novelist and biographer Vita Sackville-West to purchase the property in 1930 and with the help of her husband, Sir Harold Nicolson, the diplomat and literary critic, to create one of the most individual and influential gardens of the twentieth century. The old walls and hedges were used to create a series of intimate open-air rooms, each one planted differently, and long linking walks provide a unifying framework.

The buildings were transformed into a singular and eccentric house, its various parts scattered round the garden. The stables in the long north wing of the entrance range were formed into an atmospheric library, lined with thousands of books, many of which were Harold Nicolson's review copies. The fireplace, which now has a de Laszlo portrait of the young Vita (disliked by her) hanging above it, was made out of Elizabethan fragments found in the garden and the furniture includes copies of pieces from Knole (*see* p.188), Vita's childhood home. The family had their dining room and kitchen in the priest's house and Harold Nicolson worked in South Cottage, but the tower was Vita's retreat. Reached by a spiral staircase is the cluttered room where she wrote, its walls still lined with the books on gardening, history and travel that reflect her special interests. In summer, she would garden all day and then write into the night. From the roof there is a bird's-eye view of the garden and wider prospects over woods, fields and oast houses to a distant ridge of the North Downs, with the spire of Frittenden church in the middle distance.

LEFT The east front of Shute Barton, which is a very rare survival of an unfortified medieval manor.

ABOVE RIGHT This room in the tower, where Vita retreated to read and write, accompanied only by one of her Alsatians, is still filled with her books, furniture and ornaments.

RIGHT The romantic
Elizabethan tower that
stands at the heart of
Sissinghurst garden is a
remnant of the great
courtyard house that once
stood on this site.

Sizergh

Cumbria
3½ miles (5.6 kilometres) south
of Kendal, north-west of the
A590/A591 interchange

Sizergh is dominated by the fourteenth-century fortress at its heart. The Stricklands who have lived here for 750 years were one of the great military families of the north, and the house they constructed in about 1350 reflects both their status and the vulnerability of their estate. Only about 50 miles (80 kilometres) from the Scottish border as the crow flies, Sizergh was liable to border raids and lies in the lowland corridor that leads south between the Lakeland hills and the inhospitable North Yorkshire moors. The massive pele tower at the centre of the house rises almost 18 metres (60 feet) to the battlements. Its limestone rubble walls are still formidable despite the later mullioned windows and the softening blanket of Virginia creeper, and in the Middle Ages the castle was also protected by a moat.

Tudor and Elizabethan additions, partly hidden by a Georgian veneer, adjoin the tower and long, low Elizabethan service wings with soaring chimneys flank the entrance courtyard. Double doors that once opened into the great hall now give access to a carriageway running through the castle, with a grand stone and oak staircase rising from one side.

Early Elizabethan woodwork in several of the rooms gives Sizergh its special flavour. Superb panelling of c.1575 inlaid with Renaissance motifs in poplar and bog-oak was sold to the Victoria and Albert Museum in 1891 but was returned in 1999 and can once again be seen in its former glory in the Inlaid Chamber. Craftsmanship of similar quality is displayed in the five intricately carved armorial chimneypieces, four of which date from 1563–75. The rest of the panelling is also very fine, the oldest in the house being the oak linenfold work dating from the reign of Henry VIII in a passage room. Intriguingly, a lozenge design on the woodwork in the old dining room and a bedroom reappears on the backs of three Elizabethan oak chairs in the tower. Here, too, there are carved oak benches with unusually rich mid-sixteenth-century decoration.

A number of Stuart portraits and personal royal relics advertise the Stricklands' adherence to the Catholic faith and their loyal devotion to the Stuart cause. Refusing to desert the royal family after 1688, Sir Thomas Strickland and his wife accompanied James II into exile in France, where Lady Strickland was governess to his young son.

Terraced lawns, their retaining walls softened with shrubs and climbers, lead down from the south front to a lake that was probably created out of the former moat. Orchids and wild daffodils flowering in the grass of the meadow above the lake are part of a native limestone flora, which reflects the rock outcropping all over the estate in screes, cliffs and pavements, but the extensive rock garden was constructed of Westmorland stone in 1926 by Hayes of Ambleside, who arranged the little stream tumbling across it into the lake in a series of pools and falls.

LEFT The great pele tower which dominates the castle dates from the fourteenth century.
BELOW This beautiful Elizabethan oak screen was once the entrance to the great hall.

Smallhythe Place

Kent
At Smallhythe, 2 miles
(3.2 kilometres) south of Tenterden,
on the east side of the Rye road

This modest half-timbered sixteenth-century farmhouse belonged to the legendary actress Dame Ellen Terry for nearly 30 years, from 1899 until her death here on 21 July 1928. Appropriately, she first saw Smallhythe in the company of Henry Irving, the manager of the Lyceum Theatre in London's Covent Garden, with whom she created a famous theatrical partnership that lasted for 24 years.

Her attractive house stands at one end of Smallhythe, its steep, red-tiled roof and sturdy brick chimneys outlined against the Kentish marshes on all sides. With the sea 10 miles (16 kilometres) away as the crow flies and the once sizeable stream bordering the garden shrunk to a narrow ditch, it is difficult to believe that the farm was formerly Port House to a thriving shipyard that catered for a procession of boats unloading at the wharves along the creek. A duckweed-covered pool marks the site of the repair dock that was used for some 400 years, until the seventeenth century.

Now preserved as a theatrical museum, the house is full of mementoes of Ellen Terry's life and of the world in which she moved. In the large beamed kitchen which she used as a dining room, with traditional wheel-back chairs ranged round the walls, a refectory table in the middle of the warm red-brick floor and a high-backed settle by the fire, two walls are devoted to mementoes of David Garrick and Sarah Siddons. Other exhibits connected with famous names from the past include an affectionate message from Sarah Bernhardt – 'Merci, my dearling' – written with a flourish on the cover of a dressing-table; Sir Arthur Sullivan's monocle, with his autograph on the glass; a chain worn by Fanny Kemble and a visiting card from Alexandre Dumas, whose *La dame aux camélias* inspired Verdi's *La Traviata*. A letter in Oscar Wilde's languorous scrawl in an adjoining room begs Ellen Terry to accept 'the first copy of my first play', adding 'perhaps some day I shall be fortunate to write something worthy of your playing'. Here, too, is her make-up box; a sponge, a mirror and a large swatch of grey hair are prominent among the notably sparse contents, which seem barely adequate for someone of Terry's stature.

Upstairs there are displays of the lavish silk and velvet costumes that Irving created for Terry. Much criticised for

ABOVE This timber-framed sixteenth-century farmhouse at one end of Smallhythe village was bought by the spirited actress Ellen Terry in 1899 and is full of her theatrical mementoes and treasures.

their extravagance, they include the moss-green beetle-wing dress she wore as Lady Macbeth in 1888. The more private face of the great actress is revealed in her simple, low-ceilinged bedroom, with a view out over the marshes from the casement windows. It is still as she left it, with brightly patterned rugs on the bare boards of the floor and rotund pottery pigs on the mantelpiece. Kate Hastings's pastel portraits of Terry's mother and of her two children, Edith and Edward Gordon Craig, offspring of her liaison with the architect and theatrical designer Edward Godwin, hang above the bed with its theatrical curved Empire ends. Godwin himself designed the modest dressing table and the wooden crucifix that Edward Gordon Craig made for his mother stands on the bedside table, next to a worn copy of the Globe Shakespeare annotated in her distinctively generous hand. Something of the great actress's integrity and resolution also emerges in a much-read edition of Robert Louis Stevenson's 'Christmas Sermon', one of the many underlined passages exhorting 'If your morals make you dreary, depend upon it they are wrong.'

Snowshill Manor

Gloucestershire
3 miles (4.8 kilometres)
south-west of Broadway, 4 miles
(6.4 kilometres) west of the
junction of the A44 and the A424

The old lady who showed her grandson the family treasures hidden away in her Cantonese cabinet on Sunday afternoons could not have known that this would inspire one of the most extraordinary collections ever assembled by one person. Charles Paget Wade, born in 1883, was clearly an unusual little boy and he grew up to be an exceptional man. A talented artist and craftsman as well as a professional architect, once he had inherited the family sugar estates in the West Indies he devoted his life to restoring the Cotswold manor house he bought in 1919 and to amassing the wide-ranging exhibits now displayed here.

BELOW This eccentric display in Seraphim sets an array of Balinese and Javanese dancing masks against a collection of fine cabinets.

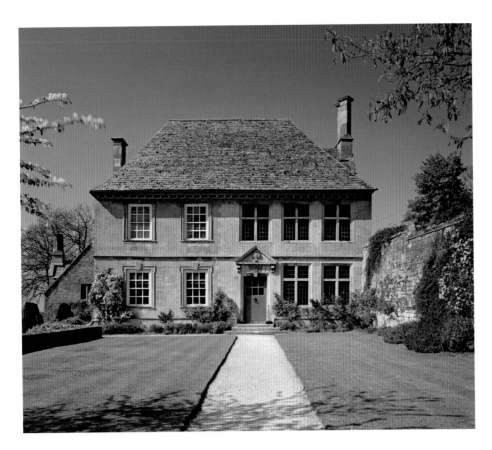

LEFT When Snowshill's south front was extended in 1720, the left-hand side of the façade was given Georgian sash windows, but the old stone-mullioned and transomed casements were kept on the right.

OPPOSITE The Blue Room, in the part of the manor that was remodelled in 1720, is lined with ornate cabinets like the one that fascinated the young Charles Wade.

Snowshill is an L-shaped building of warm Cotswold stone, with a warren of rooms on different levels leading off one another. The Tudor hall house of *c.*1500 at its heart, still evident in the huge fireplace on the ground floor and in two ceilings upstairs, was substantially rebuilt in about 1600 and altered again in the early eighteenth century, when the oddly attractive south front was created. Here, Georgian sash windows on the left side of the pedimented main entrance contrast with mullioned and transomed casements to the right, giving the house a rakish air.

Every corner from ground floor to attics is devoted to Charles Wade's acquisitions, which are packed into rooms with bizarre names such as Dragon, Meridian, Top Gallant and Seraphim. Mr Wade did not set out to accumulate things because they were rare or valuable, but saw his pieces primarily as records of vanished handicrafts. As a result, the Snowshill collection is unique, displaying an unclassifiable range of everyday objects, from tools used in spinning, weaving and lacemaking to baby minders (one for use on board ship),

prams, early bicycles, exquisite bone carvings made by French prisoners of war, eighteenth-century medicine chests cunningly contrived to carry a mass of little bottles and gaily painted model farm wagons. One room is devoted to pieces connected with the sea, such as compasses, telescopes and ship models, another to musical instruments, arranged as a playerless orchestra, and yet another (his Seventh Heaven) to many of the toys Mr Wade had as a child. Perhaps the most remarkable spectacle is in the Green Room, where suits of Japanese Samurai armour topped with ferocious masks threaten visitors in a theatrically staged display. A sense of order everywhere shows that this is no random, magpie collection but a reflection of a serious purpose.

The steeply sloping terraced garden was largely designed by Wade's friend M.H. Baillie Scott, a fellow architect with whom he had worked when employed by Raymond Unwin in London before the First World War, but Wade altered and adapted the original structure. It is laid out as a series of interconnecting but separate garden rooms, with arches and steps leading from one to another. Flagged paths, carefully contrived vistas down and across the slope, many features and centres of interest, among them a medieval dovecote with birds roosting on the steeply pitched roof, and Wade's old-fashioned planting schemes reflect the influence of the Arts and Crafts movement, with its preference for cottage-garden styles. And always there is the backdrop of a far wooded hillside across the valley.

At the top of the garden, just below the manor house, is the little cottage where Charles Wade lived. He had no electricity, a fireplace with two bread ovens being the only means of heating and cooking, and the walls and even the ceiling of his kitchen/living room are covered with a multitude of useful objects, from bowls and tankards to farm tools. Seeing these spartan conditions and the workshop where he spent so many happy hours making, among other things, the model Cornish fishing village that is now on display, it is easy to believe, as Queen Mary said after visiting Snowshill in 1937, that the most notable part of the collection was Mr Wade himself.

Speke Hall

Merseyside
On the north bank of the Mersey,
8 miles (12.8 kilometres) south-east
of the centre of Liverpool, 1 mile
(1.6 kilometres) south of the A561,
on the west side of the airport

A carved overmantel in the great parlour depicts the three generations of the wealthy gentry family who were largely responsible for this magical half-timbered moated manor house. Henry Norris to the left, accompanied by his wife and five children, carried on the building started by his father on inheriting the estate in about 1490. In the centre sits Sir William, whose considerable additions in the mid-sixteenth century may be explained by the nineteen children grouped at his feet (the son killed in battle is accompanied by a skull and bones). To the right is Edward, who recorded his completion of the house with an inscription dated 1598 over the entrance, and is shown with his wife and two of their children.

These men built conservatively, each addition merging perfectly with what had gone before and with no hint of the Renaissance influences that were becoming evident further south. Four long, low ranges enclose a cobbled courtyard, the jettied gables topped with finials that project unevenly and apparently haphazardly from the facades and the rough sandstone slabs that cover the roof all contributing to a charmingly crooked effect. Leaded panes show up as dark patches in a riot of black-and-white timberwork, among the finest in England. An Elizabethan stone bridge crosses the now grassy moat to the studded wooden doors which give access to the interior. Walking through is a surprise: two huge yews known as Adam and Eve shadow the courtyard, their branches rising above the house.

Surviving Tudor interiors live up to the promise of the exterior. In the light and airy T-shaped great hall rising to the roof, a number of plaster heads look down from the crude Gothic chimneypiece stretching to the ceiling. The naïve decoration here contrasts with the sophisticated carving on the panelling at the other end of the room, where busts of Roman emperors represented in high relief are set between elegant fluted columns. In the great parlour next door, panels in the fine early Jacobean plaster ceiling are alive with pomegranates, roses, lilies, vines and hazelnuts; bunches of ripe grapes and other fruits dangle enticingly and rosebuds are about to burst into flower. A spy-hole in one of the bedrooms and hiding places throughout the house reflect the Catholicism and royalist sympathies that brought the Norrises to the edge of ruin in the seventeenth century, when parts of the estate were sold.

After years of neglect following the death of the last of the family in 1766, the house was rescued in the late eighteenth

century by Richard Watt, whose descendants introduced the heavy oak furniture in period style which contributes to Speke's unique atmosphere. The more intimate panelled Victorian rooms in the north and west wings were created by the shipping magnate F.R. Leyland, who leased the house and carried on Watt's restoration after his early death. A noted patron of the arts, Leyland was responsible for hanging the early William Morris wallpapers that are now a feature of Speke, and he also entertained the painter James McNeill Whistler here.

The house lies buried in bracken woodland beside Liverpool airport, forming a green oasis in the heart of industrial Merseyside. A wide ride leads to the great embankment that shelters the property to the south. Those who struggle up the steep grassy slope are rewarded by a panoramic view of the River Mersey stretching away in a shining sheet of water to the smoking stacks of Ellesmere Port on the other side of the estuary.

ABOVE When the shipping magnate Frederick Leyland lived at Speke in the 1860s, he invited some 80 children from the estate to a Christmas meal in the great hall, built in the 1530s.
LEFT All of Speke Hall's half-timbered ranges are decorated with a riot of geometrical timberwork, but the patterning on each front is different. This is the south side of the house.

Springhill

Co. Londonderry
1 mile (1.6 kilometres) from
Moneymore on the Moneymore–
Coagh road (B18)

Four flintlocks used in the defence of Derry when James II's army besieged the town in 1689 are among many mementoes on show in this modest manor house which recall the staunchly Protestant family who built it and lived here for 300 years. The construction of Springhill itself, which was finished some time after 1697, may well have been interrupted by the hostilities. Although the Conynghams had acquired the estate in 1658, it was only at the end of the century, when 'Good' Will Conyngham's marriage articles bound him to build for his bride, that the property acquired a residence. (A copy of Will's marriage contract now hangs in the hall.)

Springhill is attractively set at the end of a long, straight avenue. With its peaceful whitewashed frontage, long sash windows and steeply pitched slate roof, it is difficult to believe that it was once necessary to defend this atmospheric place with a stockade. Hexagonal one-storey bays added in the eighteenth century extend the house on either side, and detached pavilions with charming Dutch gables that were once used as servants' quarters flank the entrance courtyard. Old yews shading the house are the remnants of an ancient forest that once stretched for miles along the shores of Lough Neagh, clothing the ridge on which the estate stands.

Springhill's eighteenth- and nineteenth-century interiors have many echoes of the Conyngham family and their connections. Sir Albert Conyngham, who commanded the Inniskilling Dragoons, was presented by the king with Kneller's portraits of William and Mary, which hang in the library, for his services to the Protestant cause. And the medicine chest full of bottles and drawers in this room was used by the 3rd Viscount Molesworth, who was connected to the Conynghams by marriage, during the War of Spanish Succession (1701–14), when he was the Duke of Marlborough's aide-de-camp. The exceptional collection of books, mostly acquired in the eighteenth century, includes a very early edition of Gerard's *Herbal* and first editions of Hobbes's *Leviathan* (1651) and Raleigh's *History of the World* (1614). Walnut William and Mary fiddleback chairs surround an Irish table in the dining room on the other side of the house, where a painting by Philip Wickstead, showing a group of young men on the Grand Tour in the early 1770s, also has family associations.

A gateway from the entrance court leads into the laundry yard, which still has its original slaughterhouse and turf shed. The old laundry is used to show a changing exhibition of costumes from the important collection of colourful and unusual pieces from the eighteenth to the early twentieth century that is now housed at Springhill. The little walled garden beyond the outbuildings, where herbs surround a tiny camomile lawn, is overlooked by a two-storeyed seventeenth-century barn, its interior spanned by roughly hewn oak beams.

Standen

West Sussex
2 miles (3.2 miles) south of
East Grinstead

Standen is a most unusual house, built in 1892–4 and yet not at all Victorian, built all of a piece and yet seeming to have grown out of the group of old farm buildings to which it is attached. This peaceful place on the edge of the Weald was designed by Philip Webb for the successful London solicitor James Beale, who wanted a roomy house for his large family for weekends and holidays. Standen was one of Webb's last commissions and, like Red House (*see* p.271), which was his first, is among the few unaltered examples of his work. A lifelong friend and associate of William Morris, for whom Red House was built, Webb shared Morris's views on the value of high-quality materials and craftsmanship. His aim was to design good, plain buildings, with comfortable interiors that could be lived in, an ambition that Standen fulfils in every respect.

As shown in Arthur Melville's delightful watercolour, painted when he visited the Beales for a weekend in 1896, Standen sits on a terrace, with views south over the long lake of the Weirwood reservoir to the wooded hills of Ashdown Forest. The attractive five-gabled garden front is partly built of creamy sandstone from the hill behind, but the upper storeys are weather-boarded and tile-hung in the Wealden fashion, producing a red and white effect. An arcaded conservatory is joined onto this front and there are tall brick chimneys rising almost to the height of the tower holding the water tanks.

The light, airy rooms are furnished with Morris's wallpapers and textiles, with richly coloured William de Morgan pottery, such as the red lustreware in a cabinet in the stairwell, and with a pleasing mixture of antiques and beautifully made pieces from Morris's company. The house was lit by electricity from the beginning, and many of the original fittings still exist. Webb's delicate wall lights in the drawing room hang like overblown snowdrops, casting soft pools of light on the blue and red hand-knotted carpet and on the comfortable chairs covered in faded green velvet that were supplied from Morris's workshops. A sunflower motif on the wallpaper is echoed in the embossed decoration on the plates supporting the light brackets and in the swirls of foliage and sunflowers on the copper cheeks of the fireplace. A view through to the conservatory from this room shows cane furniture set enticingly amidst a profusion of plants. All the rooms reflect Webb's meticulous concern for detail. The dining room at the end of the south front has an east-facing breakfast alcove, where the little round table flanked by oak dressers lined with china is flooded with sunshine in the early morning. Curiously, the first floor reveals that the Beales were expected still to rely heavily on washstands and hip baths: only one bathroom was provided for twelve bedrooms.

OPPOSITE, LEFT Past hostilities, among them the 105-day siege of Londonderry in 1689 which probably interrupted the building of the house, are conjured up by this show of weapons in the Gun Room at Springhill.
OPPOSITE, ABOVE Stylistically, Springhill is a mixture, with a rear facade that does not repeat the symmetry of the entrance front.
ABOVE Standen has always been lit by electricity and many of the original fittings are still in the house, among them the delicate lights in the hall by W.A.S. Benson, William Morris's protégé.
RIGHT Furnishings from Morris & Co in the drawing room include a six-legged pie-crust table and most of the easy chairs.

ABOVE Webb's water tower, which he provided with a viewing platform, links the entrance front to the weather-boarded servants' wing on the left.

The steep, south-facing garden reflects changes over several decades by a number of different hands. A fussy, gardenesque layout by the London landscape gardener G.B. Simpson, who was employed before Webb and planned his design to focus on a differently sited house, was then modified by his successor, who favoured a simpler approach concentrating on grass and trees and was responsible for the terraces that descend the hill in giant leaps, their outlines followed by stepped yew hedges. The planting, on the other hand, was undertaken by James Beale's wife Margaret. The end result, although based on no coherent overall plan, is both individual and charming, with many changes of level linked by flights of steps. The little quarry from which the stone for the house was taken is now attractively leafy and overgrown.

ABOVE A splendid pinnacled and buttressed tower stands over the west door of Staunton Harold Church, where an inscription records that this singular building was the work of Sir Robert Shirley in 1653.

Staunton Harold Church

Leicestershire
5 miles (8 kilometres) north-east of Ashby-de-la-Zouch, west of the B587

This splendid church set in parkland on the edge of a lake is one of the very few that were erected in the 20 years between the outbreak of the Civil War and the restoration of Charles II. Built in 1653, it was an act of defiance by the young Sir Robert Shirley, 4th Baronet, who was strongly opposed to Cromwell's Puritan regime and fully identified with the High Church Anglicanism of the martyred Charles I. Unfortunately for him, the church advertised both his audacity and his wealth. The incensed Cromwell retaliated by demanding money for a regiment of soldiers, throwing Sir Robert into the Tower of London when he refused to comply. There he died, aged only 27.

Staunton Harold is Sir Robert's memorial. Built in the revived Gothic style that symbolised continuity with the old Church, its prominent pinnacles, embattled parapets and imposing tower are consciously medieval in spirit, but there is also a classical west doorway, with an outspoken inscription by the young baronet above it.

Fine carved woodwork by a joiner named William Smith survives unaltered inside. Oak box pews fitted with original brass candlesticks fill the nave. Oak panelling lines the walls and faces the columns of the nave and a magnificent Jacobean screen supports the organ loft at the west end. The organ itself, which predates the church, is one of the oldest English-built instruments still in its original condition. Swirls of blue, black and white representing the elements in chaos draw the eye high overhead to a wonderfully abstract version of the Creation, dated 1655. The Puritans would have regarded both this display and the fixed altar in the chancel as idolatrous. The only two later features in the church are Robert Bakewell of Derby's ornate wrought-iron screen in the chancel arch that was an addition of the early eighteenth century and the marble tomb to Robert Shirley's great-grandson, who died of smallpox in 1714. The young man lies propped on his right elbow, as if eagerly surveying the world he has left.

ABOVE Stoneacre's gabled, half-timbered facades seem all of a piece, but much of the house was created in the 1920s by Aymer Valance, who re-used material from other Tudor buildings.

Stoneacre

Kent
At the north end of Otham village, 3 miles (4.8 kilometres) south-east of Maidstone, 1 mile (1.6 kilometres) south of the A20

Prosperous yeomen farmers and other men of moderate means in the late Middle Ages built their houses to a standard pattern, with a central hall open to the rafters and an adjoining block, or blocks, with smaller chambers on two floors. An upper room, known as the solar, is where the family would retreat from the rest of the household. This layout, which endured for generations, reconciled increasing pressures for privacy with the traditional communal life.

This attractive half-timbered Wealden house, dating from about 1480, was typical of its time. But Stoneacre's individual character, created by Aymer Vallance, biographer of William Morris, in the early twentieth century, sets it apart. Impressive timberwork spans the great hall, with a rare and beautiful king-post, devised as a cluster of columns, supporting the ridge of the roof from the gigantic tie beam which stretches the length of the room. A massive brick chimney built in the 1920s rises the height of the hall from the fifteenth-century fireplace introduced by Mr Vallance on the south side, a collection of warm-toned Hispanic plates along the chimney breast enhancing the soft pinks of the brickwork. Twelve-light windows with leaded panes, some with stained glass designed by Vallance, face east and west, bringing both morning and evening sun pouring into the hall.

In the adjoining parlour, where the Tudor fireplace was rescued from a house that was being demolished, the Arts and Crafts fabric making up the curtains, with a repeated motif of an angel blowing a trumpet, was designed by the artist and writer Herbert Horne in c.1884 for the newly formed Century Guild, devoted to the promotion of traditional crafts.

This fifteenth-century core with its solar block to the south is now the centrepiece of a much larger place. Using timber, windows and furnishings from dilapidated Tudor houses, some of which were acquired as complete buildings, Mr Vallance created half-timbered wings in complete harmony with the genuinely medieval work. Badly neglected before he began his restoration, Stoneacre is a fascinating example of creative scholarship.

Stourhead

Wiltshire
At Stourton, off the B3092,
3 miles (4.8 kilometres)
north-west of Mere

This fine Neo-classical house standing high on a ridge of the Wiltshire Downs looks out over the park to distant wooded hills. One of the first Palladian houses in England, it was built in 1721–4 by Henry Hoare I, whose wealth came from the bank founded by his father, Sir Richard Hoare, in 1672. Henry had purchased the estate in 1717, three years after it had passed out of the hands of the Stourton family who had lived here for 700 years. He immediately demolished the existing house and employed Colen Campbell, a leader of the fashionable Neo-classical revival, to design this replacement. The square main block, with its temple-like portico rising the height of the building, is flanked by pavilions added in the 1790s to house a picture gallery and library. The rather severe lines of the facade are softened only by three lead statues set above the portico and by two flights of steps rising to the entrance, their end pillars supporting stone basins surmounted by the Hoare eagle.

Sadly, fire gutted this central block in 1902, destroying much of the original decoration. More or less faithful Edwardian reconstructions of Campbell's intentions by the local architect Doran Webb and the more prestigious Sir Aston Webb who replaced him are now sandwiched between the Regency rooms in the pavilions, both of which survived virtually unscathed. The contents, a rich collection of family heirlooms with finely crafted furniture by Thomas Chippendale the Younger, reflect the interests of several generations of Hoares and the addition of pieces from Wavendon, the family's house in Buckinghamshire, in the nineteenth century.

The nucleus of paintings, sculpture and *objets d'art* acquired by Henry Hoare II to embellish his father's new house was greatly extended by his grandson Sir Richard Colt Hoare, who inherited in 1785. This eminent antiquary, scholar and county historian was an omnivorous collector, amassing a magnificent library in one of his purpose-built extensions and displaying the pick of his grandfather's art collection, together with his own acquisitions of works by Italian and British contemporaries, in the other. Although some of the finest were sold in the late nineteenth century, the paintings still hang triple-banked against pea-green walls, some simple gilt frames contrasting with florid rococo creations on the end wall. Cigoli's *Adoration of the Magi* dominates the room, an expression of great tenderness lighting the face of the grizzled king in an ermine-fringed cloak who kneels at the Virgin's feet.

Similarly, although many of his books have now been dispersed, Colt Hoare's evocative green and white library is one of the most beautiful surviving Regency rooms in England, with the arch of the high barrel-vaulted ceiling echoed in the curves of the alcoves lined with books. Thomas Chippendale's rich mahogany furniture (including massive staircase-like library steps), gilded calf bindings and the deep-green and ochre carpet all contribute to a feeling of luxurious opulence, while the muted tones are lifted by flashes of colour from the painted glass high up in the lunettes at each end of the room. Of the other treasures in the house, perhaps the most memorable is the seventeenth-century 'Pope's cabinet' designed like the facade of a Renaissance church, a framework of ebony and bronze setting off a multicoloured inlay of marble, porphyry, jasper and other ornamental stones.

At the back of the house, a door from the saloon leads to handsome stone steps designed by Aston Webb, which fan out gently to a sweep of tree-framed grass. Beyond, hidden in the trees, the ground suddenly falls away into a steep-sided valley and the magical landscape garden created here in the second half of the eighteenth century. Sheltered and enclosed by windbreaks along the rim of the combe is a serene arcadia, with classical temples and other eye-catchers set against wooded slopes and mirrored in an artificial lake. A grotto devised on the edge of the water has sombre rock pools and a sculpture of a river god. All around are the trees, with native species such as beeches and oaks mixed with exotics, among them the Norwegian maple, tulip trees, cedars, the dawn redwood and the Japanese white pine, *Pinus parviflora*.

Although later members of the family, in particular Sir Richard Colt Hoare, enriched the garden by widening the range of species and also made some more fundamental changes, Stourhead is primarily the creation of Henry Hoare II. Perhaps turned in on himself by the tragic loss of both his wives, the garden was to be Henry's absorbing interest for 40 years from 1741. The only professional engaged in its creation was the architect Henry Flitcroft, who designed the classical eye-catchers: the Doric Temple of Flora, which was the first building to be added to the garden; the domed Pantheon, with a broad flight of steps leading up to a pedimented portico; and the tall, circular Temple of Apollo, enclosed in a continuous colonnade. A Gothic cottage, its prominent traceried windows and thatched roof almost buried in vegetation, was added by Sir Richard Colt Hoare in 1806 and Sir Richard was also responsible for the impressive castellated gateway through which the house is approached. Some two miles (3.4 kilometres) away, standing high on the chalk scarp overlooking Somerset, is the triangular brick folly known as Alfred's Tower, which was also designed by Flitcroft.

Tiled cottages with mullioned windows in the estate village on the edge of the valley stretch down to the Palladian bridge over an arm of the lake. Built by Henry Hoare, they were originally hidden behind a screen of trees so that they would not intrude on his design, but now this row of buildings forms another attractive feature. Opposite the cottages is the medieval parish church, picturesquely crowned with fretwork parapets and filled with monuments to the Hoares and their predecessors, the Stourtons. Just beyond the churchyard, dominating the view over the lake, is the slender column of the medieval cross that Henry acquired from the City of Bristol in the 1760s, its tapering length suggesting the spire of a buried church. Statues of medieval kings standing round the base are carved stone replicas of the originals, which are on loan to the Victoria and Albert Museum.

BELOW The central block of Stourhead's east front, with a grand portico looking over the park, was designed to resemble the villas built by Andrea Palladio around Vicenza in Italy in the sixteenth century.
OPPOSITE The Museum of Childhood at Sudbury includes this evocation of a period schoolroom, complete with slates for each pupil.

Sudbury Hall and the National Trust Museum of Childhood

Derbyshire
6 miles (9.6 kilometres) east of
Uttoxeter at the crossing point of
the A50 Derby–Stoke and the
A515 Lichfield–Ashbourne roads

Sudbury is the most idiosyncratic of the many great houses created during Charles II's reign. It is built to a consciously outdated E-shaped plan incorporating a great hall and long gallery and yet is fashionably decorated, with rich plasterwork and woodcarving of the highest quality. The message of the exterior is similarly contradictory. The stone-mullioned and transomed windows were not yet old-fashioned when Sudbury was begun, but the diapered brickwork and carved stone ornaments over the ground-floor windows suggest a Jacobean house. By contrast, the hipped roof and gleaming central cupola, visible for miles around, show knowledge of more up-to-the-minute styles, such as the design of Roger Pratt's Kingston Lacy (*see* p.184). George Vernon, who started his new house soon after he inherited the Sudbury estate in 1660, seems to have acted as his own architect and to have adapted his original ideas over some 40 years, the result, perhaps, of being able to consult more sophisticated books and engravings and of a visit to London.

Competent but uninspired early work by local men contrasts with the skills displayed by the London craftsmen Vernon employed as time went by, in particular the woodcarvers Edward Pierce and Grinling Gibbons and the plasterers Bradbury and Pettifer. The balustrade of Pierce's virtuoso staircase, one of the finest and most elaborate of its date, is a mass of writhing foliage carved out of limewood, with baskets of fruit fashioned from elmwood set on the newel posts. Pettifer's plasterwork overhead, in which garlands of fruit and flowers and acanthus scrolls form three-dimensional encrustations, is similarly rich. And yet, 20 years after this work was finished, Vernon added a taste of the exuberant baroque style that was then popular at court by employing Louis Laguerre to paint mythological scenes in the plasterwork panels.

Another painting by Laguerre fills a plaster wreath on the ceiling of the saloon. One of the richest of Sudbury's interiors, this room is lined with family portraits, each of which is set in a gilded ornamental panel carved by Pierce, with swags of fruit and flowers above, below, and in some cases framing the pictures. But even his work is outclassed by the Grinling Gibbons carving over the fireplace in the drawing room next door, in which fruit, flowers, dead game and fish are all depicted with lifelike realism.

After so much unrelieved grandeur, the decoration of the sunny long gallery running the length of the south front is unexpected. At first glance, Bradbury and Pettifer's intricate plasterwork appears to repeat established motifs. But all is not what it seems. The classical busts portrayed along the frieze are humorous caricatures, while a lion, a horse, a boar and other animals leap gaily out of the swirls of foliage on the ceiling and grasshoppers dance playfully round the sunflower rosette in the central window bay.

The small family rooms at the east end of the house are a contrast to all this magnificence. Lady Vernon's cosy sitting room, with its leaf-green walls and tranquil view over the lake below the south front, has a communicating door to her husband's study. It is easy to imagine them talking through it, and walking together across the passage to eat in the small dining room.

Although Sudbury has lost some of its original contents, there are family portraits in almost every room, including works by Lawrence, Hoppner and J.M. Wright, and several other outstanding furnishings remain, among them walnut dining chairs of c.1735 which have been bought back for the house. In the long gallery, a seventeenth-century Flemish ebony cabinet is enchantingly decorated with scenes of the Creation by Frans Francken the Younger. The first panel shows a purple- and red-robed god hovering above an endless expanse of ocean, brooding on what he is about to unleash.

The nineteenth-century service wing by George Devey now houses the Museum of Childhood, which contains displays illustrating children's lives from the eighteenth century onwards and the Betty Cadbury collection of toys and dolls.

LEFT Sudbury, built in the 1660s, is an idiosyncratic house with an old-fashioned Jacobean exterior but work by outstanding London craftsmen mirroring the taste of the day inside.
OPPOSITE The staircase hall, with its Jacobethan staircase and array of nineteenth-century family portraits, is the heart of Sunnycroft.

Sunnycroft

Shropshire
200 Holyhead Road, Wellington

This substantial Victorian house looking south towards the wooded humps of the Wrekin hills on the outskirts of Wellington is a rare survival of a way of life that lasted from *c.*1850 to the Second World War. During this period, men from the upper middle classes, well-to-do bankers, solicitors and businessmen, acquired mini-estates on the outskirts of the towns where they worked. Here they built houses large enough to pursue a version of the landed-gentry lifestyle to which they aspired and with enough land to keep livestock and grow produce for the table as well as to have ornamental gardens. After the Second World War, when the way of life that had supported them was no longer viable, some villas became institutions; others were demolished and their land sold for building. Largely because it

was owned by the Landers from 1912 to 1997, Sunnycroft survived. The house still has many original features and contents and the grounds, 2 hectares (5 acres) in extent, are still worked, with productive areas set around and dovetailed into the ornamental parts.

Built of strident red brick, Sunnycroft is a plain, almost austere house, with large plate-glass windows, a gabled roofline and a turret over the entrance porch. A long verandah dotted with potted plants shades the main rooms and on the west side, so close to the house as to seem part of it, is an enchanting Victorian glasshouse. The earliest part, where the rooms are more modest, was built in 1880 for J.G. Wackrill, who founded the Shropshire Brewery. He sold the house to the widow of a wine and spirit merchant and in 1899 she extended Sunnycroft, adding the capacious hall, with its Jacobethan staircase, and the larger reception rooms and creating the present entrance. The

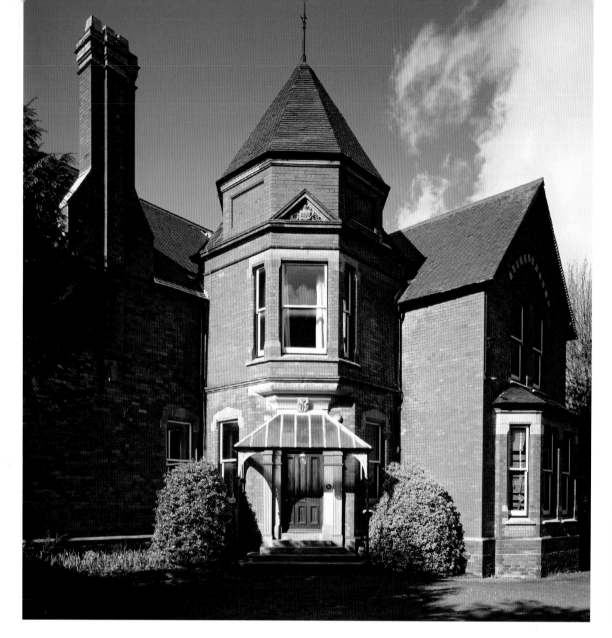

first of the Landers, John Vernon Thomas, a Wellington solicitor who used to walk into work wearing a white bowler hat and a carnation from the glasshouses, bought the property in 1912. His son Offley, who was a founder-director of an ironworks at Coalbrookdale, acquired the house on J.V.T.'s death in 1943, and then, in 1973, it was inherited by his daughter Joan, who left the estate to the National Trust.

The interior is an evocative period piece. There is much sombre decoration and substantial late-Victorian and Edwardian furniture, windows and archways are hung with heavy curtains, and the house still has original parquet and decorative tiled floors, ornamental gas brackets, its Victorian rooflight with tinted glass and cast-iron radiators, part of the up-to-the-minute technology installed in 1899. There are separate servants' quarters and the family's social aspirations come through in the billiard room with its full-size table, a masculine domain for the men of the house, and in the stately dining room where the Landers hosted five-course dinners and where lunch was held punctually at one. Something of the Landers themselves can be sensed in fine needlework by Joan, who trained as an embroiderer, and in the coat and leather gloves Offley wore when he drove to work in the black Daimler, number plate AW1, which still sits in the garage outside.

Sutton House

London
At the corner of Isabella Road and Homerton High Street, Hackney

An inner-city borough in East London is the unexpected setting for this fine Tudor red-brick house. A three-storey H-shaped building set back from the road across a paved yard, with diamond diapering marking the west wing, it sits at the west end of Homerton High Street, just where the road starts to swing north. Dating from 1534–5, Sutton House was built for the high-flying courtier and statesman Sir Ralph Sadleir (1507–87) in what was then desirable countryside on the edge of Hackney village, with open fields between here and London. Right-hand man to Thomas Cromwell, Sadleir survived his patron's fall in 1540, and was one of those who tried the ill-fated Mary Queen of Scots in 1586, when he would have been 79. His house has had a more chequered career. Remodelled in c.1700, when the Tudor gables and mullioned windows were replaced with the present elegant sashes and roofline parapet, divided into two in c.1750, partly faced in heavy stucco in the mid-nineteenth century and reunited in 1904, Sutton House has served as school, working men's institute and offices as well as one or more private dwellings. It was restored by the National Trust after a period of uncertainty and decline in the twentieth century.

The restoration exposed original features hidden behind later alterations and, apart from the great hall that once filled the bar of the H, the basic Tudor plan also survives, with staircases in the wings and a few cupboard-like garderobes. The parlour in the west wing is one of the finest Tudor interiors in London, with oak linenfold panelling running from floor to ceiling and a fireplace of carved Reigate stone. On the first floor, above what was the great hall, is the airy, high-ceilinged great chamber, lit by windows to both north and south. As in the parlour, the panelling here has been rearranged, and some of it is Jacobean rather than Tudor, but this is a striking room, its effect enhanced by Sadleir family portraits, an oak refectory table and a Charles II dresser.

Other features reflect later history. There is painted Jacobean strapwork imitating what richer folk would have had executed in stone or wood, a panelled Georgian parlour in a delicate mint green and Georgian barley-twist balusters on the east staircase, and a Victorian study. There is also one surviving leaded and mullioned Tudor window, looking out onto the secluded, stone-flagged court at the centre of the house.

The sparse furnishings are not original but all are in keeping, including a couple of reproduction seventeenth-century harpsichords. 'Finds' on display – thimbles, bobbins, scissors, pins, the odd shoe – date from the school years, and a squatter has left a sinister red and black eye on the wall of an attic room. The Wenlock Barn closing the court, a balconied hall with an open timber roof built by Lionel Crane, son of Arts and Crafts designer Walter Crane, is now a function room and a first-floor gallery is often used to show the work of Hackney's sizeable community of artists, said to be the largest in Europe.

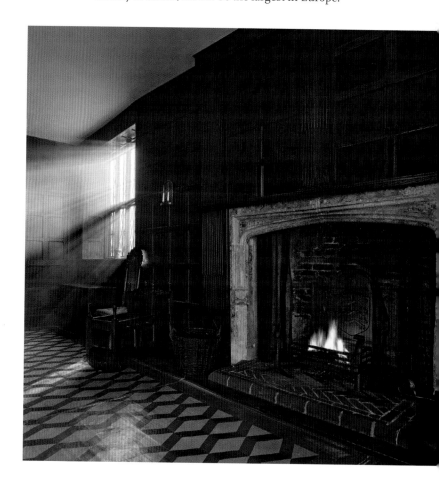

RIGHT Built for a high-flying courtier in the 1530s in what was then open countryside outside London, Sutton House has a fine Tudor parlour with linenfold panelling and a fireplace of carved Reigate stone.

Tattershall Castle

Lincolnshire
On the south side of the A153,
15 miles (24 kilometres) north-east
of Sleaford, 10 miles (16 kilometres)
south-west of Horncastle

Ralph, 3rd Baron Cromwell, was an ambitious man, reaching the climax of his career as Treasurer to Henry VI in 1433–43. His sturdy brick tower, rising prominently from the Lincolnshire Fens, is one of the most striking monuments of the later Middle Ages, all that remains of the largely brick-built castle he created here. That anything survives is entirely due to Lord Curzon, who bought the building back from speculators in 1911 and who also engineered the return of chimneypieces which had been removed from the tower and were about to be shipped to America.

Tattershall looks both forwards and backwards. By 1430, when Cromwell started on extensions to the existing buildings, keeps had gone out of fashion in England, but were to be built for another century or so in France. The magnificent products of Franco-Burgundian culture, so exquisitely illustrated in the *Très Riches Heures* of the Duc de Berry, may well have inspired the young nobleman, who would have had ample opportunity to see them while serving with the English army in the Hundred Years War. Like its French counterparts, Tattershall has an air of unreality, as if it too had stepped from a contemporary manuscript. It is essentially a status symbol, equivalent to the gatehouse towers that other men of substance were to build in the years that followed (*see*, for example, Sissinghurst and Oxburgh, pp.291 and 244).

Although outwardly defensive, girdled by two moats and with machicolated fighting galleries underneath the battlements, this is in fact a domestic country mansion masquerading as a fortress, with large and plentiful windows and several entrances. Each of the four floors above the vaulted basement is filled with one great chamber, with the Treasurer's personal bedchamber at the very top of the tower. Stone chimneypieces carved with Cromwell's arms and his treasurer's purse and elaborate window tracery point to luxuriously fitted interiors.

LEFT A spiral staircase with a finely moulded stone handrail sunk into the wall fills one of Tattershall Castle's octagonal turrets.
ABOVE The keep-like brick tower which formed the core of Tattershall Castle is a medieval country house masquerading as a fortress.

Tattershall is as significant for its material as its design. Although bricks were used in the eastern counties in the thirteenth and fourteenth centuries, they were usually concealed under plaster. Tattershall is one of the earliest examples of the deliberate choice of this material, with its decorative possibilities exploited in the rows of corbels at the top of the facades. Inside, the skill of the craftsmen Cromwell employed shows particularly in the spiral staircase that fills one of the corner turrets, with its finely moulded stone handrail fashioned in the wall, and in the brickwork of the decorative vaults.

Cromwell was a man of the world, acquiring large estates across the East Midlands and building manor houses elsewhere as well as constructing his lavishly appointed tower-house at Tattershall. He was also a creature of his age, concerned for his fate in the next world as much as his comfort in this one. Like other great men of his time, he anticipated the Last Trump by endowing a memorial college to be built close by his castle. Apart from a ruined, two-storey brick building, possibly offices and lodgings, only the beautiful collegiate church, with its armorial stained glass and mutilated brass commemorating Cromwell and his wife, survives, the attractive row of almshouses having been rebuilt in the seventeenth century (neither is owned by the Trust).

In the late Middle Ages this considerable complex of buildings, rising like an island of the civilised world from the sea of the Fens, tellingly revealed the self-importance and aspirations of the man who created them.

Tatton Park

Cheshire
3½ miles (5.6 kilometres) north of Knutsford, 4 miles (6.4 kilometres) south of Altrincham, 3½ miles (5.6 kilometres) from the M6 at the Manchester interchange

The 4th Lord Egerton, who inherited the Tatton estate in 1920, was a restless and individual man who was intrigued by the scientific discoveries of his day. Widely travelled, he staked a claim in the Yukon during the Gold Rush of the 1890s and once lived with a tribe in the Gobi Desert, but he also experimented with short-wave radio and was a pioneer aviator. His 1900 Benz proudly displaying the number plate M1 was the first car to be registered in Cheshire.

The 4th Lord's enquiring mind seems to have been an inherited trait. In all the plans for the remodelling of the house, on which Samuel Wyatt and his nephew Lewis were employed between 1774 and about 1825, the library is given particular prominence. A comfortable room filling the centre of the garden front, it was designed to be used, not admired. Books lie companionably on the reading chairs and stands, leather-padded armchairs are drawn up by the fire and a library ladder invites inspection of the topmost shelves. There is something for everyone here, including first editions of Jane Austen's novels, volumes of music, and illustrated works on the arts and classical antiquities, most of them finely bound. The nucleus of the collection is the sixteenth-century library acquired by Thomas Egerton, founder of the family fortunes, who rose from unpromising beginnings to become Lord Chancellor of England.

Lewis Wyatt's formal drawing room hung with cherry-coloured silk is much grander, with a relentless coffered ceiling and with specially commissioned gilt-framed chairs and sofas carved in a sinuous rococo style by Gillows of Lancaster that would not seem out of place in a Venetian palazzo. Van Dyck's *Martyrdom of St Stephen* seems curiously appropriate in these unrelaxed surroundings, cherubs hovering overhead to receive the saint's soul. Two moody Venetian views by Canaletto are full of delightful detail, such as the little white dog with a jaunty tail that trots purposefully along the quay in the scene in front of the Doge's Palace.

Lewis Wyatt was also responsible for the inspired treatment of the staircase in the centre of the house and for a theatrical vista through a colonnade-like series of arches on the first floor.

The Regency lifestyle for which Tatton was designed emerges strongly here, every bedroom except one sporting a dressing room. Each suite was originally distinguished by the colour of its textiles and the wood of the furniture, the pieces in the principal apartment being of mahogany inlaid with ebony.

The Wyatts' exterior is a pure Neo-classical design, with a giant pedimented portico dominating the south front, a low-pitched roof and almost no decoration except for the chaste swags in panels over the sash windows. Only the dining room designed by T.F. Pritchard, with its superb rococo plasterwork, remains from the eighteenth-century house.

The atmosphere of opulent grandeur extends into the spacious gardens with their sweeping lawns, herbaceous borders and a rich variety of trees. Grassy terraces on the south front, with shallow flights of steps descending to a fountain surrounded by an Italianate parterre, were designed by Joseph Paxton and there is an impressive range of glasshouses, including Wyatt's classical conservatory and Paxton's fernery, the roof of which has been raised to allow for the huge New Zealand tree ferns which now reach to the glass.

BELOW The servants' quarters at Tatton Park would have seen much activity in 1887 when the Prince and Princess of Wales stayed in the house and the prince planted a tree in the garden to mark his visit.

More informal planting surrounding the artificial lake known as the Golden Brook almost conceals the Japanese garden laid out here in 1910, with stone lanterns dotting a mosaic of water and islands. Another surprise is the small beech maze hidden behind a bank of rhododendrons beside the long avenue known as the Broad Walk.

The Home Farm at Tatton Dale was once the heart of the extensive Egerton estates, with pigsties, stockyards, stables and workshops surrounding the office from which nearly 1,000 tenant properties were administered. Humphry Repton produced a Red Book for the extensive park, but most of the landscaping probably dates from William Emes's work in the mid-eighteenth century, with some early nineteenth-century modifications by John Webb. There are deer and flocks of Soay and Hebridean sheep beneath the trees, and the remains of the medieval manor house are used to introduce visitors to the realities of pre-modern life.

ABOVE Like other great country houses, Tatton Park was largely self-sufficient, generating its own electricity until 1961. This intriguing calorifier was used for heating the water.
RIGHT The neo-classical Regency south front, with the colonnaded family wing added later in the nineteenth century to the left, overlooks a magnificent formal Italian garden.

Theatre Royal, Bury St Edmunds

Suffolk
In Westgate Street, Bury St Edmunds, close to the A14

This delightfully intimate theatre, seating fewer than 300, is the only surviving Regency playhouse in Great Britain. Built in 1819, it dates from an era when Bury was a provincial capital and farmers and gentry from miles around crowded into the town for the short autumn season. Comfortable red plush seats have replaced the benches in the pit, but original boxes still fill the dress circle and the stalls are steeply raked towards the stage. This little jewel is the creation of William Wilkins the Younger, an experienced theatre designer and one of the leading Neo-classical architects of his day, who was later to produce the National Gallery and the screen at King's College, Cambridge. Winged sphinxes and griffins decorate the dress circle and another classical frieze adorns the proscenium arch.

The pink, white and grey facade on Westgate Street, with a projecting glazed portico, is dwarfed by the huge buildings of the Greene King brewery, an ever-present reminder of the years the theatre lay forgotten. The coming of the railways in the 1840s, which transported those in search of good entertainment speedily to Norwich or London, hastened a decline that had set in a decade or so earlier and could not be halted even by the staging of the world première of *Charley's Aunt* here in 1892. Closing in 1925, the theatre was bought by Greene King & Sons and used as a barrel store for 40 years, but the brewery also played a prominent part in its revival in 1965 and has given the National Trust a 999-year lease on the building.

All kinds of performances have been held here ever since, but early twentieth-century alterations had deprived the theatre of some of its unique Regency features. In recent years, the 1819 design has been largely reinstated. In particular, the forestage that projected into the auditorium with boxes either side has been reintroduced, so plays of the period can once again be staged as was intended, with the actors interacting closely with the audience. The original decorative scheme has also been re-created.

RIGHT In the days when Bury St Edmunds was a provincial capital, farmers and gentry from miles around used to flock to the Regency Theatre Royal, where the original stage has recently been re-created.

Tintagel Old Post Office

Cornwall
In the centre of the village
of Tintagel, on the main street

The considerable increase in postal traffic resulting from the introduction of the penny post in 1844 led to a much-improved service in remote parts of the country. Tintagel, then a little-known village called Trevena on the wild north Cornish coast, was blessed with its first post office, set up, to receive incoming mail only, in a room in this ancient cottage. The Old Post Office is traditionally built of slate, now weathered to a uniform grey. Nothing about it is symmetrical, from the placing of the sturdy two- and three-tier chimneys to the off-centre projecting porch and the undulating roof. Dating in parts from the fourteenth century and a rare survival of local domestic architecture, it is now also one of the few remaining Picturesque buildings in Tintagel, most of the others having been ruthlessly torn down

in the late nineteenth century to be replaced with a rash of boarding houses and hotels catering for Victorian romantics in search of King Arthur. The Old Post Office itself was saved by a local artist, Catherine Johns, who bought the building in 1895, and shortly afterwards it was sensitively restored by the Arts and Crafts architect Detmar Blow according to the principles of the youthful Society for the Protection of Ancient Buildings.

The interior suggests a very small manor house, with a diminutive hall rising to the roof in the middle of the building and a passage running through the house to the little split-level garden. The rooms are furnished with local oak pieces, mostly of the sixteenth century and typical of those that would have been found in farmhouses and cottages in this part of the world.

ABOVE The little fourteenth-century building known as the Old Post Office, built of local slate and occasional pieces of granite, has a tiny medieval hall rising to smoke-blackened rafters in the roof.

Townend

Cumbria
3 miles (4.8 kilometres) south-east
of Ambleside at the south end of
Troutbeck

Townend is a rare and remarkably intact survival of the house of a family of yeoman farmers and is a fine example of domestic Lake District architecture. An L-shaped house with limewashed stone walls, oak-mullioned windows and a slate roof topped with six round chimneys, it probably dates from the late sixteenth or early seventeenth century, but has been much altered and extended since. Just across the lane, built on a much grander scale, is the homestead's stone-and-slate galleried barn, with a ramp up to the granary floor and the date 1666 carved on one of the lintels.

The Browne family who lived here for over four centuries were sheep farmers, and they seem to have gradually risen in society through careful management of their affairs and by judicious marriages. Much of Townend's attraction derives from the fact that its contents reflect slow accretion by several generations of the Brownes. In the little library, Milton rubs shoulders with Clarke's sermons, Walton's *Compleat Angler*, a history of England and volumes of farming periodicals. The collection as a whole gives a unique insight into the interests and preoccupations of a rural middle-class family.

The preservation of the house and its contents owes much to the last George Browne (1834–1914), who was both a noted antiquary and a gifted joiner and woodcarver. The rooms are filled with ornate examples of his work, from the richly carved chairs in the firehouse, the oldest part of the building, to the little spindle-fronted cupboard in one of the bedrooms, in which no two spindles are alike. Such painstakingly crafted pieces speak of long winter evenings by candlelight round the fire.

The wealth of heavy oak furniture displayed at Townend also includes the long seventeenth-century dining table in the firehouse, undoubtedly assembled *in situ*, where the Brownes would have taken meals with their farmhands and servants. From the kitchen next door, an early seventeenth-century spiral staircase made of solid blocks of oak winds steeply upwards to the austere quarters for the housekeeper and maids, with a pair of clogs set out ready for the morning by one of the beds. Charmingly naïve paintings of the family's sheep elsewhere in the house are by the local nineteenth-century artist William Taylor Longmire. Perhaps he took his models from the ancestors of the beasts that still graze the fells rising behind Townend.

The colourful little garden, with beds filled with traditional cottage-garden flowers, is a partial re-creation of George Browne's layout based on his notebooks, orders for seeds and cuttings and some surviving plans. Plums, gages and apples grow in the orchard George established.

BELOW Some of the last George Browne's wood-carving can be seen in Townend's atmospheric stone-flagged kitchen, where he made the child's chair for his youngest daughter and decorated the cupboards.

Treasurer's House

North Yorkshire
In Minster Yard, York, on the
north side of the Minster

Treasurer's House, bordering a narrow medieval cobbled street in the shadow of York Minster, was once attached to one of the wealthiest and most sought-after benefices in England. Successive treasurers of the cathedral lived in a mansion on this site from 1100 until the office was abolished under Henry VIII. Little remains of the building now except the name, but, intriguingly, the remains of a Roman road have been found in the cellars, suggesting a history of occupation going back 2,000 years.

The present elegant and airy town house incorporates some Elizabethan fabric but structurally it dates largely from c.1630, when the attractive garden front with its classical central entrance bay was built and curved Dutch gables were added to the wings either side. Extensive alterations at the turn of the century and in Georgian times account for the Venetian windows on this front and for the elegant William and Mary staircase, its beautifully carved balusters possibly the work of the local carpenter-architect William Thornton, who was responsible for the magnificent woodcarving at Beningbrough Hall (see p.51).

Among the many residents of the house at this period were the writer and literary hostess Elizabeth Montagu, who was born here in 1720, and Dr Jacques Sterne, whose nephew, the novelist Laurence Sterne, satirised the inward-looking cathedral set in his *A Political Romance* (1759), his savage attack on local ecclesiastical courts provoking the banning of the book.

In the nineteenth century the house was subdivided into at least five separate dwellings and became increasingly run down. It was rescued by the wealthy industrialist and aesthete Frank Green, who acquired it in 1897. With the help of the architect Temple Moore, Green carefully restored the house to what he thought was its original appearance, removing all nineteenth-century alterations and additions and creating a huge hall out of the two-storey central block, with a half-timbered gallery supported on classical columns. Appropriate antiques were used to form a sequence of period rooms. Furniture reflecting the craftsmanship of two centuries includes a fine oak refectory table of c.1600, a marquetry grandfather clock of 1680 and three early eighteenth-century tester beds in the rooms where Edward VII, then Prince of Wales, his wife Alexandra and their daughter Victoria slept when visiting the house in 1900. Ornate early eighteenth-century giltwood mirrors make the airy drawing room looking over the garden, with panelling painted a brilliant peacock blue, seem even larger than it is and there is a set of walnut chairs of the same period covered in contemporary needlework. The house is further enriched by English and Flemish portraits from the sixteenth to eighteenth centuries. Frank Green composed each room carefully, using stud-marks in the floors to specify where each piece of furniture stood. The house today is largely as it was when he gave it to the National Trust in 1930.

The formal walled garden fronting the principal facade was established between 1897 and 1900 by Frank Green and, like the house, is mostly as he had it. A central sunken lawn is bordered on one side by a pollarded plane-tree avenue and there are raised terrace walks along the walls. Nothing in the garden can compete with the view of the Minster towering above it.

LEFT In the early seventeenth century, the garden front of the Treasurer's House was given an elegant new facade.

Tredegar House

Newport
M4 junction 28, then exit
roundabout A48 to St Mellons

Those heading west on the M4 out of Newport get a tantalising glimpse of this striking late seventeenth-century house set at the end of an avenue of oaks leading away from the motorway. Built to replace a Tudor mansion on the same site, and approached across two courts and through a gilded wrought-iron screen and gates of c.1714–18, Tredegar was designed to impress. The long, symmetrical, red-brick entrance front, lit by huge stone-mullioned and transomed windows on both the principal floors and with projecting pavilions at both ends, is richly decorated with carved stone. Baroque spiral columns frame the central doorway, swags of fruit hang beneath the first-floor windows and heraldic cartouches flanked by charmingly realised lions and griffins crown all the ground-floor windows. A sizeable red-brick stable block closing one side of the outer court, ornamented with brick pilasters topped by pineapples and an elaborate central doorway, and with an interior that includes a riding school, is almost as imposing.

The heraldry of the entrance front relates to the upwardly-mobile Morgan family, who owned land here for over 500 years. John ap Morgan's support of Henry Tudor's bid for the English throne in 1485 brought the family power and status in south-east Wales, a position which was reflected in the grey-stone Tudor house set round three sides of a courtyard which was subsequently built here, probably in the mid-sixteenth century. One wing of the old place, with a low roofline and large stone-mullioned windows looking onto what is now an enclosed courtyard at the heart of the house, still survives, and this is where Charles I would have been entertained when he came to Tredegar in 1645. William Morgan, who greatly increased the family's wealth and landholdings by judicious marriages, commissioned the remodelling of the house, by an unknown designer-craftsman, between 1664 and 1674, a few years before his death, and the stables were probably built towards the end of the century for William's son. The Morgans were further enriched by the industrial development of this part of Wales in the late eighteenth and nineteenth centuries, when coal was mined on the estate and the family collected tolls from a lucrative tramroad across their land.

By the early twentieth century, when the Morgans had been elevated to the peerage and owned an estate of some 21,500 hectares (53,000 acres), Tredegar was at a high point and the family was known for their philanthropy as well as their wealth. But the extravagance of Courtenay Morgan, who inherited in 1913, and of his colourful son Evan, together with crippling death duties and the ever-increasing expense of maintaining Tredegar, led to the sale of the house in 1951. A school for 23 years, in 1974 Tredegar was acquired and refurbished by Newport Borough Council, who bought back, or obtained on loan, many family portraits and other original

ABOVE LEFT The main entrance to Tredegar is crowned by endearing carvings of the lion and griffin from the Morgan coat of arms.
LEFT The Gilt Room, the most ornate of the late seventeenth-century state rooms, has original paintings inset in the panelling and a spectacular chimneypiece like a baroque Italian altar.
OPPOSITE Tredegar's late seventeenth-century entrance front is set off by a gilded wrought-iron screen and gates of c.1714–18.

furnishings. In 2012 the National Trust took a 50-year lease on the house, the presentation of which is work in progress.

Much of the interior still reflects the grandeur of the late seventeenth century. State rooms interconnecting along the entrance front are as richly decorated as the exterior, although, except in the Gilt Room, the original ornamental plaster ceilings have been lost. Oak panelling in the dining room is enriched with a wide band of carved foliage full of creatures, some of them half-animal and half-human, and each panel is crowned with a scrolled broken pediment carrying the bust of a Roman emperor. The adjoining Gilt Room filling the south-west corner of the house is even more spectacular. Here pine panelling has been painted to imitate walnut and richly gilded, the chimney piece resembles a baroque Italian altarpiece, original plasterwork on the ceiling frames an allegorical painting based on one in the Palazzo Barberini in Rome, and more inset paintings, including a version of a nude by Titian, decorate the walls. Like the work on the ceiling, these paintings, a motley collection of the Seasons and Virtues, some of which seem to be based on sculptural decoration in Amsterdam Town Hall, were probably copied from books of engravings. A portrait of Sir William Morgan, whose grandson built the house, is set over the fireplace, and more family portraits hang in the other rooms along this front.

A stone-flagged, high-ceilinged room in the south-east range has been the kitchen since the house was built, the Victorian fittings here now including a gleaming copper boiler and an immensely long kitchen table. Upstairs, a suite of rooms looking out towards the lake on the east side of the house reflects Tredegar in the 1930s, when the homosexual and eccentric Evan Morgan held wild weekend parties here, during which guests of both sexes bathed in the nude, and entertained many leading artistic figures of the day, among them Augustus John, whose portraits of Evan and his mother are both in the house, H. G. Wells and Ivor Novello. In Evan's light and airy bedroom, with its cool grey and white colour scheme, photographs of the two women he married to keep up appearances stand on the mahogany keyhole desk that was made for his father, and which cunningly conceals a washstand. Other photographs immortalise creatures from Evan's menagerie, many of which, including a honeybear called Alice, were allowed to wander the grounds. A bedroom fitted out with loaned Biedermeyer furniture has been re-created with the help of Princess Olga Dolgorouky, Evan's second wife, whose room it was, and the princess also advised on the furnishing of the study next door.

To the west of the house are formal walled gardens with wide gravel walks in the style of the early 1700s. To north and east are the remnants of the park landscaped in the late eighteenth century, when the lake, its outlines now partly obscured by rhododendrons and ornamental conifers, was created.

Trerice

Cornwall
3 miles (4.8 kilometres) south-east
of Newquay, via the A392 and the
A3058

This delightful Elizabethan manor house, constructed of local buff-coloured limestone and incorporating parts of an earlier medieval and Tudor building, was completed in 1572–3. It is not grand but, despite being hidden away in the depths of Cornwall, it is built with an awareness of the latest fashions of the day. It is also largely unchanged, perhaps escaping alteration in the eighteenth and nineteenth centuries, when Cornish prosperity, based on mining, was at its height, because its owners chose to live elsewhere. Belonging to the Arundells, one of the great families of Cornwall, for over 400 years, in 1802 it passed to the Aclands, whose principal estates were in Devon and Somerset (see Killerton, p.182).

The nature of the house is heralded in an approach down a narrow winding lane, with hedges high on either side, and in the unpretentious gateway that leads into the small walled garden setting off the entrance front. This E-shaped facade has a central porch and scrolled gables in the newly fashionable Dutch style. Among the earliest such features in Britain and unusual in Cornwall, these sophisticated gables may reflect the fact that Sir John Arundell, for whom the house was built, had been a soldier in the Low Countries. Two granite Arundell lions guard the path to the front door and the bay to the left of the porch is entirely filled by the two-storey window lighting the great hall. An intricate lattice of mullions and transoms supports 576 panes, many of them still with their original sixteenth-century glass. Although the limestone of this part of the house is now all pleasingly weathered, the north wing to the right of the porch was partly demolished in the 1860s, after storm damage was thought to have made it unsafe, and was not rebuilt until the 1950s. Fortunately, the carved stonework of the scrolled gables had been preserved and these are the originals.

The interior of the house fulfils the promise of the exterior. The sunny, south-facing great chamber on the first floor is richly decorated with bold Elizabethan plasterwork over the fireplace and on the splendid barrel ceiling, which is one of the best of the period in the West Country. Apart from the long table in the hall, made for the house in the nineteenth century, none of the furniture is original, but there are some good oak and walnut pieces among the furnishings introduced by the Trust, including a longcase clock by Thomas Tompion, a Queen Anne *escritoire* and an eighteenth-century travelling case fitted out with bottles for wines and spirits, and also some fine Chinese and English eighteenth-century porcelain and glass. Paintings by John Opie, who was born at Trevallas, only 15 miles (24 kilometres) away, add an appropriately Cornish flavour, among them portraits of his two wives, Mary and Amelia. There are also many reminders of the Arundells' devotion to the royal cause in the seventeenth century. The hall is filled with Stuart portraits and a haunting picture of Charles I by Henry Stone hangs in the court chamber upstairs. The face is careworn, the eyes withdrawn and watchful. Also in the house is an enchanting Jacobean embroidery panel, believed to depict Charles and his queen, in which Henrietta is shown giving the king a bunch of flowers, while a large snail crawls between them and a long-eared rabbit looks on.

Across the cobbled courtyard behind the house lies a magnificent great barn of a size and age – it probably dates from the fifteenth century – rarely seen in Cornwall. A ramp from the flat lawn above, where the Home Guard drilled in the Second World War, leads to the loft of the former stable.

No traces remain of the geometric Elizabethan garden that would once have set off the entrance front, but steps from the grassy court in front of the house lead up onto what was a Tudor bowling-green, from where there is a roof-level view of the gables on the east front. To the south, what was the lowest of a suite of Elizabethan terraces stepping down the hill and once a formal ornamental garden is now a grassy orchard planted in a quincunx pattern, where every tree is in line with its neighbour from wherever it is viewed. An early fifteenth-century chapel has also disappeared, although its site lives on in the field name 'Chapel Close'.

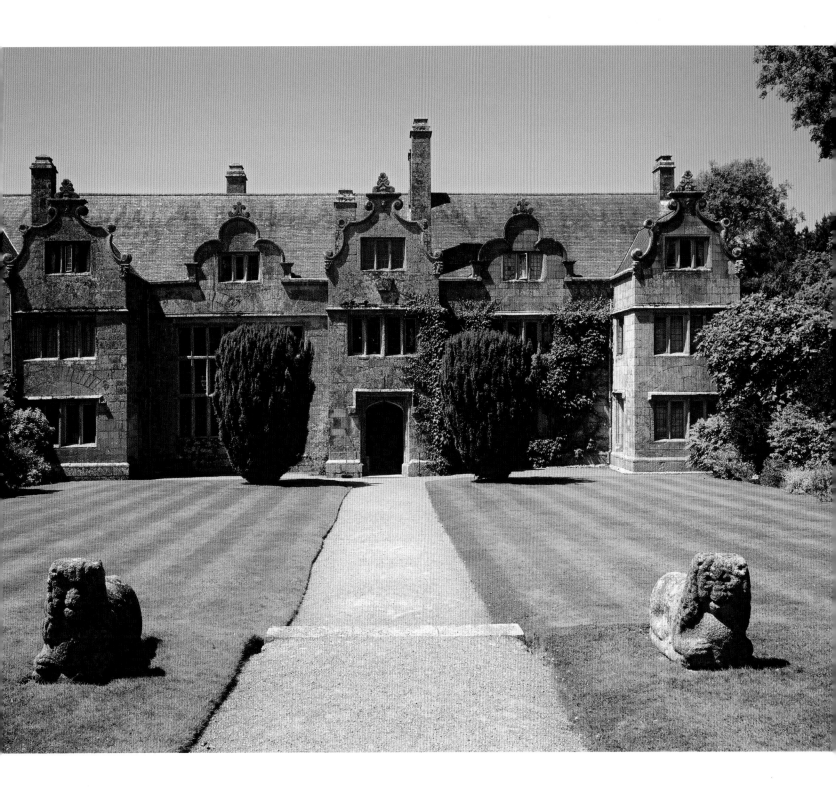

ABOVE Trerice, an unspoilt Elizabethan manor hidden away in rural Cornwall, was built by Sir John Arundell in c.1570 and has two granite Arundell lions guarding the path to the front door.

Tyntesfield

Somerset
Off the B3128, 3 miles
(4.8 kilometres) east of Nailsea

This romantic High Victorian mansion is set on steeply rising ground, with woods behind and a panoramic view south over parkland and the valley of the Yeo to the distant ridge of the Mendips. Still all of a piece with its original furnishings, decorative schemes and the accumulated possessions of the family that lived here for four generations, this memorable place is an unspoilt and largely unaltered example of a Gothic Revival country house. Windows are stone-mullioned and traceried, there are pepper-pot turrets, huge chimneystacks and fanciful Gothic dormers, and window bays and rooflines are finished off with carved friezes, pierced parapets, finials and gargoyles. Rising over the house is the steeply pitched roof of a sizeable chapel, with finialled buttresses between the Gothic windows and a west-end stair turret.

Together with 200 hectares (almost 500 acres) of gardens, park and estate, Tyntesfield was acquired by the National Trust in 2002 after a whirlwind campaign to save the property from being sold on the open market, which required the Trust to raise over £20 million in 50 days. This was only made possible by a huge public response, and a measure of the brinkmanship involved is that the contents had already been ticketed and sorted for sale by auction. Much-needed conservation and restoration has been going on ever since.

Tyntesfield is predominantly the creation of the entrepreneurial William Gibbs (1790–1875). Involved in the family firm, which had business interests in Spain and Latin America, from a young age, by 1842, when he was in his early 50s, William was in charge. In the same year, the firm's South American agent concluded the deal that was to make him a fortune, giving Gibbs and Sons a virtual monopoly in the shipment of Peruvian guano, then a fertiliser of prime importance. A growing family may have encouraged William and his wife Blanche, 28 years his junior, to look for a place out of London, and in 1843 William bought what was then a Georgian country house with some decorative Gothic touches.

Twenty years later he commissioned the architect John Norton, who had learned his trade from a pupil and friend of Augustus Welby Pugin and so had direct links with the most influential figure of the Gothic Revival, to remodel Tyntesfield.

The house is built of golden Bath stone, with roofs covered partly in tiles, partly in heavy stone slabs quarried in Wiltshire. Carved stone decoration enlivening every facade includes some finely detailed, three-dimensional work by a certain Mr Beates, who realised the plants and creatures of the gardens and estate in stone. There are primroses, cobnuts and strawberries carved on corbels in the porch, and a capital carries a dormouse, bees and a lizard. As throughout the house, the craftsmanship is of the highest quality.

William's son Antony (1841–1907), an art collector and highly skilled amateur craftsman rather than a businessman, moved into Tyntesfield in 1890 after the death of his mother. He embarked on alterations, but his chosen architect, Henry Woodyer, also worked in the Gothic Revival style and Woodyer's changes, including the substantial verandah which he had added on for Blanche in 1883, were all in keeping with the earlier work. By the next generation, a shift in taste was reflected in changes made by George Gibbs, 1st Lord Wraxall (1873–1931), who was a prominent politician and socialiser and invited members of the government down for country-house weekends. Again, though, with the exception of the drawing room, the essential character of the place was retained.

The 2nd Lord Wraxall (1928–2001) succeeded to the title when he was only 3, and his mother Ursula, Lady Wraxall ran Tyntesfield for many years. At the end of his life, Lord Wraxall was living at Tyntesfield alone and many of the main rooms were shut up, but he maintained a keen interest in the gardens and estate and cared for the fabric of the place. Most importantly, although he sold some items, he did not follow the reaction against High Victorian art that led to other houses being stripped of their contents, and he added pictures and other objects to the collection.

ABOVE LEFT The vaulted roof of Tyntesfield's cloister-like entrance hall.
OPPOSITE The beautiful library, with its soaring oak roof and comfortable chairs, was a favourite family sitting room where theatricals were sometimes staged.

ABOVE Tyntesfield's chapel is fitted out with ornate metalwork, stained glass from one of the best designers of the day, and a mosaic floor of exceptional richness, incorporating pieces of Mexican onyx and Derbyshire bluejohn. **OPPOSITE** Tyntesfield's east-facing entrance front, with the bay lighting the library to the left of the porch, is dominated by the pinnacled chapel designed by William Butterfield on the far right.

The interior is of a piece, combining original decorative schemes with much surviving Victorian furniture, some of it, such as a richly ornamented rolltop desk, by the Warwickshire cabinet-makers Collier and Plucknett, who supplied the family with furniture in the later nineteenth century. Wood and stone have been used profligately: there are open timber roofs, decorative panelling and parquet floors; monumental fireplaces, stone arches and doorways and pillars of polished marble. The main rooms are arranged around the toplit staircase hall, with clerestory windows beneath an open roof of English oak. Paintings hung thickly on the walls include a portrait of William, with white hair and side-whiskers, by his close friend Sir William Boxall, and a seascape by Sir Augustus Wall Callcott, all steely sky and blue-grey sea. The chenille stair carpet, in ribbons when the Trust acquired Tyntesfield, has been rewoven in wool, to the original design, for which 27 colours were required.

William's spirit is strong in the spacious library which fills one of the wings on the entrance front. A comfortable, welcoming room rising to an open oak roof, it has the original carpet, in deep reds and blues, by the fashionable decorators J.G. Crace and Son and this company also provided the deep-buttoned armchairs and sofa. William's seven children staged theatricals here, and the bookcases round the walls, carefully numbered in Latin numerals, are stuffed with the gilded bindings of his library. William's religious sympathies lay with the Oxford Movement, which was launched in the 1830s to return ceremony and ritual, and thus elements of beauty and mystery, to the Church of England. The main texts of the movement are here, and so too are key works on the Gothic Revival, with which it went hand in hand, including the writings of Pugin and Ruskin. Above the bookcases at the west end of the room is a striking display of Imari porcelain – blue and white, green and red.

The dining room, entered through a flamboyant carved stone doorway and lined with wallpaper imitating Spanish leather, is Antony's. But the drawing room, with a Renaissance-style fireplace and an original Crace carpet that has been dyed to match the crimson damask on the walls, was altered and refurnished by Antony's son George, 1st Lord Wraxall, and his first wife Via. Two intricately turned ivory candlesticks were made by Antony, and also on display is the finely carved Flaxley casket. Once thought to be medieval, and also made of ivory, the casket is in fact an intriguing early Gothic Revival fake. Much more relaxed in spirit is the capacious billiard room, with an array of antlered heads on the walls, skins thrown casually over ageing sofas, and a centrally heated table with an electric scoreboard.

Upstairs, a run of bedrooms along the south and east fronts includes the room used by Via, who died at the tragically early age of 39. The rose carpet was installed for her, her dressing-table set is on display, and the room is furnished with Italian and Dutch marquetry pieces that she brought with her to the house. Because of the slope of the hill, the family could walk from these first-floor rooms straight into the chapel which William commissioned from Arthur Blomfield and which was only just finished when William died in 1875. Provided with a chancel and ornate screen and richly fitted out with gleaming mosaics, stained glass and an inlaid floor, it proclaims

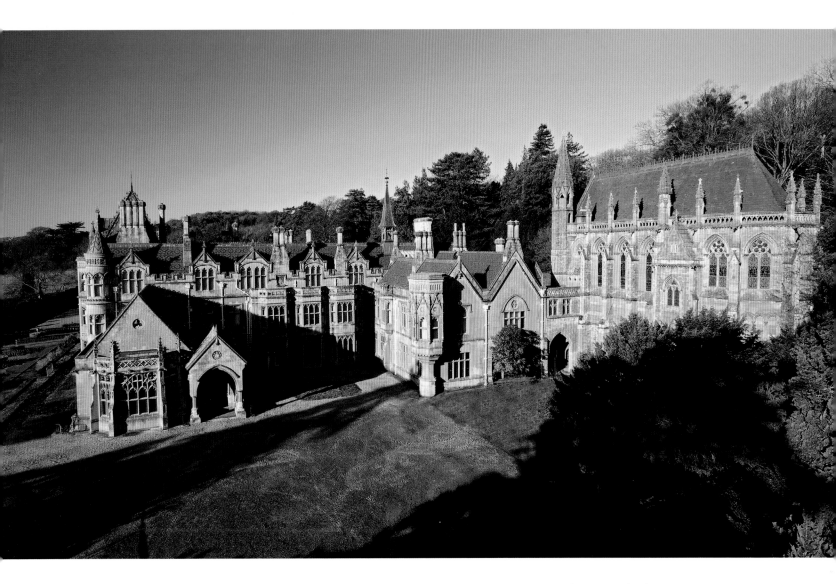

William's commitment to High Church principles. A silver communion set designed by William Butterfield in 1876 was commissioned by Blanche in memory of her husband.

The layout of the garden is still very much as it was when William died. Close to the house, billowing hollies lap the marble urns set along the lower terrace, and bright displays of bedding plants reflect the taste of the 2nd Lord Wraxall. A lone palm and luxuriant magnolias and camellias outside the billiard room mark the site of John Norton's huge conservatory, with an onion dome and gilded cupola, which was demolished after the dome collapsed in a storm in March 1916. A formal walk lined by mushroom domes of holly stretches away from the west front, past the former rose garden, and another long walk, marked by clipped Irish yews, echoes the line of the terraces, with views over the sadly waterless lake. Architectural stone Gothic seats punctuate the ends of the walks.

Everywhere in the landscaped grounds are huge specimen trees and a ha-ha allows uninterrupted views across the park and the valley beyond. Hidden from the house are the walled kitchen gardens, with greenhouses that are still very much in use, and a splendid classical orangery, of brick and stone. Cut flowers and fresh vegetables are still supplied to the house from these gardens as they always have been.

Uppark House and Garden

West Sussex
5 miles (8 kilometres) south-east of Petersfield on the B2146, 1½ miles (2.4 kilometres) south of South Harting

The serene two-storey house built in about 1690 for Ford, Lord Grey, Earl of Tankerville, owes its existence to his grandfather's invention of an effective method of pumping water to great heights, without which the commanding site on a crest of the South Downs would have been impractical. The amoral and duplicitous Lord Grey, who emerged remarkably unscathed from his involvement in the Duke of Monmouth's rebellion against James II in 1685, perhaps because he turned king's evidence, is one of many colourful characters connected with the estate. His new house, whose architect is uncertain, was in the latest Dutch style. Standing four-square like a giant doll's house, it is built of red brick with weathered, lichen-tinted stone dressings and dormer windows in a hipped roof. A pediment crowns the south front and detached mid-eighteenth-century stable and kitchen blocks balance the composition on either side.

The rich interior is mostly the work of Sir Matthew Fetherstonhaugh, who bought Uppark in 1747. This cultivated man, heir to the vast fortune of a distant relative, redecorated most of the principal rooms and enriched the house with a magnificent collection of carpets, furniture and works of art, much of it, such as portraits by Batoni and four harbour and coastal scenes by Joseph Vernet, purchased on a Grand Tour with his wife Sarah in 1749–51. The couple were responsible for the hauntingly beautiful white and gold saloon, with its delicate plaster ceiling and ivory silk brocade curtains framing the long south-facing windows, and with paintings set into fixed plasterwork frames in the Adam style. Fireplaces inlaid with Sienese marble warm both ends of the room, one of them carved with the Sienese wolf suckling Romulus and Remus. Sarah also introduced the finely crafted doll's house of c.1740, with three floors of rooms behind a pedimented facade. Every detail is accurate. Diminutive landscape paintings hang on the walls, hallmarked silver and glass gleam on the dining-room table and there are fire irons of silver and brass. Meticulously dressed dolls people the mansion, those representing the family identifiable by their wax faces, the lower orders depicted in wood.

Matthew's only son Harry inherited his parents' good taste and enriched their collection. But in other respects he was a prodigal young man, with a love of hunting and the turf which is echoed in his sporting pictures and silver-gilt cups. His close friend the Prince Regent was a guest at the lavish house parties staged at Uppark, with superb meals produced by Moget, Harry's French chef. It was on one of these occasions that the 15-year-old Emma Hart, the future Lady Hamilton, is said to have danced naked on the dining-room table. Sir Harry's liaison with Emma, whom he had discovered in London, was only brief and the letters she wrote to him after she had been sent away, six months pregnant, went unanswered. Decades later, Sir Harry caused another stir when, in his 70th year, he married young Mary Ann Bullock, his head dairymaid. Largely because of Mary Ann and her sister Frances, who joined the household, Uppark was to survive the nineteenth century little changed.

In the basement is an extensive range of service rooms. There is an authentically laid out butler's pantry, and the sunny room where H.G. Wells's mother presided as housekeeper from 1880–93 has easy chairs drawn up by the fire and tea laid on a tray. Long whitewashed tunnels, down which the young Wells chased the maids, lead to the eighteenth-century pavilions flanking the house. One was a stable block, the other a laundry and greenhouse where, in c.1815, Sir Harry installed a new kitchen. During most of the nineteenth century the present kitchen, with a long scrubbed table and gleaming pots and pans, was probably a still room, used for making cakes and drinks and for giving final touches to the dishes for upstairs after their long journey through the tunnel.

Much of Uppark's charm derives from its setting, with a great stretch of downland turf planted with mature trees sweeping away from the house and leading the eye across a rolling landscape to the sea. Humphry Repton, who added the pillared portico to the north front, was probably also responsible for Mary Ann's elegant dairy, its white tiles decorated with a blue and green frieze of clematis, and for the little Gothic summerhouse.

One of the more traumatic events in the National Trust's history was the fire at Uppark in 1989, from which most of the furniture and paintings were rescued but which destroyed much of their eighteenth-century setting. Restoration took five-and-a-half years, and required the re-learning of traditional skills. Plasterwork was re-created, intricate mouldings and architraves re-carved, new curtains woven and wallpaper printed. From the outset, the Trust aimed to maintain the air of faded elegance that makes the house so attractive. New was carefully matched to old, even to the extent of imitating picture-protected patches of wallpaper and time-darkened white paint, but almost every room has also been left with scorched floorboards and chimneypieces and other reminders of the fire, or with unfinished, newly created detail, such as an ungilded ornamental cherub. Wherever possible, fire-mangled and shattered fittings were put back together: lanterns and chandeliers that had been reduced to twisted

metal shapes and fragments of glass were painstakingly reconstructed and a scagliola table-top was pieced together, bit by bit. The house itself seems unchanged. As before, the most enduring memory is of mellow pink brick and lichened stone against a life-enhancing view. And martins have returned to nest under the eaves.

Upton House

Warwickshire
1 mile (1.6 kilometres) south of
Edge Hill, 7 miles (11.2 kilometres)
north-west of Banbury, on the west
side of the Stratford-upon-Avon
road (A422)

Walter Samuel, 2nd Viscount Bearsted, was lucky enough to inherit a fortune from his father, who had profited greatly from the expansion of trade with the Far East in the late nineteenth century and, together with his brother, had developed the Shell organisation, building it up into an international corporation. One of the twentieth century's most generous philanthropists, the 2nd Viscount used his inheritance to benefit a long list of charities, hospitals and schools. At the same time, it also enabled him to pursue his great passion for painting and the decorative arts, and to acquire one of the finest art collections of his time.

Lord Bearsted bought Upton in 1927, shortly after the death of his father, as somewhere to display his collection. At the heart of the house, making up the central seven bays of the long, sash-windowed entrance front, is the mansion built in 1695 for Sir Rushout Cullen, but this was altered substantially in the eighteenth century, when the entrance bay acquired its baroque broken pediment, and in 1927–9 the architect Percy Morley Horder reworked the place for Lord Bearsted, giving the building a strong horizontal emphasis. Morley Horder's interiors, which include a 30-metre (100-foot) long gallery on the south-facing garden front, were among the most luxurious of the period, but were deliberately bland and restrained in order to create a suitable setting for the collection. Only the first-floor suite created for Lady Bearsted, which includes a Chinese bedroom looking out over the garden and a striking

Art Deco bathroom decorated in silver, red and black, has a strong character of its own.

Lord Bearsted's collection included tapestries, furniture, silver, miniatures and many other fine things, but the rooms at Upton are now largely devoted to displaying his paintings, including some inherited from his father, and his eighteenth-century soft-paste French and English porcelain. In both areas he had an eye for the unusual and outstanding. Among a number of works by fifteenth- and sixteenth-century masters is El Greco's *El Espolio* (Flagellation of Christ), the spears of the soldiers grouped behind Our Lord suggesting a crown of thorns. In another strongly atmospheric work, Brueghel's *Dormition of the Virgin*, Our Lady is shown receiving a lighted taper from St Peter in a dimly lit room. The use of grey and black alone gives the picture a ghostly quality. Serene Dutch interiors and landscapes with diminutive figures set against immense skies include Saenredam's cool study of St Catherine's Church, Utrecht, in which beetle-like clerics and two men inscribing a stone set into the floor are dwarfed by the soaring arches of the nave.

Sporting pictures feature in the dining room. Here, too, hang Stubbs's scenes from rural life, his *Haymakers*, *Reapers* and *Labourers*, the weariness evident in the horses about to take away a laden cart as real as the chill conjured up in Hogarth's portrayal of an early winter morning in front of St Paul's, Covent Garden, one of the paintings for his engraved series, *The Four Times of Day*.

The porcelain collection is similarly wide-ranging. Here, again, perhaps reflecting Lord Bearsted's essential humanitarianism, figures feature prominently, among the most memorable being two Chelsea pieces in the long gallery depicting a wet nurse suckling a swaddled baby and a shepherd teaching his shepherdess how to play the flute, holding the instrument for her as she blows. Embroidery on the eighteenth-century-style walnut chairs in this room, depicting people involved in weaving, grape-treading and other occupations, is the work of the 3rd Lord Bearsted, who started doing it as therapy after he was badly injured in the Second World War. Art of a different kind features in the display of scenic posters produced by Shell in the 1930s which are devoted to some of England's most beautiful buildings and landscapes, several National Trust properties among them.

OPPOSITE The long gallery, created from several smaller rooms, is hung with sixteenth- and seventeenth-century Dutch paintings and displays Lord Bearsted's English porcelain.
ABOVE To imitate silver leaf, which would have tarnished, Morley Horder covered the walls and vaulted ceiling of the Art Deco bathroom at Upton House with aluminium leaf.

While the house is bland and architecturally undistinguished, the gardens are full of character. Across a broad double terrace and cedar-framed lawn on the south front, there is a sudden steep descent to a chain of ponds in the valley below. An Italianate balustraded stairway added in the 1930s leads into the depths of the combe, its lichen-stained steps overhung with wistaria. The mellow brick wall of the old kitchen garden on the slopes of the valley still carries espaliered fruit trees as it did in the seventeenth century and present renovation of the ornamental terraces above will give a 1930s flavour to the planting, with drifts of colour in the style of Gertrude Jekyll. A wilder bog garden fills a natural amphitheatre to the west of the house, sheep graze on the other side of the valley and over a mile (1.6 kilometres) away, just visible from the terrace, a lake reflects the columns of a little eighteenth-century Tuscan temple.

The Vyne

Hampshire
4 miles (6.4 kilometres) north of Basingstoke, between Bramley and Sherborne St John

This long red-brick house with purple diaperwork lacing the facades is set low in a hollow, looking north over an idyllic lake. There is a pedimented portico on the garden front and the original mullions have been replaced with mid-seventeenth-century sash windows, but the E-plan is that of a Tudor house. Dating from some time between 1500 and 1520, The Vyne was built for William, 1st Lord Sandys, whose long career in the service of Henry VIII culminated in his appointment to the office of Lord Chamberlain in 1526.

Sandys's battlemented chapel juts out conspicuously at the east end of the house. One of the most perfect private oratories in England, this lofty room rising the height of two storeys is still largely as it was built in 1518–27. Intricately carved canopied stalls facing across the chapel are fringed by intriguing early sixteenth-century Italian tiles: richly coloured in blue, yellow, orange and green, they were found in heaps in the grounds. Three magnificent stained-glass windows at the east end, seen at their best in morning sunlight, are equalled in importance only by those of similar date in King's College, Cambridge. One of them, showing Henry VIII with Catherine of Aragon, who is accompanied by a little dog, would have been hidden from view when the king came here with Anne Boleyn in 1535.

The Oak Gallery, stretching the length of the west wing on the first floor, one of the finest examples of its date in Britain, is another survival from the Tudor house. The delicate linenfold panelling which lines the walls from floor to ceiling carries a wealth of carved badges and devices, among them the Tudor rose and Catherine of Aragon's pomegranate. A more unusual emblem is the curious portcullis-like hemp bray that was used in the separation of flax fibres and which is included here because it was the crest of Sir Reginald Bray, uncle of Lord Sandys's wife. The white marble of a seventeenth-century classical fireplace in the middle of the east wall is picked up in a series of portrait busts set down the room, a mixed company in which portrayals of Shakespeare, Milton and Mary Queen of Scots rub shoulders with a typically arrogant Nero and a world-weary Seneca.

Lord Sandys's service to Henry VIII was rewarded at the Dissolution of the Monasteries with the gift of Mottisfont Abbey (*see* p.218) and it was here that the family retired when impoverishment in the Civil War forced the sale of The Vyne in 1653. The new owner was another successful and astute politician, Chaloner Chute, shortly to be Speaker in Richard Cromwell's parliament, who reduced the size of the house. He also added the classical portico on the north front, which is thought to be the earliest on a domestic building. His grandson Edward acquired the Queen Anne furniture and Soho tapestries now displayed in the house, such as the hangings in the room next to the gallery. Depicting oriental scenes, they are full of gay spotted butterflies and darting birds, and one shows a monkey sitting in a palm tree.

Chute's great-grandson John, friend of Horace Walpole, made notable alterations in about 1750, creating the theatrical classical staircase, with busts of Roman emperors on the newel posts, ornate fluted columns fringing a first-floor gallery and a moulded ceiling in pale blue and white. John Chute was also responsible for the tomb chamber off the chapel, built in honour of his distinguished ancestor. Here the Speaker lies immortalised in Carrara marble on the top of a box-like monument loosely disguised as a Greek temple. His lifelike effigy rests on an unyielding plaited straw mattress, his head supported on his right arm, one finger extended along the curve of his brow.

OPPOSITE, LEFT One of the Tudor stained-glass windows in the chapel at The Vyne shows Henry VIII, a deep blue cloak over his gilt-plated armour, kneeling in prayer beside his patron saint, Henry II of Bavaria.

OPPOSITE, RIGHT The chapel at the Vyne, built between 1518 and 1527, is a largely unaltered Tudor interior.

ABOVE The tapestry room is named after the early eighteenth-century chinoiserie hangings, which are complemented by a display of mostly oriental porcelain.

Waddesdon Manor

Buckinghamshire
6 miles (9.6 kilometres) north-west
of Aylesbury, on the A41, 11 miles
(17.7 kilometres) south-east of
Bicester

The great châteaux of the Loire made such an impression on the young Ferdinand and future Baron de Rothschild, grandson of the founder of the Austrian branch of this famous banking family (*see* Ascott, p.26), that he determined to model any house he might build on what he had seen in France. This magnificent palace designed by Gabriel Hippolyte Destailleur and built in 1874–9, when the baron was in his late 40s, fulfilled the youthful Ferdinand's dreams, its pinnacles, mansard roofs, dormer windows, massive chimneys and staircase towers reproducing the characteristic features of Maintenon, Blois and other French Renaissance châteaux. The hill on which Waddesdon is set was purchased from the Duke of Marlborough, a platform was carved out for the mansion and the slopes were planted with half-grown trees. Building materials were brought up by cable, while the timber was hauled laboriously up the hill by teams of horses.

This pastiche château has similarly extravagant, French-inspired interiors, with a procession of high-ceilinged reception rooms re-creating the elegant splendour of the pre-Revolutionary regime. Profiting from Baron Haussmann's remodelling of Paris for Napoleon III, Ferdinand was able to obtain panelling from the great eighteenth-century houses that were destroyed to form the city's new boulevards, and this elaborately carved woodwork can be seen in almost every room. Royal fleurs-de-lis feature prominently on the Savonnerie carpets, a representation of the Sun King himself appearing on one from a set that Louis XIV commissioned for the long gallery of the Louvre. Eight pieces of furniture were made for the French royal family by the great Jean-Henri Riesener, the leading cabinetmaker of his day, including a marquetry writing-table created for Marie Antoinette and a drop-front secretaire ordered for the queen by Louis XVI. Elegant little tables with delicate gazelle-like legs contrast with the baron's massive cylinder-top desk that once belonged to the dramatist Beaumarchais and a monumental black and gold secretaire surmounted by a clock and crowned by a huge gilt eagle. Tear-drop chandeliers are reflected in mirrors with ornate gilt frames and every surface is crammed with clocks, Sèvres and Meissen porcelain and *objets d'art*, among them a gold snuffbox that once belonged to Louis XV's mistress, Madame de Pompadour, with her pet dogs, Ines and Mimi, shown cavorting on the lid. Paintings by Watteau, Lancret, Boucher and Greuze help to create a sense of pre-Revolutionary France.

These French pieces are harmoniously combined with a fine collection of eighteenth-century English portraits by Gainsborough, Reynolds and Romney, and with a number of seventeenth-century Dutch paintings, such as Jan van der Heyden's tranquil view of an Amsterdam canal, with stepped red-brick gables reflected in the still waters, a garden scene by de Hooch, and Rubens's dreamy *The Garden of Love*. One of the two galleries leading from the main entrance is dominated by two huge canvases of Venice by Francesco Guardi, one a view to Santa Maria della Salute and San Giorgio Maggiore, two gilded and canopied gondolas gliding across the water between them, the other looking towards the Doge's Palace from across the lagoon. Oenophiles are tantalised by a 'library' of Rothschild vintages on view in the wine cellars; there is a display of Sèvres porcelain and a recently acquired silver dinner service that was made in Paris for George III; and a tower room is hung with panels commissioned by the late James de Rothschild from the stage designer Leon Bakst, who incorporated portraits of the family and their friends in paintings illustrating the story of Sleeping Beauty. Also shown is the Bachelor's wing, complete with smoking and billiard rooms, where Ferdinand entertained his male guests.

An extensive programme of restoration undertaken by the Rothschild family at the turn of the century returned Waddesdon's Bath stone to its original striking yellow and the house is set off by an exceptional Victorian garden. Steps from the south front lead down to a parterre with an ornate Italian fountain. The wooded park beyond, with rich plantings of specimen trees and some contemporary sculpture, is part of the extensive grounds designed by the French landscape gardener Lainé, while artificial rockwork by Pulham and Sons bordering the approach north of the house shelters an aviary in eighteenth-century style, its presence heralded by chirruping from the exotic inhabitants, many of which were bred here. The aviary is the heart of the west garden as Baron Ferdinand conceived it, with flamboyant beds and hedges giving way to tranquil glades.

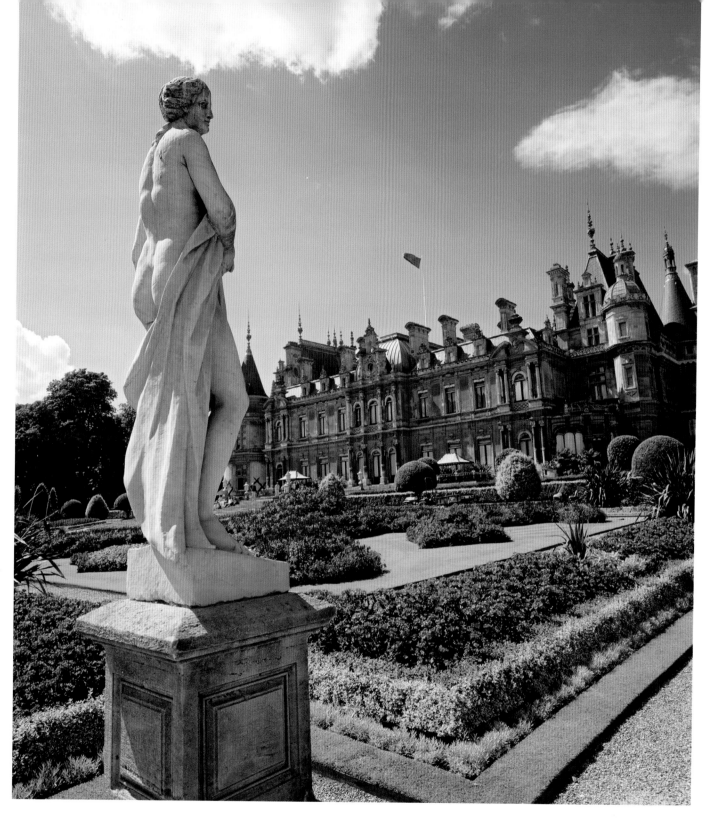

ABOVE Waddesdon Manor, built on a hill above the Vale of Aylesbury in 1874–9 for Ferdinand de Rothschild, was designed to look like a château of the Loire and is set off by a great formal parterre.

Wallington

Northumberland
12 miles (19.3 kilometres) west of
Morpeth on the B6343, 6 miles
(9.6 kilometres) north-west of
Belsay on the A696

Many country houses are hidden behind walls or screens of trees, but there is nothing secluded about Wallington. The pedimented south front of this square stone building crowns a long slope of rough grass, in full view of the public road through the park. Nor is there a lodge or an imposing gateway. The pinnacled triumphal arch built for the house was found to be too narrow for coaches and now languishes in a field.

Wallington is largely the creation of Sir Walter Calverley Blackett, 2nd Baronet, who commissioned the Northumbrian architect Daniel Garrett in *c*.1738 to remodel his grandfather's uncomfortable house. Garrett's cool, Palladian exteriors are no preparation for Pietro Lafranchini's magnificent rococo plasterwork in the saloon, where delicate, feminine compositions in blue and white, with winged sphinxes perched on curling foliage, garlands of flowers and cornucopias overflowing with fruit, suggest an elaborate wedding cake.

Oriental porcelain in the alcoves on either side of the fireplace is part of a large and varied collection, much of it the dowry of Maria Wilson, who married into the family in 1791 just a few years after Wallington had passed to Sir Walter's nephew, Sir John Trevelyan. A bizarre Meissen tea-set in the parlour features paintings of life-size insects nestling in the bottom of each cup. Even more extraordinary is Wallington's Cabinet of Curiosities, which Maria also introduced, its strange exhibits ranging from a piece of Edward IV's coffin to stuffed birds set against painted habitats and a spiky red porcupine fish like an animated pin cushion.

The hall rising through two storeys in the middle of the house reflects another era. Created in 1853–4 out of what was an internal courtyard, this individual room was the inspiration of the talented Pauline Trevelyan, whose vivid personality attracted a stream of artists and writers, including Ruskin, Swinburne and Rossetti. Under her influence, Rossetti's friend William Bell Scott was commissioned to produce the eight epic scenes from Northumbrian history which decorate the walls,

the subjects portrayed including the death of the Venerable Bede and Grace Darling in her open boat rescuing the men of the *Forfarshire*. In the canvas showing the landing of the Vikings, savage heads on the prows of the fleet emerge out of the gloom over the sea like an invasion of prehistoric monsters. Ruskin and Pauline herself, among others, painted the delicate wild flowers – purple foxgloves, brilliant-red poppies and yellow columbine – on the pillars between the pictures. The family's later connection with the Macaulays brought associations with scientists and politicians as well as artists and writers, and Lord Macaulay wrote his monumental history of England here.

Sir Walter Calverley Blackett's spirit lives on in the extensive estate, which embraces several parishes. This he transformed,

ABOVE Wallington's vast central hall was created out of what was a courtyard in 1853–4 and is painted with murals by William Bell Scott illustrating scenes from Northumbrian history.

laying out roads, enclosing fields, building cottages, planting woods and devising follies. His formal pleasure grounds were later converted into a naturalistic landscape park, possibly with the advice of the young 'Capability' Brown, who was born nearby and went to school on the estate and who, in about 1765, was employed to design the setting for the ornamental lake at Rothley. But Sir Walter himself was responsible for damming the River Wansbeck and for James Paine's imposing three-arched bridge below the house.

Sir Walter also laid out the walled garden that lies in a sheltered dell half a mile (0.8 kilometre) east of the house. Once a vegetable garden, it is now an unexpected delight of lawns and mixed herbaceous beds following the lines of the valley, with a little stream running out of a pond in a stone niche that was created in 1938. To one side a raised terrace walk carries a little brick pavilion, surmounted with the owl of the Calverley crest, and Sir George Otto Trevelyan's 1908 conservatory. A hedged nuttery on the slopes below marks the site of the former vegetable patch, while across the valley is a broad, sloping mixed border. Although this must be one of the National Trust's coldest gardens, roses, honeysuckles, clematis and sun-loving plants thrive against the south-facing walls.

Washington Old Hall

Tyne & Wear
5 miles (8 kilometres) west of
Sunderland, 2 miles
(3.2 kilometres) east of the A1,
south of the Tyne tunnel

Two nineteenth-century watercolours in the parlour show Washington Old Hall as it once was: an unassuming house on the edge of Washington village, close by the church on its wooded hill and with cornfields stretching away behind. The village has now been swallowed up by Washington New Town, but there is still a little green valley below the house with a view across it to the red-brick mansion which was the home of the Bell family, connected by marriage to the Trevelyans of Wallington (*see* p.338).

Washington Old Hall is a modest Jacobean manor with small mullioned windows and rough sandstone walls that was built in *c.*1613 on the foundations of a twelfth-century house. The interior was conventionally designed on an H-plan, with a great hall occupying the centre of the building. Two arches from the original house lead from the hall into the kitchen. The medieval building that forms the basis of the present hall was the ancestral home of George Washington, who was elected first President of the USA in 1789; his direct ancestors lived here for five generations and the property remained in the family until 1613. Mementoes of the Washington connection and the struggle for independence can be seen throughout the house. A portrait of George Washington executed on drum parchment while he was on campaign as leader of the rebel forces hangs alongside a letter from Percy, 2nd Duke of Northumberland, who served with the British troops. Upstairs, a lottery ticket signed by Washington is exhibited beside a glass case displaying a uniform of the Washington Greys.

Although none of the furniture is original, it is all in tune with the house and includes some interesting pieces, such as the seventeenth-century baby-walker in the bedroom and the beautifully embroidered stumpwork cabinet in the parlour.

A print of Mount Vernon, given by President Jimmy Carter when he visited the house in 1977, symbolises the importance of a more recent American connection. Washington Old Hall was divided into tenements in Georgian times and during the nineteenth century became increasingly dilapidated. Its condition was so bad by the 1930s that demolition was seriously considered and only a concerted campaign, instigated by the tireless Frederick Hill, saved the building. Generous gifts from across the Atlantic made restoration possible and the people of the USA continue to offer much-needed help, many of them visiting the Old Hall every year.

LEFT The ancestors of George Washington, the first president of the United States, lived in the medieval house that forms the basis of Washington Old Hall.

West Wycombe Park and Village

Buckinghamshire
2 miles (3.2 kilometres) west
of High Wycombe, on the A40

Everything about West Wycombe bears the stamp of the man who created it, the mercurial eighteenth-century dilettante Sir Francis Dashwood. Armed with the fortune his father had made trading with Africa, India and the East, Sir Francis interleaved several visits to Italy with tours as far afield as Russia and Turkey. Months of foreign travel not only gave him opportunities to indulge in the practical jokes he was fond of but also an appreciation of art and a depth of learning that led him, in 1732, to be a founder member of the Dilettanti Society, which was to have an important influence on English taste. Now remembered chiefly for his connection with the notorious Hellfire Club, which met in caves burrowed into the hill rising steeply to the north of West Wycombe, the more serious side of his character comes across in his successful political career. Although disastrous as Chancellor of the Exchequer in 1762, he proved himself a more than able joint Paymaster General in the years that followed.

Between 1735 and Sir Francis's death in 1781, the square, red-brick Queen Anne building he inherited was transformed into a classical mansion and filled with paintings and furniture acquired on his Grand Tours. The architect John Donowell supervised the remodelling until 1764, but it is not clear who was responsible for designing the house. Sir Francis undoubtedly had strong ideas of his own, but he may also have had expert advice from Giovanni Servandoni, Roger Morris and Isaac Ware, and Nicholas Revett was involved in the later stages of the work. In his remodelling, Sir Francis was no more than a man of his time; but the architecture and decoration with which he enriched West Wycombe give the house its highly individual and theatrical character. An unusual double colonnade rising to roof height stretches almost the full width of the long south front, rivalling the huge porticoes decorated with frescoes, one of which was designed by Revett in imitation of a Greek temple, that dominate the east and west facades. The richly-decorated interior, with gilded mirrors reflecting glittering vistas through the house, mixes illusion with fine craftsmanship. Sensual baroque painted ceilings by the Italian Giuseppe Mattias Borgnis, who was brought to England specially for this commission, adorn some of the principal rooms, his *Triumph of Bacchus and Ariadne* in the Blue Drawing Room a riot of overweight cherubs, heavily muscled bodies and flowing drapery. Paint was also used to imitate marble, fine plasterwork and joinery of burr walnut and satinwood and Sir Francis's Neo-classical hall and dining room, with illusionistic coffered ceilings by Giuseppe's son Giovanni, marbled walls and elaborate stone floors, were intended to evoke the houses of Roman antiquity. The hall was even fitted with hypocaust heating.

Some delicate rococo plasterwork is the real thing, and elaborate marble chimneypieces in many of the rooms include at least two by Sir Henry Cheere, who carved doves, and an owl devouring a small bird, on the one in the music room and was probably also responsible for the plaque showing cherubs warming themselves by a fire in the study, and for the grand columned doorcase of the saloon. The mahogany staircase inlaid with satinwood and ebony is similarly fine and one of very few examples of work of this kind (*see also* Claydon, p.94).

Hardly altered since Sir Francis's death, the house still displays his catholic collection of lesser Italian masters, family portraits stretching back to the seventeenth century, and views of the house painted in the 1750s by William Hannan. But much of Sir Francis's fine eighteenth-century furniture, including a state bed embellished with pineapples, was sold in 1922 by the 10th Baronet. Although the 11th Baronet, who inherited in 1963, was able to buy back some of these pieces, many of the present furnishings, all of which seem totally in keeping, are not original.

The house is set off by Sir Francis's serene landscape garden, which he created by remodelling his own earlier, more formal layout. A composition in grass, trees and water, it is focused on an islanded lake and richly embellished with ornamental buildings, many of which are as individual as the house. John Donowell was probably responsible for the gigantic grey arch of flint and stone known as the Temple of Apollo that stands next to the house, and for the octagonal tower carried on flintwork arches. Later eye-catchers designed by Nicholas Revett between 1770 and 1781 include a Doric temple on the largest island in the lake, a cottage disguised as a church and a colonnaded circular dovecote with a pyramidal roof known as the Round Temple. The 11th Baronet added

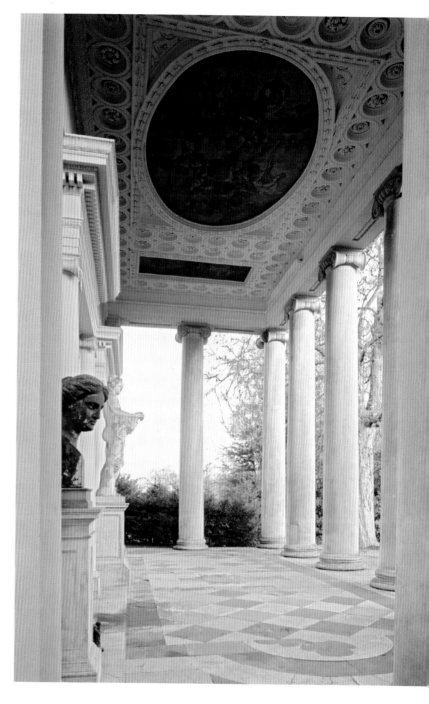

OPPOSITE The Palladian north front of West Wycombe Park is less theatrical than the other sides of the house and looks over the eighteenth-century landscape created by Sir Francis Dashwood.

ABOVE In 1771, a ceremony at West Wycombe to dedicate the dramatic west portico involved a procession of 'priests ... fauns, satyrs etc' and further celebrations in boats on the lake.

new features to the garden, such as the huge fibreglass equestrian statue on the crest of the hill above the house, and restored others that had been lost, among them the Temple of Venus on a grassy mound in the woods to the west of the lake.

From the north front of the house the ground falls away into a wooded valley, rising again to an extraordinary hexagonal mausoleum and the church remodelled by Sir Francis on the top of the hill opposite. Hidden in the valley is West Wycombe village, which was acquired by the Dashwood family, as part of the estate, in 1698. This is an exceptional place, owing much of its character to the fact that, before the building of the M40, it lay on the main route from London to Oxford, the Midlands

and Wales. Timber-framed, flint and brick cottages, many of them dating from the sixteenth century or earlier, line the long main street. One of the oldest buildings, the fifteenth-century Church Loft, was originally a rest house for pilgrims, and there are three former coaching inns.

ABOVE The huge portico on the west front of West Wycombe was designed as a replica of a Greek temple dedicated to Bacchus and has a large statue of the deity standing in the middle of the facade.
OPPOSITE The east end of the garden front at Wightwick Manor, with its rich and intricate timberwork, carved and fretted gables and soaring brick chimneys, was designed to look as picturesque as possible.

Wightwick Manor

West Midlands
3 miles (4.8 kilometres) west of
Wolverhampton, up Wightwick
Bank, beside the Mermaid Inn, just
north of the A454 Bridgnorth road

In 1848 seven young men barely out of their teens, including Holman Hunt, John Everett Millais and Dante Gabriel Rossetti, founded the Pre-Raphaelite Brotherhood, a revolt against the artistic establishment and what they perceived as the emptiness and artificiality of contemporary art. The group was short-lived, but its ideals were enormously influential, feeding into the reaction against mass production and the return to pre-industrial techniques that became identified with William Morris and the Arts and Crafts Movement. Rossetti, Ford Madox Brown and Burne-Jones were among the founders of Morris's design and furnishing company, which started life as an artist's co-operative in 1861 (*see* Red House, p.271).

Wightwick Manor is one of the best surviving examples of a house built and furnished under the influence of the Arts and Crafts Movement. Morris wallpapers, textiles and carpets and William de Morgan tiles and Benson metalwork supplied by his company set off paintings and drawings by Ford Madox Brown, Holman Hunt, Millais, Burne-Jones and Ruskin. The Jacobean furniture, oriental porcelain and Persian rugs with which the house is also furnished complement rather than compete with the nineteenth-century work, demonstrating how well Morris's work blends with good craftsmanship from other periods. There is a particularly pleasing juxtaposition of antique and Victorian in the drawing room, where rich green tiles by William de Morgan featuring a bestiary of mischievous creatures are inset into an Italian Renaissance chimneypiece.

Built in two stages in 1887 and 1893, Wightwick was commissioned by the industrialist Theodore Mander, a paint and varnish manufacturer, from the Liverpool architect Edward Ould, and was designed in a traditional, half-timbered idiom. The later, eastern half is more richly decorated and is clearly inspired by the Tudor buildings of the Welsh Marches. Decorative black-and-white timbering, in stripes, swirls and quatrefoils, rises from a plinth of local stone, with banks of spiral Tudor-style chimneys crowning the gabled roofline.

In keeping with the late-medieval character of the exterior, the heart of the house is a great parlour in the form of a feudal hall, with an open timber roof painted by the talented Charles Kempe. A minstrels' gallery across one end, a deeply recessed fireplace alcove and extensive use of panelling add to the period atmosphere. Kempe was also responsible for the glowing colours in the painted windows and the deep plaster frieze telling the story of Orpheus and Eurydice that may well have been inspired by that in the High Great Chamber at Hardwick (see p.161). Orpheus sits with his harp in a forest, enticing a whole menagerie of beasts with his music, from a trumpeting elephant and a kangaroo to a peacock with a golden tail. Morris's last woven fabric design, featuring white and pink blossom on a deep-blue ground, like a meadow full of spring flowers, hangs below the frieze. Wightwick also has a copy of Morris's last major artistic project, an edition of the works of Chaucer, published by Morris's Kelmscott Press in 1896. Burne-Jones, who was responsible for the book's intricate illustrations, is represented as well by his fine late work, *Love Among the Ruins*, which dominates the gallery end of the hall, the tendrils of briar rose in which he has entangled the young couple recalling those in his cycle of paintings at Buscot Park (see p.65). Photographs of the Pre-Raphaelites and their associates on an upstairs landing include one showing William Morris and Burne-Jones with their families in which only Janey Morris looks straight at the camera. A drawing of Scarborough by Turner that was recently found in the house and once belonged to Ruskin may also soon be on display.

The attractive 7-hectare (17-acre) garden slopes away from the house into a little valley with a stream and two pools and is shielded by trees and tall hedges from the suburbia around. First laid out on the advice of the painter Alfred Parsons, it was largely redesigned by the Edwardian landscape architect Thomas Mawson, who married strongly architectural formal gardens round the house, marked out with terraces, walls, clipped yew hedges and topiary, with an increasingly informal and natural approach to the layout and planting of the valley, which has orchards and paddocks and winding mown paths. Wisteria and other climbers flower on the house and there is a show of rhododendrons and azaleas round the two pools in the valley. A wooden bridge over the road up to the house was inspired by the Mathematical Bridge over the River Cam at Queens' College, Cambridge.

ABOVE Burne-Jones's *Love Among the Ruins*, painted in 1894, only four years before he died, hangs below the minstrels' gallery in the great parlour.

OPPOSITE Wightwick's period furnishings include a fine collection of richly coloured decorative tiles, many of them by William de Morgan.

2 Willow Road

London
Near the junction of Willow Road and Downshire Hill, Hampstead

Next to some assertive Victorian villas on the western edge of Hampstead Heath is an unobtrusive three-storey, brick and concrete rectangle with a flat roof and an uninterrupted expanse of glass lighting the first floor. Compact and all of a piece, what appears to be one house is in fact a terrace of three, with a hidden basement giving onto gardens behind.

This piece of pre-war modernism was the work of the anglophile Austro-Hungarian architect Ernö Goldfinger, who designed the central house for his artist wife Ursula Blackwell and their children and lived here from 1939 until his death in 1987. The first example of modernist architecture to be acquired by the National Trust, 2 Willow Road still has its original fixtures and fittings, including some of Ernö's prototype furniture, and the Goldfingers' important collection of contemporary art, reflecting their close links with the avant-garde. The couple met in Paris, where he had trained with Auguste Perret, known for his innovative use of reinforced concrete, and she was a student of the painter Amédée Ozenfant, who reacted to Cubism by advocating a return to a minimalist representational art, in which forms are reduced to 'pure' outline. The Goldfingers came to London in 1934, but in these pre-war years Ernö's designs, apart from some work for the toy firm Abbatt, were largely unexecuted. After the war, he was responsible for some of London's now controversial developments, notably the large office complex, now converted to housing, at Elephant and Castle and high-rise housing in North Kensington.

Willow Road probably sees Ernö at his best. Number 2 is by no means large, but there is a sense of both space and light, with the glass walls of the main rooms drawing the eye out over the heath in front and onto the south-facing balcony and gardens behind. Ernö's hand is in every detail. A spiral staircase is the backbone and main artery of the house, carrying the concrete frame. Wrapped round it on the first floor is a versatile space, with movable partitions and a change in floor level indicating dining room, studio and living room. Above is the nursery and bedroom floor, with compact internal bathrooms lit through the flat roof. Built-in wardrobes are flush with the wall, study bookshelves are recessed into a room partition and the studio has a tall cupboard for Ursula's canvases. The furniture too is functional, with upturned anglepoises either side of the low double bed in the master bedroom, a lino-topped dining-table on a lathe base, and dining-chairs made out of tubular metal and plywood.

But this is not an austere house. On the walls are some of Ursula's drawings, including a surreal vision of two huge disembodied ears, abstract and figurative works by Ozenfant, Delaunay, Max Ernst and Bridget Riley, a watercolour study for standing figures by Henry Moore, and a strong photographic portrait of Ursula by the Goldfingers' close friend Man Ray. Masks brought back from holidays in the Far East, one a grinning face surmounted by a writhing mass of cobras, provide colourful contrast and the artworks include two cars in typewriter script by Ernö's grandson Dominic. The living-room area has a parquet floor and oak-veneer panelling, and there are scarlet doors and areas of deep crimson paint. It is clear, too, that Goldfinger had a particular lifestyle in mind. The basement was designed with accommodation for two servants, and his house is the only one in the terrace to be provided with two garages, one of which has an inspection pit.

ABOVE LEFT The spiral staircase at 2 Willow Road has concrete steps supported from the wall, a brass handrail and a balustrade that is largely made out of rope.
OPPOSITE A wall of glass lights the main rooms on the first floor of the house, which look out over the leafy expanses of Hampstead Heath.

Wimpole Estate

Cambridgeshire
8 miles (12.8 kilometres) south-
west of Cambridge, 6 miles
(9.6 kilometres) north of Royston

When Rudyard Kipling visited his daughter Elsie here, a few months after she and her husband Captain George Bambridge took up residence at the house in 1936, he was moved to remark that he hoped she had not bitten off more than she could chew.

Two years later the Bambridges embarked on the restoration and refurnishing of the largest house in Cambridgeshire, whose red-brick and stone facades, three and four storeys high in the central block, stretch over 76 metres (250 feet) from end to end. A double staircase leads up to the pedimented entrance bay on the south front, which is ornamented with a Venetian window over the front door and a carved coat of arms in the pediment above. From here an immense avenue lined with young limes runs over 2 miles (3.2 kilometres) into the distance. Immediately in front of the house, urns and busts on pedestals flank the courtyard like guards standing rigidly to attention.

The remodelling of the original mid-seventeenth-century house by James Gibbs and, later, Henry Flitcroft, in the first half of the eighteenth century marks Wimpole's golden age. From 1713–40 the house was the property of Edward Harley, 2nd Earl of Oxford, who entertained a brilliant circle of writers, scholars and artists here, Swift and Pope among them, and whose household included a Master of the Horse, a Groom of the Chamber and a Master of Music. Perhaps it was for the latter and his orchestra that Lord Harley commissioned James Gibbs's baroque chapel, Bavarian in its opulence, which is such a striking feature of the house. In Sir James Thornhill's *trompe-l'oeil* decoration, statues of Saints Gregory, Ambrose, Augustine and Jerome stand in niches between pairs of classical columns, their shadows etched sharply on the stone behind. Gregory leans eagerly forward with a book in his hand, as if about to escape his perch, while half-naked St Jerome displays a splendidly muscled physique. The east wall is filled with Thornhill's *Adoration of the Magi*, in which the Three Kings are accompanied by a sizeable retinue of armed men and Mary herself sits amid a romantic classical ruin, her ruddy-faced, bearded husband watching quietly in the background.

Gibbs also designed the long library to house Harley's exceptional collection of books and manuscripts, the largest and most important ever assembled by a private individual in England and later to form the nucleus of the British Library. An oak and walnut pulpit on castors gives access to the upper shelves and a brown, pink and beige carpet picks up the subdued tones of the plaster ceiling. This room is reached through a gallery that was created by Henry Flitcroft in 1742 for Wimpole's next owner, Philip Yorke, 1st Earl of Hardwicke, as a setting for his finest paintings. Now used to display pictures particularly associated with the house, such as *The Stag Hunt* by John Wootton, who frequently visited Wimpole in Lord Harley's time, the room's long sash windows framed by red curtains and the grey-green walls help to create an atmosphere that is both restful and warm.

Wimpole's most individual interior, John Soane's Yellow Drawing Room, was added 50 years later, in the early 1790s, for Philip Yorke's great-nephew, the 3rd Earl. Running from the north front into the centre of the house, the room opens out into a domed oval at the inner end that is lit from a lantern in the roof above. Yellow silk on the walls sets off blue upholstery on the gilt chairs and on the long settees curved round two semicircular apses on the inner wall, with a large painting of cherubs at play above the chimneypiece that divides them. The overall effect is of a chapel transformed into a room of exceptional elegance and grace.

Soane's indulgent bath house, with a grand double staircase sweeping down to a tiled pool which holds over 9,000 litres (2,000 gallons) of water, is a delightful reminder of another side of eighteenth-century life.

When the Bambridges moved to Wimpole, they were faced with refurnishing a largely empty house, the contents of which had been gradually dispersed. Aided by royalties from the Kipling estate, which Mrs Bambridge inherited in 1936, they bought on their travels abroad and at auction, and Mrs Bambridge continued to buy after her husband's death in 1943. While he was responsible for two Tissots and a portrait by Tilly Kettle, she acquired portraits connected with the

OPPOSITE The magnificent library at Wimpole, finished in c.1730, was specifically designed to take Lord Harley's vast collection of books, pamphlets and manuscripts,

house and paintings by Mercier, Hudson and Romney. Porcelain figures on show are from her collection, and she also added notable books to the library, including some rare editions of Kipling's work.

Wimpole's extensive wooded park fully matches the grandeur of the house and reflects the influence of some of the most famous names in the history of landscape gardening. The great lime avenue running to the south, its unyielding lines striking through a patchwork of fields like a grassy motorway, was originally created by Charles Bridgeman, who was employed by Lord Harley in the 1720s to extend an elaborate formal layout which already included the east and west avenues to either side of the house.

Remarkably, these remains of what was once an extensive scheme of axial avenues, canalised ponds, ha-has and bastions survived the attentions of 'Capability' Brown and his disciple William Emes later in the century, both of whom set about 'naturalising' the park. The view from the north front, artfully framed by the clumps of trees with which Brown replaced a felled avenue, looks over his serpentine ornamental lake to a hillock crowned with a three-towered Gothick ruin. Built in 1774, this eye-catcher was based on designs by Sanderson Miller made 25 years before. Brown's belts of trees defining and sheltering the park were thickened and extended by Humphry Repton, who produced a Red Book for the 3rd Earl in 1801, but Repton also reintroduced a touch of formality, creating the small flower garden enclosed by iron railings on the north side of the house.

Sir John Soane's home farm to the north of the house, built in a pleasing mixture of brick, wood, tile and thatch, was also commissioned by the 3rd Earl, who was passionately interested in farming and agricultural improvement. Gaily painted wagons and carts now fill the thatched barn, but the surrounding paddocks and pens make up Wimpole's rare breeds farm.

LEFT Wimpole's palatial south front, over 76 metres (250 feet) long, looks down a great double avenue of lime trees stretching for more than two miles into the distance.
RIGHT A decorative dome carrying a lantern lights the inner end of the extraordinary T-shaped yellow drawing room.

A short distance south-east of the house is the parish church. Substantially rebuilt to Flitcroft's design in 1749, it is all that remains of the village that was swept away to create the park. In the north chapel, the only part of the medieval building not demolished in the mid-eighteenth century, the recumbent effigy of the 3rd Earl with his coronet at his feet dominates a number of grandiose monuments to successive owners of this palatial place, sleeping peacefully in the midst of all they once enjoyed. Banks and ditches in the grass to the south mark the house plots of medieval villagers who tilled the land centuries ago, the ridge and furrow they created still visible on a slope of old pasture.

Woolsthorpe Manor

Lincolnshire
At Woolsthorpe, 7 miles
(11.2 kilometres) south of
Grantham, ½ mile (0.8 kilometre)
north-west of Colsterworth, west
of the A1

The premature and sickly boy born in this modest limestone house on Christmas Day 1642 came into a world that believed that the Earth was the centre of the Universe. He grew up to be the leading scientist of his day, whose work was to lay the foundations of modern scientific thought and to show that our planet is merely a satellite of the Sun. The boy was Sir Isaac Newton, the offspring of a prosperous Lincolnshire farmer who died two months before his son's birth. While his mother raised a second family nearby, Isaac spent an isolated and introverted childhood at Woolsthorpe, cared for by his grandmother. Although he left to pursue his studies in Cambridge in 1661, he returned to Woolsthorpe again in 1665 when the university was closed by the plague. That year was to see some of Newton's most fruitful work, including the discovery of the principle of differential calculus.

With its mullioned windows and simple T-shaped plan, Woolsthorpe is a typical early seventeenth-century manor house, and was bought by Isaac's grandfather, Robert Newton, in 1623. Reflecting the inventory of Newton's mother's possessions and illustrating how simply even a moderately wealthy yeoman family would have lived at this date, its plain rooms are sparsely furnished. The young Newton is evoked in some scribbled drawings on the kitchen wall, among them a sketch of a post windmill and a rough outline of a church that may be a building he knew in Grantham, where he went to school. Upstairs is the room Isaac used when he came back from Cambridge to see his mother, now hung with a portrait of the great man by Thornhill and prints of other famous scientists of the day, many of whom fell out with their brilliant but difficult contemporary. Also here is a copy of the third edition of Newton's major work, the *Principia Mathematica*.

The original apple tree that helped Newton with his work on gravity is said to have blown down in 1820, but a gnarled old specimen in the current orchard is thought to have grown from a surviving part of the trunk. Newton's major scientific concepts are put across through some hands-on activities in the seventeenth-century threshing barn, and there is an exhibition on his life in the house.

ABOVE LEFT Woolsthorpe Manor, where the scientist Isaac Newton was born on Christmas Day 1642, is a small seventeenth-century manor house built of local limestone with original stone-mullioned windows.
ABOVE An Elizabethan table stands in the middle of Woolsthorpe's kitchen, where the young Newton is said to have covered the walls with his drawings.

Wordsworth House

Cumbria
Main Street, Cockermouth

Three men born in the early 1770s and known as the Lake Poets did much to change contemporary views of landscape, their appreciation of the wild beauty of nature suggesting new ideals for people seeking an escape from the realities of the Industrial Revolution. Of the three, William Wordsworth was the most innovative. Although he followed Robert Southey as poet laureate, Wordsworth's best work permanently enlarged the range and subject matter of English poetry, outclassing Southey's more pedestrian creations and the products of Samuel Taylor Coleridge's wayward genius. Wordsworth's love of the Lakes shows above all in the fact that he chose to live here all his life.

Although the adult Wordsworth is mainly connected with the southern Lakes, his formative years were spent in the north, in the prosperous little market town on the River Derwent where his father was agent to Sir James Lowther. The elegant Georgian house where he was born on 7 April 1770, almost two years before his sister Dorothy, stands at the west end of Cockermouth's main street, its garden stretching down to the river. Close by is the ruined castle from which William derived so much inspiration. The years he spent here, up to the age of 13, when his father died, left him with a deep love of Cumbria and also saw the forging of the intense bond with Dorothy that was so important to the poet in later life.

On the death of his father, Wordsworth and his siblings lost their home and the contents of the house were dispersed. Recent restoration has returned the interior to how it might have been when the Wordsworths lived here. The rooms are elegant but not showy, with carved overmantels and one ornamental plaster ceiling. Period colour schemes have been re-created based on paint samples taken from the house and the best rooms have been fitted out with mid- to late eighteenth-century furniture, including some pieces associated with the poet. A desk that belonged to Wordsworth's father, its surface strewn with copies of his letters and documents, dominates the panelled room by the front door that may have been his office. Upstairs, a panelled olive-green drawing room on the front of the house is graced by a set of walnut chairs that once belonged to Southey and a bureau-bookcase that was Wordsworth's; a sofa and longcase clock that belonged to the poet are also in the house. Other interiors, such as Mr Wordworth's bedroom or the re-created Georgian kitchen, are furnished with high-quality reproductions.

Luckily, the flood which swept through Cockermouth in November 2009 did not do serious damage to the house, but the garden was devastated. The greatest loss was the tree-lined terrace above the Derwent at the end of the garden where Wordsworth spent so many happy childhood hours with his beloved sister Dorothy, and which has had to be totally rebuilt. The garden has been re-created in an authentic eighteenth-century style, as it might have been in William and Dorothy's day.

BELOW All five Wordsworth children may once have slept in this large room looking onto the garden at the back of Wordsworth House, where William spent many happy hours with his sister Dorothy.

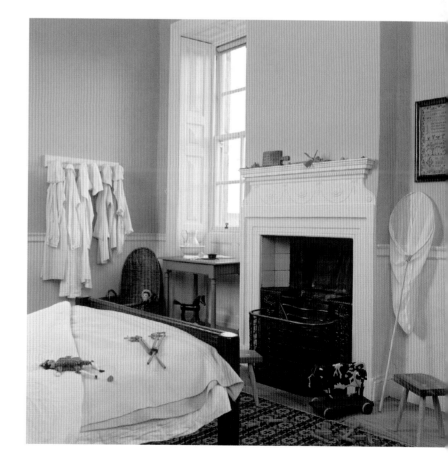

The Workhouse, Southwell

Nottinghamshire
8 miles (12.8 kilometres) from
Newark on the A617 and A612

On the eastern edge of Southwell, sitting well back from the road at the top of a gentle grassy slope, is a striking, early nineteenth-century building of mellow red brick. Three storeys tall with rows of regularly spaced iron-framed windows, massive chimneystacks and a grey slate roof, it is solid and functional, typical of the many institutional buildings of the period. It was built as a workhouse in 1824 as part of a pioneering approach to poor relief instigated by the Rev. J.T. Becher, a local magistrate. By the early nineteenth century, the existing system, based on the 1601 Poor Law that made each parish responsible for its destitute, was breaking down. Some parishes had banded together to provide workhouses, but the accent was on helping the poor to live in their own homes and this was no longer viable, partly because the scale of the problem had escalated, fuelled by agricultural depression, the return of soldiers from the Napoleonic wars and a rising population, partly because there was concern about a system that provided no incentive to work.

In Southwell, the Rev. Becher came up with a new approach that was designed to deter as well as provide relief. He tried it out first in a small workhouse just for Southwell parish, and then, in 1823, proposed a much larger institution to serve a group of neighbouring parishes. The workhouse was built on what were then open fields outside the town, with a plan that reflected the Rev. Becher's ideas on how denizens should be treated. Intended to house both the able-bodied and the aged and infirm, men, women and children, it was designed so each group would be segregated, day and night. Wives were separated from husbands, children from their parents. Inmates were made to wear a uniform, were fed the plainest of diets, and treated to a daily regime that involved hours of hard and monotonous work: breaking stones, unpicking old rope, digging the garden, or endlessly cleaning

the interior and repainting the walls. Above all, they were strictly supervised. It was a narrow and comfortless existence. All this is reflected in the plan of the workhouse, which has separate day rooms for each group on the ground floor, with segregated dormitories above. Inmates passed from one to the other by separate staircases, set side by side, and each day room gives onto a brickwalled yard, for work and exercise, with an open privy, just a hole in the ground, set behind a wall in the corner. From the yard, nothing can be seen of the outside world apart from the tops of the trees in the workhouse orchard.

The interior is shown unfurnished, as a succession of bare rooms with painted and whitewashed brick walls and stone-flagged or lime-ash floors, and is explained through an audio guide. Each room has a small fireplace. There are no

LEFT This hook on a peeling wall sums up the workhouse's desolate interior.
BELOW The food given to the inmates was laid down in dietary tables which specified what they were to have on each day of the week.
OPPOSITE A striking three-storey building with regularly spaced windows, the workhouse sits well back from the road, partly screened by its orchard.

cupboards or other fittings, just pegs in the walls where the paupers could hang their clothing. In the middle of the main range, marked by a projecting bay with a grand pedimented entrance, are the quarters for the master and the administration of the workhouse. Here the walls are plastered and there is a hierarchy of other refinements, which peaks with picture rails, skirting boards and a wooden floor in the master's office. There are cupboards, and the airy committee room where the workhouse guardians met, and where families could see each other briefly on Sundays, has a mantelpiece and a fender in front of the fire. From his rooms, the master could look down on paupers in the exercise yards, but there were some corners out of his sight, one of which has what may well be a gaming board scratched into the brickwork.

The Southwell Workhouse was studied by a Royal Commission looking into poor relief and became the prototype for a nationwide system as laid down in the New Poor Law of 1834. Hundreds of workhouses were built, 15 to 20 miles (24 to 32 kilometres) apart, each serving a group of parishes, and each operating on Becher principles. As the years passed, the focus shifted away from deterrence towards helping those who needed shelter and nursing, and the numbers needing relief declined. A red-brick building behind Southwell Workhouse was built in 1871 as an infirmary; the introduction of pensions in 1908 and national insurance in 1911 did much to alleviate the poverty of the old and unemployed; and children were moved to separate homes. Despite all this, the workhouse continued to be used into the 1990s and there is a room fitted out as a 1970s interior that would have housed an entire family.

ABOVE Oakhurst Cottage,
Surrey (see page 386).

Other Buildings

Aberconwy House

Conwy

At the junction of Castle Street and High Street in Conwy

When Edward I built his great castle at Conwy in 1283, he invited English settlers to colonise the little walled town established at its feet. This medieval house dating from the fourteenth century occupies what would have been a prime site in the new settlement, at the junction of High Street and Castle Street, the two principal thoroughfares, and close to the gate through which most of the town's trade passed down to the quay on the river. Now the oldest building in Conwy after the castle and the church, it is probably typical of the prosperous burgess houses that formed the body of the town, with two lower floors of stone supporting a half-timbered upper storey jettied out over the street. Furnished rooms illustrate life from different periods of the building's history.

Aberdeunant

Carmarthenshire

In the village of Taliaris, 4 miles (6.4 kilometres) north-east of Llandeilo, west of the B4302

Set at the head of a small valley, looking south over an undulating pastoral landscape divided by ancient hedgerows, is this traditional cruck-framed farmhouse, with rendered and limewashed walls of clay and stone and a thatched roof. Thought to be a rebuild of a late-medieval hall house with alterations in the sixteenth, seventeenth, eighteenth and nineteenth centuries, this rare survival is sited down the slope in the traditional way, with roof ridge and floors slanting noticeably from east to west. Inside, a winding stone stair leads up from the *gegin fawr*, or large kitchen, to three intercommunicating bedrooms, while a ladder from the *gegin fach*, or small kitchen, gives access to the traditional attic bedroom known as a crogloft. There is also a parlour and a small bedroom for a maid.

Outbuildings dating from the eighteenth and nineteenth centuries, mostly of stone and slate, are grouped round the house and the 59-hectare (147-acre) farm, with its mosaic of hay meadows, flower-rich pastures, unimproved marshy grassland and broad-leaved woodland, illustrates historic farming practices that have almost disappeared. Aberdeunant's survival is largely due to the Thomas family, who came here in 1852, and in particular to Gwylim Thomas, who farmed this valley until March 1997.

Ashleworth Tithe Barn (below)

Gloucestershire

6 miles (9.6 kilometres) north of Gloucester, 1 mile (1.5 kilometres) east of Hartpury (on the A417), on the west bank of the River Severn, south-east of Ashleworth

Ashleworth barn stands in a group of picturesque buildings on the banks of the River Severn, close to a riverside inn and a fine medieval house and just west of the largely fifteenth-century parish church. Although smaller than Great Coxwell or Middle Littleton (*see* pp.374 and 383), this substantial limestone building, with two projecting wagon porches, is still impressive. An immense stone-tiled roof is supported on timber trusses that stretch the width of the barn. It was built in about 1500, probably by the Canons of St Augustine's, Bristol, who were lords of the manor here.

Bembridge Windmill and Fort

Isle of Wight
Just south of Bembridge on the B3395

Set on a hill about a mile (1.6 kilometres) from the
easternmost point of the Isle of Wight, this weathered four-
storey stone mill with its great 9-metre (30-foot) sails is a
familiar landmark and has inspired generations of artists,
J.M.W. Turner among them. A fine example of an eighteenth-
century tower mill, Bembridge was built in about 1700 and
still contains original wooden machinery. The turning gear,
which rotated the wooden cap to bring the sweeps into the
wind, is still visible on the outside of the mill; the miller would
originally have operated it by walking round the building
hauling on a chain. For some 200 years until the outbreak of
the First World War the mill ground flour, meal and cattle feed
for the village and surrounding countryside. Derelict by the
1950s, it has now been partly restored and is the only
surviving windmill on the Isle of Wight.

On the downs to the south, what looks like a large
earthwork is the remains of a fort built in the 1860s as part of
Lord Palmerston's drive to strengthen the defences of the
south coast.

Blaise Hamlet

Bristol
4 miles (6.4 kilometres) north of central Bristol, west of
Henbury village, just north of the B4057

These nine rustic cottages set self-consciously around a green
were designed by John Nash, who was once heard to say that
no palace had ever given him as much pleasure as Blaise
Hamlet. His tiny settlement is certainly individual. Built in
1810–11 for the Quaker banker and philanthropist John
Harford, who had bought the Blaise Castle estate in 1789, it
was one of the first Picturesque estate villages and a reflection
of the growing appreciation of traditional vernacular
architecture. In this vision of an idealised village, each
building is different. Some are thatched, some tiled, and all
have varied rooflines, with gables and dormers at different
levels. Porches, verandahs, sheds and lean-tos ensure no
profile is repeated and contribute to the deliberate asymmetry.

Even the pump on the green is defiantly off-centre. But
everything in the hamlet is to the same scale and all the
cottages have soaring brick Tudoresque chimneys, now seen
against a backdrop of mature trees as Nash intended. And the
aged retainers whom Harford housed here were all provided
with a small garden and an outside seat where they could doze
on summer afternoons.

Boarstall Duck Decoy and Tower (below)

Buckinghamshire
Midway between Bicester and Thame, 2 miles (3.2 kilometres)
west of Brill

This enchanting three-storey tower, with hexagonal turrets
rising from each corner of the battlemented roofline, is all that
remains of the fortified moated house built here in the early
fourteenth century by John de Handlo. The only entrance to
his carefully guarded property was through this gatehouse,
its massive limestone walls, almost a metre (3 feet) thick,

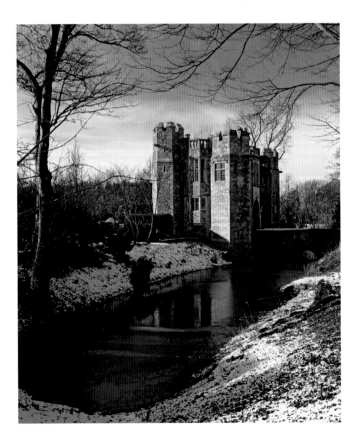

falling sheer to the waters of the moat and surviving arrow slits suggesting the formidable prospect it must once have presented.

Today Boarstall seems charmingly domestic. An array of Tudor and Jacobean windows surveys the world, octagonal chimneystacks rise almost to the height of the turrets, and a two-arched brick and cobble bridge leads over the moat. A beautiful room running 12 metres (40 feet) across the length of the third floor, now occasionally used for chamber concerts, was probably once a dormitory for the men of the establishment.

At the back of the tower, peacocks strut across romantic informal twentieth-century gardens. Just over the fields a tree-fringed lake marks Boarstall Duck Decoy, one of the few surviving working examples of a once-common feature of the English countryside, introduced from Holland by Charles II. Ducks enticed into netted-over channels leading off the lake were once an important source of winter food but are now ringed for scientific purposes.

Bodysgallen Hall Hotel
Conwy
Off the A470 above Llandudno

This tall, many-gabled stone house with stone-mullioned windows and massive chimneys stands high on a hill above Llandudno, with spectacular views of Snowdonia. The date 1620 on one of the gables flags the seventeenth-century south front, but the house also incorporates a five-storey tower which may date from the late thirteenth century, the kitchen wing was added in 1730, and in *c.*1900 Lady Augusta Mostyn, whose family had been connected with the place since the sixteenth century, restored and enlarged it for her second son Henry. Of the seventeenth-century interiors, the large entrance hall and the equally capacious chamber above, now the drawing room, survive. Bodysgallen is set off by romantic walled gardens and surrounded by 81 hectares (200 acres) of parkland. A hotel since the early 1980s, when it was acquired and restored by Historic House Hotels, the house was generously given to the National Trust by the group in 2008, together with Hartwell House and Middlethorpe Hall (*see* pp.376 and 384).

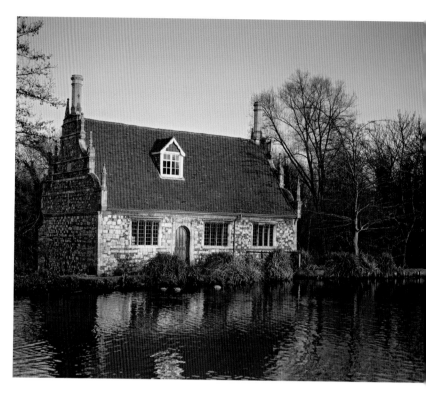

Bourne Mill (above)
Essex 1 mile (1.6 kilometres) south of the centre of Colchester, in Bourne Road, off the Mersea road (B1025)

This unusual little building with dormer windows in its steeply pitched roof and fanciful pinnacled Dutch-style gables was built by Sir Thomas Lucas as a banqueting house in 1591. Constructed of rubble and brick from the ruins of the Abbey of St John in Colchester, which had been dissolved some half a century before, the walls incorporate Roman remains and various medieval moulded stones, and the lake-like millpond may have been the monks' stewpond. A weather-boarded projecting sack hoist and the surviving machinery, including a 5.5-metre (18-foot) overshot waterwheel with 64 buckets, date from the mid-nineteenth century, when the mill was first used to grind corn. For the previous 200 years it had played a part in the East Anglian cloth industry and was used to spin yarn and for fulling woven cloth. Golden-yellow butterworts and other water-loving plants along the mill-stream and borders filled with herbs and medicinal plants contribute to the special appeal of this property.

Bradenham Village

Buckinghamshire

4 miles (6 kilometres) north-west of High Wycombe,
off the A4010

This pretty village, with flint and tile-hung cottages straggling
round a large sloping green, lies in a fold of the Chilterns
backed by beech woods on the hill above. Most of the cottages
date from the sixteenth or seventeenth century and are timber-
framed behind their later facings, while at the top of the
green, surveying all, is a fine late seventeenth-century red-
brick manor house with long sash windows and a hipped roof
and, beside it, a little flint church with elaborate Norman
carving round the south door. The manor is now offices, but
once it was the home of the writer Isaac D'Israeli, whose
oldest son, the Victorian prime minister Benjamin Disraeli,
bought the Hughenden estate just over the hill (*see* p.174).

Bradley (right)

Devon

On the outskirts of Newton Abbot, on the A381 Totnes road

From the top of Wolborough Hill just outside Newton Abbot
there is a panoramic view over rolling countryside to the
windswept heights of Dartmoor. Deep in the valley below, half
hidden by a thick blanket of oak and beech, is this L-shaped
medieval manor house, with glimpses of gables and tall
chimneys through the trees. A long, low building, home of the
Yarde family for over 300 years, it is built of roughcast local
limestone limewashed white, with granite doorways and
fireplaces and a slate roof. Despite some intrusive nineteenth-
century castellations, the striking east facade is almost entirely
fifteenth century, from the projecting chapel with a
magnificent Perpendicular window at one end to the original
cusped Gothic lights in the gables.

The interior is medieval in plan, with a screens passage
running across the house and a hall open to the rafters. The
rooms are mostly low-ceilinged and rough-walled, with a
massive granite fireplace in the old kitchen. Only the hall is
spacious, and here there is a brightly painted Tudor coat of
arms high on an end wall and a carved oak screen in the arch
leading to the chapel. In an upstairs room, lifelike depictions

of roses, tulips, primroses, acorns and beech husks in the
seventeenth-century plasterwork echo the flowers and trees in
the woods around the house. Good collections of Pre-
Raphaelite paintings and Arts and Crafts furniture are in tune
with the medieval setting.

Braithwaite Hall

North Yorkshire

1½ miles (2 kilometres) south-east of Middleham, 2 miles
(3.2 kilometres) west of East Witton

This remote seventeenth-century stone farmhouse is the
centre of a hill farm in Coverdale on the eastern edge of the
Pennines. Massive chimneystacks frame the gabled principal
facade with mullioned windows looking north to Wensleydale.
Original interior features include seventeenth-century

fireplaces, oak panelling in the drawing room and the exceptional oak staircase with turned balusters which rises from the stone-flagged hall.

Branscombe: the Old Bakery, Garden and Estate
Devon
Off the A3052, between Sidmouth and Seaton

Among the picturesque stone and cob cottages straggling along a lush green valley towards the sea which make up Branscombe are three examples of the kind of working buildings that were once found in every village. Below the church, at the bottom of the hill leading down into the village, are a working smithy and, in an orchard on the other side of the road, the old bakery (now a tea-room), both of them in thatched premises over 200 years old. Further down the valley is the stone-walled, slate-roofed manorial water mill, which once supplied the bakery with flour and is now restored to working order.

Bredon Barn
Worcestershire
3 miles (4.8 kilometres) north-east of Tewkesbury, just north of the B4080

This cathedral-like building once slumbered peacefully on the banks of the River Avon, but the ceaseless roar of traffic on the M5 has now destroyed its tranquillity. Built in 1350 for the Bishops of Worcester, lords of the manor here for about 600 years, Bredon Barn is beautifully constructed of local Cotswold stone, with stone tiles on the steeply pitched roof. It is the only aisled barn in Worcestershire: 18 great posts like the columns of a nave march down the interior, some blackened timbers being a salutary reminder of the fire that badly damaged the building in 1980.

External stone steps lead up to a room over one of the two porches on the east side, comfortably equipped with a fireplace and a garderobe. From here the bishop's reeve could look down into the barn to check on the corn being brought in and the threshers at work.

Bridge House (below)
Cumbria
In the middle of Ambleside

This tiny, two-storey building poised precariously on a bridge over the Stock Ghyll in the middle of Ambleside has been immortalised by numerous artists, including Turner and Ruskin. With rough stone walls and a slate roof, it dates from the seventeenth century and has just two rooms, one above the other. Built as a summerhouse and covered bridge for the Braithwaites of Ambleside Hall up the hill, it is said to have housed a family of eight in the mid-nineteenth century and has also served as a cobbler's shop and a tea-room. It is now a National Trust information centre.

Bruton Dovecote
Somerset
½ mile (0.8 kilometre) south of Bruton across the railway,
just west of the B3081

Nothing remains of the Augustinian abbey that once
dominated the little town of Bruton except a section of
wall and this unusual dovecote, standing alone on a hillock
in what was the abbey's deer park. Adapted by the monks
from a gabled Tudor tower with mullioned windows, it is
now roofless.

Buckingham Chantry Chapel
Buckinghamshire
On Market Hill, Buckingham

The fine Norman arch over the south door, probably brought
here from elsewhere and originally intended for somewhere
grander, is the most memorable feature of this tiny, 11.5-metre
(38-foot) rubble-built fifteenth-century chapel, the oldest
building in Buckingham. It was used as a school from the
Reformation until 1907 and was substantially restored by Sir
George Gilbert Scott in 1875.

Buscot Old Parsonage (above)
Oxfordshire
On A417 between Lechlade and Faringdon

On the banks of the Thames a mile (1.6 kilometres) or so
below Lechlade is this beautiful three-storey house of Cotswold
stone, built in 1703 to a symmetrical design. A central flight of
steps gives access to the raised ground floor and some of the
rooms have original painted panelling. Close by is the
thirteenth-century church of St Mary, with Pre-Raphaelite
stained-glass windows by Burne-Jones, whose friend William
Morris lived at Kelmscott Manor across the river.

Cartmel Priory Gatehouse
Cumbria
Cavendish Street, Cartmel

Although both the turret and battlements that once crowned
this picturesque stone gatehouse-tower straddling Cavendish
Street have been removed, it still rises imposingly above the
roofs of the surrounding houses, a reminder of the need for
protection against attacks by the Scots in the troubled border
country of the Middle Ages. Apart from the church of St Mary,

it is all that remains of the Augustinian monastery founded here in 1189–90; the strengthening of the priory's defences with the construction of the gatehouse in 1330–40 may have been prompted by Robert the Bruce's devastating raids in the neighbourhood a few years earlier. Despite the insertion of later windows and the slate roof, this former stronghold has a substantially medieval appearance and is the only secular pre-Reformation building in Cartmel. The large room over the archway was once used for manorial courts and from 1624–1790 as a school.

Chiddingstone Village (below)
Kent
4 miles (6.4 kilometres) east of Edenbridge

This leafy single-street village is one of the most attractive of the Kentish Weald. Opposite the largely seventeenth-century church of St Mary stands a perfect group of sixteenth- and seventeenth-century timber-framed buildings with overhanging upper storeys, bargeboarded gables and lichen-stained, red-tiled roofs. What is now the village shop and post office is mentioned in a deed of 1453, and most of the houses probably incorporate earlier material. Built at a time when the Wealden iron industry was at its height, Chiddingstone was originally part of a much larger settlement, but much of this was destroyed when Chiddingstone Castle park was created. The sandstone block known as the Chiding Stone, by which

local men are supposed to have chided their nagging wives, and from which the village is said to take its name, lies in the park, below the hill crowned with the Gothick castle (not owned by the National Trust).

Chipping Campden Market Hall
Gloucestershire
Opposite the police station, Chipping Campden

This little gabled and pinnacled Jacobean building stands prominently in the centre of Chipping Campden, on one side of the wide high street. Like the medieval houses of wool merchants with which it is surrounded, the market hall is built of golden Cotswold stone and roofed with stone slabs. Open arcades on all four sides give access to the cobbled floor where farmers and traders gathered to sell and buy cheese, butter and poultry.

As the coat of arms in a gable at one end signifies, the market hall was built by Sir Baptist Hicks in 1627, only two years before his death. A financier who helped support the extravagances of the court of James I, Baptist Hicks was raised to the peerage at the end of his life and is commemorated by a restrained classical monument in the south chapel of the wool church down the street.

The Church House
Devon
Widecombe in the Moor, in the centre of Dartmoor, north of Ashburton, west of Bovey Tracey

The medieval church in this over-visited Dartmoor village boasts a magnificent early sixteenth-century pinnacled tower, paid for by prosperous tin miners. The two-storey granite building known as the Church House in the tiny square by the lych gate is of much the same period, dating from 1537. One of the finest such houses in Devon, it is substantial and well proportioned, with round-headed two-light granite windows and a verandah supported on octagonal granite pillars running the length of the entrance front. Each pillar rests on a roughly hewn boulder. Originally a brew-house, it later became a school and is now partly leased as the village hall and partly used as a National Trust information centre and shop.

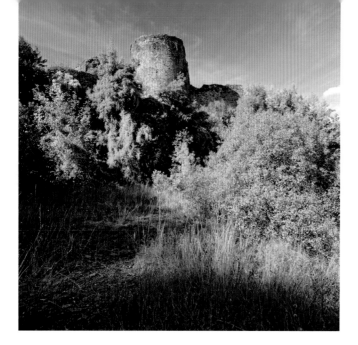

Cilgerran Castle (above)
Pembrokeshire
On rock above the left bank of the Teifi, 3 miles (4.8 kilometres) south of Cardigan, 1¹/₂ miles (2.4 kilometres) east of the A478

Like the great fortress at Durham, Cilgerran is so superbly sited that it seems a natural part of the landscape. Round towers linked by massive walls over a metre (3 feet) wide in places stand on a rocky bluff above wooded slopes plunging precipitously to the gorge of the Teifi River and its tributary the Plysgog. Only a few miles from the sea, Cilgerran could be supplied by water and also controlled the crossing point at the tidal limit of the Teifi. Once a formidable stronghold, the castle on its leafy height has for long been a romantic and picturesque ruin and has inspired a number of artists, Turner, Richard Wilson and Pieter de Wint among them.

Built by William Marshall, Earl of Pembroke, in about 1225 on the site of an earlier stronghold captured from the Welsh in the Norman conquest of Wales, Cilgerran was constructed only a few years after Skenfrith (see p.391), but already castle design had moved on. In place of a central keep, the defensive strength of the place is concentrated in the two round towers projecting from the curtain wall that encloses the tip of the promontory. The remains of a third, rectangular tower probably date from the late fourteenth century, when Edward III ordered the reinforcement of a number of Welsh castles against the threat of a French invasion. In the event, it was the south coast of England that suffered, with raids from Rye to Plymouth. A wide ditch, once crossed by a drawbridge leading to the gatehouse, separates this inner ward from the outer court; the grooves for two portcullises still mark the walls of the gatehouse. A second great ditch added further protection beyond the outer ward, where little of the original defences survives. Possibly ruined at the time of Owen Glendower's revolt in 1405, when the castle was briefly held by the Welsh, Cilgerran seems never to have been subsequently repaired.

Cobham Wood and Mausoleum
Kent
At the east end of Cobham village

Overlooking Cobham Hall (not National Trust), and set amongst open woodland where some of the mature trees date from Humphry Repton's landscaping of the park in the early nineteenth century, is an arresting stone building, with a pyramidal roof rising from columned facades. Designed by James Wyatt and built in the mid-1780s for John Bligh, 3rd Earl of Darnley, it was intended as a mausoleum for the earl and his descendants. A bridge over a dry moat leads to the chapel filling the interior; beneath it is a vaulted crypt with shelves to hold the dead. Long neglected and vandalised in the twentieth century, the mausoleum has now been restored after a 50-year struggle to secure its future. For reasons unknown, it was never consecrated and the earl and his descendants are buried in Cobham parish church nearby.

Coggeshall Grange Barn
Essex
¹/₂ mile (0.8 kilometre) south of Coggeshall, on the B1024

This majestic building, with a sweeping tiled roof above weather-boarded walls, is one of the oldest timber-framed barns in Britain. Constructed for the Savigniac monks of Coggeshall Abbey, it dates from the thirteenth century. Although the barn was extensively rebuilt in the late fourteenth century, original posts still support the roof. A thirteenth-century chapel not far away once stood outside the abbey gate, and some other monastic buildings are now part of a nearby farm. A small collection of farm carts and wagons is housed in the barn.

Coleridge Cottage

Somerset

At the west end of Nether Stowey, on the south side of the A39, 8 miles (12.8 kilometres) west of Bridgwater

The Ancient Mariner pub at the end of Lime Street flags the rather unprepossessing cottage across the road where the young Samuel Taylor Coleridge lived for three years from 1797 with his wife Sara and infant son Hartley. Once a pretty, low, thatched building, it was substantially altered at the end of the nineteenth century and only the four front rooms are relatively unchanged. Coleridge wrote some of his best poems here, including 'Fears in Solitude', 'This Lime Tree Bower My Prison', 'The Nightingale', 'Frost at Midnight', the first part of 'Christabel' and 'The Rime of the Ancient Mariner', with its many references to places in the neighbourhood. Here, too, he eagerly started to set down the opium-inspired 'Kubla Khan', the visionary epic that came to him in his sleep and that he was prevented from completing while it was still fresh in his mind by the interruption of 'a person ... from Porlock'.

Some rooms are now presented as they might have been in Coleridge's time and mementoes of the poet include his boulle inkstand, locks of his hair and letters in his distinctive hand. There are pictures of the Devon village where he was born, the church where he was married, the room in London at No. 3 The Grove, Highgate, where he died, and also of friends and acquaintances. In the little garden at the back of the house the lime-tree bower of the poem has disappeared, but the bay tree still stands as it did when Coleridge dug this plot.

Conwy Suspension Bridge (right)

Conwy

100 metres (330 feet) from Conwy town centre, adjacent to Conwy Castle

Increasing trade with Ireland in the late seventeenth and early eighteenth centuries meant that goods had to be carried to and from Holyhead along the appalling roads of North Wales and ferried across the wide estuary of the Conwy and the tide-race of the Menai Strait. The only alternative was a journey of about 15 miles (24 kilometres) upriver to the first bridge at Llanrwst. In 1811 the great engineer Thomas Telford, by then

54 years old and much in demand, was asked to survey a road to Holyhead. The route he devised through Snowdonia is a triumph. Now followed by the A5, it never exceeds the gradient of 1 in 50 which allowed a stagecoach to make a steady 10 miles (16 kilometres) an hour.

Six years later, when Telford designed a bridge to carry the road across the Menai Strait, he opted for a suspension bridge, producing only the third such structure to be built in the British Isles. His scheme for Conwy came shortly afterwards, his early plan for conventional arches soon abandoned in favour of another suspension bridge. The site of the crossing is magnificent. On the wooded left bank of the river the bridge seems to spring from the rocky crag crowned with medieval Conwy Castle. With their battlements and machicolations, the turrets supporting the road look like extensions of the castle itself. Between them stretches the 100-metre (327-foot) span of the bridge, suspended from the graceful curve of the original chains.

The bridge was opened in 1826, the same year that the Menai Bridge was badly damaged in a storm, convincing the old engineer that a length of 183 metres (600 feet) was the limit (although young Brunel's design for the Clifton Bridge over the Avon was to exceed this span in Telford's lifetime). The bridge and toll-house have been restored to their nineteenth-century glory and the road surface reconstructed to a contemporary specification.

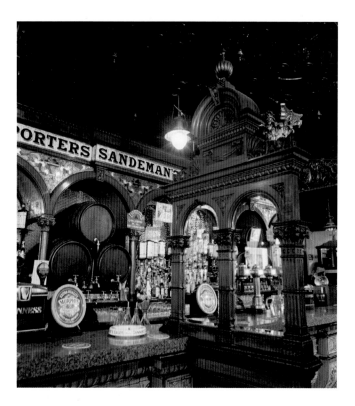

The Crown Bar (above)
Belfast
Great Victoria Street, Belfast

The Crown Bar glitters and gleams. Coloured glass in bright blues, oranges and reds sparkles behind the bar, mirrors reflect tiles and polished wood, and the shiny finish on the moulded ceiling is a kaleidoscope of changing patterns set up by the lively clientele below. Originally the Railway Tavern, designed to serve thirsty travellers disgorged from the terminus of the Great Northern railway across the street, the Crown was renamed in 1885 and remodelled in 1898 to produce this High Victorian fantasy, one of the greatest late nineteenth-century public houses in the British Isles.

Classical pilasters, a parapet topped with urns and a portico crowned with finials and supported by cast-iron columns add theatrical touches to the exterior, suggesting an affinity with Frank 'Matchless' Matcham's opera house close by. Inside, drinkers can be convivial or sit in secluded intimacy. A long bar runs down one side of the room, its inward curve designed for the comfort of those perched on stools along its length.

Facing the bar is a row of snugs enclosed by screens of wood and coloured glass, guarded by crouching heraldic beasts and fitted out with upholstered benches and tables. With the door shut, the snugs become private drinking compartments. Mellow gaslight, bar staff in waistcoats and bow ties and a menu board offering Irish broth and oysters in season all contribute to the individual atmosphere.

Cwmmau Farmhouse
Herefordshire
Near Brilley Mountain, 4 miles (6.4 kilometres) south-west of Kington between the A4111 and the A438

Winding lanes lead to this half-timbered black-and-white farmhouse set in a slight hollow in the hillside in one of the most beautiful and remote areas of the Welsh borders. Although for many years a farmhouse, as the eighteenth-century barns and other outbuildings grouped round a yard to one side confirm, this attractive and substantial place was built in the 1620s as a hunting lodge for Philip Holman, who had bought the estate in 1621 and became High Sheriff of Herefordshire a few years later.

The wattle and daub which originally infilled the timber framing was replaced with brick in the early nineteenth century. At that time the farm employed a sizeable workforce, but after a sale in 1918, when the estate which then owned it was broken up, Cwmmau was increasingly neglected and derelict and some original features, including oak panelling, the huge oak front door (the frame for which can still be seen), the staircase and doors to the rooms upstairs, were sold to America. The house was rescued by George Menges, a Lloyds underwriter, who bought it in 1934 and, together with his wife Ianthe and sister-in-law Phyllis Jerrold, meticulously restored it and added panelling to the south-facing parlour. Phyllis enriched the house with paintings and needlework, examples of her work here now including a coverlet embroidered with flowers in one of the bedrooms, a honeysuckle painted on panelling in the hall, and a wax crayon mural of the story of Genesis in the little room over the porch, to which George and Ianthe contributed the decorative borders.

Cwmmau came to the National Trust on George's death in 1964 and is now fitted out as holiday accommodation.

Dalton Castle
Cumbria
At the top of the high street in Dalton-in-Furness

Overlooking the market place in the middle of Dalton-in-Furness is this arresting rectangular tower, built of limestone rubble with sandstone dressings. With walls 1.5 metres (5 feet) thick and a roofline parapet pierced with arrow loops corbelled out from the walls, the tower looks defensive but, although dating from the fourteenth century, when this part of the world was much troubled by Scottish raids, it was built as a manorial courthouse for Furness Abbey. Originally it included a guardroom and a dungeon (the pit for which can still be seen) as well as the abbot's courtroom. There is some medieval stonework in the traceried windows and weathered sandstone figures at each corner of the parapet are carvings of fourteenth-century men-at-arms; a grinning head is the only survivor of the ten gargoyles that once marked the base of the parapet. The abbey was dissolved in 1537, and drastic remodelling in 1856 by the 5th Duke of Buccleuch, whose family had acquired the place in 1767, resulted in two of the three upper floors being removed and a new staircase built to supplement the original stone spiral stair in the thickness of the west wall. A collection of sixteenth- and seventeenth-century armour was introduced at about this time.

Manorial courts continued to be held here until 1923. Today, there is a small museum of local history on the ground floor.

Derrymore House (above right)
Co. Armagh
On the A25, off the Newry–Camlough road at Bessbrook, 1½ miles (2.4 kilometres) north-west of Newry

Set on a natural terrace with fine views over Newry and to the Mourne Mountains beyond is this delightful example of the kind of artfully rustic buildings that were added to many Irish estates in the late eighteenth century. Often these *cottages ornées* were just designed to be garden ornaments or eye-catchers in the park, but a few, Derrymore among them, were intended to be lived in.

One-storey ranges like diminutive cottages enclose three sides of an oblong courtyard. There are plentiful windows in

the primrose yellow walls, including a huge polygonal bay looking out over the park, and each side of the house is separately thatched. The interior is plainly decorated with simple ornamental mouldings and there is a marble fireplace in the drawing room.

The architect of this attractive place is unknown, but John Sutherland, who laid out the naturalistic landscape park, may well also have designed the house. It was built for the politician Isaac Corry, who represented Newry in the Irish Parliament for 30 years and rose to be Chancellor of the Exchequer in 1799. Despite his own generously fenestrated house, he introduced a window tax.

Derwent Island House
Cumbria
In Derwentwater, Keswick

This intriguing house, reachable only by boat, is set on the largest of the four wooded islands that dot the length of Derwentwater. It dates from the late eighteenth century, when the wealthy Joseph Pocklington, who had inherited a fortune from his banker father, built a pedimented villa here, and it was then extended in an Italianate style in the 1840s by Anthony Salvin, who fitted out the interiors with restrained classical decoration. Salvin was working for Henry Cowper Marshall, whose father had founded the Leeds flax-spinning industry, and Marshalls continued to live here until the house came to the National Trust in 1951. Some of the original furnishings are still here, among them the 1850s mahogany and carved oak pieces supplied by the Leeds cabinet makers John Kendell

& Co. in the dining room and the English and Dutch paintings, including works by Charles Eastlake, Edwin Landseer, Jacob Storck and Jan Steen, which hang in Salvin's capacious staircase hall. And Henry Marshall was responsible for the landscaped grounds and fine trees that set off the house.

Most evocative is Pocklington's first-floor drawing room, which was designed to have views across the lake in three directions. From here, and from the terrace added by Salvin at one end of the room, there are panoramic vistas north to Skiddaw, west to the ridge of Catbells and south down the water to the fells at the heart of the Lake District, showing how this magical scenery, for so long unappreciated, was beginning to be admired in the late eighteenth century.

Dinton Park and Philipps House
Wiltshire
In Dinton, 9 miles (14.4 kilometres) west of Salisbury, on the north side of the B3089

This severe Neo-classical house in the Vale of Wardour was designed by Jeffry Wyatt (later Sir Jeffry Wyatville), who is better known for his work in the neo-Gothic style and particularly for his alterations to Windsor Castle. Philipps House, built between 1814 and 1817, does not show this versatile architect at his most inspired. Built of local Chilmark limestone, from the same quarry that had produced the stone for Salisbury Cathedral 600 years previously, it is a plain two-storey rectangle with rows of sash windows and a parapet concealing the hipped roof, the only notable feature being a pedimented portico rising the height of the building on the south facade. A curved kitchen wing curling away from the house adds a welcome touch of asymmetry.

Wyatt's interiors are similarly austere and unadorned, the fine mahogany doors and marble chimneypieces restrained and stylised. His coolly elegant staircase, top-lit from a circular lantern, rises through the heart of the house, the grand lower flight sweeping imperiously upwards from the centre of the hall to divide at a half-landing into two parallel stairs to the first floor. Brass outlets in the flags of the hall below are remnants of the original underfloor heating system, installed in the 1820s, and there is some fine Regency furniture. The house was created for William Wyndham IV, whose family had

been at Dinton since 1689 and lived here until 1917. The undulating parkland was landscaped in the eighteenth century and contains some magnificent specimen trees.

Duffield Castle
Derbyshire
On the northern edge of Duffield village

A defensible spur between the River Derwent and its tributary the Ecclesbourne at the north end of Duffield village was once crowned by the stone keep of a formidable Norman castle. Built by William Ferrers in 1177–90 to replace earlier work in timber, the great keep, with walls up to 4.6 metres (15 feet) thick, was razed to the ground during the Montfortian rebellion of the 1260s. The castle mound, built on a prominent knoll overlooking the Derwent and reached up a long and steep flight of steps, is impressive still and gives spectacular views across the river valley, but there are no visible remains of the keep, some stones on the top of the mound outlining the foundations probably having been put in place in the nineteenth century. Two ditches which defined the bailey to the west have now been engulfed by housing, but a small fragment of ditch still survives in the grounds of Castlehill House to the south.

Dunstanburgh Castle (right)
Northumberland
9 miles (14.4 kilometres) north-east of Alnwick

No roads lead to Dunstanburgh. This magnificent ruin stands lonely and isolated on the Northumbrian coast and can be reached only by walking along a grassy track beside the sea from Craster to the south or Embleton to the north. Built where the Great Whin Sill reaches the sea in a bold outcrop of basalt, the castle occupies a natural defensive site. To the north, soaring cliffs fall sheer to the waves breaking on the rocks below; to the west the ground drops almost as precipitously to the patchwork of fields stretching away to the Cheviots; and on the east the sea is again a natural barrier, although the shore slopes gently here. The castle was most vulnerable to the south, where it now overlooks land that is marshy and cut off from the sea but where once there was a deep inlet that was used as a harbour.

Dunstanburgh's might is concentrated in massive towers set along the walls enclosing the castle's outer ward. An impressive gatehouse-keep with two D-shaped towers bulging out round the entrance passage guards the castle's south-west corner and further towers project from the curtain wall running east along the southern side of the site. To the north the long finger of the Lilburn Tower stands silhouetted against the sky on the highest point of the bluff.

Dunstanburgh was built between 1313 and 1316 for Thomas, 2nd Earl of Lancaster and grandson of Henry III. But the earl had little time to enjoy his castle: following his defeat by his cousin Edward II at the Battle of Boroughbridge, he was executed in 1322. Strengthened by John of Gaunt in the late fourteenth century as a stronghold against the Scots, Dunstanburgh's defences were put to the test in the Wars of the Roses, when the Yorkists besieged Lancastrian forces here in 1462 and 1464. Severely damaged in these engagements, the castle was barely repaired; too remote to be useful, it was quarried for building materials and gradually decayed into an empty shell. It is now a hauntingly beautiful place, the restless murmur of the sea and the plaintive cries of seabirds wheeling overhead adding to its enchantment.

Eastbury Manor House
London
In Eastbury Square, Barking, ¹/₄ mile (0.4 kilometre) south of Upney station

This arresting, three-storey, red-brick building, now surrounded by a municipal housing estate, is a fine example of an Elizabethan manor house. Dating from *c.*1572, it has mullioned windows, finialled Dutch-style gables, huge chimneystacks and an original spiral staircase. With the exception of some early seventeenth-century wall paintings, few original interior features remain. West of the house a Tudor-style kitchen garden has recently been created, and the walled garden to the east survives.

Elizabethan House Museum
Norfolk
4 South Quay, Great Yarmouth

The elegant early nineteenth-century brick frontage of this three-storey house, with a classical portico sheltering the front door and ironwork balconies decorating the sash windows on the first floor, is only a facade. Behind lies an Elizabethan building dating from 1596 in which many original features, such as oak panelling, carved chimneypieces and moulded plaster ceilings, survive. The house is now a museum of domestic life run by Norfolk Museums and Archaeology Service.

Finch Foundry (right)
Devon
At Sticklepath, 4 miles (6.4 kilometres) east of Okehampton, off the A30

Now bypassed by the busy A30, Sticklepath stands on the old route from Exeter to Okehampton, where the youthful River Taw has carved a deep valley into the northern flank of the Dartmoor massif. The nineteenth-century Finch Foundry, housed in rugged buildings of granite and cob, is the only survivor of the village's once flourishing water-powered industry. Used to produce agricultural implements and tools for the local mining and china clay industries, the foundry is still in working order, its three overshot wheels driving huge tilt hammers, a grindstone, metal-cutting shears and a polishing wheel. In business from 1814 to 1960, the foundry was always a Finch family affair, and there was much ad hoc patching-up of machinery and buildings. Demonstrations are given every hour.

Flatford: Bridge Cottage (below)
Suffolk
On the north bank of the River Stour, 1 mile (1.6 kilometres)
south of East Bergholt

This gentle countryside on the banks of the lower Stour, with
its meadows, ponds and pollarded willows and a cluster of
half-timbered houses and cottages, is where the artist John
Constable spent his boyhood and where he painted some of
his most evocative work. The National Trust's holding of some
200 hectares (495 acres) includes the eighteenth-century
water-mill which was owned by Constable's father and which
the artist painted, and also the substantial Suffolk farmhouse
known as Willy Lott's House, which appears in *The Hay-Wain*.
These and other buildings are let to the Field Studies Council
and are not open, but there is a small permanent exhibition on
John Constable and his links to Flatford at Bridge Cottage and

visitors to the area can experience Constable's viewpoints for
themselves. There are gentle walks along the valley towards
Dedham through the meadows fringing the Stour.

The Fleece Inn
Worcestershire
In Bretforton, 4 miles (6.4 kilometres) east of Evesham,
on the B4035

The delightfully irregular, black-and-white half-timbered
facades of this little village pub with a partly tiled, partly
thatched roof date back to *c*.1400, when the inn started life as
a one-storey long house, sheltering a farmer and his stock
under the same roof. Owned by the same family from the
Middle Ages until it was bequeathed to the National Trust in
1978, the building is crammed with furniture, crockery and
farming implements handed down through the generations.
It has been an inn since 1848, when Henry Byrd Taplin
decided to become a publican rather than a farmer, and what
was once the byre for the animals is now the beer cellar at the
south end of the building. Beer was still being brewed for sale
in the back kitchen well into the twentieth century.

George Stephenson's Birthplace
Northumberland
8 miles (12.8 kilometres) west of Newcastle, 1½ miles
(2.4 kilometres) south of the A69, at Wylam

George Stephenson, the engineer whose revolutionary *Rocket*
of 1829 paved the way for the development of the modern
locomotive, was born in this little stone tenement beside the
River Tyne in 1781. At the time the now-green valley was an
industrial slum, despoiled with coal pits, ironworks and slag
heaps. George's father was an impoverished colliery worker,
and the Stephensons lived in just two rooms, sharing the
tenement with three other families. George himself started
work at the age of 10. Lying half a mile (0.8 kilometre) east of
Wylam village, the cottage is still accessible only on foot or by
bicycle. Immediately in front of the house is the track of the
old Wylam colliery wagonway, now a riverside walk, for which
the Cornish engineer Richard Trevithick had produced an
earlier, less successful steam engine.

Grange Arch (above)
Dorset
At Creech, 3 miles (4.8 kilometres) west of Corfe Castle,
4 miles (6.4 kilometres) east of Worbarrow Bay

This simple early eighteenth-century folly, a pierced wall of
lichen-stained grey Portland stone, stands on a crest of the
Purbeck Hills, with magnificent views south to the sea and
north over the unspoilt wooded Dorset countryside. A central
round-headed arch is flanked by smaller rectangular openings
on either side and the stepped profile is crowned with
battlements and obelisks. Also known as Bond's Folly after its
creator Denis Bond, the arch was specifically designed to be
silhouetted against the skyline as seen from Creech Grange,
the Bond family house nestling in the woods below.

Grantham House
Lincolnshire
In the centre of Grantham, immediately east of
St Wulfram's church

The earliest part of this attractive town house, one of the oldest
buildings in Grantham, dates from the same period as the
fourteenth-century parish church across the road, with its
soaring tower and spire. But, apart from the central hall, built
in c.1380, most of the building is Elizabethan or Georgian.
Sixteenth-century mullioned windows in the entrance front
were the result of alterations by the Halls, a family of wealthy
wool merchants, while the long garden facade facing the River
Witham, with its elegant sash windows and central pedimented
doorway, was largely the result of remodelling by Anne, Lady
Cust soon after 1734, when her son John bought the house for

her. She was probably also responsible for panelling the
drawing room and introducing the three large still-lifes by G.B.
Ruoppolo in the hall, thought to have come from Belton House
just to the north of Grantham, which she subsequently
inherited (*see* p.49). A walled garden runs down to the river.

Gray's Monument
Buckinghamshire
At Stoke Poges, off the B473, east of the churchyard

James Wyatt's massive monument, a classical sarcophagus on
a square plinth inset with inscribed panels, stands on the edge
of a field just east of the churchyard which Thomas Gray
immortalised in his 'Elegy' and where he chose to be laid to
rest next to his mother. It was erected in 1799, 28 years after
the poet's death in Cambridge from 'severe internal gout', and
was commissioned by John Penn, who lived nearby.

Gray's Printing Press
Co. Tyrone
49 Main Street, Strabane

The words 'GRAY PRINTER' set above an early nineteenth-
century shop front in the main street of this little border town
advertise the only survivor of the printing concerns that
flourished here when Strabane was an important publishing
centre in the late eighteenth century. At one time there were
no fewer than ten printing businesses here and Strabane had
both the *Strabane Journal* and the *Strabane Newsletter* before
Londonderry, its larger neighbour about 15 miles (24
kilometres) to the north, began producing its own newspaper.

The works were housed on the upper floor of the long,
whitewashed building across a yard at the back of the shop.
John Dunlap, who printed the American Declaration of
Independence in 1776 and started the first daily newspaper in
the United States, is said to have served his apprenticeship
here, one of the many who learnt their trade on Strabane's two
newspapers and ten presses before emigrating to America and
the colonies to set up successful printing and publishing
businesses. The former works is now used to display
nineteenth-century printing machinery and a fine collection of
wood and metal type.

Great Coxwell Barn (above)
Oxfordshire
2 miles (3.2 kilometres) south-west of Faringdon between the A420 and the B4019

On the edge of Great Coxwell village is a mid-thirteenth-century 46-metre (152-foot) monastic barn which once belonged to the Cistercian abbey of Beaulieu. Built of Cotswold stone and oak, it has buttressed walls and a soaring stone-tiled roof that more than doubles the height of the building. Inside, stone piers some 2 metres (7 feet) high carry the slender oak posts that support the roof timbers. Projecting porches either side of the barn, one graced with a dovecote, house the original doors, those at each end of the building being insertions of the eighteenth century designed to accommodate the larger wagons of the day.

The Greyfriars
Worcestershire
Friar Street, Worcester

Thomas Grene, a wealthy Worcester brewer, built himself this fine town house on a site next to a Franciscan monastery in 1480, recording his initials on the jetties either side of the entrance. Although one of the two ranges running back from the street is Elizabethan, the present casement windows were probably inserted in the early seventeenth century and there were some later additions, the Greyfriars is none the less a very good example of the medieval timber-framed buildings that must once have housed Worcester's wealthier citizens, the upper floor jettied out over the lower and the timbers on the long street facade set expensively close together. A double gateway large enough to take a coach gives access to a cobbled passage leading to a little courtyard.

None of the original furnishings has survived, the appearance of the house today being the work of Mr Matley Moore and his sister Elsie, who took on the derelict building from the Worcester Archaeological Society in 1943 and gradually restored it. Seventeenth-century furniture and sixteenth-century tapestries in the great hall contrast with the rare Georgian hunting wallpaper in the dining room. Upstairs, a fine frieze of carved dragons is a reminder that this is Welsh borders country.

Hadrian's Wall and Housesteads Fort (right)
Northumberland
6 miles (9.6 kilometres) north-east of Haltwhistle

In about AD122, 80 years after the Roman conquest of Britain, the Emperor Hadrian ordered the construction of a wall from Tynemouth to the Solway Firth to mark the northern limit of the empire. Some 73 miles (117.5 kilometres) long, the wall was built for much of its length on the Whin Sill, a doleritic outcrop with a steep and craggy northern face, and runs along a succession of cliffs and ridges in a wild and beautiful landscape of vast distances and panoramic views.

Over 5 miles (8 kilometres) of the most dramatic section of the wall, where it rises over Hotbank Crags and Steel Rigg, are in National Trust ownership, and so too is the substantial and well-preserved fort at Housesteads (maintained and managed for the Trust by English Heritage). One of what were only sixteen permanent bases along the wall, Housesteads conjures up an evocative picture of Roman life on this northern frontier. There are considerable remains of the commanding officer's house and of barracks for the ranks, and a forest of stone pillars once supported the floor of a granary. Hadrian's Wall faded quietly away. By the mid-fourth century troops were being withdrawn from Britain to defend Rome and, 50 years later, in AD410, the Emperor Honorius unceremoniously instructed the Britons to fend for themselves. Like the trappings of Roman civilisation, the wall gradually decayed, its stone plundered for building material and gentler sections ploughed out, melting into history.

Hailes Abbey (below right)
Gloucestershire
2 miles (3.2 kilometres) north-east of Winchcombe, 1 mile (1.6 kilometres) east of the B4632 Broadway road

Set beneath the wooded western edge of the Cotswolds are the scant remains of one of the last Cistercian houses to be established in England. Apart from seventeen cloister arches and parts of the chapter house, the extensive and elaborate buildings of this once great abbey are now no more than outlines in the grass. But at one time pilgrims from all over Europe flocked to this now-secluded spot to worship at the shrine of the Holy Blood, built to house a relic given to the community in 1270 by Edward of Cornwall, whose father Richard had founded the abbey in 1246. The foundations of the five radiating chapels which once enclosed the ambulatory where the phial of Christ's blood was displayed can be seen outlined in the turf at the east end of the church, and in the little museum are floor tiles displaying the arms of the community's rich patrons and intricately carved bosses, an indication of how splendid the monastery once was. A deep stone-lined channel still carries the little stream which provided the monks with water.

Pilgrim donations helped to pay for fine fifteenth-century cloisters, but years of prosperity were brought to an abrupt end in the autumn of 1538, when Henry VIII's commissioners visited Hailes and removed the phial of Holy Blood, subsequently declaring it to be 'honey clarified and coloured with saffron'.

The abbey is managed and maintained by English Heritage.

Hardy Monument
Dorset
6 miles (9.6 kilometres) south-west of Dorchester, on the Martinstown–Portesham road

What from a distance might appear to be the chimney of a factory desecrating the South Dorset Downs is in fact a monument to Vice Admiral Sir Thomas Masterman Hardy, Flag Captain of *HMS Victory* at Trafalgar, who was immortalised by Nelson's dying words. Designed by A.D. Troyte and erected by public subscription in 1846, it stands boldly on the crest of Black Down, from where there are glorious views over Weymouth Bay.

Hartwell House Hotel (left)
Buckinghamshire
2 miles (3.2 kilometres) south-west
of Aylesbury on A418

A sweeping drive leads to this dignified and attractive house set in a hollow in the Vale of Aylesbury and surrounded by 36 hectares (90 acres) of parkland. Regular sash-windowed facades in a warm, honey-coloured stone were created by James Gibbs, who remodelled an H-shaped Jacobean house in the mid-eighteenth century for Sir Thomas Lee. Pediments are used sparingly over some of the windows and ground-floor openings in the central bay of the long south front are set within round-headed arches framed by colonnettes. The north-facing, grey-stone entrance front, with a splendid, semi-circular oriel window over the central doorway, is a survival of the Jacobean house, although the original gables were removed in the eighteenth century and replaced with a parapet and cornice.

Inside, Gibbs designed the great hall of c.1740, with its fine plasterwork ceiling, but the morning room and drawing room, with their rococo plasterwork, were created by Henry Keene in the 1750s for Sir William Lee and Keene was also responsible for the library, where the bookcases still have their original gilt-bronze wirework encasing the shelves. The most striking feature of the house is the grand staircase, which has 24 carved wooden figures, each just under a metre (2½ feet) high, arranged along the newel posts, and balusters carved as caryatids. This piece of showmanship may be Jacobean, but may also be an eighteenth-century pastiche. Likenesses of Winston Churchill, complete with a cigar, and, bizarrely, G.K. Chesterton, are modern replacements for two of the balusters.

A thousand years ago Hartwell was a royal manor, and royalty returned briefly in the nineteenth century when the exiled Louis XIII of France took refuge here, with his queen and some of his court, in 1809–14. After a sale of the contents in 1938, Hartwell was bought by the reclusive Ernest Cook with the aid of the fortune he had inherited from his grandfather, the entrepreneurial Thomas Cook, and the freehold of the house is now vested in a Trust bearing Ernest Cook's name. A school from 1956–83, Hartwell was then acquired by Historic House Hotels who, with the help of the architect Eric Throssell, have restored both the house and the surrounding landscape park, with its eyecatchers, and in 2008 presented Hartwell to the National Trust. The house continues to be a hotel.

Hawford Dovecote
Worcestershire
3 miles (4.8 kilometres) north of Worcester, ½ mile
(0.8 kilometre) east of the A449

Like Kinwarton 15 miles (24 kilometres) or so to the east (see p.380), Hawford was once a monastic grange belonging to the Abbey of Evesham. The dovecote, a three-storey half-timbered square building standing on a sandstone plinth, with four gables pierced by mullioned windows, probably dates back to the sixteenth century. Unusually large doors on the ground floor gave access to a storage area, the birds being accommodated in the two upper storeys, where only a few of the wooden nesting boxes now survive.

Hawkshead Courthouse
Cumbria
At the junction of Ambleside and Coniston roads, ½ mile
(0.8 kilometre) north of Hawkshead on the B5285

This modest two-storey gatehouse, set back from the road just outside Hawkshead, is all that remains of the medieval grange from which the monks of Furness Abbey, some 20 miles (32 kilometres) to the south, once administered their extensive estates between Lake Windermere and Coniston Water. For the most part dating from the fifteenth century, Hawkshead Courthouse is a plain rectangular building of rough slate rubble. Carved sandstone forms the central archway, the large traceried window in the south gable and the trefoil-headed windows on the east facade. An exterior flight of slate steps at the north end of the building leads to a large upper room where manorial courts are said to have been held.

Heelis (below)
Wiltshire
Kemble Drive, Swindon

One of the most significant milestones in the recent history of the National Trust was the decision to move their headquarters from an imposing building overlooking leafy St James's Park in central London to newly constructed brick offices in the heart of Swindon, which were opened in 2005. Other central offices were also relocated to Swindon at the same time. The name Heelis, by which the building is known, is that of one of the Trust's best-known benefactors, Beatrix Potter, whose married name was Heelis and whose friend Canon Rawnsley was one of the three founders of the organisation.

Set on the site of the works built by Isambard Kingdom Brunel in the 1840s to produce steam engines and rolling stock for the Great Western Railway, the new offices, by architects Feilden Clegg Bradley, were designed both to fit harmoniously with the remaining brick facades by Brunel and his colleague David Gooch and to meet the Trust's desire for a sustainable, environmentally friendly building that is also visually pleasing. Set off by clumps of silver birch that were part of the overall scheme, it features prominent vents for natural ventilation on a series of pitched roofs covered with solar photo-voltaic cells and the open-plan interior, focused on an airy atrium, makes full use of natural light.

Holnicote Estate (right)
Somerset
Astride the A39, between Minehead and Porlock

The vast 4,856-hectare (12,000-acre) Holnicote estate runs for 4 miles (6.4 kilometres) along the Somerset coast, from Porlock Bay up onto the heights of Exmoor, and inland over a succession of picturesque villages where houses, cottages and farm buildings seem rooted in the landscape. At first glance, the thatched cream-washed stone cottages of Selworthy, set in a steep wooded valley on the northern fringes of the moor, seem all of a piece with the vernacular architecture of this part of the West Country but, unlike the neighbouring villages, Selworthy was largely rebuilt in 1828 by Sir Thomas Acland of Killerton (*see* p.182), who designed a group of cottages in a local idiom set loosely round a long green. A philanthropist who wished to provide housing for the pensioners on his Holnicote estate, Sir Thomas was probably inspired by his friend John Harford, who had commissioned Nash to design Blaise Hamlet for his aged retainers 20 years earlier (*see* p.360).

Both settlements are examples of the cult of the Picturesque, but they could hardly be more different. Whereas Nash's cottages are self-consciously flamboyant and exaggerated, those at Selworthy are gentle variations on the vernacular, with tall chimneys, deep thatched eaves, eyebrow dormers and projecting ovens. At the top of the village is the fifteenth-century church of All Saints, from where there is a view over a patchwork of thatched roofs and neat cottage gardens to the heather- and bracken-covered heights of Dunkery Beacon, the highest point on the moor.

Holy Jesus Hospital
Tyne and Wear
On City Road in the centre of Newcastle

This arresting three-storey brick building, with a 30-arch colonnade at street level and small-paned casements lighting the two upper storeys, is now fronted by an elevated section of

City Road, but once looked over a garden towards the River Tyne. Funded by public subscription in the late seventeenth century, this individual place was erected as a charitable institution to house the town's retired Freemen, their widows and unmarried dependent children. Inside there were 42 rooms, each with a south-facing window, a fireplace and its own front door. Most of these survive, although largely without original fittings. Ground-floor rooms open onto the colonnade, those above onto corridors running the length of the building on the north side. A staircase, originally open to the street, leads up from the colonnade. The residents were governed by strict rules and church attendance was compulsory, but they had the luxury of a room each and could furnish them as they chose. The stonework of the decorative pump which was the residents' only source of water now stands on the pavement in front of the hospital, but originally it was in the garden.

Opened in 1682, the hospital continued to operate until 1937, when residents were moved to 40 bungalows in a more salubrious area of Newcastle. After being left empty and derelict for some years, the hospital was restored in the late 1960s and linked with the adjoining late nineteenth-century soup kitchen and Tudor tower to accommodate the John George Joicey Museum, which was housed here from 1971 to 1993. Then, in 2000, the Trust leased all three buildings from Newcastle City Council. The National Trust's Inner City Project, aimed at helping those who live in the inner city to enjoy and appreciate the countryside, is now based here. Remains of the Augustinian friary established on this site in the early fourteenth century are incorporated in the Tudor tower.

Horsey Windpump
Norfolk
15 miles (24 kilometres) north of Great Yarmouth on Horsey Road, 4 miles (6.4 kilometres) north-east of Martham

On the eastern edge of the Norfolk Broads, little more than a mile (1.6 kilometres) from the sea, is Horsey Mere and a broadland landscape of marshes and reed beds, of great importance for wildfowl. This impressive red-brick drainage mill, five storeys high and with panoramic views from the top, stands at the south-eastern edge of the mere. Built in 1912 on the foundations of an older mill, and now operated by

electricity, it is used for pumping water rather than grinding corn and is part of the intricate and extensive drainage system of dykes, waterways and rivers in this part of England. A south-east wind allows the water to escape from the mere naturally but a north-west wind, particularly during spring tides, holds up the natural flow, and pumping is necessary if flooding is to be avoided. Intriguingly, although the coast is so close, the water runs by a tortuous route south to Great Yarmouth, on a 23-mile (37-kilometre) journey.

Horton Court (below)
South Gloucestershire
3 miles (4.8 kilometres) north-east of Chipping Sodbury, 3/4 mile (1.2 kilometres) north of Horton, 1 mile (1.6 kilometres) west of the A46 Bath–Stroud road

When Robert de Beaufeu was a prebend at Salisbury Cathedral in the early twelfth century, he would have travelled some 60 miles (96 kilometres) from his living at Horton, snuggled in the lee of the southern Cotswolds, to Old Sarum, built within Iron Age and Norman defences high on a hill above the River Avon, and worshipped in the church that is now no more than outlines in the grass. It was this worldly ecclesiastic, who wrote a poem in praise of beer, or his successor, who built the Norman hall at Horton. This remarkable one-storey building, now attached to a Cotswold manor house, stands close to the church for which the prebends were responsible, two carved Gothic doorways and Norman windows set high in the buttressed walls giving the hall itself the look of a simple chapel. Probably the oldest rectory in England, it looks back to the single-storeyed manor halls of the Anglo-Saxons.

Just as remarkable is the 15-metre (50-foot) detached loggia in the garden of the manor, built some 400 years after the hall, when the prebend, William Knight, combined his ecclesiastical responsibilities with a high-flying career in the king's service. Appointed chaplain and then private secretary to Henry VIII, Knight was employed on several diplomatic missions, culminating in a visit to Pope Clement VII in 1527 in an attempt to negotiate the king's divorce from Catherine of Aragon. Knight's first-hand knowledge of Italian culture undoubtedly inspired the charming Renaissance features that he added to his manor at Horton. The open arcade of his Italian-style loggia is decorated with stucco caricatures of classical worthies, including a portrait of a bearded Hannibal, and the doorway of the manor house is carved with helmets, weapons and foliage. Although Knight seems to have had a particular affection for Horton, one of several rich livings he enjoyed, he must have had little time to visit the magnificent thirteenth-century cathedral at Salisbury, laid out on a virgin site by the Avon as the centrepiece of a new town.

Houghton Mill
Cambridgeshire
In village of Houghton, signposted off the A1123

One of a handful of surviving mills along the River Great Ouse, this unusually large four-storey brick and timber building rises from an artificial island 2 miles (3.2 kilometres) downstream of Huntingdon, the tarred weather-boarding of the upper storeys standing high above the flat water meadows bordering the river. There has been a corn-mill on this site, once a property of Ramsey Abbey 10 miles (16 kilometres) to the north, for at least 1,000 years, although the present building dates only from the seventeenth century. Three breastshot wheels powered the ten impressive pairs of millstones on the first floor and the hoists in the projecting gables, which raised sacks of grain for storage at the top of the

building. The wheels were removed when the mill ceased working in the 1930s, but the north waterwheel has now been reinstated and once again turns a pair of millstones, which are used to grind corn.

Keld Chapel
Cumbria
1 mile (1.6 kilometres) south-west of Shap village, by the River Lowther

The little hamlet of Keld, on the eastern edge of the Cumbrian fells, was once part of the estates of Shap Abbey, now an isolated ruin about a mile (1.6 kilometres) away, and this modest stone and slate building by the River Lowther was probably built by the abbey in the late fifteenth or early sixteenth century for the people of the village. Occasional services are once again held in the chapel, which was long used for other purposes.

King John's Hunting Lodge (right)
Somerset
In the Square at Axbridge, on the corner of High Street

Like contemporary towns in East Anglia (*see* Paycocke's, p.248), Axbridge, Trowbridge, Bradford on Avon and other centres of the medieval wool trade in the West Country were once filled with prosperous merchants' houses such as this misleadingly named example of *c.*1500. A three-storey timber-framed building on the corner of Axbridge's market place, it is jettied out over the street in a double overhang. A small museum of local history and archaeology run by the Axbridge and District Museum Trust is now housed here.

King's Head
Buckinghamshire
At the north-west corner of Market Square in Aylesbury

A narrow passage from Aylesbury's busy market square leads to this lovely old coaching inn dating back to 1455. A large, cobbled stable yard has its original mounting block, there is a priest's hole, and the large mullioned and transomed window which lights the bar, once the hall of a medieval house, has fragments of fifteenth-century glass.

Kinver Edge and the Rock Houses (below)
Staffordshire
On edge of Kinver village, 4 miles (6.4 kilometres) west of Stourbridge

The National Trust owns some 114 hectares (283 acres) of this prominent red sandstone escarpment above the village of Kinver. A mosaic of woodland and heath, with wide views to the Clent Hills and Wenlock Edge, the escarpment is notable for the unusual rock dwellings that honeycomb the soft, crumbly sandstone. Cave houses at Holy Austin Rock to the north of the Edge, occupied into the 1960s, have been restored and furnished as they would have been in 1900. There is also a terrace of gabled cottages built into the cliff at the top of the escarpment.

Kinwarton Dovecote (right)
Warwickshire
1½ miles (2.4 kilometres) north-east of Alcester, just south of the B4089

This substantial fourteenth-century circular dovecote sitting proudly in a field at the end of a muddy lane probably once belonged to the Abbey of Evesham some 12 miles (19.3 kilometres) away to the south, and is the only survivor of a former monastic grange. Doves are still housed in some of the 580 nesting holes built into the limestone walls, filling the air with their cooing and perching picturesquely on the red-tiled conical roof. An ingenious manoeuvrable ladder supported on a pivoting central post gives access to all the nesting boxes. Apart from this rare survival, the dovecote is also notable for its fine ogee doorway.

Knowles Mill
Worcestershire
Next to Dowles Brook in the centre of Wyre Forest, Bewdley

Rutted tracks lead to this isolated mill in a clearing surrounded by oak trees in the depths of Wyre Forest. Built of sandstone rubble with brick dressings in the late eighteenth century and last worked, for grinding corn, in 1897–8, the mill still has much of its machinery, but this is no longer in working order and only the frame of the overshot waterwheel that was powered by a leat from the Dowles Brook survives. A late eighteenth-century cottage with casement windows and a piggery sit beside the mill, forming a group of buildings of great charm.

The Kymin
Monmouthshire
1 mile (1.6 kilometres) east of Monmouth between the A466 and the A4136

The prominent hill known as The Kymin is renowned for its wide-ranging views, said to embrace nine counties, over the Wye and Monnow valleys. The National Trust owns a piece of the high ground and the two structures that crown it. In the late eighteenth century members of a local dining club formed the habit of meeting here on summer evenings for a cold supper and in 1794 built the round battlemented banqueting house on the brow of the hill for use in bad weather, each of its windows placed so as to enjoy a spectacular panorama. Nelson's victory over the French in the Battle of the Nile four years later inspired the construction of the little temple in honour of the British navy that stands nearby, its pyramidal stepped roof suggesting an Egyptian summerhouse. A prominent statue of Britannia crowns the structure and medallions record the names and principal achievements of sixteen great eighteenth-century admirals. When Nelson himself visited this spot in 1802, he thought it was one of the most beautiful places he had ever seen. History does not record the feelings of Emma Hamilton and her husband Sir William, who were accompanying Nelson on his journey down the Wye.

Lawrence House
Cornwall
9 Castle Street, Launceston

This modest Georgian brick house in the shadow of the remains of Launceston's great Norman castle was built in 1753 by the wealthy local lawyer Humphrey Lawrence and is typical of houses of the period seen in small country towns throughout England. Once the home of Caroline Pearse, a prolific Victorian author, it is now leased to the Town Council as a local museum and civic centre.

Leith Hill Tower (above right)
Surrey
1 mile (1.6 kilometres) south-west of Coldharbour, off the A29 and B2126

This battlemented Gothic folly stands on the highest point in south-east England. The monkey puzzles and Scots pine which once also crowned the sandstone ridge were flattened by the storms of 1987 and 1990, opening up magnificent views over the wooded landscape of the Weald to the South Downs, with glimpses of the English Channel beyond. First built by Richard Hull of Leith Hill Place in 1766, as a tablet

over the door records, the tower was subsequently heightened and now rises to 313.5 metres (1,029 feet) above sea level. Over 1,000 years ago, in 851, a Saxon army secured this strategic site under cover of darkness, giving them the advantage in a great battle with invading Danes.

On the wooded southern slopes of the hill is the rhododendron wood planted by Josiah Wedgwood, grandson of the famous potter, which survived the great storms. Leith Hill Place, the childhood home of Ralph Vaughan Williams (not open), lies just below.

Letocetum Roman Baths and Museum
Staffordshire
In the village of Wall on the north side of the A5

The little Romano-British town of Letocetum grew up round a posting station on Watling Street, the main imperial route to Chester and North Wales. Of the remains visible at Wall, the communal bathhouse is the most complete example of its kind in Britain, the extensive facitilies on offer including the Roman equivalents of a Turkish bath and a sauna, cold baths, an undressing room and an exercise hall. A courtyard building nearby, destroyed by fire in AD160–170, was probably an inn. Finds from excavations here and from another Roman site, at Shenstone, a short distance to the south-east, are exhibited in a small museum. Both remains and museum are in the guardianship of English Heritage.

Little Clarendon (above)
Wiltshire
In Dinton, 1/2 mile (0.8 kilometre) east of the church,
close to the post office

Stone built, with a projecting porch, mullioned windows and a stone-tiled roof, Little Clarendon dates back to the late fifteenth century, when it was built for a family of some local importance. There were alterations in the seventeenth century and then, in the late nineteenth century, it was divided into two, probably to house local farm labourers. In a state of decay, and with many of its original features obscured, the house was rescued by the Rev. George Engleheart and his wife Mary, who bought the property in 1901 and set about reopening blocked fireplaces, taking down room partitions, re-exposing beamed ceilings and generally restoring it. A brick-built cart shed close by was converted into a little Roman Catholic chapel and George Engleheart, who was fascinated by daffodils, experimented with new strains of narcisi here, raising them in greenhouses and long numbered beds separated by grassy walks. The three rooms on show – hall, dining room and parlour – are crammed with the Englehearts' collection of oak furniture, in particular a fine array of corner cupboards. The greenhouses and daffodil field have gone, but in spring the pretty triangle of grass behind the house, viewable from the footpath beside the garden wall, is covered with the Rev. Engleheart's narcisi hybrids, and more of his daffodils flower along the woodland walk to the north.

Long Crendon Courthouse
Buckinghamshire
2 miles (3.2 kilometres) north of Thame, via the B4011,
close to the church

Long Crendon Courthouse lies in one of the most attractive and unspoilt villages in Buckinghamshire, its long timber-framed facade with a jettied upper storey blending perfectly with the sixteenth- and seventeenth-century thatched cottages that line the street winding down to St Mary's church. Red handmade tiles form a warm streak of colour above the whitewashed walls. Steep wooden stairs lead directly from the street to the large room, open to the roof and floored with undulating oak boards, which runs most of the length of the upper storey.

Dating from the early fifteenth century, or even the end of the fourteenth, the courthouse seems originally to have been built for the cloth trade, to store wool from Oxfordshire destined for the weavers of East Anglia. The first floor was being used to hold manorial courts in the first half of the fifteenth century, and manorial business continued to be conducted here into Victorian times, while the ground floor was frequently used to accommodate the village poor.

Loughwood Meeting House
Devon
4 miles (6.4 kilometres) west of Axminster via the A35, 1 mile (1.6 kilometres) south of Dalwood, 1 mile (1.6 kilometres) north-west of Kilmington

In the seventeenth century people walked miles to attend Baptist meetings in this little flint and sandstone building dug into the hillside, risking imprisonment, transportation or even death until the Toleration Act of 1688 legalised nonconformist forms of worship. Built in 1653 by Baptists from the nearby village of Kilmington, who needed a safe refuge where they could practise their faith, Loughwood was originally buried in dense woodland and approached only along narrow footpaths. Sited in a deeply rural part of Devon, it seems remote even today.

A homely thatched roof and round-headed clear-glass windows give this unassuming chapel the appearance of a cottage rather than a church, despite the surrounding burial ground and the buttressed walls. Inside, it is cheerful and airy, dominated by the preacher's raised pulpit set above the baptismal pool. Unvarnished pine box pews fill the body of the chapel and the whitewashed walls and barrel roof are undecorated. Those who came from a long way away passed the time between services on Sundays in the retiring rooms underneath the musicians' gallery at the back of the building; those lucky enough to have horses quartered them in the detached stone and cob stable.

Maister House
Humberside
160 High Street, Hull

Until the building of the first commercial dock on the River Humber in 1770 led to its gradual decline, Hull's old harbour was the focus of the town's considerable trade, with grand merchants' houses lining the narrow, winding thoroughfares along the river. This fine Palladian house on the High Street is one of the few surviving from this era. Rebuilt for the merchant Henry Maister after a fire in 1743, and substantially unaltered, it is a plain three-storey classical building fronted by railings and with a stone parapet concealing the roof. The only sign of ostentation is the fine pedimented doorcase in the centre of the facade.

This severe and dignified exterior and the sober pine-panelled counting house on the ground floor act as a foil for the staircase, richly decorated with plasterwork by Joseph Page, leading to what would have been the Maister family apartments. A statue of Ceres by John Cheere in a niche above the first flight surveys swags of drapery suspended from lion masks, festoons of shells and acanthus-leaf medallions and scrolls. The coved ceiling above the gallery on the second floor is similarly richly stuccoed and a fine ironwork balustrade was supplied by Robert Bakewell. The work of a highly competent architect, the design of Maister House was probably influenced by Lord Burlington, who knew Henry Maister and whose Yorkshire home was 25 miles (40 kilometres) away.

Market House
Derbyshire
In main street of Winster, about 4 miles (6.4 kilometres) west of Matlock, on the south side of the B5057

This ruggedly attractive two-storey building is one of the few clues to Winster's former importance as a market town. Built in the late seventeenth or early eighteenth century, the Market House is a pleasing mixture of brick and stone, with thick sandstone slabs covering the steeply pitched roof and mullioned and transomed windows lighting the first floor. As was traditional with such buildings, the ground floor was originally open, but its five pointed arches are now filled in. Still the dominant feature of Winster's long main street, the Market House was bought in 1906, as the Trust's first acquisition in the Peak District. It is now a National Trust information centre.

Middle Littleton Tithe Barn (below)
Worcestershire
3 miles (4.8 kilometres) north-east of Evesham, east of the B4085

Produce from the fertile Vale of Evesham once filled this barn of coursed Lias limestone in market-gardening country on the banks of the River Avon. Some 96 metres (315 feet) long and buttressed like a church, it is both one of the largest and one of the finest barns in the country, although not all its wagon porches have survived.

Inside, oak framing forms an aisled bay at either end and eight base-cruck trusses divide the nine intermediate bays. The barn was built by the Benedictine monks of Evesham Abbey and may date from *c*.1300 or even earlier. Like Ashleworth (*see* p.359), it is part of a picturesque group of buildings which includes an Elizabethan manor.

Middlethorpe Hall Hotel
North Yorkshire
Bishopthorpe Road, York

This charming William and Mary house next to York racecourse is all of a piece. Built of mellow red brick with limestone dressings, and with an array of sash windows standing out white against the brickwork, the house rises three storeys to a gently sloping hipped roof. Designed by an unknown architect, Middlethorpe was built in *c*.1699–1701 for the aspiring Thomas Barlow, master cutler, who had bought the estate in 1698 and wanted a house that would help him establish himself as a country gentleman. The eagle of the Barlow family crest surmounts both north and south facades.

In the mid-eighteenth century Francis Barlow, High Sheriff of Yorkshire, added the one-storey wings ornamented with pilasters and a roofline balustrade which flank the front looking onto the gardens; a pedimented porch on the entrance front was added in the nineteenth century and the railings and gates enclosing a forecourt on this side of the house are recent embellishments. Original features inside the house include a splendid carved oak staircase; fine panelling, that in the dining room, ornamented with Ionic pilasters, being particularly noteworthy; and the ballroom that fills one of the two wings.

Once the home of the eighteenth-century socialite and wit Lady Mary Wortley Montagu, known for her entertaining and erudite letters, Middlethorpe was acquired in the late twentieth century, after years as a girls' school and then a night club, by Historic House Hotels, who have furnished it sympathetically and restored the gardens and parkland, creating a ha-ha and lake and repairing a seventeenth-century dovecote. The group generously gave Middlethorpe to the National Trust, together with Bodysgallen Hall and Hartwell House (*see* pp.361 and 376), in 2008, but continue to run the house as a hotel.

Morville Hall
Shropshire
3 miles (4.8 kilometres) west of Bridgnorth, off the A458

The eighteenth-century sash windows, giant pilasters and pedimented Doric porch on the entrance front of this beautiful three-storey stone house standing next to the Norman church of St Gregory disguise an originally Elizabethan, E-shaped building. There are still polygonal sixteenth-century staircase turrets in the angles of the facade and the pilasters, created by the architect William Baker when he remodelled Morville in the 1740s, disguise Elizabethan buttresses on the ends of the two projecting wings. Baker was also responsible for designing the delightful cupola-topped pavilions that are joined to the main house by curving screen walls, but the porch was added in the 1770s and alterations at this time also account for the addition of the top floor. An elaborate plasterwork ceiling dating from the 1580s in what is now the kitchen may be by the same craftsmen who worked at Wilderhope Manor nearby (*see* p.397), and there is some fine oak panelling.

Moulton Hall (below)
North Yorkshire
5 miles (8 kilometres) east of Richmond

This compact and elegant stone manor house, standing about a mile (1.6 kilometres) east of the A1, was built in 1650 and is noteworthy for its large Dutch gables and very fine carved staircase.

Nether Alderley Mill

Cheshire

1½ miles (2.4 kilometres) south of Alderley Edge, on the east side of the A34

Nether Alderley is a most unusual water-mill. On one side, a long, sweeping stone-tiled roof reaches almost to the ground, giving just a glimpse of warm sandstone walls. On the other, the mill is wedged right up against a wooded bank, the dam of the little reservoir that provides the water to turn the wheels. The stream on which the mill was sited was too small and irregular to power the machinery effectively and this ingenious solution, with the later addition of three more reservoirs, was devised when Nether Alderley was first built, in the sixteenth century. The mill is noteworthy, too, for having a pair of waterwheels, set one below the other, a short trough leading from the first to the second. Both are 3.5 metres (12 feet) in diameter and, like all the mill machinery, date from the nineteenth century.

Four dormer windows in the sloping roof light the interior, the most remarkable feature of which is the Elizabethan oak woodwork that supports the roof. Wooden pins hold the structure together and the numbers used by the carpenters when assembling the frame can still be seen on some of the timbers. A floor of finely perforated tiles is the remains of a kiln for drying wet grain, a feature more usually seen in Scottish mills.

Nether Alderley was operating up to 1939, almost 650 years after the earliest mention of a mill here in 1290. The machinery and the culvert from the reservoir have been restored and there are demonstrations of flour-grinding.

Newtown Old Town Hall (above right)

Isle of Wight

Midway between Cowes and Yarmouth, 1 mile (1.6 kilometres) north of the A3054

Despite being called Newtown, this shadow of a place on an arm of the Newtown estuary dates back over 700 years. Founded by the Bishop of Winchester in 1256 and laid out to a grid plan, much like a French bastide, it was at its height in the mid-fourteenth century when a community of some 300

prospered on the revenue from oyster beds, salt works and the ships using the magnificent natural harbour of the estuary, regarded as the best in the Isle of Wight. Now there is just a scatter of buildings here, with grassy lanes marking the lines of the town's former streets and cattle grazing on what were medieval house plots, their outlines still visible in the turf. It seems Newtown never recovered from a disastrous French raid in 1377, gradually losing its trade and importance to Newport.

Surrounded by fields, oddly isolated from the rest of the village, is the little brick Town Hall of 1699, a relic of the days when Newtown elected two Members of Parliament despite its tiny population, the franchise granted in 1584 perhaps an attempt to stem the community's decline. Lit by four long, round-headed windows down each side and crowned by a steeply pitched hipped roof, this simple building on an earlier stone basement was dignified by the addition of a classical portico in the late eighteenth century. By this time, elections were increasingly controlled by two families and Newtown's political life came to an end with the Reform Act of 1832, under which it was declared a 'rotten borough' and disenfranchised.

One of the National Trust's properties initially rescued from dereliction by Ferguson's Gang (*see* p.391), the building is used to display an exhibition about this anonymous group, whose exploits benefited the Trust in the 1920s and '30s. Not far away is Noah's Ark, a stone house of *c*.1700 that was once an inn and is now the oldest building in the village, most of the others having been rebuilt in the nineteenth century.

Oakhurst Cottage (see page 358)
Surrey
In the village of Hambledon, 5 miles (8 kilometres) south
of Godalming

This picturesque little timber-framed building in a leafy
village on the fringes of London's affluent commuter belt
dates from the sixteenth century. A rare survival that has
escaped modernisation, it is furnished as a labourer's cottage
of the mid-nineteenth century and illustrates a now-vanished
way of life. The front door opens straight into the quarry-tiled
kitchen which is the main room. There is a substantial dresser
with shelves of willow-pattern china, samplers decorate the
walls and a huge pot hangs over the hearth. A steep staircase
leads directly up to one of the bedrooms in the roof, both of
which are lit by dormer windows. In the little back kitchen,
where clothes were once washed and ironed, a low bench
known as a hog-form is where the hair was scraped from the
family pig after it had been slaughtered, a prelude to the
annual pork feast enjoyed by wealthier cottagers and so vividly
described by Flora Thompson in her book *Lark Rise to
Candleford*.

The Old Coastguard Station
North Yorkshire
In Robin Hood's Bay, on the slipway of the old village

On the edge of the sea, at the bottom of the steep and cobbled
main street leading down to the beach, is a small, two-storey
sandstone house with a pantiled roof and a rendered and
whitewashed frontage. This apparently typical piece of
vernacular architecture was in fact built in the late 1990s to
replicate a building which had stood here until the 1960s,
when Leeds University replaced it with a modern marine
research laboratory. The coastguard service was set up in the
original building in 1829 in a bid to combat the smuggling for
which the inhabitants of Robin Hood's Bay were notorious,
and coastguards continued to operate from here until the early
1900s. A century earlier, the station had been a public house
and it was divided into three tenements by the time the
coastguards took over. It is now a visitor and education centre.

The Old Manor, Norbury (above)
Derbyshire
4 miles (6.4 kilometres) south-west of Ashbourne

Behind the Carolean red-brick manor house in this leafy
village on the River Dove is a low medieval building with
rough buttressed stone walls dating from *c*.1250. Above an
undercroft and cellars is an airy first-floor hall. Original Gothic
two-light windows with stone window seats survive in the west
wall and a rare king-post roof spanning the room may have
been installed here in the seventeenth century, when the
Tudor manor was demolished. From the little knot garden
below, there is a good view of the tower of the fine fourteenth-
century church where monuments to generations of the
Fitzherbert family who held the manor of Norbury for over
650 years begin with a stone effigy of Sir Henry Fitzherbert,
who enlarged the hall house in the early fourteenth century.

Old Soar Manor
Kent
2 miles (3.2 kilometres) south of Borough Green on the A25;
approached via the A227 and Plaxtol

The rectangular solar block attached to a red-brick early
Georgian farmhouse is all that remains of the manor house of
c.1290 which stood here until the eighteenth century. The

solar over the barrel-vaulted undercroft was once the apartment of a medieval knight, a private retreat away from the noise and company in the great hall. Rough walls of Kentish ragstone rise to an open timber roof, there is a bare flagged floor and openings at the corners of the room lead to two projecting chambers, a chapel and a garderobe.

Orford Ness (below)
Suffolk
On the coast between Aldeburgh and Orford

Stretching 10 miles (16 kilometres) south of Aldeburgh, with a gentle curve westwards opposite Orford, this long shingle spit is one of the most desolate and lonely places along an often wild and inhospitable coastline. Separated from the mainland by the River Ore, which it forces ever further south, the bank is fluid and impermanent, changing shape in the winter storms that sweep in from the North Sea.

In 1993 the National Trust acquired 5 miles (8 kilometres), or some 627 hectares (1,550 acres), of the northern end of the spit. Apart from its great natural-history interest, this stretch of shingle bank includes the remains of a top-secret military research station and airfield that was in use for some 80 years. During the First World War, parachutes were tested and night flights pioneered from this site, while in the interwar years, as well as being used to test aeroplanes, ballistics and aerial combat techniques, the Ness is where, in a timber hut, Robert Watson-Watt and his team did pioneering work on the development of radar in 1935–6, which helped win the Battle of Britain. The station continued to be used up until the 1990s, the wide-ranging research conducted here including the testing of technology for the British atomic bomb.

Eerily futuristic concrete pagodas were built to absorb the blast should a test carried out in the cavernous pits beneath them go wrong. Some structures have now been demolished, others are gently decaying, a symbol of the futility of war and Man's destructiveness.

Patterson's Spade Mill
Co. Antrim
On the A6, 2 miles (3.2 kilometres) south-east of Templepatrick

This unusual relic of Ireland's agricultural past is the last water-driven spade mill in the country. Founded in 1919 to produce a range of implements, from light tools for flower beds to heavy-duty spades for cutting turf, Patterson's Mill was run as a family business for over 70 years. It was acquired by the National Trust with all machinery and fittings intact and spades are once again being made here.

Penshaw Monument
Tyne & Wear
Halfway between Sunderland and Chester-le-Street, close to the A183

Conspicuously sited on a hilltop, and visible for miles around, this roofless classical temple surveys the landscape of Tyneside, the honey-coloured sandstone of which it was built now blackened and sombre. Some 30 metres (100 feet) long and 15 metres (50 feet) wide, this impressive eye-catcher was the work of local architects John and Benjamin Green and was erected in 1844 to commemorate the radical statesman John George Lambton, 1st Earl of Durham, one-time Governor General of Canada, who had died four years earlier.

The Pepperbox

Wiltshire

5 miles (8 kilometres) south-east of Salisbury, on the north side of the A36

A steep rutted track off the A36 leads to the long tongue of Brickworth Down and this red-brick octagonal three-storey tower, with a weathervane crowning the pyramidal slate roof. Built by Giles Eyre in 1606, the Pepperbox may be the earliest folly in England, or it may have been intended as a viewpoint from which ladies could follow the hunt in comfort. Both the open arches on the ground floor and the windows of the room at the top of the tower have now been bricked in, but the views are still magnificent, the vista north-west taking in the soaring spire of Salisbury Cathedral.

Pitstone Windmill (below)

Buckinghamshire

1/2 mile (0.8 kilometre) south of Ivinghoe, 3 miles (4.8 kilometres) north-east of Tring, just west of the B488

This fascinating little building, bearing the date 1627, is Britain's oldest post mill, an example of the earliest form of windmill that was developed in the Middle Ages. Unlike later mills, such as that at Bembridge (*see* p.360), the sails are brought into the wind by turning the building as a whole, rather than by simply revolving the cap on the top of the mill.

Pitstone's two-storey timber body, reached by a ladder, is perched some 2.5 metres (8 feet) above the ground on a massive wooden post, the lower half of which is enclosed in a brick roundhouse. The building projects alarmingly on either side of its support, as if it might topple over at any moment. The tail pole sweeping down to the ground – a long beam with a wheel on the end – acted as a lever for turning the mill.

Two pairs of grinding stones, one pair used for producing coarse meal, the other for fine white flour, are now in working order, but the mill cannot at present be turned into the wind.

Priest's House, Easton on the Hill

Northamptonshire

In Easton on the Hill, 2 miles (3.2 kilometres) south-west of Stamford, off the A43

This little two-storey stone building, with fireplaces to warm the chambers on both floors, predates the Reformation of the mid-sixteenth century, which turned the Church upside down. Originally intended for celibate clergy, it would have been lived in by married priests after the Reformation and was superseded by the handsome Georgian rectory standing nearby. A small museum illustrating past village life is housed on the upper floor.

Priest's House, Muchelney (above right)

Somerset

In Muchelney, 1¹/2 miles (2.4 kilometres) south of Langport

The Somerset hamlet of Muchelney, once on an island in the Sedgemoor marshes, boasts a clutch of medieval buildings. On one side of the fine fifteenth-century church are the remains of the abbey of Muchelney, which may have been founded as early as the seventh century (in Somerset, only Glastonbury is older). On the other side, facing the church across a small green, is this thatched stone cottage, built by monks of the abbey in 1308 to house the vicar of the parish. Like Alfriston (*see* p.14), which it resembled in plan, this priest's house was no mean dwelling, even before it was modernised in the early sixteenth century. Although the interior is much altered and the hall that once rose to the roof in the centre of the house is now floored over, the exterior still displays original features: a Gothic doorway, mullioned windows and the magnificent two-tiered window to the hall, with trefoil heads to the upper lights.

Priory Cottages
Oxfordshire
1 Mill Street, Steventon, 4 miles (6.4 kilometres) south of Abingdon

These timber-framed medieval buildings set round a little courtyard are the remains of a small Benedictine priory. Essentially no more than a house of the period that was lived in by two monks, the buildings are now divided into two cottages, one of which contains the priory's great hall.

Rainham Hall
Essex
The Broadway, Rainham, just south of the church, 5 miles (8 kilometres) east of Barking

This elegant Georgian house, set back from the road behind beautiful wrought-iron gates and railings, was completed in 1729 for the merchant and shipowner John Harle. In the domestic Dutch style, with red-brick facades, stone dressings

and dormers in the hipped roof, the exterior has only one exceptional feature, a carved wooden porch with Corinthian columns. Inside, the house has been little altered, original doorcases, fireplaces and softwood panelling helping to convey a strong sense of period.

Ramsey Abbey Gatehouse (below)
Cambridgeshire
Abbey School, at the south-east edge of Ramsey, at the point where the Chatteris road leaves the B1096, 10 miles (16 kilometres) south-east of Peterborough

In 969 St Oswald, Archbishop of York, and Ailwyn, foster brother of King Edgar, founded a Benedictine abbey on a remote island in the Fens. Only fragments survive, the remains of an ornate late fifteenth-century gatehouse with a richly carved oriel window above the entrance doorway suggesting how sumptuous the abbatial buildings must once have been. A small room to the right of the gateway is filled with an impressive mid-thirteenth-century marble tomb, with a frost-damaged effigy clutching a huge key in its right hand. An intriguing mystery surrounds the identity of the figure, which was once taken to represent Ailwyn.

Rosedene (left)
Worcestershire
Victoria Road, Dodford,
near Bromsgrove

The mid-nineteenth-century working-class movement known as Chartism, which led to petitions for political equality and social justice being presented to Parliament, also spawned some practical experiments in land reform. Fergus O'Connor's land plan, developed in the 1840s, aimed to settle working-class families on smallholdings that would allow them to be self-supporting. From 1845 the Chartist Co-operative Land Society, later the National Land Company, began to acquire land, the money for which was obtained by selling shares to would-be smallholders. The estates were parcelled up into 4-acre (1.6-hectare) plots, with narrow lanes to give access, and a one-storey brick cottage was built at the head of each plot. The smallholdings were initially allocated by ballot, but a more inequitable system involving the payment of entry bonuses was introduced after a time.

Dodford, where Rosedene was built, was the last of the National Land Company's five settlements. The estate was purchased in 1848 and the first tenants moved in a year later, when this little cottage was first occupied. The smallholders, who grew strawberries and early vegetables for sale in Birmingham, only 13 miles (20.9 kilometres) away, were the most successful of the Chartist settlers and enjoyed an Indian summer during the First World War, when the strawberry crop was used to make jam for the army. Generally, though, the plots were found to be too small for self-sufficiency and for keeping an essential cow, for milk and manure, and most families had to supplement their income as best they could. Largely unaltered since it was built, Rosedene shows the kind of conditions in which the early Chartists lived, its period features including a working range, water pump and closet. There is a restored vegetable garden and orchard on the plot.

St George's Guildhall
Norfolk
In King's Lynn, on west side of King Street, close to the Tuesday Market Place

Medieval King's Lynn was a market town and port of considerable importance, trading in wool and agricultural produce across the North Sea and to Scandinavia. The Guild of St George was one of the largest of the 60 or so that flourished here in late medieval times, and this substantial building by Tuesday Market, the biggest surviving medieval guildhall in England, is a graphic illustration of the wealth and status of the fraternity.

Although the 32.5-metre (107-foot) great hall on the first floor is now a theatre, many original fifteenth-century features survive, such as the five massive buttresses against the north wall and the open timber roof. There are also traces of the Georgian theatre constructed here in 1766.

St John's Jerusalem
Kent
3 miles (4.8 kilometres) south of Dartford at Sutton-at-Hone, on the east side of the A225

After the noise and traffic of Dartford, this charming place, set amongst undulating lawns, shaded by magnificent trees and moated by the River Darent, appears as an oasis of peace and serenity. A huge cedar of Lebanon, probably planted by Abraham Hill in the late seventeenth century at the same time as he made alterations to St John's, frames the first view of the house, a pleasant two-storey stuccoed building with dormers in the steeply pitched roof. The sash windows and rich interior plasterwork were later additions by Edward Hasted, the eminent local historian, who lived here from 1755–76.

The oldest part of St John's is the medieval chapel, with buttressed flint walls and tall lancet windows, which is joined onto the east end of the house. It is all that remains of the former Commandery of the Knights Hospitallers of the Order of Saint John of Jerusalem that was established here in 1199. Dissolved at the Reformation, the order lives on in the name of this delightful property.

Segontium

Gwynedd

On the A4085 on the south-east outskirts of Caernarfon

Edward I's great castle at Caernarfon was partly built of dressed stone plundered from the Roman fort of Segontium on the top of a hill about half a mile (0.8 kilometre) to the east. One of over 30 forts built to control the rebellious tribes in the valleys west of the Rivers Severn and Dee, Segontium was sited in a commanding position on the Menai Strait, and on a route inland to the much larger garrison at Chester. Founded in AD78, it was held until about 390, longer than any other Roman fort in Wales, which probably reflects its strategic importance. Over the years, the clay rampart flanked by a ditch that originally marked the perimeter was gradually replaced in stone, to strengthen the defences.

The 2.2-hectare (5½-acre) site is crossed by the Caernarfon to Beddgelert road and only the ground plan of part of the northern half is excavated. The fort was of the usual playing-card shape and laid out to a standard design, with barracks for the men in tidy rows either side of the commander's house and the headquarters building in the middle of the compound, the latter displaying the remains of an underfloor heating system. Nothing can be seen of the two large granaries which housed a year's supply of corn for the garrison (up to 1,000 strong), but a rather basic bath suite added in the late third or early fourth century shows facilities here were less lavish than at Letocetum (*see* p.381). The fort is in the guardianship of Cadw and the site museum is not National Trust.

Shalford Mill

Surrey

1½ miles (2.4 kilometres) south of Guildford, on the east side of the A281

This large eighteenth-century water-mill sits confidently astride the Tillingbourne, a tributary of the River Wey. Two timber-framed upper storeys attractively hung with warm red tiles are built on a brick ground floor, with three brick arches on the upstream side channelling the water of the river through the mill. A prominent projecting gable at third-floor level housed the hoist, which once raised sacks of grain for storage in the large bins running the length of the attic.

All the principal machinery is still intact, but the mill can no longer be worked as only the top half of the 4.5-metre (14-foot) breastshot waterwheel remains. A vertical shaft made from a single pine trunk transmitted power from the wheel to three pairs of millstones, one of which is still complete, and to the hoist in the attic and winnowing and grading machinery on the second floor.

Shalford Mill is of particular interest because it is one of the properties presented to the National Trust by the anonymous band of conservationists known as Ferguson's Gang, who used to meet here in the 1930s. Part of the building is now converted into a house and is privately let.

Skenfrith Castle (below)

Monmouthshire

6 miles (9.6 kilometres) north-west of Monmouth, 12 miles (19.3 kilometres) north-east of Abergavenny, on the north side of the B4521 Ross road

The remains of some 80 castles scattered across South Wales are echoes of the drawn-out conflict between the Welsh and the English following the Norman Conquest. The little early thirteenth-century fortress of Skenfrith, set on low ground by the River Monnow, is one of the more important survivals; together with White Castle to the south and Grosmont to the north, it protected a natural routeway into Wales. Washed by the river on one side, the castle is protected by a wide moat, now a dry ditch, on the other three. Above these defences rise the remains of the massive curtain wall, best preserved along the river, which encloses a trapezoid-shaped area: ruined circular towers, from which attackers could be subjected to deadly

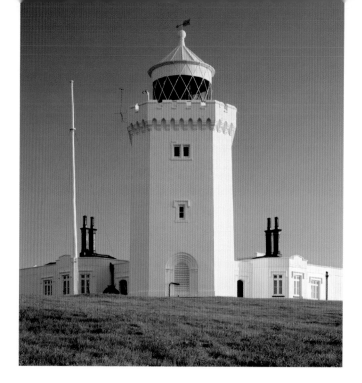

raking fire, project boldly from each of the corners. In the centre of the castle is a large round keep, in the style of those being built by the French king at this period, the mound on which it is built probably a survival from a more primitive fortress established here in the decades after the Conquest.

Skenfrith is the work of Hubert de Burgh, Earl of Kent, who was granted the 'Three Castles' by King John and may have been influenced in his design by what he had seen while imprisoned in France. Like the builder of Bodiam away to the east (*see* p.60) two centuries later, the Earl of Kent was concerned with acquiring a nobleman's residence as well as a fortress and his castle includes a great hall range, the foundations and lower walls of which can still be seen against the west curtain wall. Little changed since it was built, Skenfrith is a splendid example of the castles that foreshadowed the formidable symmetry of Edward I's great fortresses.

Souter Lighthouse
Tyne and Wear
2½ miles (4 kilometres) south of South Shields, on the A183

Just south of the Tyne estuary, overlooking a stretch of unspoilt limestone coastline owned by the National Trust, is a prominent cliff-top lighthouse, its 23-metre (76-foot) tower painted in bold red and white stripes. Built in 1870, it was the first lighthouse to be powered by an alternating electric current and could be seen from some 19 miles (30.5 kilometres) out to sea. A focal point on a stretch of open grassy cliff-top, the lighthouse dominates a row of nineteenth-century coastguard cottages and other ancillary buildings. A nearby array of lime kilns is a reminder of former quarrying along these cliffs, and there was once a colliery village here too.

South Foreland Lighthouse (above)
Kent
3 miles (4.8 kilometres) east of Dover, between St Margaret's Bay and Langdon Cliffs

This lighthouse set on downland on South Foreland Point is a conspicuous landmark on the White Cliffs of Dover. Sited to guide mariners past the shifting shoals and banks of the notorious Goodwin Sands, the lighthouse dates from 1843, when the light was an oil lamp. Marconi used the 21-metre (69-foot) tower for his first successful trials in radio navigation, making contact with the East Goodwin lightship, 10 miles (16 kilometres) away, on Christmas Eve 1898. There are views over Dover docks and the Channel from the balcony round the light, and walkers along the cliffs between here and Dover can take a zigzag path down to the shore and the wreck of the sailing ship *Preussan*, which ran aground here in 1910.

Stembridge Tower Mill
Somerset
2 miles (3.2 kilometres) north of Langport, ½ mile (0.8 kilometre) east of High Ham

This substantial four-storey stone tower set high above Sedgemoor, with a reed-covered peaked cap supporting the sails, is the last thatched windmill in England. Dating from about 1822, the mill continued to work until the early years of the twentieth century, although its wind power was being augmented with steam by the 1890s.

A pulley system, used to turn the cap, has not survived, nor has most of the milling machinery. The earth platform on which the mill stands was intended to stop livestock or people wandering too close to the sails. A bake-house and miller's cottage (not open) stand nearby and a little privy was used until modern conveniences were installed in 1970.

Sticklebarn Tavern

Cumbria

On the B5343 in Great Langdale, north of Skelwith Bridge, 7 miles (11.2 kilometres) north-west of Ambleside

Now a pub much patronised by those walking the fells, this sizeable, rugged stone building set at the foot of the Langdale Pikes in some of the most beautiful upland scenery in England was built as a two-storey bank barn, with an upper floor accessed from the higher ground against which it is placed (the double doors by which the first floor was entered are still in place). Like the dry-stone walls criss-crossing the valley floor, the barn was constructed of surface-gathered material. The slate-covered pentice roof which shelters weary walkers sitting at the tables at the front of the tavern once protected the openings to the stables and byres of the lower floor. Just 15 metres (50 feet) behind the barn are the remains of a fifteenth-century fulling mill, which was powered by a leat off the Stickle Ghyll.

Stoke-sub-Hamdon Priory (below)

Somerset

2 miles (3.2 kilometres) west of Montacute between Yeovil and Ilminster

An archway from the road leads to this picturesque group of buildings set round a grassy farmyard. On one side is a buttressed, two-storey house with a projecting porch and stone-

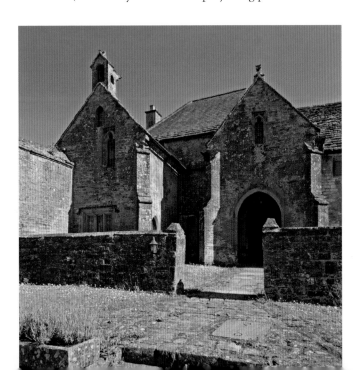

mullioned windows. Farm buildings closing the other sides and set round a second yard behind include a magnificent great barn, the ruins of a cart shed, granary and cattle shed, and a splendid circular dovecote, now roofless, fitted out with 500 nesting boxes. This enchanting complex, mostly of mellow Ham Hill stone, dates from the early fourteenth century, when the five chaplains of an Augustinian chantry founded by the Beauchamp family in 1304 were housed here and supported by income from the farm. A medieval hall open to the rafters which forms one wing of the house dates from this period, but most of the house is of the fifteenth century or later. When the chantry was dissolved, in 1548, the complex continued as a farm.

Templetown Mausoleum

Co. Antrim

In Castle Upton graveyard, Templepatrick

This perfect Neo-classical temple, erected by Sarah Upton in 1789 in memory of the Hon. Arthur Upton, who had died 20 years earlier, dominates the quiet graveyard at Castle Upton. On the dignified entrance facade, urns in niches flank a rusticated arch and three more stand on the parapet above the simple inscription. Coade stone plaques commemorate other members of the Upton family. One of the finest monuments ever designed by Robert Adam, the mausoleum is also one of the few examples of the architect's work in Ireland. Adam was commissioned to give a new look to Castle Upton (not owned by the National Trust), but the house was subsequently remodelled and only his castellated stables near the graveyard have survived.

Town Walls Tower

Shropshire

Overlooking the River Severn close to the centre of Shrewsbury

Despite Edward I's conquest of Wales in the late thirteenth century, towns in the Welsh borders still needed to be defended against possible attack by rebels from the west. This fourteenth-century four-storey tower overlooking a great loop of the Severn on the south side of Shrewsbury is one of the few remaining fragments of the fortified walls studded with twelve watchtowers which once protected the town.

Treasurer's House, Martock
Somerset
Opposite the church in the middle of Martock village;
1 mile (1.6 kilometres) north-west of the A303 between
Ilminster and Ilchester

Of the clutch of late medieval priests' houses owned by the National Trust (*see*, for example, p.388), this comfortable building of mellow Ham stone, marked by a traceried two-light window and set back from the street through an archway, is perhaps the grandest. Across a spacious courtyard is a late thirteenth-century great hall, open to an arch-braced timber roof dating from the fifteenth century and with windows of *c*.1350. A screens passage divides the hall from the earlier solar block set at right angles to the south, in fact a hall house of *c*.1260 with a first-floor hall above what was originally an undercroft. In what would have been a private chamber is a wall painting of the crucifixion. A kitchen block tacked on at one corner was built in the fifteenth century. All three buildings can be seen from a second courtyard west of the great hall.

This substantial medieval survival has been linked to the village church since at least the thirteenth century, when the treasurer of Wells Cathedral lived here and acted as Martock's rector and patron. In later years the house and associated farmland were tenanted, but a succession of treasurers continued in the same roles until 1840.

Tudor Merchant's House (left)
Pembrokeshire
Quay Hill, Tenby

This narrow, late fifteenth-century three-storey building looking down Bridge Street just above the harbour is typical of the prosperous medieval dwellings that would have crowded the lanes of this little town when it was a thriving port in the fourteenth and fifteenth centuries.

Sturdily built of roughly coursed rubblestone, the house still boasts a garderobe turret rising to the height of the building, its original jointed roof trusses

and a circular chimneystack characteristic of this part of Wales. Although the interior has been much altered, a late medieval trailing flower pattern painted in red, black and yellow on wet plaster emerged from beneath no fewer than 23 coats of whitewash on the only surviving original partition. A recreated merchant's shop on the ground floor and specially-commissioned reproduction furniture show how the house might have looked when first built.

Tŷ Mawr Wybrnant (below)
Gwynedd
At the head of the little Wybrnant Valley, 3½ miles
(5.6 kilometres) south-west of Betws-y-Coed via the A470,
2 miles (3.2 kilometres) west of Penmachno

This little sixteenth-century farmhouse hidden away on the eastern edge of the Snowdon massif, with its rough granite walls, slate roof, massive chimneys and small, deep-set windows, is typical of Wales's scattered upland dwellings. Today it is remote, but at one time drovers taking animals from the fertile Llŷn peninsula to the markets of the Welsh borders would have regularly passed down the valley.

This tranquil spot was the birthplace of Bishop William Morgan, whose translation of the Bible into Welsh is still in use today. In 1563, realising that the Welsh had no alternative to the Latin service, Elizabeth I ordered the four Welsh bishops and the Bishop of Hereford to produce a translation of the Prayer Book and the Bible within three years. The New Testament published in 1567 was a stilted, pedantic text, bearing no comparison to William Morgan's triumphantly fluid masterpiece produced in Armada year (1588), with a dedication to his queen. Alas, although the bishop was born and grew up in this remote valley, the farmhouse almost certainly post-dates him, although fragments of an earlier, cruck-framed hall house are embedded within the structure. A re-created Tudor garden is stocked with herbs, fruit, vegetables and flowers of the period.

575 Wandsworth Road (right)
London

On the south side of Wandsworth Road, screened by a leafy front garden, is a small and unobtrusive brick-built early nineteenth-century terraced house, with two floors over a semi-basement and a steep flight of steps up to the front door. This unexceptional frontage conceals rich and elaborate interiors created by the Kenyan novelist and poet Khadambi Asalache (c.1935–2006), who bought No. 575 in 1981 and over a period of 20 years, from 1986, turned his home into a work of art. Almost every surface, from walls and ceilings to shelves, doors and kitchen drawers, is embellished with fretwork patterns and motifs, which Khadambi carved by hand from pine floorboards and door-panels rescued from skips and from wine crates. The designs are mostly abstract, but included within them is an abundance of realistic detail, often small enough to need searching out: here a tiny frieze of jazz musicians, or a *corps de ballet*, there a couple of moon-shaped masks peering from a corner, or a gaggle of geese. In places, such as where Khadambi has added fragile shelving to the walls, the texture becomes many-layered and overlapping. Like anything that is created by hand, no two motifs are ever exactly the same. There is delicate painted decoration too, such as a frieze of meadow flowers in the basement bathroom and another, of giraffes, hippos and elephants in the African bush, in the spare bedroom.

Furnishings and ornaments contribute to the striking effect. In the double reception room that runs across the raised ground floor, cushions in deep reds and purples are flung across a low sofa, there are richly coloured kelims on the floor and pierced Moorish lampshades, an array of pressed and moulded glass inkwells on a low table, and shelves of pink and copper lustreware reflect and diffuse the light. Coarsely woven hangings from Senegal on the walls are painted with naïve depictions of African birds and animals that could have inspired Picasso and there is a collection of silver Coptic crosses from Ethiopia, and of antique glasses with twisted stems.

Although No. 575 is an entirely individual creation, Khadambi's rich artistic imagination was influenced by the Africa of his childhood, where traditional houses in Lamu and Mombasa were characterised by carved niches filled with Chinese porcelain; by the Moorish architecture of Andalusia, such as the filigree woodwork found in the Alhambra; and by the wooden houses, or *yali*, of Istanbul. Intriguingly, though, Khadambi started ornamenting the house for practical rather than artistic reasons. Unhappy with the look of some old floorboards that he had used to conceal persistent patches of damp in the basement, he came up with the idea of disguising them with fretwork. It was this inspired solution to a particular problem that led to his unique creation.

Khadambi trained as an architect in Nairobi and studied fine art in Europe. When he came to London, in 1960, he combined teaching and working for the BBC with writing, publishing his important novel, *A Calabash of Life*, in 1967. He then worked as a civil servant in the Treasury, creating his exquisite interiors in his spare time. A partly decorated ceiling, which Khadambi started to embellish in 2005 but was never able to complete, is a poignant reminder of the lung cancer from which he died a year later. Poignant, too, is the intricate window screen he carved on which his initial is intertwined with that of his partner, Susie Thomson.

Wellbrook Beetling Mill (above)
Co. Tyrone
4 miles (6.4 kilometres) west of Cookstown, ¹/₂ mile
(0.8 kilometre) off the A505 Cookstown–Omagh road

Like the wool industry in medieval England, linen manufacture was of major importance in eighteenth-century Ireland, particularly in the north, where new landowners from England and Scotland were anxious to maximise the return on their estates. Official encouragement included the setting up of a Linen Board in 1711, the removal of duty on Irish linen imported into England, and a body to fund development. Although some spinning and weaving continued to be done in the home, the industry was increasingly mechanised, with many mills established on the rivers around Belfast. Beetling was the last stage in the process, in which the cloth was pounded with heavy hammers for up to two weeks to give it a gleaming sheen.

This functional isolated building in a remote valley west of Cookstown is the only surviving part of the once-extensive Wellbrook linen works. Built in 1765 and modified in the nineteenth century, it continued operating until 1965, although the main bleaching mill closed about a hundred years earlier. Seven beetling engines, their hammers resembling rows of organ pipes, were powered by a large breastshot waterwheel, 5 metres (16 feet) in diameter, set against the eastern gable of the long two-storey mill. Water for the wheel was brought from a weir on the Ballinderry River a short distance away, with an impressive wooden aqueduct on brick piers to transport it the last 15 metres (50 feet) or so. After beetling, the cloth was hung to dry on the upper floor, where the airing racks and louvred windows still survive. The linen was then folded on a special table for dispatch.

Now restored to working order, the mill once again reverberates to the heavy pounding of the beetling hammers. There is also a display illustrating the Irish linen industry.

Wellington Monument
Somerset
2 miles (3.2 kilometres) south of Wellington on the A38, just west of the Wellington–Hemyock road

Anyone travelling south-west along the M5 or by train from Taunton to Exeter will recognise this stark stone obelisk, which rises prominently from the Blackdown Hills on the Devon–Somerset border. Designed in 1817 by Thomas Lee, the architect of Arlington Court (*see* p.23), and some 53 metres (175 feet) high, it was commissioned by a group of local gentry to commemorate the achievements of the Duke of Wellington, who had defeated Napoleon at the Battle of Waterloo two years before. The Iron Duke would probably have appreciated the military advantages of such a splendid position, with breathtaking views in all directions. Alas, the monument's present fragile state means visitors can no longer climb the spiral staircase to the top.

Westbury College Gatehouse
Bristol
In College Road, Westbury-on-Trym

This battlemented, four-storey gatehouse close to the parish church is one of the few remains of the magnificent buildings set round a quadrangle on the banks of the Trym that were built in the second half of the fifteenth century to house secular priests of the college established here in 1194. Westbury's benefactor, who paid for the college and improvements to the church, was John Carpenter, Bishop of Worcester, whose seated figure sits in a niche on the church tower. One of the college's more notable priests was the theological reformer John Wycliffe, who was a canon here from 1362 to 1384. When the college was dissolved in 1544, the buildings were converted into a grand mansion, but this was largely burned down in the Civil War.

Westwood Manor

Wiltshire

1½ miles (2.4 kilometres) south-west of Bradford on Avon, in Westwood village

The sixteenth century was a golden age for the west of England, when men amassed considerable fortunes in the profitable cloth trade with Antwerp and built the many fine but unpretentious houses that are such a feature of towns and villages in this part of the country. One of these men was Thomas Horton, who acquired a little fifteenth-century manor built by a prosperous Wiltshire farmer and transformed it into a house more fitting for someone of his status and position. Further embellishment in the early seventeenth century resulted in the fluid plasterwork now found in many of the rooms, and some fine panelling.

Westwood is both dignified and welcoming. A modest L-shaped building of warm local stone, its low ranges frame a grassy court crossed by flagged paths and there is a great medieval barn close by the house. One of the most satisfying rooms is the parlour over the hall, with its unusual interior porches, an elaborate plaster ceiling and a show of early keyboard instruments. The long, low window giving onto the courtyard from this room has a beautiful view of the little village church and over the valley of the River Frome beyond.

Wichenford Dovecote (left)

Worcestershire

5½ miles (8.8 kilometres) north-west of Worcester, north of the B4204

Perhaps built at the same time as the adjoining farmhouse was given its elegant late seventeenth-century facades, this tall timber-framed black-and-white dovecote strikes a similarly domestic note, with mown grass surrounding the sandstone plinth on which it stands. A lantern crowning the steeply pitched roof admitted birds to some 550 nesting boxes stacked on short brick piers.

Wilderhope Manor

Shropshire

7 miles (11.2 kilometres) south-west of Much Wenlock, 7 miles (11.2 kilometres) east of Church Stretton, ½ mile (0.8 kilometre) south of the B4371

This tall, gabled Elizabethan manor stands on the southern slope of Wenlock Edge, deep in the remote wooded Shropshire landscape evoked so vividly in the work of the local novelist Mary Webb, who used Wilderhope Manor as her model for Undern Hall in *Gone to Earth* (1917).

Built of local grey limestone with tall brick chimneys and a stone-tiled roof, this is a delightfully asymmetrical house, with an off-centre entrance, marked by a curious detached pediment, in the south-east front and projecting bays of varying widths. Large mullioned and transomed windows on this side of the building look out over the River Corve deep in the valley below.

Apart from the notable circular wooden staircase capped by a conical roof which ascends right through the house, the main feature of the interior is its unexpected plasterwork ceilings, executed with such skill that they were once thought to be the work of Italian craftsmen rather than a provincial team. The initials of Francis and Ellen Smallman, who built Wilderhope in about 1586, recur frequently in the moulds punctuating the plaster ribs, alternating with standard motifs such as the Tudor rose, the fleurs-de-lis and the portcullis. Of the original contents, only a bow rack survives.

The spot known as the 'Major's Leap' on Wenlock Edge nearby commemorates Francis and Ellen's descendant, Thomas Smallman, a supporter of the Royalist cause in the Civil War, who was imprisoned at Wilderhope. Escaping into the garden, probably by means of an old garderobe flue, he evaded his pursuers by riding his horse over Wenlock Edge. Although his unfortunate mount was killed, the major's fall is said to have been broken by a crab-apple tree.

Willington Dovecote and Stables

Bedfordshire

In Willington, 4 miles (6.4 kilometres) east of Bedford, just north of the A603

The serrated roofline of this imposing sixteenth-century dovecote built by Sir John Goshawk, Cardinal Wolsey's Master of the Horse, can be seen for miles across the flat Bedfordshire countryside. Built on a scale commensurate with the large mansion to which it was once attached, the dovecote's kidney-shaped nesting boxes set into the thickness of the stone walls could accommodate some 1,500 birds. Showy, crow-stepped gables are supported on thirteenth-century corbels that were probably filched from local priories at the Dissolution of the Monasteries. Across the road is a contemporary barn-like building with similarly ornate gables and late Gothic windows. The young John Bunyan, born at Elstow only 5 miles (8 kilometres) to the west, once stayed here, leaving his signature and the date, 1650, etched on a stone fireplace. The architecture of both dovecote and stables is exceptionally flamboyant for their apparent purposes, and it is likely they were built by Sir John for a visit by Henry VIII in 1541 and that the stables were originally designed as a banqueting house.

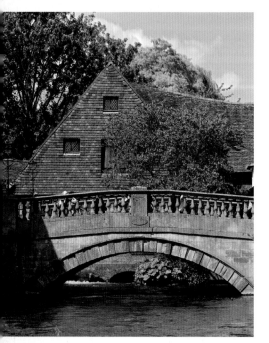

Winchester City Mill (left)

Hampshire

At the foot of Winchester's High Street, beside Soke Bridge

This attractive brick corn-mill with tile-hung gables and a delightful island garden was built over the River Itchen by Soke Bridge in 1743 on a site that has been occupied by a succession of mills since Saxon times. The fast-flowing river, which emerges in a spectacular mill-race, once powered several medieval mills in the city, a reflection of Winchester's early importance as capital of England and as a market for grain and wool. Already in decline by the late fourteenth century as a result of the ravages of the Black Death and the removal of the English wool staple to Calais, the town never recovered its former prosperity.

One of a number of Winchester mills recorded in Domesday Book as being connected to the Church, the Soke Bridge mill was then a property of the Benedictine nunnery of Wherwell a few miles north of the city, passing to the Crown when the monastery was dissolved in 1538–9. Some years later, in 1554, it was given to the city by Mary I in partial recompense for the expense of her marriage to Philip of Spain in Winchester Cathedral. The current mill, with its undershot waterwheel, has been restored to working order.

Wray Castle

Cumbria

In Low Wray, 2 miles (3.2 kilometres) south of Ambleside

This battlemented and turreted baronial fantasy rising above the trees on the western side of Lake Windermere is like an oversized toy castle. Every feature, including the plentiful arrow slits, is exaggerated. Built in the 1840s for Dr James Dawson, a retired Liverpool surgeon, and his wife Margaret, it was designed by the Liverpool architect John Jackson Lightfoot and is largely constructed of slate rubble, with slate ashlar facings on some façades and limestone dressings. Inside, a central hall rises dramatically into the lantern tower that dominates the castle and grand living rooms are endowed with doors, skirtings, mouldings and other fittings on a scale as massive as the exterior detailing. In the 1880s, when Beatrix Potter was in her late teens and twenties, this was one of the places where the family came for summer holidays and which introduced the lonely girl to the lakes and fells amongst which she would spend most of her adult life (*see* p.168). Beatrix painted a watercolour of the castle library and her father's photographs of the interior, which is currently unfurnished, help to conjure up how the castle would have looked in its heyday. The castle has its own jetty on the lake, to which visitors can come by boat from Ambleside.

ᴠᴇ Montacute House,
ᴇʀset (see page 214).

Maps

G H I J K L

1

2

3

4

5

6

7

8

Market
Rasen
A631
Louth
Mablethorpe
A1500
A46
A158
A16
A157
LINCOLN
A57
Horncastle
A158
Ingoldmells
Gunby Hall
Skegness
A607
Washingborough
Coningsby
A607
A17
Tattershall
Castle
A153
Boston
A16
Sleaford
A17
A52
A52
Belton
House
Grantham
Grantham House
A52
A18
Holbeach
Woolsthorpe
Manor
A151
A1
A151
Spalding
Bourne
A17
King's
Lynn
Wisbech
Peckover
House
Hunstanton
A149
A148
Fakenham
Blakeney
Wells-
next-the-
Sea
A148
Cromer
Felbrigg Hall,
Gardens and Estate
North Walsham
Blickling Estate
Aylsham
A140
Horsey
Windpump
A606
Stamford
Priest's House,
...ston on the Hill
A16
A47
Peterborough
A47
A1073
A47
Downham
Market
A1122
March
Swaffham
Oxburgh
Hall
East
Dereham
A1065
Walton
Wymondham
NORWICH
A47
A146
A143
Great Yarmouth
Elizabethan House
Museum
Attleborough
A11
Lowestoft
Oundle
Corby
Lyveden
New Bield
Kettering
Ramsey Abbey
Gatehouse
Huntingdon
Chatteris
Littleport
Ely
Brandon
A1066
Diss
Bungay
Beccles
Southwold
Halesworth
Eye
A143
Saxmundham
A12
A1120
Rushden
A14
St Ives
Waterbeach
Burwell
A14
Newmarket
Bury St Edmunds
Theatre Royal
Bury St Edmunds
Leiston
St Neots
Histon
CAMBRIDGE
Ickworth
Stowmarket
Aldeburgh
Willington
Dovecote
and Stables
Bedford
A428
Anglesey Abbey
and Lode Mill
IPSWICH
Woodbridge
Wimpole
Estate
Haverhill
Melford Hall
Long
Melford
Lavenham
Guildhall
Orford Ness
Newport
Pagnell
Milton Keynes
M1
Royston
Saffron
Walden
Sudbury
Flatford:
Bridge
Cottage
Felixstowe
Harwich
Baldock
Letchworth
Hitchin
A1(M)
Stevenage
M11
Bishop's
Stortford
Coggeshall
Grange Barn
and Paycocke's
A120
Braintree
Colchester
Clacton-on-Sea
...pel
...tt
Luton
Shaw's
Corner
A507
A602
Welwyn
Garden
City
A120
Witham
West
Mersea
Pitstone Windmill
St Albans
Hertford
Ware
Harlow
Maldon
...esbury
...House
Hemel
Hempstead
M10
Hatfield
Hoddesdon
Chelmsford
A414
Burnham-on-Crouch
Hughenden
High Wycombe
M1
M25
Fenton House
and Garden
2 Willow Rd
Brentwood
Rayleigh
M25
Gray's Monument
M25
Sutton House
Basildon
Southend-on-Sea
Osterley
Park
Slough
M4
Carlyle's House
Eastbury Manor House
Rainham Hall
Canvey Island
Ham House
George Inn
575 Wandsworth
Road
Red House
St John's Jerusalem
Sheerness
Whitstable
Herne Bay
Margate
Windsor
The Homewood
M25
Owletts
Cobham Wood
and Mausoleum
Rochester
A2
Faversham
Ramsgate
A257
...atchlands Park
Clandon Park
M25
Quebec
House
M25
Knole
M26
Old Soar
Manor
Ightham Mote
Maidstone
A20
M2
Canterbury
Deal
...alford Mill
Guildford
Polesden
Lacey
A25
Chartwell
Stoneacre
A20
South Foreland
Lighthouse
Leith Hill
Tower
A23
Chiddingstone
Village
Tunbridge Wells
Ashford
Dover
Oakhurst Cottage
Standen
Scotney
Castle
Sissinghurst
Castle
A2070
M20
Folkestone
Nymans
Hayward
Heath
Smallythe Place
Tenterden
Hythe
A272
Billingshurst
Bateman's
Bodiam Castle
New Romney
Petworth
House
A27
Battle
Rye
Lamb House
A259
Midhurst
A27
A22
A271
Lewes
Hailsham
A259
Hastings
A26
Hove
Monk's House
Bexhill-on-Sea
Littlehampton
Worthing
Brighton
Alfriston Clergy House
Bognor
Regis
Newhaven
Eastbourne
Selsey
...nill

Map references

Aberconwy House 400 C1
Aberdeunant 400 C4
A La Ronde 400 D7
Alfriston Clergy House 401 H6
Anglesey Abbey and Lode Mill 401 H3
Antony 400 C7
Ardress House 402 B4
The Argory 402 B4
Arlington Court 400 C6
Ascott 400 F4
Ashdown House 400 F5
Ashleworth Tithe Barn 400 E4
Attingham Estate 400 D2
Avebury 400 E5
Baddesley Clinton 400 E3
Barrington Court 400 D6
Basildon Park 400 F5
Bateman's 401 H6
Bath Assembly Rooms 400 E5
The Beatles' Childhood Homes 402 F6
Beatrix Potter Gallery 402 F4
Belton House 401 G2
Bembridge Windmill and Fort 400 F7
Beningbrough Hall and
    Gardens 403 H5
Benthall Hall 402 F8
Berrington Hall 400 D3
Birmingham Back to Backs 400 E3
Blaise Hamlet 400 D5
Blickling Estate 401 I2
Boarstall Duck Decoy and
    Tower 400 F4
Bodiam Castle 401 H6
Bodysgallen Hall Hotel 402 E6
Bourne Mill 401 H4
Bradenham Village 400 F4
Bradley 400 C7
Braithwaite Hall 403 G4
Branscombe: The Old Bakery, Garden
    and Estate 400 D7
Bredon Barn 400 E4
Bridge House 402 F4
Brockhampton Estate 400 E3
Bruton Dovecote 400 E6
Buckingham Chantry Chapel 400 F4
Buckland Abbey 400 C7
Buscot Old Parsonage 400 E4
Buscot Park 400 E4
Calke Abbey 400 F2
Canons Ashby 400 F3
Carlyle's House 401 G5

Cartmel Priory Gatehouse 402 F4
Castle Coole 402 A4
Castle Drogo 400 C7
Castle Ward 402 C4
Charlcote Park 400 E3
Chartwell 401 G5
Chastleton House 400 E4
Chedworth Roman Villa 400 E4
Cherryburn 403 G3
Chiddingstone Village 401 H6
Chipping Campden Market
    Hall 400 E4
Chirk Castle 400 D2
The Church House 400 C7
Cilgerran Castle 400 B4
Clandon Park 401 G5
Claydon 400 F4
Clevedon Court 400 D5
Cliveden 400 G5
Clouds Hill 400 E7
Clumber Park 400 F1
Cobham Wood and
    Mausoleum 401 H5
Coggeshall Grange Barn 401 H4
Coleridge Cottage 400 D6
Coleton Fishacre 400 C7
Compton Castle 400 C7
Conwy Suspension Bridge 402 E6
Corfe Castle 400 E7
Cotehele 400 C7
Coughton Court 400 E3
Cragside 403 G2
Croft Castle and Parkland 400 D3
Croome 400 E3
The Crown Bar 402 C3
Cwmmau Farmhouse 400 D3
Dalton Castle 402 F5
Derrymore House 402 B4
Derwent Island House 402 F4
Dinefwr 400 C4
Dinton Park and Philipps
    House 400 E6
Downhill Demesne and Hezlett
    House 402 B2
Duffield Castle 400 F1
Dudmaston Estate 400 E3
Dunham Massey 403 G6
Dunstanburgh Castle 403 G2
Dunster Castle 400 C6
Dyrham Park 400 E5
Eastbury Manor House 401 H5

East Riddlesden Hall 403 G5
Elizabethan House Museum 401 I2
Erddig 400 D1
Farnborough Hall 400 F3
Felbrigg Hall, Gardens and
    Estate 401 I2
Fenton House and Garden 401 G5
Finch Foundry 400 C7
Flatford: Bridge Cottage 401 I4
The Fleece Inn 400 E4
Florence Court 402 A4
Fountains Abbey and Studley
    Royal 403 G5
Gawthorpe Hall 403 G5
George Inn 401 G5
George Stephenson's
    Birthplace 403 G3
Gibside 403 G3
Godolphin 400 A8
Grange Arch 400 E7
Grantham House 401 G2
Gray's Monument 401 G5
Gray's Printing Press 402 A3
Great Chalfield Manor 400 E5
Great Coxwell Barn 400 E5
Greenway 400 C7
The Greyfriars 400 E3
Greys Court 400 F5
Gunby Hall 400 H1
Hadrian's Wall and Housesteads
    Fort 403 G3
Hailes Abbey 400 E4
Ham House 401 G5
Hanbury Hall 400 E3
The Hardmans' House (Mr
    Hardman's Photographic
    Studio) 402 F6
Hardwick Hall 400 F1
Hardy Country 400 E7
Hardy Monument 400 D7
Hartwell House Hotel 400 F4
Hatchlands Park 401 G5
Hawford Dovecote 400 E3
Hawkshead Courthouse 402 F4
Heelis 400 E5
High Cross House 400 C7
Hill Top 402 F4
Hinton Ampner 400 F6
Holnicote Estate 400 C5
Holy Jesus Hospital 403 G3
The Homewood 401 G5

Horsey Windpump 401 I2
Horton Court 400 E5
Houghton Mill 401 G3
Hughenden 401 G5
Ickworth 401 H3
Ightham Mote 401 H5
Kedleston Hall 400 F2
Keld Chapel 402 F4
Killerton 400 C6
King John's Hunting Lodge 400 D5
King's Head 400 F4
Kingston Lacy 400 E6
Kinver Edge and the Rock
    Houses 400 E3
Kinwarton Dovecote 400 E3
Knightshayes 400 C6
Knole 401 H5
Knowles Mill 400 E3
The Kymin 400 D4
Lacock Abbey, Fox Talbot Museum
    and Village E5
Lamb House 401 H6
Lanhydrock 400 B7
Lavenham Guildhall 401 H3
Lawrence House 400 B7
Leith Hill Tower 401 G6
Letocetum Roman Baths and
    Museum 400 E2
Levant Mines and Engines 400 A8
Lindisfarne Castle 403 G1
Little Clarendon 400 E6
Little Moreton Hall 400 E1
Llanerchaeron 400 C3
Lodge Park 400 E4
Long Crendon Courthouse 400 F4
Loughwood Meeting House 400 D6
Lyme Park, House and
    Garden 403 G6
Lytes Cary Manor 400 D6
Lyveden New Bield 401 G3
Maister House 403 I5
Market House 401 E1
Melford Hall 401 H3
Middle Littleton Tithe Barn 400 E3
Middlethorpe Hall Hotel 403 H5
Mompesson House 400 E6
Monk's House 401 G6
Montacute House 400 D6
Morville Hall 400 E2
Moseley Old Hall 400 E2
Mottisfont 400 F6

Moulton Hall 403 G4
Mount Grace Priory 403 H4
Mount Stewart 402 C3
Mr Straw's House 400 F1
Needles Old and New Batteries 400 F7
Nether Alderley Mill 403 G7
Newark Park 400 E5
Newtown Old Town Hall 400 F7
Nostell Priory and Parkland 403 H6
Nuffield Place 400 F5
Nunnington Hall 403 H4
Nymans 401 G6
Oakhurst Cottage 401 G6
The Old Coastguard Station 403 H4
The Old Manor, Norbury 400 D2
Old Soar Manor 401 H5
Orford Ness 401 I3
Ormesby Hall 403 H4
Osterley Park 401 G5
Overbeck's 400 C8
Owletts 401 H5
Oxburgh Hall 401 H2
Packwood House 400 E3
Patterson's Spade Mill 402 C3
Paycocke's 401 H4
Peckover House 401 H2
Penrhyn Castle 400 C1
Penshaw Monument 403 G3
The Pepperbox 400 E6
Petworth House 401 G6
Pitstone Windmill 401 G4
Plas Newydd 400 C1
Plas yn Rhiw 400 B2
Polesden Lacey 401 G5
Powis Castle 400 D2
Priest's House, Easton on the
    Hill 401 G2
Priest's House, Muchelney 400 D6
Priory Cottages 400 F5
Quarry Bank Mill and Styal
    Estate 400 E1
Quebec House 401 G5
Rainham Hall 401 H5
Ramsey Abbey Gatehouse 401 G3
Red House 401 H5
Rosedene 400 E3
Rufford Old Hall 402 F6
St George's Guildhall 401 H2
St John's Jerusalem 401 H5
St Michael's Mount 400 A8
Saltram 400 C7

Picture credits

2, 119, 201 © National Trust Images / Paul Harris; 7, 172, 173 (left and right) © National Trust Images / Stuart Cox; 10, 33, 34, 167, 184, 185, 187 (top and bottom), 192, 377 (left) © National Trust Images / James Dobson; 12, 15, 26–27, 35, 90, 98, 136, 153, 154, 155, 156, 161, 174 (left), 191, 193, 232, 233 (left and right), 244, 259, 262, 271, 277, 279, 280, 285, 291, 312 (right), 314, 327 © National Trust Images / John Hammond; 13, 288, 389 (right) © National Trust Images / John Blake; 14, 166 (right), 294, 358, 361, 364, 372, 374 © National Trust Images / John Miller; 16–17, 46 (bottom), 89, 100, 103, 157 (left and right), 158, 182, 238 (bottom), 284, 295, 297, 311, 316–317, 348, 349 © National Trust Images / Dennis Gilbert; 18 (top and bottom), 146 (left), 376, 395 © National Trust Images / Cristian Barnett; 18–19, 36, 37, 50, 63, 91, 95, 105, 110, 118, 120 (top), 144, 148 (left), 170, 177, 183, 228, 229 (right), 239, 242, 265, 270, 272–273, 310, 322 (top), 323, 342, 344 © National Trust Images / Andrew Butler; 20, 22, 46 (top), 47, 73, 74, 86, 127, 159, 160, 202, 254, 275, 298–299, 300 (right), 356 (left and right), 357, 367, 394 (right) © National Trust Images / Arnhel de Serra; 21, 23, 30–31, 53, 78, 80, 108, 124, 130, 134 (top), 139, 175, 180, 205, 230–231, 238 (top), 248, 249, 252, 286, 331, 338 © National Trust Images / Matthew Antrobus; 24–25, 55, 58–59, 72, 85, 92, 115, 117 (bottom), 126, 131, 133 (bottom), 138, 148 (right), 162, 204, 211, 301 (left), 332, 355 © National Trust Images / Nadia Mackenzie; 28, 334 (left) © National Trust Images / Derrick E. Witty; 29 © National Trust Images / Flo Smith; 32, 41, 44, 45, 49, 51, 67, 70, 79, 81, 84, 94, 113, 125, 128, 151, 171, 174 (right), 189, 190, 195, 200 (left), 206, 218, 219, 229 (left), 230, 247, 250 (left and right), 253, 258, 267, 274, 293 (right), 300, 301 (right), 307, 313, 318, 322 (bottom), 328, 333, 335, 339, 340, 351, 353, 396 © National Trust Images / Andreas von Einsiedel; 38, 65, 290 © National Trust Images / David Dixon; 39, 57, 69, 76, 82, 140, 141 (top), 141 (bottom), 142, 196, 197, 227, 268, 309, 381 © National Trust Images / John Millar; 40 © National Trust Images / Raymond Lea; 42, 226, 299 © National Trust Images / Geoffrey Frosh; 43, 54, 68, 83, 87, 96, 114, 117 (top), 129, 137, 186, 188, 210, 214 (right), 302, 326 © National Trust Images / Rupert Truman; 48 © National Trust Images / Alex Black; 56, 62, 112, 121, 132, 133 (top), 163, 164, 165, 178, 181, 220, 234–235, 245, 261, 308, 362, 380 (right), 386, 390 © National Trust Images / Robert Morris; 60, 365 © National Trust Images / Alasdair Ogilvie; 61, 243, 281, 282–283, 383, 389 (left) National Trust Images / David Sellman; 64, 111 © National Trust Images / George Wright; 71 © National Trust Images / Mark Bradshaw; 75 © National Trust Images / Patrick Prendergast; 77, 334 (right) © National Trust Images / James Mortimer; 88, 371 © National Trust Images /Ian Shaw; 93 National Trust Images / Anthony Parkinson; 96–97, 179 © National Trust Images / Paul Mogford; 99 © National Trust Images / Dave Zubraski; 102, 304, 393 © National Trust Images / Brian and Nina Chapple; 104, 145 (left and right) © National Trust Images / Mark Bolton; 106–107 © National Trust Images / Don Bishop; 109, 216, 237, 325, 369, 379, 391 © National Trust Images / Derek Croucher; 101 © National Trust Images / Jerry Harpur; 120 (bottom), 198, 276 © National Trust Images / David Noton; 122 © National Trust Images / Michael Caldwell; 123, 166 (left), 240, 255, 354 (right) © National Trust Images / Bill Batten; 134 (bottom), 203, 207, 208, 260, 263, 287, 306, 320, 377 (right), 397 © National Trust Images / Nick Meers; 135 © National Trust Images / Angelo Hornak; 143, 289, 312 (left) © National Trust Images / Mike Williams; 146 (right), 147 © National Trust Images / Aerial-Cam; 149, 150, 209 (left and right), © National Trust Images / Nick Guttridge; 168 © National Trust Images; 169 © National Trust Images / Stephen Robson; 194 © National Trust Images / David Sullivan; 200 (right), 341, 366, 370, 392 © National Trust Images / Joe Cornish; 212, 213 © National Trust Images / Eric Crichton; 214, 388 © National Trust Images / Neil Campbell-Sharp; 215 © National Trust Images / W H Rendell; 217 © National Trust Images / Phil Evans; 221 © National Trust Images / Mark Sunderland; 222–223, 225 © National Trust Images / Alex Ramsay; 224 © National Trust Images / Peter Aprahamian; 246 © National Trust Images / Keith Hewett; 251 © National Trust Images / Rod Edwards; 264 © National Trust Images / Paul Highnam; 266, 394 (left) © National Trust Images / Erik Pelham; 269 © National Trust Images / Alan Novelli; 278 © National Trust Images / David Levenson; 280 (left) © National Trust Images / A C Cooper; 292 © National Trust Images / Jonathan Buckley; 293 (left) © National Trust Images / Val Corbett; 296, 314–315, 337 © National Trust Images / Andy Williams; 303, 343 © National Trust Images / John Bethell; 319 © National Trust Images / Rob Talbot; 329 © National Trust Images / Giraffe Photography; 345, 346, 347 © National Trust Images / Paul Raeside; 352 © National Trust Images / Megan Taylor; 354 (left) © National Trust Images / Tessa Musgrave; 359 © National Trust Images / Oliver Benn; 360 © National Trust Images / David Hall; 363 © National Trust Images / Tony West; 368 © National Trust Images / Will Webster; 373 © National Trust Images / Fay Godwin; 375 (left) © National Trust Images / Paul Wakefield; 375 (right) © National Trust Images / Colin Sturges; 378 © National Trust Images / Jason Ingram; 380 (left) © National Trust Images / Roger Hickman; 382 © National Trust Images / Ian West; 384 © National Trust Images / John Boothroyd; 385 © National Trust Images / Nick Carter; 387 © National Trust Images / Paul Barker; 398 © National Trust Images / Phil Ripley; 399 National Trust Images / Robert Morris.

Images reproduced by kind permission of: Sir Evelyn de Rothschild (pages 26–27); © Estate of Rex Whistler. All rights reserved, DACS 2012 (pages 219 and 259); © The Estate of Stanley Spencer 2012. All rights reserved DACS (page 280).

Index